LAW AND THE RESTORATION

LAW AND THE RESTORATION

Law and Latter-day Saint History

Nathan B. Oman

Greg Kofford Books
Salt Lake City, 2024

Cover design by Loyd Isao Ericson.

Published in the USA.

ISBN: 978-1-58958-796-0 (paperback); 978-1-58958-810-3 (hardcover)
Also available in ebook.

Greg Kofford Books
P. O. Box 1362
Draper, UT 84020
www.gregkofford.com
facebook.com/gkbooks
twitter.com/gkbooks

Library of Congress Cataloging-in-Publication Data

Names: Oman, Nathan, author. | Oman, Nathan. Law and the Restoration ; v. 1

Title: Law and Latter-Day Saint history / Nathan B. Oman.
Description: Salt Lake City : Greg Kofford Books, 2024. | Series: Law and the Restoration | Includes bibliographical references and index. | Summary: "Law and the Restoration: Law and Latter-day Saint History is a profound exploration of the intricate legal history of The Church of Jesus Christ of Latter-day Saints. In this first of two volumes, Nathan B. Oman delves into the unique intersection of law and religion, uncovering how legal frameworks have shaped and been shaped by the experiences of Latter-day Saints. Through a series of meticulously researched essays, Oman reveals the profound impact of legal conflicts and developments on the growth and identity of the Church. From the early struggles for legal recognition and the battles over polygamy to the establishment of corporate entities and the role of religious courts, this book offers a comprehensive and enlightening narrative of the Church's legal journey. Oman's scholarly work extends beyond mere historical recounting; it situates the Mormon legal experience within the broader context of American legal history. By examining the ways in which the Latter-day Saints navigated the legal challenges posed by a predominantly Protestant legal system, Oman provides invaluable insights into the broader themes of religious freedom, church-state relations, and legal pluralism. Each chapter is a testament to the resilience and adaptability of the Church, highlighting pivotal moments and key figures who influenced its legal standing"-- Provided by publisher.
Identifiers: LCCN 2024024040 (print) | LCCN 2024024041 (ebook) | ISBN 9781589587960 (paperback) | ISBN 9781589588103 (hardcover) | ISBN 9781589587977 (ebook)
Subjects: LCSH: Latter Day Saints--Legal status, laws, etc.--United States--History. | Church and state--Church of Jesus Christ of Latter-day Saints--History. | Church of Jesus Christ of Latter-day Saints--History. | Church of Jesus Christ of Latter-day Saints--Customs and practices. | Ecclesiastical courts--United States--History. | Latter Day Saint churches--Doctrines.
Classification: LCC KF4869.M6 O43 2024 (print) | LCC KF4869.M6 (ebook) | DDC 342.7308/52893--dc23/eng/20240730
LC record available at https://lccn.loc.gov/2024024040
LC ebook record available at https://lccn.loc.gov/2024024041

For Heather.

"Behold, there shall be a record kept among you . . ."
(Doctrine & Covenants 21:1)

Contents

Preface

This is the first of a two-volume work written by a law professor. A lawyer inflicting so many words on the world requires some kind of defense or, at the very least, an explanation. I first encountered issues around law and Mormonism as an undergraduate at Brigham Young University, where then-professor Paul Edwards introduced me to the nineteenth-century polygamy cases that The Church of Jesus Christ of Latter-day Saints fought to the US Supreme Court before capitulating to federal pressure in 1890. I was fascinated and chose to pursue a career as a legal scholar, in large part, as a result of that experience. These volumes are the consequence. In the two decades since graduating from law school, I have written and published extensively on law and the Latter-day Saint tradition. The purpose of this volume and the next is to collect those materials into a single place. Some of the chapters that follow appeared in Mormon studies journals, but many of them were published in law reviews where many students of Mormonism are unlikely to see them. Two chapters are published in this volume for the first time.

While each chapter is meant to be read on its own, my hope is that gathering these essays into a single place will be both helpful to readers and illustrative of the possibilities of Latter-day Saint legal thought. My goal has never been to provide a comprehensive summary of Mormon positions on disputed jurisprudential questions, to articulate an integrated Mormon vision of the law, or to write a legal history of Mormonism. Rather, these essays are meant to model ways in which disciplined reflection on the relationship between law and Mormonism might be conducted given the eclecticism of legal thought.

This first volume focuses on Mormon legal history. Rather than starting with the abstractions of theology or the intricacies of normative legal arguments, one can begin with Mormon legal experience. Looking at nineteenth-century Mormonism, there are at least two interrelated stories that can be told about the law. The first is the story of the various ways in which the law was used by outsiders as a tool to suppress or control Mormonism. This began with legal actions brought against Joseph Smith during the opening months of his ministry, and it continued through much of the nineteenth century, reaching a dramatic crescendo in the 1880s when the federal government used the full panoply of post-Reconstruction legal mechanisms to coerce the Church into abandoning polygamy. The second story looks at the ways in which Mormonism has used law as a mechanism for defining itself and advancing its own religious agendas. This story begins with the organization of the Church in 1830 under the laws of the state of New York. At the height of their independence in Utah during the 1850s and 1860s, the Latter-day Saints in effect established their own legal system consisting of a mixture of territorial legislation and ecclesiastical adjudication. In addition, law played a key role in the development of various Mormon cooperatives and other economic experiments in the nineteenth century, whose structure was often decisively influenced by legal requirements.

Both of these narratives focus on the nineteenth-century experience of Latter-day Saints, which has garnered the lion's share of academic attention devoted to Mormon legal experience. From a scholarly point of view, the twentieth-century legal experience of Latter-day Saints remains largely terra incognita. During this period, however, the Church began to permanently expand overseas, bringing to the fore questions of how Mormonism interacts with non-American legal systems. Also, as the Church has gained power and self-confidence, it has been involved as a political actor in seeking to shape the law. In the United States, its most dramatic interventions came with its opposition to the Equal Rights Amendment in the late 1970s and its involvement in debates over same-sex marriage in the 1990s and 2000s. Abroad, it has had to deal with occasional harassment under anti-cult laws, as well as legal opposition from incumbent religions eager to shield themselves from what they perceive as American competition.

Latter-day Saint legal thinkers need to claim and understand this past. The first step in doing so, however, requires that it be viewed in less overtly Mormon terms. Much of the scholarship that has been done on Mormon legal experience is structured by an implicit apologetic agenda. This has taken several different forms. On one hand, there is work that seeks to examine long-standing accusations of Mormon misbehavior, recast the accusations as a legal claim, and then demonstrate that the legal claim is false, thus vindicating the Latter-day Saints. The classic example of such work is Dallin H. Oaks's 1965 article in the *Utah Law Review* on the suppression of the *Nauvoo Expositor*, an anti-Mormon newspaper whose destruction at the hands of the Latter-day Saints directly led to Joseph Smith's murder.[1] In his article, Oaks demonstrated that Smith's actions as mayor of Nauvoo

---

1. See Dallin H. Oaks, "The Suppression of the Nauvoo Expositor," *Utah Law Review* 9 (1965): 862–903.

in suppressing the paper were constitutional under then-current applications of the First Amendment. Alternatively, Mormon writers have examined the actions of historical opponents of Mormonism, arguing either that they acted illegally or that the legal means they employed would or should be rejected today. Hence, for example, one of Oaks's students has examined the proceedings that led to the incarceration of Joseph Smith in Liberty Jail in 1838 and concluded that they were illegal.[2] Likewise, in their book-length legal history of nineteenth-century Mormonism, Ed Firmage and Collin Mangrum provide an analysis under modern law of the government's legal position in the 1880s, concluding that it would fail to pass constitutional muster today.[3]

Mormon legal history must move beyond this apologetic paradigm if it is to be useful in thinking constructively about the law. Rather, scholars must place the Mormon legal experience in a broader historical context, showing the ways in which Latter-day Saints' stories followed and diverged from the experience of non-Mormons. Only by asking the question of what Mormon legal history tells us about the story of the law can that history begin to form a basis for Latter-day Saint legal thought. The apologetic paradigm necessarily narrows the significance of Mormon legal experience and restricts its ability to act as a fruitful starting place for Latter-day Saint reflection on the law. Indeed, even as an apologetic it is likely to fail, as law is ultimately a tool ill-suited for establishing religious legitimacy. Rather, work on Latter-day Saint legal history should instead focus on what the Latter-day Saint legal experience tells us about legal history, the relationship between law and religion, or the role of law in the rise of a new religious tradition. My hope is that the chapters that follow model what such an approaches might look like.

Except for minor stylistic changes, the previously published articles are presented here as they first appeared. The one exception is chapter 4, which I have taken the liberty of expanding.[4] Excessive footnoting is

2. See Gordon A. Madsen, "Joseph Smith and the Missouri Court of Inquiry: Austin A. King's Quest for Hostages," *Brigham Young University Studies* 43, no. 4 (2004): 92–136.

3. See, e.g., Edwin Brown Firmage and Richard Collin Mangrum, *Zion in the Courts: A Legal History of the Church of Jesus Christ of Latter-Day Saints, 1830–1900* (Urbana: University of Illinois Press, 1988), 156–59.

4. Truth be told, my expansion is the restoration of materials on the broader historical context that were deleted for the more popular audience of the BYU Religious Studies Center, where the piece was first published. See Nathan B.

one of the many vices of legal scholarship, and I have removed footnotes required by law review conventions that I deemed excessive or distracting. I am grateful to the publishers of the articles listed below for permission to include them in this volume:

Nathan B. Oman. "'The Blessing That's Anticipated Here Will Be Realized in the Next Life': The Development of Modern Latter-Day Saint Marital Sealing Rules." *Journal of Mormon History* 49, no. 3 (2023): 103–40.[5]

Nathan B. Oman. "Salt, Smurthwaite, and Smith: The Origins of the Legal Identity of the Church of Jesus Christ of Latter-day Saints." *Journal of Mormon History* 48, no. 1 (2022): 92–122.

Nathan B. Oman. "'Established Agreeable to the Laws of Our Country': Mormonism, Church Corporations, and the Long Legacy of America's First Disestablishment." *Journal of Law and Religion* 36, no. 2 (2021): 202–29.

Nathan B. Oman. "'We the People of the Kingdom of God': Constitution Writing in the Council of Fifty." In *The Council of Fifty: What the Records Reveal about Mormon History*, 55–72. Provo & Salt Lake City: Religious Studies Center, Brigham Young University & Deseret Book, 2017.

Nathan B. Oman. "International Legal Experience and the Mormon Theology of the State, 1945–2012." *Iowa Law Review* 100 (2015): 715–50.

Nathan B. Oman. "Natural Law and the Rhetoric of Empire: Reynolds v. United States, Polygamy, and Imperialism." *Washington University Law Review* 88, no. 3 (2011): 661–706.

Nathan B. Oman. "Preaching to the Court House and Judging in the Temple." *Brigham Young University Law Review* 2009, no. 1 (2009): 157–24.

Oman, "'We the People of the Kingdom of God': Constitution Writing in the Council of Fifty," in *The Council of Fifty: What the Records Reveal about Mormon History* (Provo & Salt Lake City: Religious Studies Center, Brigham Young University & Deseret Book, 2017), 55–72.

5. The published article contained a dating error at note 104, which has been corrected in this volume. I am grateful to Katie Gibson Jacobsen for pointing out the error.

CHAPTER 1

Three Generations of Mormon Legal History

Introduction

This chapter is on the past practice and the future possibilities of Mormon legal history. For most legal scholars, the fact that there even is such a thing as "Mormon legal history" comes as a surprise, and the idea that it "should be proved . . . to be worthy of the interest of an intelligent man"[1] may sound dubious at best. In part, such a reaction stems from the marginal status of Latter-day Saints. At a broader level, however, the invisibility of Mormon legal history is simply part of the broader problem of the discussion of religion within the legal academy. While there is a deep literature on traditional questions of church and state, discussions of religious legal experience or thought have been less prominent. Many legal scholars, if they were to consider the question, would assume that there is not any there there. An anecdote by Harold Berman illustrates the issue:

> In 1951, as an assistant professor, I asked the formidable Dean Erwin Griswold [of Harvard Law School] whether it would not be a good idea to introduce a course in law and Christianity, since Christianity had had such an important influence on the origin and development of our legal institutions. He replied, "Well, perhaps it could be an extracurricular seminar, not for credit."[2]

With the waning of mid-century certainties about the onward march of secularization, however, the legal academy has been more open to the possibilities of studying religious legal thought and experience.[3]

---

1. See Oliver Wendell Holmes, Jr., *The Essential Holmes: Selections from the Letters, Speeches, Judicial Opinions, and Other Writings of Oliver Wendell Holmes, Jr.*, ed. Richard A. Posner (Chicago: University of Chicago Press, 1997), 265 (noting that his goal in writing The Common Law was to persuade readers that law was "worthy of the interest of an intelligent man").

2. Harold J. Berman, "Foreword," in *Christian Perspectives on Legal Thought*, ed. Michael W. McConnell, Robert F. Cochran, Jr., and Angela C. Carmella (New Haven: Yale University Press, 2001), xii. Berman's anecdote, of course, overstates academic indifference to religion, even at Harvard Law School in the 1950s. See, e.g., Mark DeWolfe Howe, *The Garden and the Wilderness: Religion and Government in American Constitutional History* (Chicago: University of Chicago Press, 1965). (Howe was a law professor at Harvard.)

3. Of course, some scholars remain intensely skeptical about the legal academy's ability to accommodate religious legal perspectives. For example, William J.

This is fortunate because there is much in the legal past of Mormonism that should be of interest to legal scholars. For example:

- During the nineteenth century, Latter-day Saints settled and governed much of the Intermountain West, creating a religious commonwealth that covered much of the country from Canada to Mexico and from the crest of the Rockies to the crest of the Sierra Nevadas. For at least four decades they sought to create a theocratic government within the context of the United States, producing their own legal codes and institutions.[4]

Stuntz has written, "Religion is not a topic of much conversation in the law school world; what little discussion there is tends to treat serious religious commitment as a disease—call it the germ theory of religion—perhaps especially if the religion is Christianity." William J. Stuntz, "Christian Legal Theory," *Harvard Law Review* 116 (2003): 1707. The appearance—and generally respectful reception—of the book that Stuntz was reviewing in the quoted article, however, suggests that his view is far too dour. See, e.g., Mark Tushnet, "Distinctively Christian Perspectives on Legal Thought?," *Michigan Law Review* 101, no. 6 (2003): 1858–68. The presence of other religious voices in the pages of the law reviews and the academic presses also suggests that religion is not viewed as quite the noxious disease that Stuntz suggests. See, e.g., David A. Jr. Skeel and William J. Stuntz, "Christianity and the (Modest) Rule of Law," *University of Pennsylvania Journal of Constitutional Law* 8, no. 4 (2006): 809–40; R. J. Araujo, "Thomas Aquinas: Prudence, Justice, and the Law," *Loyola Law Review* 40, no. 4 (1995): 897–922 (Catholic); Harold J. Berman, "The Spiritualization of Secular Law: The Impact of the Lutheran Reformation," *Journal of Law and Religion* 14, no. 2 (1999): 313–49 (Protestant); David A. Funk, "Traditional Islamic Jurisprudence: Justifying Islamic Law and Government," *Southern University Law Review* 20, no. 2 (1993): 213–94; Suzanne Last Stone, "In Pursuit of the Counter-Text: The Turn to the Jewish Legal Model in Contemporary American Legal Theory," *Harvard Law Review* 106, no. 4 (1993): 813–94 (Jewish).

4. See David Bigler, *Forgotten Kingdom: The Mormon Theocracy in the American West, 1847–1896*, 1st ed. (Logan: Utah State University Press, 1998) (recounting Mormon efforts to create a theocratic commonwealth in the Great Basin and the ultimately successful efforts of non-Latter-day Saints to suppress it); Leonard J. Arrington, Feramorz Y. Fox, and Dean L. May, *Building the City of God: Community and Cooperation Among the Latter-day Saints*, 2nd ed. (Urbana: University of Illinois Press, 1992) (discussing the economic and political organization of the nineteenth-century Mormon commonwealth in the Great Basin); Dale L. Morgan, *The State of Deseret* (Logan: Utah State University Press with the Utah State Historical Society, 1987) (discussing the history of the Mormon commonwealth in the Great Basin and reproducing all of the legislation passed by the State of Deseret).

- From 1862 until 1890, the federal government waged a massive legal campaign against the practice of polygamy. For three decades the Latter-day Saints tried one legal and political gambit after another to avoid prosecution. Hundreds of polygamists were incarcerated, and the Supreme Court issued a series of decisions that defined, for the first time, the religion clauses of the first amendment. It was the longest and most intense conflict between law and religion in American history.[5]
- During the last half of the nineteenth century, as outside legal authority in the shape of federal laws and officials increasingly penetrated "Mormon country," Latter-day Saints abandoned the secular courts as the forum for resolving their civil disputes. The result was the rise of the Mormon ecclesiastical court system that, for at least two generations, functioned as the primary civil dispute resolution mechanism for the Latter-day Saints and some non-Latter-day Saints. In terms of geographic and temporal extent and breadth of subject matter, it was perhaps the largest religious legal system in American history, as well as one of the largest private American legal systems.[6]

The thesis of this chapter is that the limited visibility of Mormon legal history stems less from a lack of interest in religious legal experiences in general or in Mormon legal experiences specifically, than from the idio-

---

5. See Sarah Barringer Gordon, *The Mormon Question: Polygamy and Constitutional Conflict in Nineteenth-Century America* (Chapel Hill: University of North Carolina Press, 2002) (recounting the federal government's crusade against polygamy in the decades after the Civil War); Orma Linford, "The Latter-day Saints and the Law: The Polygamy Cases, Part I," *Utah Law Review* 9, no. 2 (1964): 308–71 (same as previous); Orma Linford, "The Latter-day Saints and the Law: The Polygamy Cases, Part II," *Utah Law Review* 9, no. 3 (1965): 543–92 (same as previous); Ray Jay Davis, "The Polygamous Prelude," *American Journal of Legal History* 6, no. 1 (1962): 1–27 (same as previous).

6. See Edwin Brown Firmage and R. Collin Mangrum, *Zion in the Courts: A Legal History of the Church of Jesus Christ of Latter-Day Saints, 1830–1900*, 1st ed. (Urbana: University of Illinois Press, 1988), 263–370 (providing a detailed summary of the functioning of Mormon ecclesiastical courts from 1846 to 1900); Raymond T. Swenson, "Resolution of Civil Disputes by Mormon Ecclesiastical Courts," *Utah Law Review* 1978, no. 2 (1978): 573–95 (same as previous); C. Paul Dredge, "Dispute Settlement in the Mormon Community: The Operation of Ecclesiastical Courts in Utah," in *Access to Justice: The Anthropological Perspective: Patterns of Conflict Management: Essays in the Ethnography of Law*, ed. Klaus-Friedrich Koch, vol. 4 (n.p.: Giuffrè Editore/Sijthoff/Noordhoff, 1979) (same as previous).

syncratic intellectual development of Mormon legal historiography itself. By explaining that development and introducing the work that has already been done on Mormon legal history, I hope to assist future scholars in better integrating Mormon legal experience into the mainstream discussions of the legal academy.

The remainder of this chapter has three goals: first, to provide an introduction to the literature on legal history that has been produced in the small but growing field of Mormon studies; second, to show how the intellectual development of that literature has limited its usefulness to those outside of the field of Mormon history; and third, to argue that the discussion within Mormon studies has reached a point at which it can and should be of interest to the legal academy.

A Brief History of Mormonism and its Historians

The history of Mormonism can be simplified and summarized thus:[7] The Church was founded in 1830 in upstate New York by a young man named Joseph Smith. Fueled by the revivals of the Second Great Awakening, Smith's spiritual journey began with a vision of God and Jesus Christ in 1820, instructing him not to join any of the competing evangelical sects. In the mid-1820s, he had another series of visions that culminated in the publication of the Book of Mormon as an additional book of scripture to the Bible in 1830.[8] Thereafter, Smith attracted converts and controversy as he moved his headquarters first to Ohio and then to Missouri. Producing additional revelations that were added to the expanding Mormon canon, Smith taught that his followers had to gather to build up the New Jerusalem in preparation for Christ's second coming. This concentration of Mormon population (and political power),

7. For one-volume histories of Mormonism, see Claudia Bushman and Richard L. Bushman, *Building the Kingdom: A History of Latter-day Saints in America* (Oxford: Oxford University Press, 2001); Klaus J. Hansen, *Mormonism and the American Experience* (Chicago: University of Chicago Press, 1981); Leonard J. Arrington and Davis Bitton, *The Mormon Experience: A History of the Latter-Day Saints*, 1st ed. (New York: Knopf, distributed by Random House, 1979). For a historically informed treatment of Mormonism from the perspective of religious studies, see Jan Shipps, *Mormonism: The Story of a New Religious Tradition* (Urbana: University of Illinois Press, 1985).

8. See Richard Lyman Bushman, *Joseph Smith and the Beginnings of Mormonism* (Urbana: University of Illinois Press, 1984) (discussing the early history of Mormonism in New York).

coupled with theological innovations and fiery rhetoric by Mormon preachers, finally led to violent mobs in Missouri and the ultimate expulsion of the Latter-day Saints from the state by the governor.[9] They found refuge in Illinois, where they founded the city of Nauvoo, briefly the largest city in the state. The same tensions with neighbors, exacerbated by the quasi-secret introduction of polygamy by Smith, led to his murder at the hands of a mob in 1844 and the expulsion of the Latter-day Saints from Illinois in 1846.[10]

Under the leadership of Brigham Young, the Latter-day Saints emigrated en mass to the American west, where they founded a vast religious commonwealth in the Great Basin which included much of present-day Utah, as well as parts of Idaho, Wyoming, Colorado, Arizona, New Mexico, Nevada, California, and—at its greatest extent—settlements in both Canada and Mexico.[11] The theocratic government, polygamous marriage system, and economic communitarianism of the Latter-day Saints, however, attracted the attention of Protestant reformers. In 1857, the federal government dispatched an army to put down a Mormon "rebellion." Ultimately, a peaceful settlement between Latter-day Saints and federal troops was negotiated, but not before a fearful group of Latter-day Saints in a remote area of Utah had murdered a company of California-bound immigrants in the so-called Mountain Meadows Massacre.[12] Thereafter federal pressure mounted in the form of increasingly stringent legislation aimed at Mormon polygamy, as well as Mormon economic and political

---

9. See R. J. Robertson, "The Mormon Experience in Missouri, 1830–1839, Part I," *Missouri Historical Review* 68, no. 3 (1974): 280–98; R. J. Robertson, "The Mormon Experience in Missouri, 1830–1839, Part II," *Missouri Historical Review* 68, no. 4 (1974): 393–415; Stephen C. LeSueur, *The 1838 Mormon War in Missouri* (Columbia: University of Missouri Press, 1987) (discussing the conflict between Latter-day Saints and non-Latter-day Saints in Missouri).

10. See generally Glen M. Leonard, *Nauvoo: Place of Peace, a People of Promise* (Salt Lake City: Deseret Book Co., 2002) (discussing the history of Mormonism during the Illinois period); Robert Bruce Flanders, *Nauvoo: Kingdom on the Mississippi* (Urbana: University of Illinois Press, 1975) (same as previous).

11. See Leonard J. Arrington, *Brigham Young: American Moses*, 2nd ed. (Urbana: University of Illinois Press, 1991) (recounting the story of Mormon settlement in the Great Basin).

12. See Norman F. Furniss, *The Mormon Conflict, 1850–1859* (New Haven: Yale University Press, 1960) (recounting the so-called "Utah War"); Juanita Brooks, *The Mountain Meadows Massacre* (Stanford: Stanford University Press, 1950) (recounting the murder of the California-bound immigrant train and its aftermath).

power. Ultimately, hundreds of Latter-day Saints were jailed and disenfranchised, the Church was legally disincorporated, and its property was confiscated by federal officials. In the face of this pressure, the Church relented in 1890, publicly abandoning polygamy.[13] Despite continued public suspicion—and the clandestine practice of polygamy by some Latter-day Saints for another ten to fifteen years—tensions between the Latter-day Saints and the nation gradually relaxed.[14] Mormonism reconstructed itself from a marginal monster into the epitome of middle-American wholesomeness and focused on a world-wide missionary effort which has resulted in a massive international expansion with millions of converts, largely in developing countries.[15]

From its inception, Mormonism has been a historically self-conscious faith. In 1831 Smith published a revelation in which God called one of his associates to "continue in writing and making a history of all the important things which he shall observe and know concerning my church."[16] During his lifetime Smith composed several autobiographical sketches, as well as an incomplete history of the Church.[17] In addition to the of-

---

13. See Gordon, *The Mormon Question* (discussing the history of the federal government's crusade against the Latter-day Saints).

14. See Kathleen Flake, *The Politics of American Religious Identity: The Seating of Senator Reed Smoot, Mormon Apostle* (Chapel Hill: University of North Carolina Press, 2004) (discussing political controversies involving Latter-day Saints in the early 1900s); Thomas G. Alexander, *Mormonism in Transition: A History of the Latter-Day Saints, 1890–1930* (Urbana: University of Illinois Press, 1996) (discussing the shift from nineteenth- to twentieth-century Mormonism).

15. See Gregory A. Prince and Wm. Robert Wright, *David O. McKay and the Rise of Modern Mormonism* (Salt Lake City: University of Utah Press, 2005) (discussing Mormon history in the twentieth century, particularly after World War II).

16. See *Doctrine and Covenants of the Church of Jesus Christ of Latter-Day Saints* (Salt Lake City: The Church of Jesus Christ of Latter-day Saints, 1981), 69:3. The Doctrine and Covenants contains revelations published by Smith and his successors as presidents of the Church. It is accepted as canon by Latter-day Saints, giving it the same status as the Bible and Book of Mormon in LDS theology.

17. See Joseph Smith and Dean C. Jessee, *The Personal Writings of Joseph Smith*, revised edition (Salt Lake City: Deseret Book Co, 2002); Joseph Smith Jr. and Dean C. Jessee, *The Papers of Joseph Smith*, vol. 1 (Salt Lake City: Deseret Book Company, 1989); Joseph Smith, Jr., *The Papers of Joseph Smith*, vol. 2 (Salt Lake City: Deseret Book Company, 1989); Brigham H. Roberts, *A Comprehensive History of the Church of Jesus Christ of Latter-Day Saints*, 6 vols. (Provo: Brigham Young University Press, 1965).

ficial recordkeeping of the Church hierarchy, individual Latter-day Saints have a long tradition of journal keeping and personal histories.[18] These two streams of recordkeeping have combined to create a vast literature of genealogical and devotional history explicitly aimed at a Latter-day Saint audience.[19] Alongside this literature has grown a vast body of polemical works on Mormon history, aimed at debunking its religious claims.[20]

Beginning about 1950, a new genre of Mormon history began to appear. Written by university-trained academics or those employing the methods of academic history, the genre sought to extricate itself from the battles between devotional writers and anti-Mormon polemicists and to present Mormonism as a subject of inherent intellectual interest independent of its religious truth claims. To be sure, most—but by no means all—of the practitioners of the so-called New Mormon History have been Latter-day Saints of one stripe or another. Nevertheless, the ambition of this history has been to speak in a secular—or neutral—voice for a general academic audience. The result has been a torrent of monographs, books, and articles.[21] Several peer-reviewed journals have sprouted up, as well as a professional group called the Mormon History Association that sponsors annual conferences for those working in the area.[22] After a half-century of work, it is safe to say that Mormon history has emerged as a legitimate academic subfield with

---

18. See Davis Bitton, *Guide to Mormon Diaries & Autobiographies* (Provo: Brigham Young University Press, 1977) (summarizing Mormon diaries and autobiographies held by various research libraries).

19. The most sophisticated and enduring example of this genre has been the six-volume *Comprehensive History of the Church* written for the Church's 1930 centennial by Brigham H. Roberts, a member of the Church hierarchy and an autodidact philosopher, historian, and theologian.

20. Some sense of the scope of the literature on Mormonism can be seen in Chad J. Flake, ed., *A Mormon Bibliography, 1830–1930; Books, Pamphlets, Periodicals, and Broadsides Relating to the First Century of Mormonism.* (Salt Lake City: University of Utah Press, 1978), which lists literally thousands of books, articles, and pamphlets.

21. An extensive and electronically searchable bibliography of this material is maintained by Brigham Young University at http://mormonhistory.byu.edu.

22. The main peer-reviewed academic journals in Mormon studies are *The Journal of Mormon History*, *Brigham Young University Studies*, and *Dialogue: A Journal of Mormon Thought*. In addition, there are numerous smaller academic journals devoted to Mormon topics such as *Element: The Journal of the Society for Mormon Philosophy and Theology*.

a substantial body of high-quality literature.[23] Indeed, in what is perhaps a sign of intellectual maturation, a number of works tracing the trajectory of Mormon historiography have appeared.[24] None of these works, however, have dealt with the development of Mormon legal history.[25]

23. See, e.g., Scott McLemee, "Latter-Day Studies: Scholars of Mormonism Confront the History of What Some Call 'the Next World Religion,'" *The Chronicle of Higher Education*, March 22, 2002, sec. A14 ("The field of Mormon studies displays an abundance of energy, attracting not just specialists in American studies or religious history, but social scientists and cultural theorists as well"). This is not to suggest, of course, that the study of Mormon history or of Mormonism is not beset with tensions and difficulties. See Seth Perry, "An Outsider Looks in at Mormonism," *The Chronicle of Higher Education*, February 3, 2006, sec. B9 ("The academic study of religion is itself relatively new, beset with a number of interpretive problems that have not been fully sorted out—issues of faith and scholarship, of the status of insiders and outsiders, of the parochialism that religion often brings out in scholars as much as in everyone else—and those problems are displayed in particularly stark relief with respect to the study of Mormonism").

24. See Newell G. Bringhurst and Lavina Fielding Anderson, *Excavating Mormon Pasts: The New Historiography of the Last Half Century*, 1st ed. (Salt Lake City: Greg Kofford Books, 2004); Ronald W. Walker, David J. Whittaker, and James B. Allen, *Mormon History* (Urbana: University of Illinois Press, 2001); D. Michael Quinn, *The New Mormon History: Revisionist Essays on the Past* (Salt Lake City: Signature Books, 1992); Davis Bitton and Leonard J. Arrington, *Latter-day Saints and Their Historians* (Salt Lake City: University of Utah Press, 1988); James B. Allen, "Since 1950: Creators and Creations of Mormon History," in *New Views of Mormon History*, by Leonard J. Arrington, Davis Bitton, and Maureen Ursenbach Beecher (Salt Lake City: University of Utah Press, 1987), 407; Thomas G. Alexander, "Toward the New Mormon History: An Examination of the Literature on the Latter-Day Saints in the Far West," in *Historians and the American West*, by Michael P. Malone (Lincoln: University of Nebraska Press, 1983). For an earlier historiographic treatment, see Marvin S. Hill, "The Historiography of Mormonism," *Church History* 28, no. 4 (1959): 418–26. The New Mormon History has also sparked a lively debate within Mormonism about the relationship between religious faith and professionalized history. See generally George Smith, ed., *Faithful History: Essays on Writing Mormon History* (Salt Lake City: Signature Books, 1992).

25. The recent work on Mormon historiography does mention Mormon legal history in passing, but there is no real attempt to analyze that work independent of its place within Mormon history generally. See, e.g., Martha Sonntag Bradley, "Out of the Closet and into the Fire: The New Mormon Historians Take on Polygamy," in *Excavating Mormon Pasts*, 303, 317–18 (briefly summarizing the work of legal historians dealing with the issue of polygamy in the context of a general review of the literature on Mormon polygamy).

The Possibilities of Mormon Legal History

Contemporary legal scholarship is largely a story of intellectual arbitrage. To be sure, the legal academy retains the much-maligned tools of doctrinal analysis and traditional legal reasoning, and so long as it is in the business of training lawyers and digesting the work of the courts, in no doubt it always will. Nevertheless, many of the most fruitful legal research agendas of the last few decades have taken the form of intellectual imports from beyond the law which have been adapted to a new jurisprudential surrounding. To give an example, economists have pursued research on the idea of perfectly specified contracts; untangling the strategic puzzles involves designing a hypothetical contract that would explicitly set forth the rights between the parties under any possible future state of affairs. Legal scholars, in turn, have taken these highly abstract game-theoretic discussions and used them to think about the way the law provides default terms for parties who could not possibly write fully specified contracts in the real world.[26] This is the way that legal thought is fertilized by new ideas. Hence, much of a legal scholar's work consists of finding untapped sources of ideas for thinking about the law.

Mormonism is one of the most colorful threads running through American history. In a country supposedly dedicated to religious pluralism, it sought to create a theocratic commonwealth based on religious unity and solidarity. In the face of national narratives about the sanctity of monogamous marriage and free enterprise, nineteenth-century Latter-day Saints radically re-imagined family relationships and sought to create large-scale communal economic experiments at the height of the Gilded Age. At the same time, Mormonism bears the marks of the American culture from which it emerged. Part of that cultural inheritance was the American tradition of legalism. Hence, many key aspects of Mormon experience were mediated through legal events or legal concepts. For at least fifty years, Mormonism has attracted sustained academic attention. The result is a wealth of documentation and analysis of the Mormon past. The fruit of this industry includes a haul of material on the legal aspects of that past. Nevertheless, it is only comparatively recently that any attempts

26. See, e.g., Robert E. Scott and George G. Triantis, "Incomplete Contracts and the Theory of Contract Design Symposium: Incomplete Contracts: Judicial Responses, Transactional Planning, and Litigation Strategies," *Case Western Reserve Law Review* 56, no. 1 (2005): 187–202. See also the articles included in the *Case Western Reserve Law Review* symposium issue of which the Scott and Triantis article is a part.

have been made to relate this research to on-going debates within the legal academy. In short, the New Mormon History represents a potential area of intellectual arbitrage that has yet to be fully tapped.

I will confine myself to one example. Traditionally, legal scholars have focused their attention on formal, governmental structures. Law, so the thinking has gone, is something that states do, and to study the law is to study the rules promulgated by governments. This state-centric vision of the law, however, is something of a historical accident, an inheritance from John Austin, Oliver Wendell Holmes, and other state-obsessed jurisprudes of the nineteenth century. Harold Berman, for example, has shown that many of the key features of the Western legal tradition developed outside of—and indeed in opposition to—the authority of the state.[27] Thus the ecclesiastical law of the medieval Catholic Church proved at least as influential on later legal developments as royal law.[28] (In Anglo-American law this influence can be traced back through the ideas of equity.) Likewise, the great medieval revival in Roman law began not in the royal chanceries but in the universities.[29] Finally, the earliest antecedents of modern commercial law are found not in the decisions of the royal courts but rather in the lex mercatoria, or law merchant, developed and administered by the businessmen who organized the fairs of medieval Europe.[30] More prosaically, many practicing lawyers know that certain classes of disputes never make it into the courts, but rather are handled by private tribunals applying rules developed by those who are "in the trade."[31] Furthermore, some communities seem to resolve potentially legal disputes without recourse to formal adjudication of any kind.[32]

---

27. See Harold J. Berman, *Law and Revolution: The Formation of the Western Legal Tradition* (Cambridge: Harvard University Press, 1983).

28. See Berman, 199–224. See also James Gordley, *The Philosophical Origins of Modern Contract Doctrine* (New York: Oxford University Press, 1993) (arguing that the law of contracts finds its ultimate intellectual origins in the work of late-medieval theologians).

29. Berman, *Law and Revolution*, 120–64.

30. Berman, 332–56.

31. See, e.g., Lisa Bernstein, "Private Commercial Law in the Cotton Industry: Creating Cooperation through Rules, Norms, and Institutions," *Michigan Law Review* 99, no. 6 (2001): 1724–90.

32. See, e.g., Robert C. Ellickson, *Order without Law: How Neighbors Settle Disputes* (Cambridge: Harvard University Press, 1991) (discussing dispute resolution among cattle ranchers in Shasta County, California).

Legal scholars have recognized that understanding "law" requires studying these ubiquitous non-state mechanisms that serve legal functions. For example, Lisa Bernstein has produced a string of excellent studies examining the structure, rules, and procedures of private legal systems in the diamond, cotton, and grain and feed industries.[33] What she has uncovered, in turn, challenges key assumptions on which much of modern commercial law is based.[34]

Mormon legal history dramatically raises the issue of private legal systems. Nineteenth-century Latter-day Saints were hostile to the common-law system that they inherited. Joseph Smith spent essentially his entire adult life being sued by one person or another, and he seems to have transmitted an understandable antipathy toward lawyers to his followers. Brigham Young was strident in his denunciations of the evil of the Latter-day Saints "going to law" with one another. The origins, however, of Mormon antipathy toward the secular courts go deeper than simple dislike of lawyers. Rather, nineteenth-century Mormon theology centered around the concept of Zion, a vision of the godly society that was to be achieved through the consecrated efforts of the Latter-day Saints in the here and now. Given such a totalizing social vision, the Latter-day Saints unsurprisingly created their own alternatives to the secular courts.[35] The result was the Mormon ecclesiastical court system, staffed by the local lay leaders of the Church and serving as a full-service private legal system for the Latter-day Saints. The most extensive account of the court system summarizes it thus:

---

33. See Bernstein, "Private Commercial Law in the Cotton Industry"; Lisa Bernstein, "Merchant Law in a Merchant Court: Rethinking the Code's Search for Immanent Business Norms," *University of Pennsylvania Law Review* 144, no. 5 (1996): 1765–1821; Lisa Bernstein, "Opting out of the Legal System: Extralegal Contractual Relations in the Diamond Industry," *Journal of Legal Studies* 21, no. 1 (1992): 115–58.

34. See Bernstein, "Merchant Law in a Merchant Court" ("This Article draws on a case study of merchant law in a merchant court to reexamine, and, ultimately, to challenge, the fundamental premise of the Uniform Commercial Code's adjudicative philosophy, the idea that courts should seek to discover 'immanent business norms' and use them to decide cases"). See also Lisa Bernstein, "The Questionable Empirical Basis of Article 2's Incorporation Strategy: A Preliminary Study," *The University of Chicago Law Review* 66, no. 3 (1999): 710–80.

35. See generally Edwin Brown Firmage, "Reflections on Mormon History: Zion and the Anti-Legal Tradition," *Dialogue: A Journal of Mormon Thought* 31, no. 4 (Winter 1998): 53–62.

> After they migrated to the deserts of the Great Basin, the Saints pursued their radical theory of Zion as an alternative to the social experiment of pluralistic America. A critical part of this effort was the establishment and maintenance of their own court system. Through their ecclesiastical courts Latter-day Saints were able to offer an alternative to the divisive influence of the adversarial legal system with its technical pleadings, rules of evidence, and pettifogging lawyers. More importantly Latter-day Saints were able to introject their own notions of community and temporal affairs into the resolution of social conflict. The ecclesiastical court systems facilitated a radical change in the laws governing the distribution of land, water, and other natural resources. Church courts also permitted religious perspectives to be determinative in conflicts arising out of contractual or tortious disputes. Finally, the courts provided forums for the mediation of conflict in polygamous families. In each of these substantive law areas, the existence of the church courts enhanced the independence of the church from the state, thereby lending credibility to the theological concept of Zion.[36]

This summary of the Mormon courts gives some sense to their temporal, geographic, and jurisdictional scope. They functioned as the main Mormon adjudicators from at least 1846 until about 1900.[37] Geographically, they covered the entirety of Mormon country, making them one of the primary "legal" actors in the region of the United States stretching from the Sierra Nevadas to the Rockies and from the Snake River in the north to the Colorado River in the south.[38] Finally, with the exception of criminal cases, the ecclesiastical courts sought to exercise virtually unlimited jurisdiction over all Latter-day Saints. They also provided adjudication for non-Latter-day Saints who preferred the informality of the ecclesiastical courts to the slower pace of the secular courts.[39] Indeed, the Mormon courts did not hesitate to take jurisdiction over even govern-

---

36. Firmage and Mangrum, *Zion in the Courts*, 261.

37. Firmage and Mangrum, 264–67.

38. This is in some ways a conservative description of the area of Mormon settlement and influence, which extended into western Wyoming and well south of Colorado into central Arizona. In addition, Latter-day Saints sent out colonies far to the north and south of the Mormon heartland, founding settlements in northern Mexico and southern Alberta. See generally S. Kent Jackson Brown, Donald Q. Cannon, and Richard H. Jackson, *Historical Atlas of Mormonism* (New York: Simon & Schuster, 1994) (discussing the extent of Mormon settlement); Wallace Stegner, *Mormon Country*, ed. Richard W. Etulain, 2nd edition (Lincoln: Bison Books, 2003) (same as previous).

39. Firmage and Mangrum, *Zion in the Courts*, 264–67.

mental entities when those entities were composed of Latter-day Saints. For example, a Mormon court adjudicated a dispute over fees between the City Council of Ogden, Utah, and an attorney that it had retained, and another ecclesiastical tribunal declared invalid a fishing-rights monopoly granted by a local county government.[40] None of the private legal systems studied by Bernstein, for example, have had anything like the scope and longevity of the nineteenth-century Mormon court system.[41]

Despite the apparently natural link between the history of the Mormon court system and the debate over the role and meaning of private legal systems, no work has yet sought to use this aspect of Mormon legal history as a way of thinking about the role of non-governmental "law."[42] Rather, the literatures on both subjects pass like ships in the night.[43] For example, Bernstein's research revealed that unlike the Uniform Commercial Code, the private legal systems set up by merchants do not resolve contractual disputes by looking to practice in the trade or other imminent business norms.[44] Rather, they seem to adopt what looks to post-Realist lawyers like a very rigid and formalistic approach to contract adjudication. This is not, she concludes, because the merchants are actually rigid and formalistic in their business treatment of contracts. Quite the opposite seems to be the case: the merchants seem to operate under a two-tiered set of norms, with one set of flexible and equitable norms that govern on-going

40. Firmage and Mangrum, 272, 277 (city council dispute and fishing rights, respectively).

41. Since the nineteenth century, the Church has retained its judicial system, but its jurisdiction is now confined to more traditional questions of church discipline, and the Church, while continuing to take an ambivalent attitude toward litigation, counsels its members to avail themselves of the secular courts. See generally Kif Augustine-Adams, "The Web of Membership: The Consonance and Conflict of Being American and Latter-Day Saint," *Journal of Law and Religion* 13, no. 2 (1998): 567–602 (discussing the role of ecclesiastical and secular adjudication in modern Mormon thought).

42. In addition to *Zion in the Courts*, the Mormon ecclesiastical court system has been extensively discussed in works by Swenson and Dredge. Swenson, "Resolution of Civil Disputes by Mormon Ecclesiastical Courts"; Dredge, "Dispute Settlement in the Mormon Community: The Operation of Ecclesiastical Courts in Utah."

43. One notable exception is Jerold S. Auerbach's book *Justice Without Law?* See Jerold S. Auerbach, *Justice Without Law?* (New York: Oxford University Press, 1983), 54–56 (discussing the Mormon court system).

44. See Bernstein, "Merchant Law in a Merchant Court," 1771–82.

relationships, and another rigid and formalistic set of norms that govern the end of relationships. The rigidity of adjudication can be explained by the fact that it is the forum of relationship-ending norms rather than relationship-maintaining norms.[45]

The nineteenth-century Mormon court system would seem to offer an excellent test case for this theory. As suggested above, one of the primary justifications for the capacious jurisdiction of the ecclesiastical courts was to maintain the cohesion of the Mormon community and to assist in the religious ambition of "establishing Zion." In short, the Mormon judiciary seems to have been self-consciously conceived as a forum of relationship-maintaining norms. Bernstein's theory would predict that Mormon contract adjudication would eschew formality in favor of a search for the more flexible norms of on-going relationships. To a certain extent, research on Mormon courts seems to confirm this prediction. For example, Mormon courts were more likely to look to secular law in contract cases than in other areas precisely because the secular law was deemed to represent ordinary business practices, a move that in some ways pre-figured the approach ultimately taken by the Uniform Commercial Code.[46] Other evidence of relationship-maintaining norms can be seen in Mormon contract adjudication. For example, in one case a Mormon court ordered a defendant in a contract case to pay less than the stipulated amount of interest on the contract in light of the fact that payment of the full amount would place him in financial distress. Lorenzo Snow, then president of the Church and a judge in the case, then personally paid the plaintiff the difference between the interest ordered by the Church court and the amount to which the plaintiff was entitled by the contract. The defendant in the case then subsequently paid Snow for this amount. Hence, Mormon judges went to the extraordinary length of becoming personally involved in the financing of remedies in order to maintain good feelings between the parties.[47]

Yet despite this emphasis on maintaining harmony among the parties in the dispute, in many ways Mormon contract adjudication was more aggressive than the secular legal system in enforcing contract terms. As late as 1908, Mormon courts were regularly enforcing contracts that had

---

45. Bernstein, 1787–96.

46. Firmage and Mangrum, *Zion in the Courts*, 339–40 ("The civil rules were considered helpful because they reflected normal commercial practices and would help make business practices in the Great Basin more consistent").

47. Firmage and Mangrum, 349 (discussing the case).

been discharged by bankruptcy.[48] Likewise, in an 1879 case, the ecclesiastical court required a widow to pay on a contract of her dead husband's that was unenforceable under the secular law of succession.[49] Perhaps most strikingly, in some cases the Mormon courts went so far as to award punitive damages for breach of contract based on the blameworthiness of the promisor's conduct.[50] This formalism cannot be explained on the basis of some general Mormon preference for formalistic adjudication. Indeed, the broad jurisdiction of Mormon courts was generally justified by the need to eschew the pettifogging technicalities of the secular courts, and in other substantive areas, the preference for compromise solutions that maintained communal harmony seems to have been stronger. In short, despite their apparently overriding concern for what Bernstein has labeled relationship-maintaining norms, there seems to have been something about contracts in particular that called forth more formalistic modes of adjudication.

This excursion into the Mormon ecclesiastical court system comes nowhere close to exhausting its possibilities as a vehicle for thinking about the nature of private legal systems or about the substantive areas of law like contracts. Indeed, without further research it is difficult to answer the question that I raised above, namely the strikingly formalistic nature of contractual adjudication even in a context devoted to relationship-maintaining norms.[51] What it does illustrate, however, is the capacity of

---

48. Firmage and Mangrum, 342–44.

49. Firmage and Mangrum, 341–42.

50. Firmage and Mangrum, 344.

51. Further research on the Mormon court system is complicated by the fact that while there are extensive records of these cases, the records are not generally available to researchers. The records are held in the archives of the Church, which regards them as subject to rules of pastoral confidentiality similar to the priest-penitent confidentiality of the Roman Catholic Church. See generally Richard Turley, "Confidential Records," in *Encyclopedia of Mormonism*, by Daniel H. Ludlow (New York: Macmillan, 1992). Furthermore, the Church generally regards this requirement of pastoral confidentiality as extending even to parties long dead. For their work on *Zion in the Courts*, Firmage and Mangrum were apparently granted extraordinary access to the documents, but only on the condition that the parties not be named. Hence, in their research, parties are identified only by initials. Some pre-Utah records of Mormon ecclesiastical courts, however, have been published, but in this period the full extent of the Church courts' later jurisdiction had not been totally worked out. See, e.g., Donald Cannon and Lyndon W. Cook, eds., *Far West Record: Minutes of the Church of Jesus Christ of Latter-Day Saints, 1830–1844* (Salt Lake City: Deseret

Mormon legal history to pose problems and questions for conversations that ultimately have little to do with the interpretation of Mormon history per se. Solving the puzzle of formalism in Mormon contract adjudication would do more than simply deepen our understanding of the Mormon past. It would allow us to use that past to understand aspects of our legal present. Given such possibilities, the question arises of why Mormon legal experience has remained relatively invisible within the legal academy. The remainder of this chapter answers that question by providing an intellectual history of Mormon legal historiography that shows how it developed an internal logic which has, until recently, kept it basically separate from mainstream legal scholarship.

First Generation Mormon Legal History

There is a sense in which Mormon legal history is inevitable. The lifeblood of history is sources. A gifted historian can find the universe contained in what appears to be a grain of sand, but every practitioner of the craft needs documents of one kind or another with which to construct their narratives and theories about the past. Hence one of the great vices and frustrations of the law becomes its abiding virtue in the eyes of historians: law produces paper. While no one is naive enough in this post-modern age to believe that a historian simply "lets the sources speak," there is a real sense in which the availability of materials dictates the course of historical debate. One is always arguing about the interpretation of sources and their lacunae, and in Mormon history these sources are frequently legal in origin. It was the widespread reliance of historians of Mormonism on legal documents that gave rise to the first generation of Mormon legal history.

Finding origins is always a tricky business, but 1950 is probably as good a date as any to mark the beginnings of the modern academic discussion of Mormon history. In 1946, Fawn Brodie published her path-breaking biography of Joseph Smith, *No Man Knows My History*. In 1950, Juanita Brooks published her study *The Mountain Meadows Massacre*, and toward the end of the decade Leonard Arrington's *Great Basin Kingdom* appeared. All of these works relied on legal materials. Brodie told the story of Joseph

Book Co., 1983) (printing the records of the Far West, Missouri, High Council from the 1830s, including records of some ecclesiastical trials). Hence, while the Church is not hostile per se to the study of its ecclesiastical courts, any research must cope with the religious imperatives that govern access to the records.

Smith's 1826 trial for money digging.[52] She also noted that "[d]uring his short, tumultuous career Joseph was haled into court more than a score of times, on charges varying from disturbing the peace to treason," and her book relied on the records generated by these cases.[53] John Dee Lee's successive trials for his role in the Mountain Meadows Massacre were a central part of Brooks's narrative.[54] Perhaps most decisively, Arrington's massive study of Latter-day Saint economic history relied extensively on court records to piece together key parts of his narrative of nineteenth-century Mormon communitarianism.[55]

Leonard Arrington's 1952 article "The Settlement of the Brigham Young Estate, 1877–1879" in the *Pacific Historical Review* provides a good example of first-generation Mormon legal history.[56] There are a number of reasons for this. First, it is devoted to a legal subject. Second, it was published just as the New Mormon History was being born. Third, Arrington was hugely influential on later Mormon historians both through his writings and as a formal and informal mentor for graduate students and younger scholars. Finally, because of his expertise in economic history, Arrington is an unusually sophisticated lay person when it comes to legal materials and is adept at tracing out the complex transactions that form the heart of many legal disputes. In short, his *Pacific Historical Review* article represents the first generation of Mormon legal history at its best.

Arrington announces his interest in studying the dispute over Brigham Young's estate as inquiring into the "unique arrangement [that] existed between the Church and private enterprise in which the two worked together as one in providing for the material wants of the Mormon people."[57] When the Latter-day Saints moved to the Great Basin, they initially organized themselves as the "State of Deseret." The legislature of

---

52. See Fawn McKay Brodie, *No Man Knows My History: The Life of Joseph Smith, the Mormon Prophet* (New York: A. A. Knopf, 1945), 30–31.

53. See Brodie, viii.

54. See Brooks, *The Mountain Meadows Massacre*, 188–210 (discussing the successive trials of John D. Lee).

55. See, e.g., Leonard Arrington, *Great Basin Kingdom: An Economic History of the Latter-Day Saints, 1830–1900* (Cambridge: Harvard University Press, 1958), 353–79 (discussing the federal campaign against polygamy and Mormon political and economic power).

56. Leonard J. Arrington, "The Settlement of the Brigham Young Estate, 1877–1879," *Pacific Historical Review* 21, no. 1 (1952): 1–20.

57. Arrington, 1.

this "state" granted a corporate charter to the Church in 1851. After Utah Territory was organized, the territorial legislature confirmed the charter, which among other things gave the Church an unlimited ability to hold property, thus repudiating the long tradition of mortmain laws in English and American jurisprudence. In 1862, Congress passed the Morrill Anti-bigamy Act, which revoked the Church's corporate charter and limited the amount of property that it could hold. Through the collection of tithing donations, the Church was far and away the largest concentration of capital in pioneer Utah. Church leaders, in turn, used this wealth to capitalize local economic development to a large degree. This was done as part of the Church's religious mission to care for its members and to "build up Zion." In the face of congressional limits on the corporate church's ability to hold property, Brigham Young and his associates took personal possession of Church property. Upon his death, there was a dispute between the Church and some of Young's heirs as to what property properly belonged to the Church and what belonged to Young.

Arrington's article lays out the story of this dispute. He provides a simplified and accurate account of the legal maneuverings, albeit one largely drawn from secondary sources. He then goes on to use the story as a way of illustrating the nature and extent of Mormon economic activity in pioneer Utah, as well as the commercial relationship between Church leaders and the Church. (Although Brigham Young and his associates worked more or less full time for the Church, they received no formal salary or stipend. Rather, they seemed to have received compensation in the form of interest-free loans for various business enterprises, many of which had some sort of a communal goal or element.) Arrington then generalizes from his account, showing that many commonly held perceptions about Brigham Young—that he had vast personal wealth, that he owned many business enterprises in Utah, etc.—are mistaken, as most of this wealth was not personal, but rather consisted of the Mormon Church's attempts to circumvent federal law. He goes on to point out the incongruity of the federal policy:

> Freedom of enterprise and private property—those great catchwords and slogans of post-Civil War America—may have been permitted to the Standard Oil, New York Central Railroad, and American Tobacco companies. They did not apply to the Corporation of the Church of Jesus Christ of Latter-day Saints.[58]

---

58. Arrington, 20. Historians since Arrington have explored the connections between political opposition to the kind of post-Civil War big business that

In short, Arrington's article is an admirable and concise bit of historical research that demonstrates a mastery of the sources and the ability to synthesize them into an illuminating historical narrative.

Legally speaking, there are several striking features of Arrington's discussion. He makes no effort to provide a technically precise account of either the legal arguments involved in the case or in the course of the litigation. He provides a basic outline of how the relevant laws functioned, but there is no discussion in his article about how the laws governing the Church and the Brigham Young estate related to American law or its history as a whole. For example, there is no evidence that Arrington was aware of the long tradition of mortmain laws limiting the property that could be held by religious corporations, nor of the historic use to which such laws had been put. (They were instrumental in Henry VIII's breakup of the English religious orders, and they reinforced congregational Protestantism in America by making it difficult—if not impossible—for legally integrated ecclesiastical structures to develop.) Rather, Arrington's concern is relentlessly focused on Mormon history, and the law serves only as a convenient documentary springboard for his discussion of Mormon economic relations. The single sentence in his work that aims at a legal generalization is confined to a footnote and reads, in its entirety, "It is probable that no estate in America presented so many difficulties and complications as this one, because of the interests involved, the number of heirs, and the types of property involved."[59] The article, however, does not discuss how the unique situation of Brigham Young's estate challenged the American law of succession, and what that challenge reveals about the nature or development of that law.

Ironically, despite numerous discussions of the legal aspects of Mormonism, the first generation of Mormon legal history was marked by a basic disinterest in the law. This disinterest in the law is a limitation but not necessarily a fault of this work. Arrington and those who followed him were not legal historians or even lawyers. The law was simply not their concern. Furthermore, calling such work "first generation" legal history suggests, erroneously, that it is somehow obsolete or anachronistic. This, of course, is not the case. For example, Richard Bushman's excellent 2005 biography of Mormonism's founder, *Joseph Smith: Rough Stone Rolling*, contains repeated discussions of Joseph Smith's legal difficulties that are

---

Arrington referred to and opposition to the concentration of Mormon wealth in the Church. See, e.g., Gordon, *The Mormon Question*, 200–206.

59. Arrington, "The Settlement," 8 n26.

biographically important, even if Bushman makes no conscious effort to use the legal aspects of his narrative as a springboard for any broader jurisprudential discussion.[60] More subtly, given the paucity of early contemporary Mormon sources, there is a reason beyond Bushman's scholarly interest in farming in the early republic that so much of the early aspects of his narrative focus on the real-estate transactions of the Smith family.[61] The simple fact of the matter is that the legal records of these events are some of the only contemporary documents we have relating to Joseph Smith and his family prior to 1830. Accordingly, they are the grains of sand in which Bushman is forced to find the early life of Mormonism's founder. There is no reason to suppose that such use of legal materials by historians of Mormonism will abate in the future, nor is there any reason to wish that it should.

Second Generation Mormon Legal History

Yet the legal past of Mormonism is more than a fortunate producer of documents for historians. It is also a series of legal events that can be studied using the traditional tools of legal analysis. From this insight sprang the second generation of Mormon legal history, which has its genesis in Dallin H. Oaks's 1965 *Utah Law Review* article, "The Suppression of the *Nauvoo Expositor*."[62] As Joseph Smith's theological teachings became increasingly radical after the Latter-day Saints' move to Nauvoo in 1838, internal dissension within the Church accelerated. By 1844, secret teachings about polygamy and public teachings about the nature of God had driven some of Smith's closest former associates into public opposition. On June 7, 1844, they published the first and only issue of the *Nauvoo Expositor*, which declared its aim "to explode the vicious principles of Joseph Smith, and those who practice the same abominations and whoredoms."[63] Smith

60. See Richard Lyman Bushman, *Joseph Smith: Rough Stone Rolling* (New York: Alfred A. Knopf, 2005), 734 (an extensive list of references under the index heading "Smith, Joseph Jr.—court appearances of").

61. See, e.g., Bushman, 17–18, 32 (discussing real estate transactions by the Smith family). Cf. Richard Lyman Bushman, "Farmers in Court: Orange County, North Carolina, 1750–1776," in *The Many Legalities of Early America*, by Christopher L. Tomlins and Bruce H. Mann (Chapel Hill: University of North Carolina Press, 2001), 388 (discussing the legal difficulties of early American farmers).

62. Dallin H. Oaks, "The Suppression of the Nauvoo Expositor," *Utah Law Review* 9 (1965): 862–903.

63. Quoted in Bushman, *Rough Stone Rolling*, 539.

and his associates were frightened that the paper—particularly its exposé of then-secret polygamous marriages—would ignite the growing resentment and suspicion among local non-Latter-day Saints into the kind of open warfare that had driven the Latter-day Saints from Missouri. The Nauvoo City Council voted to suppress the *Nauvoo Expositor* as a public nuisance and destroy the press, which was subsequently done by city officials acting on Smith's orders (at the time he was mayor of Nauvoo as well as president of the Church).

It was widely assumed at the time that the actions of Smith and the Nauvoo City Council were illegal, and subsequent historians of Mormonism had generally counted the suppression of the *Nauvoo Expositor* as an instance of Mormon conflict with the "law of the land." Then a professor at the University of Chicago Law School, Oaks subjected this claim to an exacting legal analysis. After providing a detailed historical background to the suppression, Oaks identified three main legal objections to the actions of Smith and his associates: (1) the power of the city council to abate nuisances; (2) the propriety of classifying a newspaper as a public nuisance; and (3) the constitutionality of suppressing a paper. Oaks then provided an exhaustive and lawyerly summary of the controlling law in 1844, showing that there was substantial precedent supporting both the city's power to summarily abate nuisances and to treat defamatory papers as nuisances. Turning to the constitutional guarantee of freedom of the press, Oaks noted that the First Amendment did not apply to the states prior to the Civil War. He went on to analyze the question under the press guarantee of the Illinois state constitution. Tracing the history of that provision to the Pennsylvania constitution of 1790, Oaks concluded that prior to the twentieth century, the dominant interpretation of all such provisions was that they prohibited prior restraints on publication, but they did nothing to protect editors and publishers from ex-post legal consequences for what they published, including suppression. Oaks concluded:

> [T]he common assumption of historians the action taken by the city council to suppress the paper as a nuisance was entirely illegal is not well founded. Aside from damages for unnecessary destruction of the press, for which the Nauvoo authorities were unquestionably liable, the remaining actions of the council, including its interpretation of the constitutional guarantee of a free press, can be supported by references to the law of their day.[64]

---

64. Oaks, "The Suppression of the Nauvoo Expositor," 903.

Oaks' article did two important things. First, it provided a paradigm in which to ask legal questions about the Mormon past. Second, it demonstrated how the traditional tools of doctrinal legal analysis could be deployed to answer these questions. The paradigm that Oaks provided was essentially apologetic. His insight was to see that many of the claims made about the Mormon past—Joseph Smith acted illegally in suppressing the *Nauvoo Expositor*, Latter-day Saints were deprived of their legal rights by mobs, etc.—were essentially legal claims whose truth or falsity could be established by legal argument. The apologetic portion of the analysis came from the ability of such arguments to demonstrate that common charges made against Latter-day Saints by contemporaries and later historians were false, or alternatively, that Latter-day Saints were illegally treated by those that opposed them. For example, in a later article, Oaks and one his students, Joseph Bentley, examined the bankruptcy of Joseph Smith and concluded that "[a]lthough plagued by misfortune in business and bad advice about the law, Joseph Smith was nevertheless untainted by the wrongful conduct with which his enemies charged him."[65] It would be a mistake to assume that the apologetic edge to "second generation" Mormon legal history means that it can be dismissed as little more than a Mormon brief in long-dead legal disputes. The work of Oaks and those that followed him is thoroughly researched and objective in its treatment of the merits of the legal issues. It is perfectly willing to label the legally untenable claims of Latter-day Saints as such.[66] Yet much of its interest comes precisely from its ability to adjudicate long-standing disputes about the legal rightfulness of events in Mormon history.

The method of Mormon history that Oaks provided has been extremely influential on later Mormon legal history, providing a model for several industrious scholars—some of them Oaks's students—who have followed in his footsteps.[67] One recent example is Gordon Madsen's article

---

65. Dallin H. Oaks and Joseph I. Bentley, "Joseph Smith and Legal Process: In the Wake of the Steamboat Nauvoo," *Brigham Young University Law Review* 1976 (1976): 781.

66. See, e.g., Oaks, "The Suppression of the Nauvoo Expositor," 886 ("There are two reasons why Joseph Smith's argument was not well founded and why the council's action cannot be justified on the basis of the judicial powers of some of its members").

67. Oaks himself has become enormously influential within the Church. After serving as an assistant dean at the University of Chicago Law School, he was tapped to serve as president of Brigham Young University, the Church's flagship

"Joseph Smith and the Missouri Court of Inquiry: Austin A. King's Quest for Hostages."[68] When the Latter-day Saints were driven out of Missouri in 1838, Joseph Smith and several of his associates were captured by the Missouri militia and were subjected to a court of criminal inquiry before a Missouri magistrate for treason and other crimes. Ultimately, Joseph Smith was incarcerated awaiting a full trial, and he spent the winter of 1838–39 in prison before being allowed to escape to join the rest of his people in Illinois. In his article, Madsen meticulously documents the inquiry against Smith and his associates, canvassing the testimony introduced at the trial and the controlling Missouri law of the period. He concludes, "The order binding Joseph and the others over for treason . . . fails for at least six reasons," which he goes on to list.[69] The marks of Oaks's paradigm are clear in the article. It transforms a persistent theme in Mormon history ("Latter-day Saints were deprived of their legal rights by Missouri officials") into a legal question ("Was the proceeding against Joseph Smith legal?") and then deploys the tools of doctrinal analysis to answer the question.

Like the first generation that it builds on, second generation Mormon legal history has its own limitations and virtues. In large measure, it derives its interest from Mormon history itself. While second generation Mormon legal history is much more legally sophisticated than the work that preceded it, it too is largely unconcerned with making connections to broader debates in legal history or jurisprudence. The focus remains largely fixed on the internal questions and concerns of Mormon history, albeit now translated into much more legally sophisticated form. One of the greatest virtues of second generation Mormon legal history is that, by recasting questions of Mormon history in legal terms, it has provided an additional reason for ferreting out the legal details of the Mormon past, which now take on significance *as legal materials* rather than as simply fodder for economic or biographical studies. The haul has been enormous. For example, contrary to Brodie's estimate of a "score of times," it now

school. After stepping down as president of the university, he served a brief stint as a professor at BYU Law School before being tapped for the Utah Supreme Court. He served there until 1984, when he was chosen by Spencer W. Kimball, then president of the Church, to become a member of the Quorum of the Twelve Apostles, the second-highest council within the Church.

68. Gordon A. Madsen, "Joseph Smith and the Missouri Court of Inquiry: Austin A. King's Quest for Hostages," *Brigham Young University Studies* 43, no. 4 (2004): 93.

69. Madsen, 119.

appears that Joseph Smith was involved in over 150 lawsuits during the course of his life.

Third Generation Mormon Legal History

The third generation of Mormon legal history marks the expansion from questions purely internal to Mormon studies to engagement with broader themes in legal history and jurisprudence. For both first- and second-generation Mormon legal history, Mormonism was the dependent variable, the thing to be explained, and the law was invoked in one way or another as an independent variable that could be used to illuminate the nature of the Mormon past. In contrast, third generation Mormon legal history takes Mormonism as its independent variable and seeks to show how it can be used to explain or illuminate legal issues that are not inherently Mormon or primarily related to the history of Mormonism.

To his credit, Oaks also helped to pioneer this aspect of Mormon legal history. In 1975, he and Marvin Hill published *Carthage Conspiracy*.[70] The book followed the story of the 1845 Illinois trial of those accused of murdering Joseph Smith in 1844. After the death of Joseph Smith, the level of tension in western Illinois around the city of Nauvoo (renamed by the Latter-day Saints "The City of Joseph") was extremely high. Contrary to the fears of many at the time, the Latter-day Saints did not mobilize their militia for a massive counterstrike against Smith's killers, concentrating instead on the internal leadership crisis created by his death and the completion of their temple in Nauvoo. Nevertheless, agitation to excise the Mormon presence in Illinois continued. Eventually, mobs and informal militias attacked Latter-day Saints on outlying farms, and Brigham Young, who had emerged as Joseph Smith's chief successor, determined that the Latter-day Saints must abandon Illinois and settle far outside the borders of the United States, in the Great Basin. This was the environment of tension and uncertainty in which the non-Mormon officials of the state sought to prosecute Smith's accused murderers.

Joseph Smith had been killed while being held in the protective custody of state officers after Thomas Ford, the governor of Illinois, had guaranteed that he would not be harmed. In the face of these facts, the Latter-day Saints had no confidence in state officials, mainly absenting themselves from the proceedings. For their part, state officials were in an

---

70. Dallin H. Oaks and Marvin S. Hill, *Carthage Conspiracy: The Trial of the Accused Assassins of Joseph Smith* (Urbana: University of Illinois Press, 1975).

extremely difficult situation. The public reputation of the state demanded that they take some action against those that had murdered Smith while in state custody. At the same time, they lacked the coercive capacity to maintain order in western Illinois if the simmering hatred against the Latter-day Saints erupted into fully fledged mob violence. In the end they found a middle course by unsuccessfully prosecuting the ringleaders of the anti-Mormon mob that killed Smith. This allowed them to deny the state's complicity in the murder while avoiding the explosion that might have resulted from convictions for what many residents viewed as an entirely legitimate form of democratic violence against the Latter-day Saints. This was done in essentially two ways. First, the judge in the case refused to empanel a jury selected from the region as a whole, as it would have included a large number of Latter-day Saints, picking instead jurors from the largely anti-Mormon crowd that gathered at the courthouse on the day of the trial. Second, the counsel for the defense argued that the murderers of Smith were acting as legitimate representatives of the community and had rid it of a dangerous man that the law could not reach.

Oaks and Hill transcended previous Mormon legal scholarship in two ways. First, they offered a legally sophisticated account of the maneuvers at trial. Indeed, it was their familiarity with legal technicality that allowed them to uncover the mechanisms by which the compromise was worked out. Second, and more importantly, they explicitly linked their discussion to broader jurisprudential issues. In particular, they located the strategies adopted by the defense within the American tradition of jury nullification, writing:

> Prominent legal theorists like Roscoe Pound and John H. Wigmore have praised the jury's power to disregard the law in certain cases. In their view, this was necessary "to enable a verdict to be rendered which will accord with the moral sense of the community" and to remedy the inevitable conflict between law and justice by supplying "that flexibility of legal rules which is essential to justice and popular contentment."[71]

They then went on to canvas the history of jury nullification from the refusal of Boston juries during the American Revolution to convict those violating English laws deemed tyrannical to "[a] more recent and notorious example of . . . the failure of white southern juries to indict or convict whites shown to be guilty of crimes against Negroes or civil rights

71. Oaks and Hill, 211 (internal citations omitted).

workers."[72] The trial of Smith's alleged murderers fit into this history, illustrating the way in which the jury acted as a ceremonial and institutional mediator between the law and extra-legal democratic violence.

For the anti-Mormon defendants tried and acquitted in Carthage, the jury, as voice of the community, had provided a ceremonial cleansing by which the defendants could return to society absolved of the stigma of murder and fully qualified to function in a community soon to be rid of the Latter-day Saints. Many years later, when Thomas C. Sharpe was asked after a long and creditable career in politics and government if he had murdered Joseph Smith, his only response was fully relevant—"Well, the jury said not." The democratic version of higher law—popular sovereignty—had been applied to his case; its spokesman, the jury, had fully exonerated him of any sense of guilt.[73] In this analysis of the trial and its significance, there is a sense in which Mormonism ceases to be the primary subject. Rather than looking to legal materials for what they reveal about Joseph Smith and the religion he founded, Oaks and Hill looked to the legal experience of Latter-day Saints to see what it revealed about the nature of American law.

Another very important transitional work is *Zion in the Courts: A Legal History of the Church of Jesus Christ of Latter-day Saints, 1847–1900* by Edwin Brown Firmage and Richard Collin Mangrum. In some ways, this is the most ambitious piece of Mormon legal history that has yet been produced, as it seeks to provide a comprehensive account of Mormon legal experience in the nineteenth century. In many ways, Firmage and Mangrum provide a synthesis of first- and second-generation work on Mormon legal history, canvassing the productions of the New Mormon History for every treatment of a legal theme and then stitching these together into a single, explicitly legal narrative. Both Firmage and Mangrum, however, are law professors. Accordingly, they have a much greater appreciation for legal nuance than the non-specialist historians on whose work they frequently rely. Their interpretation of the anti-polygamy battles of the late nineteenth century, in particular, bear the marks of second-generation history. They provide a summary of all the most important cases at the Territorial and United States Supreme Court level, as well as describing the evolution of anti-polygamy legislation between 1862 and 1890. However, rather than aggressively situating their discussion within the historical context of other movements in nineteenth-century American jurisprudence, they in-

72. Oaks and Hill, 212.
73. Oaks and Hill, 214.

stead evaluate the correctness of nineteenth-century Supreme Court cases in light of later doctrinal developments. Still, by dint of its sheer scope, *Zion in the Courts* transcended previous work on Mormon legal history.

To date, the most fully realized example of third-generation Mormon legal history is Sarah Barringer Gordon's book *The Mormon Question: Polygamy and Constitutional Conflict in Nineteenth Century America.*[74] Beginning with the Republican Platform of 1856, Mormon polygamy—dubbed one of the "twin relics of barbarism"—emerged as a national political issue. Beginning in 1862, anti-polygamy agitation was transformed into federal legislation, and thereafter the drive to suppress the Mormon marriage system became increasingly legalized. Federal officials sought to prosecute Latter-day Saints for polygamy, and the Latter-day Saints responded with political and legal gambits to frustrate their efforts. The federal government responded with additional waves of legislation to deal with the obstacles thrown up by Mormon lawyers and politicians. Between 1862 and 1890 the level of legal pressure continuously intensified. By 1890, hundreds of Latter-day Saints had been incarcerated for polygamy and "unlawful cohabitation," the Church lay in financial ruin with essentially all of its assets confiscated by the federal government, tens of thousands of Latter-day Saints had been disenfranchised, and Congress stood poised to pass legislation that would purge all Latter-day Saints from the voting rolls. Faced with institutional annihilation and permanent political subjugation for his people, Wilford Woodruff, then president of the Church, issued the so-called "Manifesto," which began the tortuous process of abandoning plural marriage and Mormonism's nineteenth-century utopian ambitions.

Gordon's theme is the story of this confrontation and its role in shaping American law. Drawing on much of the literature produced by the New Mormon History, she relates it to the discussions that have animated the general study of nineteenth-century American law, particularly as it relates to matters of religion and family. In doing so, she adopts the stance of Oaks and Hill. No longer is Mormonism the ultimate subject of her

---

74. For reviews of Gordon's book, see Anthony S. Winer, "A Tale of Two Epochs and a Thread That May Still Run True," *William Mitchell Law Review* 29, no. 4 (2003): 1519–48; David R. Down and Jose I. Maldonado, "How Many Spouses Does the Constitution Allow One to Have? The Mormon Question: Polygamy and Constitutional Conflict in Nineteenth Century America," *Constitutional Commentary* 20, no. 3 (2003–2004): 571–678; Nathan B. Oman, "The Story of a Forgotten Battle," *Brigham Young University Law Review* 2002, no. 3 (2002): 745–58.

inquiry. Rather, Mormon legal experience becomes a lens through which we can see the development of American law in dramatic new ways. She summarizes her conclusions thus:

> The conflict over polygamy forces us to reassess the strength of national legal and political movements after the Civil War and to appreciate the role of faith in nineteenth-century legal interpretation and political culture. The breadth of issues both sides addressed is astounding—religion, sexuality, slavery, moral relativism, freedom, consent, democracy, women's rights. The conflict included disputes over the relationship of political legitimacy to private structures of governance and state control over marriage, as well as the moral meaning of religious liberty and separation of church and state, all issues that have dogged lawyers and constitution theorists for a century and more. By recovering important constitutional questions, this book begins to explain why such issues provoked tangled and enduring questions. Legal scholars and constitutional historians have focused on the abolition of slavery, the failure of Reconstruction, and the jurisprudence of race, all important topics but not capable of yielding an understanding of the role of religion in the development of constitutional law and federal power. They have neglected slavery's "twin relic of barbarism," as contemporary Republicans called polygamy, missing the conflict over religion that remade legal history and constitutional law in the second half of the nineteenth century.[75]

One can argue, of course, with Gordon's conclusions and interpretations, but her claims place Mormon legal history in the heart of contemporary scholarly debates about America's legal history and the role of religion in legal developments. In so doing, she provides an attractive model for the possibilities of Mormon legal history, showing how it can transform itself from a niche position within the subfield of Mormon studies into a source of ideas and perspectives in the broader conversations of the legal academy.

Conclusion

Richard Bushman, Joseph Smith's most accomplished biographer, has argued that the importance and usefulness of studying Smith's life depends largely on the context in which he is placed.[76] Seen, for example, as a village seer and mystic whose context is confined to upstate New York in the 1820s, Smith becomes of merely parochial or local interest. In contrast,

75. Gordon, *The Mormon Question*, 12–13.

76. See Richard Lyman Bushman, "The Visionary World of Joseph Smith," *Brigham Young University Studies* 37, no. 1 (1997): 183–205.

some scholars have placed Smith in a dramatically larger context, seeing him as a nineteenth-century manifestation of currents of religious and philosophical thought with their roots in the Radical Reformation and the late Renaissance.[77] In this larger context, the study of Smith's life and thought takes on new interest, allowing us to examine a much broader range of phenomena.

The same is true of Mormon legal history. Hitherto, the context for Mormon legal history has mainly been taken to be Mormonism itself. This basic approach has generated a wealth of fascinating and suggestive materials. It has not, however, been an interpretive framework that lends any significance to Mormon legal history for the study of the law. On the other hand, when Mormon legal history is placed in an essentially jurisprudential context, so that its field of relation is not other aspects of the Mormon past but rather the law itself, it holds the promise of answering questions about the law in surprising and ultimately illuminating ways.

---

77. See, e.g., John L. Brooke, *The Refiner's Fire: The Making of Mormon Cosmology, 1644–1844* (New York: Cambridge University Press, 1996).

CHAPTER 2

Preaching in the Courthouse and Judging in the Temple

On the evening of September 9, 1831, two men arrived in the small county seat of Jacksonville, Illinois. It was court day, and "there were a great many country people in the village."[1] Some had no doubt come to settle disputes before the state's travelling judiciary. Illinois law required that all members of the state supreme court hold a circuit court in each county seat at least twice a year. In their wake came the lawyers who "rode circuit" with the judges, picking up clients at the local tavern and hurriedly conferring with them before rising to make their arguments about this man's failure to pay on a note or the damage done by that man's wandering cow. Others came to watch the spectacle of the court. This September evening, however, afforded the citizens of Morgan County a different kind of performance. The first of the two men was a schoolteacher turned preacher named William McLellin; his companion was Hyrum Smith, brother of the Mormon prophet Joseph Smith Jr.[2] McLellin recorded:

> [A]s soon as they found out who we were, they gathered around us; we separated and talked with them about two hours. I cut some of them so close with the truth that a ruffian fellow rolled up his sleeves and swore that he could give it to me but a gentleman prevented him and took him away.[3]

The two Mormon elders made an appointment to "preach next day in the Courthouse."[4] At the designated time, a "numerous concourse of people" gathered, and McLellin recorded his trepidation at having "to ascend the judges bench, and face Judges, Lawyers Doctors Priests and people," but he added, "I arose with confidence in Elijah's God and gave them a brief history of the book of Mormon."[5]

---

1. Jan Shipps and John W. Welch, eds., "The Manuscripts of William E. McLellin (1831–36), Journal I, July 18, 1831–November 20, 1831," in *The Journals of William E. McLellin, 1831–1836*, 1994, 29–60.

2. See John W. Welch, "The Acts of the Apostle William McLellin," in *The Journals of William E. McLellin, 1831–1836*, ed. Jan Shipps and John W. Welch, 1994, 13–26 (giving biographical information on McLellin and his companion).

3. Shipps and Welch, "The Manuscripts of William E. McLellin (1831–36)," 39.

4. Shipps and Welch, 39.

5. Shipps and Welch, 39.

Five years later, a larger group of Mormon elders gathered in Kirtland, Ohio, then the headquarters of the Church. They made their way to the recently completed Kirtland Temple, which sat on a bluff overlooking the Chagrin River flowing toward Lake Erie a few miles to the north. The building differed markedly in its religious significance from the New England churches that it architecturally resembled. Anxious to avoid anything that smacked of "Popery," the Puritans had insisted that their meetinghouses were just that: places to meet without any special sanctification. The Mormon edifice, in contrast, had been dedicated in an elaborate set of ceremonies that identified it with Old Testament temples, their priestly ceremonies and inner sanctuaries.[6] In the dedicatory prayer, Joseph Smith implored God that the temple "may be sanctified and consecrated to be holy, and that thy holy presence may be continually in this house; and that all people who shall enter upon the threshold of the Lord's house may feel thy power and feel constrained to acknowledge that thou hast sanctified it, and that it is thy house, a place of thy holiness" (D&C 109:12–13). Hence the Mormon elders who made their way to the temple on March 29, 1837, were not simply "going to meeting." Rather, they were entering the sanctified center of their religious community. Yet despite the geographic and symbolic distance between them and the judges, lawyers, and village rowdies of Morgan County, the Kirtland elders were also essentially a judicial gathering. After opening with prayer, they turned to the case of *Cahoon v. Green*. Elder Cahoon charged Elder Green "1st for Disturbing the Sining Scoll several times 2nd for Swearing and calling the Complainant a liar. . . ."[7] Green denied the charge of disturbing the peace but admitted to the swearing and slander. After considering and rejecting Green's defense that Cahoon was in fact a liar, the assembled elders voted to withdraw their fellowship from him.[8]

The juxtaposition of Mormon elders preaching in the courthouse and adjudicating in the temple illustrates the fluidity of the boundaries between law and religion in nineteenth-century America. During the colonial period and the nineteenth century, numerous religious groups sought to opt

6. See generally Taylor Petrey, "Christian Temple Builders and the Latter-Day Saints," in *Archive of Restoration Culture: Summer Fellows' Papers 2000–2002*, ed. Richard Lyman Bushman (Provo: Joseph Fielding Smith Institute for Latter-day Saint History, 2005), 139.

7. Lyndon W. Cook and Milton V. Backman, eds., *Kirtland Elders' Quorum Record 1836–1841* (Provo: Grandin Book Co., 1985), 25.

8. Cook and Backman, *Kirtland Elders' Quorum Record 1836–1841*, 25–26.

out of the secular legal system, moving civil litigation between co-religionists into the hands of their churches.[9] No group was entirely successful in doing so, but some—particularly the Quakers and the Mormons—were able to forge ecclesiastical courts that proved remarkably robust over long periods of time. Their stories have been told as paeans to alternative dispute resolution.[10] Believers, so the explanations go, wished to avoid the expense of formal litigation and turned to religious fora as convenient alternatives to the courts. There is, of course, some truth to this view. Yet McLellin's injection of religion into the civic ritual of court day, preaching from the bench to the judges, lawyers, litigants, and spectators, and the relocation of adjudication to the symbolic heart of their religion by the Kirtland elders problematizes any attempt to reduce religious tribunals to simply another player in the perpetual quest for low-cost dispute resolution. Rather, the move to bring litigation within the fold of the Church played out against a much richer context of civic and religious symbols and institutions, a fact powerfully illustrated by the Mormon experience.

---

9. See generally Jerold S. Auerbach, *Justice Without Law?* (New York: Oxford University Press, 1983), 19–47 (discussing the resolution of civil disputes in religious fora).

10. See, e.g., Auerbach, *Justice Without Law?*, 19–47 (lauding ecclesiastical courts as attractive alternatives to the civil court system); George S. Odiorne, "Arbitration and Mediation Among Early Quakers," *Arbitration Journal* 9 (1954): 161–69 (lauding the Quakers' system of ecclesiastical adjudication as an early example of alternative dispute resolution). Cf. William M. Offutt, Jr., *Of "Good Laws" and "Good Men": Law and Society in the Delaware Valley, 1680–1710* (Urbana: University of Illinois Press, 1995), 147 (referring to "panegyrics composed of anecdotal evidence on alternative, community-based dispute resolution systems"). For discussions of the Mormon ecclesiastical court system in the nineteenth century, see Edwin Brown Firmage and R. Collin Mangrum, *Zion in the Courts: A Legal History of the Church of Jesus Christ of Latter-Day Saints, 1830–1900*, 1st ed. (Urbana: University of Illinois Press, 1988), 263–370 (providing a detailed summary of the functioning of Mormon ecclesiastical courts from 1846 to 1900); Mark P. Leone, *Roots of Modern Mormonism* (Cambridge: Harvard University Press, 1979), 111–48 (discussing ecclesiastical courts among Mormon settlers in nineteenth-century Arizona); C. Paul Dredge, "Dispute Settlement in the Mormon Community: The Operation of Ecclesiastical Courts in Utah," in *Access to Justice: The Anthropological Perspective: Patterns of Conflict Management: Essays in the Ethnography of Law*, ed. Klaus-Friedrich Koch, vol. 4, 1979, 191 (discussing ecclesiastical courts in early Utah); and Raymond T. Swenson, "Resolution of Civil Disputes by Mormon Ecclesiastical Courts Note," *Utah Law Review* 1978, no. 2 (1978): 573–96.

The story of the rise and fall of the jurisdiction of Mormon courts over ordinary civil disputes provides us with a number of insights into the interaction between law and religion in nineteenth-century America. It dramatically illustrates the fluidity of the boundaries between law and religion early in the century and the hardening of those boundaries by its end. The Mormon courts initially arose in a context in which the professional bar had yet to establish a monopoly over adjudication. Rather, churches felt confident in their ability to create a "legal" apparatus of judges and lawsuits. By century's end, however, the increasing complexity of the legal environment pushed the Mormon courts out of the business of resolving civil disputes, hardening the boundaries around the legal profession's claimed monopoly over adjudication. Equally important for the decline of the Mormon courts was the fact that allegiance to the common-law courts became a prerequisite of assimilation into the American mainstream. While hostility to the secular courts had been a hallmark of a major stream of American Protestantism during the colonial period as well as the first decades of the Republic, by the end of the nineteenth century, Mormons' rejection of those courts marked them as dangerous outsiders. Part of the price of their acceptance into the national mainstream was the abandonment of legal distinctiveness. The story of the Mormon courts also illustrates the importance of law for the development of religious beliefs and practices. Nineteenth-century Mormons expended an enormous amount of theological and institutional energy on legal issues. Other scholars have documented the "public law" side of this story, showing how the federal government's effort to eradicate Mormon polygamy was central to the Mormon experience in the last half of the nineteenth century and ultimately forced a revolution in Mormon beliefs and practices.[11] The rise and fall of the Mormon court system, however, shows that private law—subjects like contract, tort, and property—could exercise no less of a power over the religious imagination.

---

11. See generally Sarah Barringer Gordon, *The Mormon Question: Polygamy and Constitutional Conflict in Nineteenth-Century America* (Chapel Hill: University of North Carolina Press, 2002); Elizabeth Harmer-Dionne, "Once a Peculiar People: Cognitive Dissonance and the Suppression of Mormon Polygamy As a Case Study Negating the Belief-Action Distinction," *Stanford Law Review* 50, no. 4 (1998): 1295–1347; Douglas H. Parker, "Victory in Defeat—Polygamy and the Mormon Legal Encounter with the Federal Government," *Cardozo Law Review* 12, no. 3–4 (1991): 805–20.

Finally, the story told here challenges the standard narrative within Mormon history concerning the rise of the Church court system and the anti-legalism of nineteenth-century Latter-day Saints. In their extensive study of civil disputes in Mormon ecclesiastical courts, Professors Richard Collin Mangrum and Edwin Firmage explain the genesis and rise of Mormon courts entirely in terms of the internal imperatives of Mormon theology and communitarianism.[12] They write, "After they migrated to the deserts of the Great Basin, the Saints pursued their radical theory of Zion as an alternative to the social experiment of pluralistic America. A critical part of this effort was the establishment and maintenance of their own court system."[13] This narrative, however, unduly emphasizes the uniqueness of the Mormon experience and fails to acknowledge the important continuities between the Mormon court system and the experience of discipline-oriented Protestant churches. Accordingly, this chapter emphasizes the way in which the emergence of the Mormon court system must be seen within the broader context of American and even Atlantic religious history. Only by examining the Mormon courts in this broader context can we see the way in which they both continued and sharply departed from earlier ecclesiastical practices. Mangrum and Firmage, likewise, rightly emphasize the anti-lawyer rhetoric of nineteenth-century Mormon leaders, but they fail to appreciate the way in which Mormon attorneys resisted their designation as social parasites.[14] In contrast, this chapter shows how Latter-day Saint lawyers crafted their own legitimating religious narratives, insisting that "true lawyers" could work harmoniously within Mormon norms. In time, Church leaders adopted this self-conception of Mormon attorneys in place of their earlier blanket denunciations of the legal profession, and it provided an important rhetorical bridge between the extensive jurisdiction of Church courts in the nineteenth century and their abandonment at the beginning of the twentieth century.

The remainder of this chapter will proceed as follows: part I will trace the origins of the Mormon court system, locating it within the intellectual and theological context of early America; part II will discuss the effort to move civil litigation between Mormons into the ecclesiastical courts; finally, part III will discuss the transformation of Mormon adjudication, tracing the ultimate abandonment of Church-based litigation.

---

12. Firmage and Mangrum, *Zion in the Courts*, 1–2.
13. Firmage and Mangrum, 261.
14. Firmage and Mangrum, 16–18, 271–74.

I. The Rise of the Mormon Judiciary: 1526–1886

The Mormon court system emerged from the much older tradition of ecclesiastical discipline among the English Protestants who settled North America. Under English law, ecclesiastical courts were integrated into the judicial machinery of the state. Certain kinds of issues—mainly dealing with family law and certain aspects of probate—lay exclusively within the jurisdiction of the courts of the Church of England. These courts enforced their decisions by excommunicating recalcitrant parties, and excommunication would then carry certain civil penalties.[15] The Church of England, however, made comparatively little effort to police the spiritual or moral purity of church members. The assumption was that attempts to enforce ecclesiastical purity through church discipline were unnecessary. Indeed, those who called for more aggressive church discipline were labeled "Donatists" (after an early Christian sect condemned by Augustine for their insistence on ecclesiastical purity) and treated as dangerous heretics.[16] Accordingly, the sanctions of church courts were reserved for the ordinary legal cases falling within their jurisdiction. Virginia and other colonies where Anglicanism was the dominant religion continued this easy-going attitude toward church discipline.[17] Since they did not have bishops of their own, these American churches came under the jurisdiction of the Bishop of London. The geographic distance from ecclesiastical courts made it all but impossible for them to exercise even ordinary functions, thus strengthening the tendency to ignore problems of religious impurity.[18] This judicial neglect by the Church of England does not seem to have bothered Virginians very much. For example, when the Reverend James Blair, founder of The College of William and Mary, tried to create

---

15. According to William Blackstone: "[W]ith us by the common law an excommunicated person is disabled to do any act, that is required to be done by one that is probus et legalis homo. He cannot serve upon juries, cannot be a witness in any court, and, . . . cannot bring an action, either real or personal, to recover lands or money due to him." William Blackstone, Commentaries *102.

16. See Edmund S. Morgan, *Visible Saints: The History of a Puritan Idea* (Ithaca: Cornell University Press, 1963), 2–4.

17. See Stephen Botein, *Early American Law and Society* (New York: Knopf, 1983), 19–21.

18. See Botein, 19 ("[C]olonies south of New England . . . failed to replicate the Anglican ecclesiastical system . . . The Church of England did not help matters along by trying to govern colonial religious institutions out of the bishopric of London instead of creating a diocese in the New World").

local ecclesiastical courts to discipline "all cursers Swearers and blasphemers, all whoremongers fornicators and Adulterers, all drunkards ranters and profaners of the Lords day," his proposal was treated with horror by the planter elite and was quickly squashed.[19]

The English Protestants who founded the colonies to the north, however, rejected the lax attitude of Anglicanism toward church discipline. The roots of their dissatisfaction lay in a radical wing of the German Reformation: the Anabaptists.[20] In the sixteenth century, the Anabaptists were most notable for their rejection of infant baptism and the apocalyptic theocracy of the city of Munster, which was bloodily suppressed by the local Catholic bishop in 1535. The Anabaptists, however, also insisted that discipline was the mark of a true church.[21] In particular, they focused on the eighteenth chapter of Matthew in which Christ commands, "If your brother sins against you . . . tell it to the church; and if he refuses to listen even to the church, let him be to you as a Gentile and a tax collector" (Matt. 18:15–17).[22] Adult baptism, insisted one Anabaptist pamphleteer in 1526, would be "no better than infant baptism had been if fraternal admonition and excommunication did not go along with it."[23] In Geneva, John Calvin regarded the Anabaptists as one of his chief theological rivals, but he nevertheless imbibed their emphasis on church discipline from an early teacher with strong Anabaptist connections.[24] (Calvin also married an Anabaptist widow.[25]) He wrote, "as the saving doctrine of Christ is the soul of the church, so does discipline serve as its sinews."[26] He did, however, try to distinguish himself from "Donatists and Anabaptists" who "in an impious

---

19. See Botein, 20. Cf. Joseph C. Robert, "Excommunication, Virginia Style," *South Atlantic Quarterly* 40, no. 3 (1941): 243, 251 (noting that the discipline of Virginia's Anglican churches was known only for its laxity).

20. See generally Kenneth R. Davis, "No Discipline, No Church: An Anabaptist Contribution to the Reformed Tradition," *The Sixteenth Century Journal* 13, no. 4 (1982): 43–58 (discussing the Anabaptists' influence on reforming trends of the day).

21. See Davis, 45.

22. See Davis, 44–45. The Anabaptists also relied on the parable of the wheat and the tares contained in Matthew 13. They insisted that the parable applied only to the world and not the Church, which could not include both believers and unbelievers.

23. Davis, 47.

24. Davis, 56–57.

25. See Patrick Collinson, *The Reformation* (London: Weidenfeld & Nicolson, 2003), 91.

26. John Calvin, *Institutes of the Christian Religion*, ed. John T. McNeill, trans. Ford Lewis Battles (Philadelphia: Westminster John Knox Press, 1960), 1230.

schism separated themselves from Christ's flock" and "under the pretense of their zeal . . . subvert whatever edification there is."[27] With the English break from Rome, Calvinist and Anabaptist ideas made their way across the Channel. Among the Puritan criticisms of the Anglican settlement was their insistence that "every church should exclude and expel the wicked."[28]

Like their Anglican cousins to the south, the Puritans of New England dispensed with the courts of the Church of England, moving matters of traditional ecclesiastical jurisdiction entirely into the secular courts.[29] Their early insistence on the purity of the church, however, meant that Puritans kept alive ecclesiastical discipline, excommunicating church members who failed to live godly lives.[30] The practice of formal church discipline among Puritans, however, was ultimately limited. Early Puritan theology required that church members demonstrate that they had been predestined to salvation, an exacting spiritual requirement that few congregants met. Accordingly, few of the people in Puritan pews were actually members of the church and therefore subject to its discipline.[31] The so-called Halfway Covenant, a form of partial church membership, eventually relaxed the prerequisites for church membership, increasing the number of congregants potentially subject to discipline. However, the Halfway Covenant

---

27. Calvin, 1239.

28. Morgan, *Visible Saints*, 12.

29. See Edmund S. Morgan, *The Puritan Dilemma: The Story of John Winthrop* (Boston: Little, Brown & Co., 1958), 95–96 ("Though the ministers enjoyed a powerful influence over their congregations, the shadow of Rome still lay heavily on the Puritans. None of them wanted a 'theocracy' in the sense of government by the clergy. Indeed, of all the governments in the Western world at the time, that of early Massachusetts gave the clergy least authority"). The relationship between ecclesiastical and secular courts in Puritan Massachusetts was complicated. Although ecclesiastical courts had limited de jure authority, secular courts punished offenses such as blasphemy, and on some issues—such as sumptuary regulation—secular tribunals only stepped in when the Church courts failed to deal with such issues "at home." See generally George Lee Haskins, *Law and Authority in Early Massachusetts: A Study in Tradition and Design* (New York: Macmillan Co., 1960), 87–93.

30. See David C. Brown, "The Keys of the Kingdom: Excommunication in Colonial Massachusetts," *New England Quarterly* 67, no. 4 (1994): 531, 540–47.

31. See Morgan, *Visible Saints*, 107–9 (discussing the varied reactions of settlers to the newly imposed requirements of church membership).

itself seems to have dampened the fervor for ecclesiastical purity, and with it, the widespread practice of church trials and excommunication.[32]

The same could not be said of the churches that sprouted among dissenters from Puritan orthodoxy and other dissenting English Protestants. Despite Calvinist antipathy toward Anabaptism, its ideas and adherents found their way to New England in the first years of settlement. English Separatists in Holland had come into contact with Anabaptists in the Low Countries during the 1610s and 1620s, and in 1638, Roger Williams established an early Baptist congregation in Rhode Island that drew on this Separatist tradition.[33] From these beginnings, American Baptists spread around the fringes of New England, and in the 1690s, Baptists from New England formed the first Baptist congregation in the southern colonies at Charleston, South Carolina.[34] While divided in their allegiance to Calvinist theology (some Baptists followed the Dutch theologian Jacob Arminius, who rejected predestination), Baptists retained the early Anabaptist conviction in the need to maintain the purity of the church, and prior to the later part of the nineteenth century, Baptist congregations aggressively disciplined their members. Before 1840, eight percent of white male Baptists may have "passed under the church's rod of discipline" each year.[35]

The Quakers provide another instance of a well-developed church judiciary emerging from the Radical Reformation. Quakerism came out of the radical fringes of British Protestantism during the religious and political upheavals that accompanied the English Civil War. After decades of intermittent persecution in England, the Quaker philanthropist William Penn established the colony of Pennsylvania as a refuge for the Friends, as Quakers called themselves. Like the radical New Englanders to their north, Quaker congregations in America aggressively disciplined their members.[36] The basic ecclesiastical unit was the so-called "Monthly

32. Indeed, by the end of the seventeenth century, Puritan congregations largely ceased to excommunicate their members. See Brown, "The Keys of the Kingdom," 556–57.

33. See Bill J. Leonard, *Baptists in America* (New York: Columbia University Press, 2005), 8–9, 13–14.

34. See Leonard, 13–14.

35. Gregory A. Wills, *Democratic Religion: Freedom, Authority, and Church Discipline in the Baptist South, 1785–1900* (New York: Oxford University Press, 1997), 54.

36. See Jack Donald Marietta, "Ecclesiastical Discipline in the Society of Friends, 1682–1776" (unpublished PhD dissertation, Stanford University, 1968), 4–5 (on file with the author).

Meeting," which would inquire into the actions of members and could formally withdraw fellowship from those who did not live up to the standards of the Society.[37] Several monthly meetings were collected into so-called "Quarterly Meetings" and "Yearly Meetings," which exercised appellate jurisdiction as well as promulgated rules to govern church discipline.[38] In many ways, Quaker discipline was aggressive even by the standards of discipline-oriented churches. For example, in addition to traditional concerns such as lying, swearing, or sexual impropriety, Quakers were subject to discipline for traveling without first informing their local "Meeting" or for failing to attend Quaker services while visiting a different region.[39]

Scholars have long argued that the origins of Mormonism lie in New England.[40] Although the Church of Christ (later rechristened The Church of Jesus Christ of Latter-day Saints) was organized in upstate New York in April, 1830, its founder, Joseph Smith Jr., was born in Vermont of old New England stock.[41] Perhaps more importantly, many of the earliest converts to the new faith in western New York and Ohio were displaced New Englanders whose family roots lay in the "radical fringe" of Connecticut, Rhode Island, New Hampshire, and Vermont, precisely

---

37. Marietta, 1–2.
38. Marietta, 1–2.
39. See Marietta, 12–13.
40. See David Brion Davis, "The New England Origins of Mormonism," *The New England Quarterly* 26, no. 2 (June 1, 1953): 147. Writing in the shadow of Perry Miller's magisterial works on Puritan thought, Davis conceptualized Mormonism as a populist—and somewhat silly—attempt to recapture Puritanism in the nineteenth century. See Davis, 158 ("Mormonism can be seen as the extreme result of the evils of literal-mindedness. . . . This anachronistic residue of seventeenth-century New England just did not understand the meaning of individualism"); Cf. Charles L. Cohen, "The Post-Puritan Paradigm of Early American Religious History," *The William and Mary Quarterly* 54, no. 4 (1997): 695, 701 ("Miller conceived of Puritanism as a fixed intellectual configuration . . . and he diagnosed alterations in sentiment, doctrine, rhetoric, or practice as degeneration from this initial scheme. Declension theory's explanatory force derives from its deducing Puritanism as an a priori unity from which every departure must necessarily signify decay").
41. See Richard Bushman, *Joseph Smith: Rough Stone Rolling*, 1st ed. (New York: Alfred A. Knopf, 2005), 8–29 (discussing the New England background of Joseph Smith Jr.'s family).

the regions where Anabaptist and Quaker influence was the strongest.[42] Likewise, Joseph Smith found early followers in Ohio and the upper reaches of the Susquehanna River, regions peopled largely by settlers from Quaker Pennsylvania. These early converts carried their forbearers' emphasis on church discipline into the new movement. The earliest rules for the government of the Church were contained in the "Articles of the Church of Christ" composed in late 1829.[43] The "Articles" endorsed the baptism of adult believers and insisted on the importance of disciplining recalcitrant members.[44] "Therefore if ye know that a man is unworthy," the Articles stated, "if he repenteth not he shall not be numbered among my people that he may not destroy my people."[45] A few months later, the newly organized Church adopted an expanded "Articles and Covenants." This document directed that "[a]ny member of the church of Christ transgressing, or being overtaken in a fault, shall be dealt with as the scriptures direct . . . [a]nd also, if any have been expelled from the church . . . their names may be blotted out of the general church record of names."[46]

The emphasis on ecclesiastical purity and church discipline meant that adjudication emerged almost immediately as an important facet of Mormon religious experience. The earliest judicial procedures used by the Latter-day Saints, however, cannot be found in the quasi-constitutional "Articles and Covenants." Rather, the Mormons simply adopted procedures used by other discipline-oriented churches. Prior to any formal ac-

---

42. This theory of early Mormon demography was first advanced by John Brooke in 1994. See John L. Brooke, *The Refiner's Fire: The Making of Mormon Cosmology, 1644–1844* (New York: Cambridge University Press, 1996), 59–88. Since then, Brooke's demographic thesis has been significantly supported by a much more comprehensive study by Val D. Rust. See Val D. Rust, *Radical Origins: Early Mormon Converts and Their Colonial Ancestors* (Urbana: University of Illinois Press, 2004).

43. See Scott H. Faulring, "An Examination of the 1829 'Articles of the Church of Christ' in Relation to Section 20 of the Doctrine and Covenants," *Brigham Young University Studies* 43, no. 4 (Winter 2004): 57. The full text of the "Articles of the Church of Christ" is reproduced in Faulring's article.

44. See Faulring, 77 ("Now therefore whosoever repenteth and humbleth himself before me [that is, Jesus Christ] and desireth to be baptized in my name shall ye baptize them" is a quote from the transcript of the 1829 Articles of the Church of Christ. Brackets not in original).

45. Faulring, 78.

46. *Doctrine and Covenants of the Church of Jesus Christ of Latter-Day Saints* (Salt Lake City: The Church of Jesus Christ of Latter-day Saints, 1981), 20:80, 83.

tion, teachers "labored" with refractory members, urging them to confess their transgressions without formal disciplinary action.[47] If this did not work, then the erring brother or sister would be brought before the local "conference" for trial.[48] These proceedings were presided over by a "moderator" who was elected for the meeting.[49] The moderator was a familiar character from both Protestant churches and New England town meetings, and his purpose was less to act as a judge than to run the meeting. Generally, the moderator among Protestants was the minister, but with an entirely lay clergy, the office seems to have rotated from meeting to meeting among the Mormons.[50] There were no formal evidentiary or procedural rules. Rather, evidence was presented by the parties in the case.[51] The assembled members would then vote on the verdict.[52] The congregational

---

47. For example, the business of an 1834 meeting of teachers in Kirtland consisted entirely of appointing brethren to labor with particular members: "[T]he conference then appointed brothers John Taylor and Benjamin Johnson to labor with Orva Cartwright for making use of tobacco, also brother Joseph Ceehum (?) was appointed to labor with both Bates & wife also brothers G. Johnson & A.C. Graves was appointed to labor with the widow Shaw." "Teachers Quorum Minutes, Dec. 1834–Dec. 1845," n.d., Church Archives, The Family and Church History Department of The Church of Jesus Christ of Latter-day Saints, Salt Lake City, Utah. See also Donald Cannon and Lyndon W. Cook, eds., *Far West Record: Minutes of the Church of Jesus Christ of Latter-Day Saints, 1830–1844* (Salt Lake City: Deseret Book Co., 1983), 38 (a conference voted two elders to mediate between two quarrelling members).

48. See, e.g., Cannon and Cook, 15 ("Ezra being absent . . . Cowdery be dispatched . . . [to] bring him before this conference immediately").

49. See, e.g., Cannon and Cook, 27 ("Br Sidney Rigdon appointed moderator").

50. See Cannon and Cook, e.g., 26–31. Between November 1, 1831, and November 13, 1831, there were six conference meetings in Kirtland all with different moderators. However, the role of moderator seems to have attached fairly quickly to particular priesthood officers. See, e.g., Cannon and Cook, 65 ("The Bishop Edward Partridge was acknowledged to be at the head of the Church of Zion at present consequently will be our Moderator in councils or conferences by virtue of his office").

51. See, e.g., Cannon and Cook, 15 ("After hearing the relations of all the parties, the conference requested them to withdraw while they should investigate the testimony & pass their decision").

52. See, e.g., Cannon and Cook, 12 ("Upon testimony satisfactory to this conference it was voted that Ezra Booth be silenced from preaching as an Elder in this Church").

basis and the vocabulary used by these earliest Mormon courts were very similar to meetings of Baptists or Quakers.

While this early pattern of church discipline was retained throughout the nineteenth century by Latter-day Saints in Europe and the British Isles,[53] the Mormon judiciary rapidly began diverging from its Protestant antecedents in ways that reflected the religious radicalism of Mormonism. Joseph Smith had founded his Church on the claim that God had chosen him to "restore" the Christian gospel in its original purity. Hence, in some sense, Mormonism was simply an extreme manifestation of the basic Protestant anxiety about the corruption of the Christian church. In other respects, however, the new movement broke radically with the Protestant tradition from which it emerged. First, Smith insisted that he was not a reformer but rather a prophet on the biblical model who received knowledge directly from angelic visitors and waking theophanies.[54] On this basis, Smith claimed the right to add additional scripture to the biblical canon, which he did first with the Book of Mormon and subsequently in a series of written "revelations" given in response to specific questions or problems. Second, Smith rejected the notion of a priesthood of believers, insisting instead that authentic ecclesiastical authority could come only by the "laying on of hands" by those who could trace their authority through an unbroken chain of ordination back to Christ, authority that Smith claimed to have received from visiting angels. Both of these claims marked Mormonism as

53. See Richard L. Jensen, "Church Councils and Governance," in *Mormons in Early Victorian Britain*, ed. Richard L. Jensen and Malcolm R. Thorp (Salt Lake City: University of Utah Press, 1989), 179. The first Mormon missionaries arrived in England in 1837, and the new religion garnered tens of thousands of converts in Great Britain and Scandinavia over the following decades.

54. To contemporary ears, Smith's repeated claims to visions and revelations sound startling and unique, marking him to modern Mormons as a miraculous figure, and to many non-Mormons, a transparent fraud. See Jan Shipps, "The Prophet Puzzle: Suggestions Leading Toward a More Comprehensive Interpretation of Joseph Smith," *Journal of Mormon History* 1 (1974): 3 (discussing the problem of the prophet-fraud dichotomy in the context of Joseph Smith and early Mormonism). However, while Joseph Smith was certainly recognized as a religious radical and was accused of being an imposter in his own lifetime, he nevertheless operated in a religious milieu in which claims to visions and visiting angels were frequent, indeed commonplace. See Richard Lyman Bushman, "The Visionary World of Joseph Smith," *Brigham Young University Studies* 37, no. 1 (1997): 183 (discussing the role that stories of visions and angels played in the religious economy of Jacksonian America).

a heretical sect in the eyes of American Protestantism, and both of them contributed to the unique elaboration of the Mormon judiciary.

Smith's position as prophet and conduit of priesthood authority centralized a great deal of ecclesiastical power in his hands. Equally, if not more important, however, was the way in which Smith dispersed prophetic and priestly authority. He insisted that everyone had the right to receive personal revelation from God, and essentially all Latter-day Saint males were given the priesthood. He also set up a slew of independent councils that were to receive revelation and direct affairs within their appointed areas.[55] The result was the widespread dispersal of authority away from Joseph Smith. As one biographer has observed, "Joseph's presence was not required to make [the councils] work. Instead of councils relying on him to give the last word, they met, deliberated, and made policy decisions in his absence."[56] Much of the work done by these councils was adjudicative, either inquiring into the worthiness of individual Mormons accused of sin or settling disputes between Mormons. As a result, Mormon ideas of personal revelation and priesthood authority became intertwined with the emerging Mormon judiciary, which was divided into various specialized councils as opposed to the earlier congregational procedures.

These special councils began developing early in the history of the new movement. In 1831 Joseph Smith made Edward Partridge a "bishop." Thereafter, other men were ordained to the same office. Initially, the bishops were associated only with the "temporal affairs of the church," namely the emerging experiments with communal economics among Mormons in Ohio and Missouri.[57] The bishop also, however, became a judicial officer. For example, an 1835 revelation stated that he was "to be a judge in Israel . . . to sit in judgment upon transgressors upon testimony as it shall be laid before him according to the laws" (D&C 107:72). In addition, as Smith elaborated various priesthood offices—deacons, teachers, priests,

---

55. Richard Lyman Bushman, "The Theology of Councils," in *In Revelation, Reason, and Faith: Essays in Honor of Truman G. Madsen*, ed. Donald W. Parry, Daniel C. Peterson, and Stephen D. Ricks (Provo: Foundation for Ancient Research and Mormon Studies, Brigham Young University, 2002), 433, 439–41.

56. Bushman, 433, 440. See also Bushman, 443 ("In bringing conciliar government into being, Joseph not only distributed authority to the councils, but he dispensed the divine gift of revelation as well").

57. See Leonard Arrington, *Great Basin Kingdom: An Economic History of the Latter-Day Saints, 1830–1900* (Cambridge: Harvard University Press, 1958), 6–17 (discussing early Mormon communitarianism and the role of bishops).

elders, seventies, and high priests—the men in a given area holding each office gathered in quasi-fraternal organizations called "priesthood quorums." Each of these quorums was presided over by a president, and the quorum as a body had limited judicial authority. Although it could not excommunicate an erring brother, it could formally withdraw the fellowship of the quorum, and adjudication emerged as one of their main activities.[58]

Smith also established a series of superior councils that eventually gelled into a two-tiered appellate structure for the Church judiciary. In 1832, he announced a revelation to create a body called "the First Presidency" consisting of himself and two counselors, which would acquire final appellate jurisdiction in the Church. In 1834, Smith further refined the Mormon judiciary by creating a body known as "the high council," a group of twelve high priests presided over by a president, which was to settle "important difficulties which might arise in the church, which could not be settled by the church or the bishop's council to the satisfaction of the parties" (D&C 102:2). A year later, Smith underlined the centrality of discipline and adjudication to the emerging ecclesiastical structure by announcing a revelation creating a special procedure for excommunicating the President of the Church (Smith himself) should it become necessary, that "none shall be exempted from the justice and the laws of God, that all things may be done in order and in solemnity before him, according to truth and righteousness" (D&C 107:84).[59]

58. See Proceedings Before the Committee on Privileges and Elections of the United States Senate in the Matter of the Protests Against the Right of Hon. Reed Smoot, a Senator from the State of Utah, to Hold His Seat, S. Doc. No. 486, 59th Cong., 1st Sess. (1906), at 3:23 [hereinafter Smoot Hearings] (testimony by James E. Talmage stating that "[a]fter proper trial any quorum may disfellowship one of its members"). See generally Cook and Backman, *Kirtland Elders' Quorum Record 1836–1841* (recording numerous disciplinary actions by the Kirtland Elders' Quorum).

59. The sometimes-fluid nature of the Mormon judiciary is illustrated by the disagreements over the years about precisely how the procedure for excommunicating the President of the Church should work. At a meeting of the Twelve Apostles and the First Presidency on December 24, 1902, Apostle Rudger Clawson recorded:

> Elder Smoot [that is, Reed Smoot] said that there was a diversity of opinion in Utah Stake as to who would sit in judgment if the President of the church were placed on trial. Some claimed that it would be the right of the Presiding Bishopric to try him. Elder Smoot said he did not coincide with this view. The matter might be considered inappropriate for discussion, but he thought

However, while the refinement of the Mormon judiciary pushed adjudication away from the earlier congregational model into specialized tribunals, the possibility of trial by a general vote of the membership remained. Joseph Smith taught that "[w]hen there is no Bishop, [those subject to discipline] are to be tried by the voice of the Church."[60] Similarly, extraordinary cases could be decided by a general vote of the Church even when other tribunals were functioning. For example, in 1886 Joseph Q. Cannon, then a counselor to the presiding bishop of the Church, was excommunicated for adultery by vote of "the public congregation in the Big Tabernacle."[61]

> the council ought to be agreed as touching this question. Elder Smoot said that the revelation which directed that in case the President of the High Priesthood should [be] put upon trial, the Presiding Bishop associated with twelve high priests should constitute the trial court, was given before the church was fully organized and before the Twelve had been chosen. Pres. Smith [that is, Joseph F. Smith] suggested that the matter be taken under advisement for one week, which was done.

Stan Larson, ed., *A Ministry of Meetings: The Apostolic Diaries of Rudger Clawson* (Salt Lake City: Signature Books, 1993), 525–26 (second brackets in original). Clawson did not record the outcome of the special committee. However, in 1904, Joseph F. Smith, a nephew of Joseph Smith, Jr. and the then President of the Church, testified before the US Senate as part of the controversy surrounding the seating of Mormon Senator Reed Smoot. Responding to questions asked by the Senators, he stated that he could be tried for his membership before his local bishop's court like any other member, with appeal lying to his stake president, and from thence to a special council. See Smoot Hearings, 1:352. In an influential work on Church government published a few decades later, however, Apostle John A. Widtsoe described a special procedure based on the 1835 revelation to Joseph Smith, Jr. See John A. Widtsoe, *Priesthood and Church Government* (Salt Lake City: Deseret Book Co., 1939), 217.

60. Gregory A. Prince, *Power From on High: The Development of Mormon Priesthood* (Salt Lake City: Signature Books, 1995), 198 (citation omitted).

61. Dennis B. Horne, ed., *An Apostle's Record: The Journals of Abraham H. Cannon* (Urbana: University of Illinois Press, 2003), 85–86. In his 1904 testimony before the Senate, James E. Talmage also suggested that a vote of the general conference of the Church also constituted a method of extraordinary appeal:

> An appeal would lie from the first presidency to the assembled quorums of the priesthood; that is to say, the church as a body is the supreme court before which the cases involving church [*sic*].

The proliferating councils eventually settled into a single integrated judicial structure. In 1838, after years of intermittent violence, the Mormons were driven out of Missouri and settled in Illinois along the banks of the Mississippi river where they founded the city of Nauvoo. Eventually a bishop was assigned to each of Nauvoo's municipal wards, mainly to look after the needs of the poor and to provide a bishop's court for local members. These bishops were under the direction of the president of the Nauvoo Stake of Zion and his high council. This high council had appellate jurisdiction over decisions by the bishop's courts and local priesthood quorums, as well as original jurisdiction in difficult cases.[62] Other areas of concentrated Mormon settlement were organized into other "stakes" with a similar judicial structure. In some cases, the high council had a president who was different than the president of the stake.[63] For much of the nineteenth century, there were also "traveling bishops" who operated independent of particular wards or congregations.[64] The First Presidency then exercised appellate jurisdiction over all of the various high councils. In addition, certain councils, such as the Presiding Bishopric, retained jurisdiction independent of stake organizations.[65] With minor

---

> The assembled quorums or organizations of the priesthood may be said to be in session at every general conference of the church. But, of course, in the same assembly with the quorums of the priesthood standing and church rights may be tried.

Smoot Hearings, 3:21 (testimony of James E. Talmage); see also T. B. H. Stenhouse, *The Rocky Mountain Saints* (New York: D. Appleton and Co., 1873), 564–66 ("[T]here is also an appeal to the 'quorum' of the 'First Presidency,' and from that, if desired, to the Church collectively in General Conference").

62. See generally William G. Hartley, "Nauvoo Stake, Priesthood Quorums, and the Church's First Wards," *Brigham Young University Studies* 32, no. 1–2 (1991): 57–80 (illustrating examples of high council appellate jurisdiction in Nauvoo).

63. See William G. Hartley, "Brigham Young and Priesthood Work at the General and Local Levels," in *Lion of the Lord: Essays on the Life & Service of Brigham Young*, ed. Susan Easton Black and Larry C. Porter (Salt Lake City: Deseret Book Co., 1995), 338, 358.

64. See Hartley, 338, 358.

65. The office of Presiding Bishop is independent of the office of an ordinary bishop. After the Nauvoo period, bishops emerged as essentially congregational leaders, although local ecclesiastical structures remained quite fluid into the late 1870s. However, Joseph Smith published a revelation in 1841 which created an office of Presiding Bishop, who was to oversee the temporal affairs of the Church

refinements, this three-tiered structure of bishops' courts, high councils, and the First Presidency has survived in the Church to the present day.[66]

Unlike the Protestant structures from which it emerged, the mature Mormon judiciary was more than a simple, congregationally based method of policing ecclesiastical purity. It was a single, institutionally integrated system that was ideologically related to key aspects of Mormon theology. In February 1834, the Kirtland High Council met and "[Brother] Joseph . . . said he would show the order of councils in ancient days . . . as shown him by vision the law by which to govern the Council of the Church of Christ."[67] Smith went on to explain that "Jerusalem was the seat of the Church Council in ancient days" and that the procedures he was instituting were those that had been used by the apostle Peter, who "was appointed to this office by the voice of the Savior."[68] In reaching their decisions, the council was to "speak precisely according to the evidence and according to the teaching of the Spirit of the Lord."[69] Likewise, "in cases of difficulty respecting doctrine or principles if there is not a sufficiency written to make clear to the mind of the council, the president may inquire and obtain the mind of the Lord by Revelation."[70] The institutional structure of Mormon courts was thus central to the theological narrative of pristine Christianity and authentic priestly authority restored in the latter days. Likewise, the process of decision-making in Mormon courts explicitly rested on claims to continuing and immediate revelation from God. In short, Mormon courts became a key location in which Latter-day Saints experienced the divine and enacted the theological narratives that structured their religious beliefs. When the Kirtland Elders Quorum chose the temple as the location to hear the case of *Cahoon v. Green*, they were giving concrete expression to this central religious role of adjudication.

---

at a general level. See Doctrine & Covenants, 124:20–21, 141; see also Hartley, "Brigham Young and Priesthood Work," 356–58 (discussing the evolution of the office of Presiding Bishopric).

66. For many years there was a fourth level in the appellate structure: the Salt Lake Stake was considered "the center Stake of Zion" and the Salt Lake High Council had appellate jurisdiction over other high councils, which placed it in a position between the ordinary high councils and the First Presidency. See Hartley, "Brigham Young and Priesthood Work," 359.

67. "Kirtland High Council Minutes (Dec. 1834–Nov. 1837)," n.d., Church History Library, Salt Lake City, Utah.

68. "Kirtland High Council Minutes (Dec. 1834–Nov. 1837)."

69. "Kirtland High Council Minutes (Dec. 1834–Nov. 1837)."

70. "Kirtland High Council Minutes (Dec. 1834–Nov. 1837)."

II. Suing Before the Ungodly and Suing Before the Church

A suspicion of secular courts and a preference for church tribunals emerged within the first generation of Christianity. In his first letter to the Corinthians, Paul rebuked the early Christians for their litigiousness, noting with horror that "brother goes to law against brother, and that before unbelievers" (1 Cor. 6:6) He asked rhetorically, "When one of you has a grievance against a brother, does he dare to go to law before the unrighteous instead of the saints?" (1 Cor. 6:1) These passages from the New Testament captured the imagination of discipline-minded churches. The emphasis of these churches on ecclesiastical purity meant that adjudication was already an important part of their religious experience. Equipped with the institutional machinery and social practices to manage lawsuits between members, they combined Paul's attack on litigation with a deep-seated suspicion of the common-law courts. The result was a series of attempts to create religious alternatives to the civil courts, of which the Mormon judiciary became an exemplar.

The Puritans made some attempts to resolve civil litigation in church courts. For example, in 1635 the First Church of Boston excommunicated one of its members "for extortion, deceipt [*sic*], and lying, in and about Iron Worke which he made for one Mr. Jacob."[71] In the end, however, Puritan churches did not become heavily involved in resolving civil cases for the same reasons that their church discipline as a whole was less vigorous than other sects. Early Puritan congregations were made up mainly of non-members, and the theological accommodation marked by the Halfway Covenant dampened the practice of church adjudication. Congregationalist churches, however, did provide arbitrators from time to time,[72] and as late as the 1840s, Presbyterian churches, which merged with the Congregationalists under the 1801 Plan of Union, "frequently viewed questionable business practices, even if technically legal, as breaches of discipline."[73] Baptists were even more aggressive in using their disciplinary machinery to resolve civil disputes:

---

71. Haskins, *Law and Authority in Early Massachusetts*, 90.

72. See, e.g., L. Kinvin Wroth and Hiller B. Zobel, eds., *The Adams Papers: The Legal Papers of John Adams* (Cambridge: Belknap Press, 1965), 20–21 (discussing a dispute over timber submitted to arbitration before a church committee).

73. Glenn C. Altschuler and Jan M. Saltzgaber, *Revivalism, Social Conscience, and Community in the Burned-Over District: The Trial of Rhoda Bement* (Ithaca: Cornell University Press, 1983), 155.

> Rules prohibited quarreling, litigation between fellow members without church consent, the evasion of just debts, especially by taking advantage of the statute of limitations in order to circumvent legal collection. An important function of the church was to serve as a jury in the settlement of difficulties among its members. . . .[74]

The Quakers initially absented themselves from the English legal system because their literal interpretation of Christ's injunction, "swear not," (Matt. 5:34) meant that they refused to take the oaths that formed a necessary part of common-law procedure.[75] The result was a turn away from the secular courts and toward what the Quakers called "The Gospel Order," a comprehensive system for resolving intra-Quaker disputes without litigation.[76] For example, rules adopted by the New England Yearly Meeting in 1697 stated that "when any friend or friends shall hear of any . . . difference betwixt any friends . . . they [shall] forthwith speak to and tenderly advise, the persons between whom the differences is, to make a speedy end thereof."[77] If friendly persuasion did not work, the rules called for ad hoc arbitrators. "[T]hey should each choose an equal number of different, impartial and judicious friends, to hear and speedily determine the same; and that they do bind themselves to stand to their award and determination."[78] The Gospel Order, however, placed onerous sanctions on any Quaker who instituted a civil lawsuit against another "friend" without submitting the dispute to arbitration: "[I]f any person professing truth with us, shall . . . sue . . . at law, any other of our members, before he hath proceeded in the methods herein before recommended . . . then he be disowned by the meeting."[79]

Any Quaker thus disciplined could appeal to the quarterly and yearly meetings.[80] Although there is reason to suppose that intra-Quaker litigation was considerably more common than the "Gospel Order" would

74. Robert, "Excommunication, Virginia Style," 248 (describing church discipline among eighteenth- and nineteenth-century Baptists).

75. Offutt, Jr., *Of "Good Laws" and "Good Men,"* 147.

76. Offutt, Jr., 147. See also Odiorne, "Arbitration and Mediation Among Early Quakers," 161 (describing arbitration proceedings among the Quakers).

77. *Society of Friends New England Yearly Meeting, Rules of Discipline of the Yearly Meeting Held on Rhode Island for New England* (n.p.: n.p., 1849), 3–4.

78. *Society of Friends New England Yearly Meeting*, 3–4.

79. *Society of Friends New England Yearly Meeting*, 5–6.

80. *Society of Friends New England Yearly Meeting*, 1 (setting forth the procedures in appeals).

suggest,[81] one nineteenth-century author insisted that "[c]ases, where property is concerned to the amount of many thousands, are determined" according to the Gospel Order.[82]

The earliest recorded case of a civil dispute in a Mormon tribunal was an action for debt, resolved by an Indiana conference in December 1831. The minutes of the meeting record that "Brs. George Heartley & Oliver Walker then withdrew to settle the difficulty between themselves but could not agree[.] Therefore decided that two should be appointed by the Moderator."[83] After an attempt at mediation failed, the parties "agreed to abide the decision of John & Thomas who concluded that Oliver Walker pay George Heartly which was his just due."[84] The decision of the arbitrators "was laid before the Conference," and it was only with "much cavilling" that the losing party was persuaded "to stand or hold fast to his agreement."[85] In the end, however, "they came together as brothers and disciples & all matters were settled & buried."[86]

Mormon courts soon moved from arbitration for two willing parties to direct jurisdiction over a case. A strikingly high proportion of these earliest complaints were for defamation of one kind or another. For example, in December 1833 Joseph Smith heard a complaint against a

> Bro. Ezekiel Rider . . . who had said many hard things against Bro. Whitney, the Bishop of the Church—he said that Bro. Whitney was not fit for a Bishop and that he treated the Brethren who came into the store with disrespect that he was overbearing and fair would walk on the necks of the Brethren &c.[87]

---

81. See Offutt, Jr., *Of "Good Laws" and "Good Men"*, 174–81 (providing a demographic analysis of litigation in the Delaware valley which suggests widespread intra-Quaker lawsuits).

82. Thomas Clarkson, *A Portraiture of Quakerism: Taken from a View of the Education and Discipline, Social Manners, Civil and Political Economy, Religious Principles, and Character of the Society of Friends* (New York: Samuel Stansbury, 1806), 70.

83. Cannon and Cook, *Far West Record*, 38.

84. Cannon and Cook, 38.

85. Cannon and Cook, 38.

86. Cannon and Cook, 38. Interestingly, this earliest foray of Mormon tribunals into arbitration does not seem to have been entirely successful. Cannon and Cook write, "Although the problem was considered 'buried' at this conference, it surfaced again and was a matter of business in Kirtland in December 1834." Cannon and Cook, 38n4.

87. "Kirtland High Council Minutes (Dec. 1834–Nov. 1837)."

In the Quaker context, it has been theorized that the heavy preponderance of defamation cases in the ecclesiastical docket reflects procedural advantages offered by church courts. A plaintiff bringing such an action in a secular court risked a defendant who "attempt[ed] to prove the truth of the alleged defamatory statement, broadcasting to the court crowd further attacks on the plaintiff's reputation."[88] While nineteenth-century Mormon courts were not entirely private affairs, they could offer a less glaringly public rehearsal of the original insults. In addition, early Mormons operated in an often-violent frontier "culture of honor" that "bred deep loyalties to friends and family while instilling a fierce urge to avenge insults."[89] Church courts provided a way of managing the conflict this culture created by transforming insults from a private *causus belli* into ecclesiastical litigation.

During the 1830s, church courts heard increasing numbers of cases involving civil claims such as actions for debt, but the "secular" issues in these disputes were frequently tied up in religious and political struggles of central importance to the Church. For example, after Mormons were violently pushed out of Jackson County, Missouri, one Mormon lawyer found himself disciplined after agreeing to represent non-Mormons in Jackson County trying to collect debts against fellow Mormons.[90] After the Mormons moved to Illinois, they dominated political and legal offices in Nauvoo. Joseph Smith was elected mayor and served as a judge, studying law for a time and boasting that "I am a lawyer; I am a big lawyer and comprehend heaven, earth and hell, to bring forth knowledge that shall cover up all lawyers, doctors and other big bodies."[91] He also, however, preached that "as long as I have a tongue to speak I will expose the iniquity of the Lawyiers [*sic*] and wicked men."[92] Also, for the first time in Nauvoo, Church courts began treating the mere filing of a civil lawsuit by one Mormon against another Mormon as a matter for discipline. Using

---

88. Offutt, Jr., *Of "Good Laws" and "Good Men"*, 172.

89. Bushman, *Rough Stone Rolling*, 295. Cf. David Hacket Fischer, *Albion's Seed: Four British Folkways in America* (New York: Oxford University Press, 1989), 765–71 (discussing honor and violence among backcountry settlers).

90. See Cannon and Cook, *Far West Record*, 163.

91. Joseph Fielding Smith, ed., *Teachings of the Prophet Joseph Smith* (Salt Lake City: Deseret Book Co., 1967), 279.

92. Andrew F. Ehat and Lyndon W. Cook, eds., *The Words of Joseph Smith: The Contemporary Accounts of the Nauvoo Discourses of the Prophet Joseph* (Salt Lake City: Bookcraft, 1980), 324.

a formula that would be repeated countless times in succeeding decades, in November 1842 a member filed a complaint with the Nauvoo High Council to "prefer a charge" for "instituting a suit at Law against me," an action "derogatory to the character of a Christian."[93]

These Church councils became increasingly important as the Mormons were driven west in the 1840s. A mob murdered Joseph Smith in 1844, and the Mormons abandoned Nauvoo in 1846. Their final destination was the Great Salt Lake valley, but they first crossed Iowa to the banks of the Missouri River and founded a temporary settlement dubbed "Winter Quarters." Brigham Young, Joseph Smith's successor, established the "Municipal High Council" to govern the settlement. Formally identical to earlier high councils, the Winter Quarters High Council exercised an extremely expansive jurisdiction, resolving all civil disputes and meting out criminal punishments.[94] When the vanguard of Mormons arrived in the Salt Lake Valley in 1847, they replicated this system. John Smith was made president of the Salt Lake Stake with a high council that exercised both civil and criminal authority. The Mormons made an early bid for statehood, drafting a constitution modeled on that of Illinois and setting up a government for the provisional "State of Deseret" in 1849.[95] By early 1850, the courts of Deseret took over from the Salt Lake High Council. Hence from 1846 until 1850, Mormons lived under high councils that had full civil and criminal power.

Congress rejected the State of Deseret and organized the Territory of Utah as part of the Compromise of 1850, providing the legal context in which the Mormon courts operated for more than four decades. The Territorial Legislature was locally elected and dominated by Mormons. The Territorial Supreme Court, in contrast, was staffed with non-Mormon federal appointees, as was the territorial executive after President James Buchanan replaced Brigham Young as Territorial Governor in 1857. The treatment of civil cases by the high councils, however, showed basic con-

93. "Nauvoo Stake High Council Court Papers (1839–44)," Church History Library, Salt Lake City, Utah.

94. See Edward L. Kimball and Kenneth W. Godfrey, "Law and Order in Winter Quarters," *Journal of Mormon History* 32, no. 1 (2006): 180–81 (discussing the legislative, executive, and judicial powers of the Winter Quarters High Council).

95. See Peter Crawley, *The Constitution of the State of Deseret* (Provo: Friends of the Harold B. Lee Library, 1982); Dale Morgan, *The State of Deseret* (Logan: Utah State University Press, 1987), 7–29 (discussing the manner in which the Mormons formed the State of Deseret and appealed for statehood).

tinuity throughout the period. Plaintiffs filed simple written complaints with the clerk of the bishop's court or high council. Clerks issued summons to the defendants. Defendants who refused to appear risked disfellowshipment or excommunication for "contempt of the priesthood."[96] The parties presented evidence, and the council issued decisions. Appeals could be taken to the high council and the First Presidency, which both tried cases de novo. A Mormon sued by another Mormon in a secular court could file a counter-complaint before a Church court alleging "unChristian-like conduct."[97] The Church court would then take jurisdiction over the entire dispute and resolve the underlying lawsuit on the merits. Failure to carry the Church judiciary's final decision into effect resulted in excommunication.

As might be expected, losing parties were not always satisfied with the decisions of Church courts. For example, in 1847 when one victorious plaintiff called at a defendant's house to claim property to which the high council had declared him entitled, the irate defendant responded, "The Council might go to hell and be damned[!]"[98] In another case, a diarist recorded that a losing party in a high council case "was dissatisfied with their judgment and told them that it was no better than robery [*sic*]."[99] However, one non-Mormon observer insisted that "[i]n ninety-nine cases out of a hundred the parties are satisfied."[100] Indeed, occasionally, "Gentiles," as Mormons called non-Mormons, sued Mormons in Church courts rather than secular fora. For example, in one case an influential bishop had run-up several thousand dollars of debt to a Gentile merchant. The merchant "brought suit against the bishop in [a Church court] in preference to going to law."[101] After a ninety-minute trial, the Church court ruled that "the bishop should pay the full amount within twenty-eight days, or be

96. See Firmage and Mangrum, *Zion in the Courts*, 289 (discussing sanctions for refusals to submit to the jurisdiction of Church courts).

97. See Firmage and Mangrum, 264–67 (discussing one representative dispute spanning both secular and Church courts).

98. Nicholas Groesbeck Morgan, ed., *The Old Fort: Historic Mormon Bastion, the Plymouth Rock of the West* (Salt Lake City: Nicholas Groesbeck Morgan, 1964), 82 (showing the reprinted minutes from the Great Salt Lake City High Council).

99. Juanita Brooks, ed., *On the Mormon Frontier: The Diary of Hosea Stout 1844–1861* (Salt Lake City: University of Utah Press, 1964), 433.

100. Execution of the Laws in Utah [To accompany bill H.R. No. 1089.], H.R. Rep. No. 21, at 1 (1870) (testimony of Franklin Head, Feb. 28, 1870).

101. Edward W. Tullidge, *History of Salt Lake City: Biographies* (Salt Lake City: Star Printing Company, 1886), 169.

suspended from his bishopric."[102] The merchant was satisfied with the decision and offered to pay court costs "which [was] declined, for suits in this court were without costs."[103]

Although Church courts referred to "the law of the Church" and "the law of the Lord," it was unclear what rules—if any—they looked to in resolving cases. The basic procedures used by the high councils had been given by Joseph Smith in 1834 and remained quite stable. During the period of 1846 to 1850, high councils promulgated written rules to govern Mormon communities; however, they ceased to do so once the legislature began operating.[104] Even the treatment of these rules, however, reveals ambivalence toward formal legislation. For example, the Salt Lake High Council promulgated a law dealing with stray livestock that imposed substantial fines on the owners of the animals. The council subsequently determined that the rule was too harsh and left the bishops who applied it with too little discretion. Accordingly, the council repealed the rule; however, they "also . . . imposed a fine of 25 dollars on any one of the Council who divulged the same as they wished to let the force of the law do all the good possible after it was repealed."[105]

One Mormon tried to explain the rules applied in Church courts by saying "[t]he laws of the church are revelations. . . . No rule, however, is of binding effect until it has been adopted by the people to whom it applies."[106] In reality, appeals to formally canonized revelations decided few cases. In 1870, a Gentile observed more accurately that bishop's courts applied "a sort of wild equity, that is generally not far from just."[107] Occasionally, Church courts looked to biblical rules, for example by requiring four-fold compensation for theft.[108] In one case a party appealed

102. Tullidge, 169–70.

103. Tullidge, 170.

104. See, e.g., *Ordinances Passed by the Legislative Council of Great Salt Lake City, and Ordered to Be Printed* (n.p.: n.p., 1849) (showing a collection of ordinances adopted by the Salt Lake High Council).

105. Brooks, *On the Mormon Frontier*, 334–35.

106. "Proceedings Before the Committee on Privileges and Elections of the United States Senate in the Matter of the Protests Against the Right of Hon. Reed Smoot, a Senator from the State of Utah, to Hold His Seat" (Washington, DC, 1906), 20 (testimony of James E. Talmage).

107. Execution of the Laws in Utah [To accompany bill H.R. No. 1089.], H.R. Rep. No. 21, at 1 (1870) (testimony of Franklin Head, Feb. 28, 1870).

108. In some cases, Mormon tribunals applied the biblical rules in unusual circumstances. John Nebeker described one such case decided in 1847 or 1848:

to "known and justly established usages of law and equity in civilized nations."[109] In some instances Church courts followed secular law,[110] but they did not hesitate to abandon it, for example, by enforcing debts discharged in bankruptcy[111] or by forging a new system of water rights better suited to the arid Great Basin.[112] The upper reaches of the Church's hierarchy did attempt to create some uniformity. For example, in some instances bishops or high councils facing a difficult issue wrote the First Presidency, and the letters sent in reply evidence consistent positions on some points. The Church's then official organ, *The Deseret Evening News*, also printed articles occasionally, presumably penned by Church leaders, instructing that certain rules be applied in particular situations. Finally, high Church officials regularly traveled from stake to stake, preaching and instructing local leaders on, among other things, the proper way of conducting Church courts and resolving disputes among the Latter-day Saints.[113] These meetings also provided opportunities to raise questions of substance and procedure with the visiting leaders. Despite these mechanisms, however, the Mormons never came close to promulgating anything like a religious law code governing disputes in their courts.

This Mormon ambivalence toward substantive legislation was linked to Mormon theology. On this point, Mormonism can be usefully compared with Islam.[114] Both religions claim to be completions of the monotheis-

---

> There was one case that created a great deal of fun. A certain man persisted in keeping a dog. Now a dog would eat pretty much of what, under the circumstances, could be eaten by the people and therefore all could not afford to keep dogs. This dog stole some biscuits from a man and the fellow borrowed a shot gun and shot the dog. The case was brought before me for arbitration, and I gave the man who had lost the biscuits the full benefit of the law, namely, allowed him four fold—or 16 biscuits, which kept the fellow a whole week.

John Nebeker, "Early Justice in Utah," *Utah Historical Quarterly* 3, no. 3 (1930): 87–89.

109. Cannon and Cook, *Far West Record*, 204.

110. Firmage and Mangrum, *Zion in the Courts*, 339–40.

111. Firmage and Mangrum, 342–43.

112. Firmage and Mangrum, 321.

113. See, e.g., Horne, *An Apostle's Record*, 322 (recording sermons given to stake leaders on conduct of Church courts by Apostle Francis M. Lyman and President George Q. Cannon).

114. The comparison was ubiquitous, if universally pejorative, in the nineteenth century. See generally Arnold H. Green, "Mormonism and Islam: From Polemics

tic tradition, and both were founded by prophets who offered the world new sacred texts. Islam, however, developed an elaborate jurisprudential theory, the *usul al-fiqh*, which sought to derive a comprehensive legal code from the Qur'an and the example (*sunna*) of the prophet Mohammed.[115] There was no comparable effort in Mormonism to derive detailed substantive rules from Mormon scripture or its founding prophet. Of course, it took Islam several centuries to develop a fully elaborated jurisprudence.[116] Hence, one might argue that Mormonism is still too young to invite useful jurisprudential comparison to Islam.

There are deeper differences at work, however, than simply age. Islam never developed a corporate identity similar to the Christian idea of a church. Rather, as one scholar has written, "every person, as such, with no exceptions, was summoned in his own person to obey the commands of God: there could be no intermediary, no group responsibility, no evasion of any sort from direct confrontation with the divine will."[117] Despite this radically individualistic view of human relation to the divine, the notion of a unified community of the believers (*ummah*) remained a vital part of Islam. These seemingly incommensurable aspirations were mediated in part through the *usul al-fiqh*, which allowed a professional class of jurists to impose sufficient consistency to keep Islam's theological individualism from undermining the communal cohesion of the believers.[118]

---

to Mutual Respect and Cooperation," *Brigham Young University Studies* 40, no. 4 (2001): 199, 200–209 (discussing the ways in which Mormonism and Islam were related to one another during the nineteenth and early twentieth centuries).

115. See generally Noel J. Coulson, *A History of Islamic Law* (Edinburgh: Edinburgh University Press, 1964). For a detailed account of Islamic legal reasoning, see Wael B. Hallaq, *A History of Islamic Legal Theories: An Introduction to Sunni Usul al-Fiqh* (Cambridge: Cambridge University Press, 1997).

116. The prophet Mohammed died in 632 AD. See Coulson, *A History of Islamic Law*, 22–23. The *usul al-fiqh*, however, is dated to a much later period. For example, Ahmad ibn Hanbal, the founder of the last of the great schools of classical Islamic jurisprudence, died in 855 AD. Coulson, 71. See also Marshall G. S. Hodgson, *The Venture of Islam: Conscience and History in a World Civilization, The Classical Age of Islam*, vol. 1: The Classical Age of Islam (Chicago: University of Chicago Press, 1974), 319 (providing a brief chronology of the development of the four schools of classical Islamic jurisprudence—Maliki, Hanifi, Shafi, and Hanbali—between 700 and 855 AD).

117. Hodgson, *The Venture of Islam*, 1: The Classical Age of Islam: 318.

118. To put the point in Weberian terms, the *usul al-fiqh* served to control and limit the charisma of members of the Islamic *ummah*. See generally Hallaq, *A*

Mormonism faced many of these same tensions. Like Islam it contains a radically individualistic conception of the human relationship to the divine, albeit on a very different metaphysical basis. Mormon scripture teaches that the human spirit is uncreated and co-eternal with God, and that every individual is entitled to direct, personal revelation from God. The potentially fragmenting consequences of such ideas emerged early in Mormon history. In response to one associate who had begun receiving revelations directed at the new church, Joseph Smith published a counter-revelation stating "no one shall be appointed to receive commandments and revelations in this church excepting my servant Joseph Smith, Jun., for he receiveth them even as Moses" (D&C 28:2).[119] Over time, Smith created an ever more elaborate ecclesiastical structure—of which the Church courts were a key part—and endowed it with enormous theological significance, ultimately identifying the Church as a corporate body with the kingdom of God in "the dispensation of the fullness of times" (D&C 128:20–21).[120] Thus, in Mormonism the living prophet and the institutional Church performed the function that the *usul al-fiqh* performed in Islam, protecting the religious community from the anarchic forces of its own individualistic theology. As Remi Brague has put it:

> In Islam . . . the development of a more and more precise *sharia* that demanded more and more clearly a direct connection to the origins and become more and more incarnate in a class of jurists ended up rendering superfluous a caliph who claimed to unite in his person the political authority of the head of state and the religious authority of the successor to the Prophet.[121]

In contrast, Mormons felt no religious need to elaborate a clear body of substantive law. Indeed, to the extent that such a body of law would have placed the exegesis of sacred texts in competition with living prophets, or the church as an institution, it was anathema to Mormon theology. In

History of Islamic Legal Theories, 21–35 (introducing the *usul al-fiqh* as it relates to the different communities of Islam).

119. See also Bushman, *Rough Stone Rolling*, 120–22 (discussing the confrontation between Joseph Smith and Hiram Page that gave rise to this revelation).

120. For an excellent discussion of the tension within Mormon culture between individualistic and corporate or authoritarian elements of Mormon theology, see Terryl L. Givens, *People of Paradox: A History of Mormon Culture* (New York: Oxford University Press, 2007), 3–19.

121. Rémi Brague, *The Law of God: The Philosophical History of an Idea*, trans. Lydia G. Cochrane (Chicago: University of Chicago Press, 2007), 258.

contrast, the largely ad hoc approach that Mormon courts adopted—"a sort of wild equity"[122]—was both sufficient to the dispute resolution needs of frontier society and consonant with their own religious beliefs.

The Mormons struggled to create effective enforcement mechanisms for their Church courts. Previous writers have tended to assume that, with the exception of the 1846–1850 interlude, the threat of excommunication was the only method by which the decisions of Church courts could be enforced.[123] To be sure, in the context of closely knit Mormon communities, excommunication carried a heavy cost, including social ostracism and even commercial boycott.[124] But this is not the whole story. Prior to 1874, the Church courts were only one part of a web of Mormon legal institutions and practices. Mormons dominated the Territorial Legislature, and they used their power to limit the authority of lawyers and the common law they represented. First, the Legislature very pointedly refused to pass a reception statute making the common law binding in the territory, instead commanding that "no laws nor parts of laws shall be read, argued, cited, or adopted in any court . . . except those enacted by the Governor and Legislative Assembly."[125] They also abolished technical common-law pleadings.[126] Next, they struck at lawyers by stating that no person em-

---

122. Execution of the Laws in Utah [To accompany bill H.R. No. 1089.], H.R. Rep. No. 215, at 1 (1870) (testimony of Franklin Head, Feb. 28, 1870).

123. See, e.g., Firmage and Mangrum, *Zion in the Courts*, 287 ("The church court system relied on the voluntary submission of church members to its decision. While the state courts enforced decisions with fines, imprisonment, and even death, church courts could only disfellowship or excommunicate recalcitrant church members").

124. See, e.g., Richard S. Van Wagoner and Mary C. Van Wagoner, "Orson Pratt, Jr.: Gifted Son of an Apostle and an Apostate," *Dialogue: A Journal of Mormon Thought* 21, no. 1 (1988): 84, 91 (mentioning the boycott of the business of an apostate Mormon in a remote southern Utah settlement); Ronald G. Watt, "Sailing 'The Old Ship Zion': The Life of George D. Watt," *Brigham Young University Studies* 18, no. 1 (1977): 48 ("In 1874, however, Watt lost his membership in the Church. . . . After his excommunication, old friends ignored him and his obscurity began").

125. Michael W. Homer, "The Judiciary and the Common Law in Utah Territory, 1850–61," *Dialogue: A Journal of Mormon Thought* 21, no. 1 (1988): 97, 102 (internal quotations omitted).

126. An Act Concerning the Judiciary, and for Judicial Purposes § 10, in Acts, Resolutions, and Memorials Passed by the First Annual and Special Sessions of the Legislative Assembly of the Territory of Utah (1852) [hereinafter 1852 Acts]

ploying an attorney "shall be compelled by any process of law to pay the counsel so employed."[127] The same law rejected the adversary system by requiring lawyers to "present all the facts in the case, whether they are calculated to make against his client or not."[128]

In addition, the legislature created Mormon-dominated courts as an alternative to the Gentile-dominated Territorial Supreme Court and district courts. They did this in two ways. First, the congressional act creating Utah Territory gave the legislature the power to create probate courts. Building on a practice common in many western territories dissatisfied with carpet-bagging judges, the legislature gave these probate courts "power to exercise original jurisdiction both civil and criminal."[129] The probate judges, in turn, were chosen by the legislature, and were almost always Mormon.[130]

("Immaterial variancies [*sic*], errors, or defects, may be disregarded . . ."). See generally Homer, "The Judiciary and the Common Law," 97 (discussing the history of the common law in nineteenth-century Utah).

127. An Act for the Regulation of Attorneys § 2, in 1852 Acts. In addition, the Territory's homestead exemption preserved "the proper tools, instruments, or books of any farmer, mechanic, surveyor, physician, teacher, or professor." An Act Concerning the Judiciary, and for Judicial Purposes § 22, in 1852 Acts. The books of lawyers and attorneys may have been pointedly omitted.

128. An Act for the Regulation of Attorneys § 5, in 1852 Acts. A lawyer failing to comply with this provision was to "be liable to all the penalty hereinbefore provided for, and the further penalty of not less than one dollar at the discretion of the court."

129. An Act in Relation to the Judiciary § 30, in 1852 Acts. See Earl S. Pomeroy, *The Territories of the United States, 1861–1890* (Philadelphia: University of Pennsylvania Press, 1947), 59–60. See also Jeffery Ogden Johnson, "Was Being a Probate Judge in Pioneer Utah a Church Calling" (Mormon History Association Annual Meeting, Casper, Wyoming, 2006), 1 (noting that other territories created locally staffed courts as a way of undermining the control of federally appointed judges).

130. See generally James B. Allen, "The Unusual Jurisdiction of County Probate Courts in the Territory of Utah," *Utah Historical Quarterly* 36 (1968): 132–42 (exploring the Mormon Church's influence on civil affairs as a result of probate judges being elected by the legislature); Elizabeth D. Gee, "Justice for All or for the 'Elect'? The Utah County Probate Court, 1855–72," *Utah Historical Quarterly* 48, no. 2 (1980): 129, 136 (noting that most of the judges presiding over the probate court also held high Church offices); Johnson, "Was Being a Probate Judge in Pioneer Utah a Church Calling," 177; Jay E. Powell, "Fairness in the Salt Lake County Probate Courts," *Utah Historical Quarterly* 38 (1970):

Second, the legislature adopted a series of laws apparently designed to make the decisions of Church courts legally binding. They did this by taking an extremely liberal attitude toward arbitration. "By the consent of the Court and the parties, any person may be selected to act as Judge for the trial of any particular cause or question," stated the territory's first judiciary act.[131] Elsewhere, the law declared that "[a]ny matter involving litigation may be referred to arbitrators" chosen by either the parties or the court.[132] These arbitrators had extensive powers. A judge chosen by the parties, said the law, "shall possess all the powers of the District Judge in the case."[133] Likewise, arbitrators had the "authority to subpoena witnesses, administer oaths, or affirmations, and issue process as the Court."[134] Decisions of arbitrators were to be treated by clerks and marshals "in the same manner, as if the case had been prosecuted and decided in the usual manner."[135] Most intriguingly, a special law called for each county to "elect a council of twelve select men as referees, whose duty it shall be to decide all cases in litigation which may come before them by the mutual consent of the parties."[136] This body of men sounds tantalizingly like a local high council, which also consisted of twelve men.[137] In addition to the number chosen, the territorial act borrows language from one of Joseph Smith's revelations on Church courts, declaring that once the referees make a decision it "shall be the end

---

256–62 (examining the impartiality of probate court in Salt Lake during its early years of operation); Jay Emerson Powell, "An Analysis of the Nature of the Salt Lake County Probate Court's Role in Aggravating Anti-Mormon Sentiment, 1852–1855" (honors thesis, Department of History, University of Utah, 1968) [hereinafter Powell, Anti-Mormon Sentiment] (analyzing the operation of the Salt Lake County Probate court during those years).

131. An Act in Relation to the Judiciary § 11, in 1852 Acts.

132. An Act in Relation to the Judiciary § 45.

133. An Act in Relation to the Judiciary § 11.

134. An Act in Relation to the Judiciary § 45.

135. An Act in Relation to the Judiciary § 45.

136. Resolution in Relation to Election of Twelve Select Men, or Referees, in 1852 Acts.

137. See Powell, "Anti-Mormon Sentiment," 28–29 ("There has been some speculation that the effect of this resolution may have been to give legal status to the decisions of local high councils, but there is not enough evidence concerning the selection or actions of these men to permit drawing any conclusions").

of all controversy in the matter."[138] In a sermon denouncing litigation, Brigham Young explicitly associated the Church courts with this territorial legal structure:

> There is not a righteous person, in this community, who will have difficulties that cannot be settled by arbitrators, the Bishop's Court, the High Council, or by the 12 Referees (as provided in Resolution No. 4, page 390 of Utah Laws), far better and more satisfactory than to contend with each other in law courts . . .[139]

Under territorial law, however, the jurisdiction of such arbitrators was neither wholly voluntary nor were their decisions wholly hortatory. Rather, parties could be required by a court to submit to arbitration,[140] arbitrators exercised the procedural powers of secular judges,[141] and their decisions were legally binding.[142] Hence, to the extent that church courts acted as the arbitrators under any of these laws, in theory they exercised a power substantially identical to that held by secular trial judges.

It is not at all clear, however, that this legal machinery ever functioned as intended. There are no reported cases invoking the provisions governing arbitration. Furthermore, ultimate control of the territorial judiciary lay in the hands of Gentile appointees who were often actively hostile to the Territorial Legislature. One of the earliest of these judges declared "that

---

138. Resolution in Relation to Election of Twelve Select Men, or Referees, in 1852 Acts. Cf. Doctrine & Covenants, 107:83 ("And their decision upon his head shall be an end of controversy concerning him").

139. Brigham Young, June 8, 1856, *Journal of Discourses*, 26 vols. (London and Liverpool: LDS Booksellers Depot, 1854–86), 3:238.

140. An Act Concerning the Judiciary, and for Judicial Purposes § 11, in 1852 Acts.

141. See An Act Concerning the Judiciary, and for Judicial Purposes § 11 (a person chosen to decide a case "shall possess all the powers of the District Judge in the case"); An Act Concerning the Judiciary, and for Judicial Purposes § 45 ("[A]rbitrators have authority to subpoena witnesses, administer oaths, or affirmations, and issue process as the Court").

142. See An Act Concerning the Judiciary, and for Judicial Purposes § 45 ("And when they shall have made their decision, shall report the case . . . to the Clerk of the County in which the case has arisen . . . and it shall be the duty of the Clerk . . . [to] proceed in the same manner, as if the case had been prosecuted and decided in the usual manner"); Resolution in Relation to Election of Twelve Select Men, or Referees, in 1852 Acts.

the Utah laws are founded in ignorance" and could thus be ignored,[143] insisting in one case that "[t]he law must be construed by men learned in the Law, and not by virtue of any Priesthood."[144] A later court declared that the Mormons had "tacitly agreed upon maxims and principles of the Common Law suited to their conditions," despite the explicit earlier territorial legislation to the contrary, which the court ignored.[145] Finally, in 1874, Congress passed an act abolishing the extensive jurisdiction of the probate courts as part of an effort to facilitate polygamy prosecutions by increasing Gentile control of the territorial judiciary.[146] In short, the courts disregarded the statutes passed by the Territorial Legislature, which were also met with congressional hostility.

It is difficult to gauge how successful the Mormons ultimately were at suppressing intra-Mormon litigation. In his annual message to the Legislature in 1850, then-Governor Young reported proudly that not a single lawsuit had been heard before the district courts of the territory.[147] The diary of Hosea Stout, a Mormon attorney active in this period, however, records numerous lawsuits.[148] Unfortunately, virtually all

---

143. "Letter from Samuel W. Richards, Member of the Utah Legislature, to His Brother (Dec. 7, 1855)," in *History of Salt Lake City*, by Edward W. Tullidge (Salt Lake City: E. W. Tullidge, 1886), 145.

144. People v. Green, 1 Utah 11, 15 (1876).

145. First Nat'l Bank v. Kinner, 1 Utah 100, 107 (1873) (holding that the Statute of Frauds had been tacitly accepted in Utah). Ironically, while the Territorial Supreme Court essentially ignored early territorial enactments attempting to exclude the common law, those territorial statutes have been invoked more recently by the Utah Supreme Court as aids in interpreting the Utah State Constitution. See Craftsman Builder's Supply, Inc. v. Butler Mfg. Co., 974 P.2d 1194 (Utah 1999) (citing territorial statutes).

146. See Poland Act, Act of June 23, 1874, ch. 469, 18 Stat. 253 (1874). At about the same time, a case reached the Utah Territorial Supreme Court on the jurisdiction of the Utah probate courts. The justices ruled that the Territorial Legislature had exceeded its power under Utah's Organic Act by endowing the probate courts with unlimited subject-matter jurisdiction. See Cast v. Cast, 1 Utah 112, 119–20 (1873).

147. Homer, "The Judiciary and the Common Law in Utah Territory," 98.

148. Homer, 2:364 (entry for Mar. 9, 1850: ". . . I also prosecuted another Suit H. S. Eldrege V.S Mr Long for killing an ox which did not belong to him"); Homer, 2:367 (entry for Apr. 22, 1850: "Attended a trial Dan Jones Vs E. Williams in matter of debt as council for Jones"); Homer, 2:370 (entry for May 30, 1850: "Attending to Legal business Sally Murdoc V.S. S. O Holmes in

of the records of civil cases by the Utah Territorial Courts were either lost or destroyed. Hence it is difficult to compile an accurate picture of civil litigation in Mormon country during the nineteenth century. Records of the Mormon-dominated probate courts do exist, and detailed studies of two of the most important of these courts reveal an ambiguous picture.[149] Analysis of the Utah County Probate Court shows that Gentiles were much more likely to institute civil litigation than Mormons were. Seventy-three percent of the plaintiffs were Gentiles, who never constituted more than seventeen percent of the population prior to 1874 when the jurisdiction of the probate courts was sharply limited.[150] On the other hand, of civil cases litigated to judgment, more than half involved Mormons suing other Mormons.[151] A study of the Salt Lake County Probate Court between 1852 and 1855 revealed that intra-Mormon litigation constituted thirty percent of all litigation involving Mormons.[152] It is possible, of course, that this intra-Mormon litigation only occurred after trying to unsuccessfully resolve the case in a Church court, which would be in line with ecclesiastical procedure.[153] A more likely interpretation, however, is that while the Church judiciary limited litigation among Latter-day Saints, it never came close to eliminating it.

In part, the Mormon attempt to opt out of civil litigation reflected dissatisfaction with the expense and contentiousness of common-law adjudication. For example, Church President Wilford Woodruff wrote to one stake president in 1896 that "[h]eartburnings, bitterness, and ill-feel-

---

matter of debt"); Homer, 2:378 (entry for Aug. 21, 1850: "Still engaged in Legal business Bullar vs Tolton in debt on part of Tolton").

149. See generally Gee, "Justice for All or for the 'Elect'?" (examining the records of the Utah County Probate Court); Powell, "Anti-Mormon Sentiment" (examining the records of the Salt Lake County Probate Court).

150. Gee, "Justice for All or for the 'Elect'?," 139.

151. See Gee, 144 (showing that for the period studied, twenty-one cases involving Mormon plaintiffs and Mormon defendants were litigated to judgment, while only nineteen other civil cases received a final judgment on the merits).

152. Powell, "Anti-Mormon Sentiment," 74 (showing twenty-five resident vs. resident cases out of a total of eighty-three cases involving residents); Powell, 48 ("While residency and membership in the Mormon Church can be generally equated during this period, there were undoubtedly a few non-member residents. What the Utah emigration list yields is specifically Mormon emigration; so technically what we have is a Mormon/non-Mormon split").

153. Firmage and Mangrum, *Zion in the Courts*, 267–71 (discussing procedures that allowed intra-Mormon litigation).

ing invariably attend lawsuits, whichever way they terminate, and we are desirous to stop litigation among the members of the church."[154] Likewise, one prolific critic of Brigham Young and Mormonism nevertheless insisted that "[t]he judicial department of the priesthood . . . has saved the brethren and sisters all the trouble and expense of lawsuits when differences have arisen among them."[155] Another key concern was communal unity. The strenuous efforts of nineteenth-century Mormons were directed toward "the building up of Zion," a vision of the godly society that was to be achieved by the Latter-day Saints in the here and now of Jacksonian Missouri and later in the expanses of the Great Basin.[156] Central to the idea of Zion was the need for harmony and unity. "[I]f ye are not one," God declares in the text of one of Joseph Smith's revelations, "ye are not mine" (D&C 38:27). The "heartburnings" of litigation were a threat to this unity, and the expansive jurisdiction of Church courts sought—with uneven success to be sure—to maintain the communal harmony central to this vision of Zion. They also served to heighten the divide, so important for nineteenth-century Mormons, between the Saints and "the World." The secular courts represented the Babylon out of which the Latter-day Saints had been gathered, while the Church courts were identified with the Zion to which they had fled.

---

154. Smoot Hearings, 17.

155. Stenhouse, *The Rocky Mountain Saints*, 564. Likewise, J. H. Beadle, the editor of The Corrine Reporter and an activist in anti-Mormon politics, testified before Congress:

> Well, I will do our bishop—we call him "our bishop" in accordance with the universal custom—the credit to say that, where no special interests of his religion are involved, he generally does substantial justice. He knows nothing of law; but in ordinary cases, when not instructed by the "council," he will use his best judgment, and generally do nearly right.

Laws in Utah, Additional Testimony, H.R. 21, at 10–11, Serial Set Vol. No. 1436, Session Vol. No. 1, 41st Cong. (2d Sess. 1870) (testimony of J. H. Beadle, Feb. 11, 1874). Note that from Beadle's testimony it is difficult to tell if he is referring to the local bishop's court or the local probate court of which the bishop was a judge.

156. See generally Arrington, *Great Basin Kingdom*, 84 (discussing the concept of Zion and its relationship to the communitarianism of Mormon economic experiments); see also Leonard J. Arrington, Feramorz Y. Fox, and Dean L. May, *Building the City of God: Community and Cooperation Among the Mormons*, 2nd ed. (Urbana: University of Illinois Press, 1992) (same as previous).

The Mormon objection to "suing before the ungodly" was also tied up with the spectacle of litigation. "Court day" was an important civic ritual in nineteenth-century America. Few towns had permanent magistrates above the level of justices of the peace, and more complicated cases were handled by circuit courts that met—usually twice a year—at county seats. These gatherings were major social, economic, and political events. During the colonial period, they served to enact social hierarchies, with genteel magistrates decked out in the regalia of royal authority. In Massachusetts, for example, traveling justices were met at the county line by the sheriff, who would accompany them to the courthouse, where "[t]rumpets and drums or firearm volleys announced the justices' arrival in town."[157] After independence, court day continued to enact social hierarchies,[158] but it also developed into a rollicking democratic carnival.[159] Court sessions were accompanied by peddlers on the courthouse square hawking their wares, which generally included a generous amount of alcohol. Drunken fights were common. Indeed, they were part of the appeal of court day, as one diarist complained in 1807: "a very Poor Court, no fighting or Gouging, very few Drunken people."[160] One veteran lawyer described Illinois court

---

157. Martha J. McNamara, *From Tavern to Courthouse: Architecture & Ritual in American Law, 1658–1860* (Baltimore: Johns Hopkins University Press, 2004), 12.

158. See, e.g., Ariela Julie Gross, "Pandora's Box: Slavery, Character, and Southern Culture in the Courtroom, 1800–1860" (unpublished PhD dissertation, Stanford University, 1996), 205–17 (on file with author) (discussing the role of the planter elite in court-day rituals in Nachez, Mississippi, during the 1830s).

159. See, e.g., "Life in the Backwoods: Scraps from the Note-Book of a Missouri Lawyer," *Spirit of the Times: A Chronicle of the Turf, Agriculture, Field Sports, Literature and the Stage*, September 19, 1846, 355–56 ("A session of the Circuit Court not only draws together the parties litigant, their witnesses and friends, but a host of others, who attend out of curiosity, or for a frolic, or to trade horses, or to make up a scrub race, or to make a promised settlement; for 'Court week' is the time generally designated for a settlement of accounts"); "Sketches of Life in Missouri," *Spirit of the Times: A Chronicle of the Turf, Agriculture, Field Sports, Literature and the Stage*, February 29, 1840, 614 ("The Circuit Court for the district had that day commenced its sittings, and the town, a neat little germ of a hamlet, was thronged with suitors, witnesses, lawyers, and the farmers from the surrounding country. . . . [T]he busy 'hum of preparation' could be heard in every quarter of the town").

160. Carl R. Lounsbury, *The Courthouses of Early Virginia: An Architectural History* (Charlottesville: University of Virginia Press, 2005), 8. See also David Herbert Donald, *Lincoln* (New York: Simon & Schuster, 1995), 105–6 (discussing

days in the 1840s and 1850s, noting that "the local belles came in to see and be seen" and the work continued in the courthouse "from 'early morn till dewy eve'" while ribaldry in the tavern continued "from dewy eve to early morn."[161] George C. Cooke's 1834 painting Patrick Henry Arguing the Parson's Case in the Hanover County Courthouse anachronistically provides an image of the kind of communal drama associated with a nineteenth-century court day.[162] The lawyer stands in a small but packed courtroom. The spectators, who are intently focused on his oratory, crowd around a rough-hewn bench where the lawyers sit. They spill out the open door into the square beyond. In the foreground a pair of children play in the courtroom with a hoop and stick, while in the background we see the sign for a tavern that waits to refresh the crowd of thirsty spectators. Indeed, there was a symbiotic relationship between courthouses and taverns. Many frontier courts sat in the public rooms of taverns in the absence of courthouses.[163] Likewise, in some cases taverns were purposefully established close to courthouses to service the people who gathered to watch the judges and lawyers.[164] In short,

> [c]ourtroom trials . . . provided prime entertainment for the community. Courtrooms were always crowded because the drama, tragedy, and comedy of real life occurred there. With judges and lawyers as the star actors, the courtroom substituted for theater, concert halls, and the opera. Spectators in the courtroom expected a good show from the lawyers, the judges, the witnesses and the other participants.[165]

It was precisely this theatrical aspect of litigation that concerned the Mormons.

---

court day in antebellum Illinois and noting the abundance of whiskey, gambling, and fighting).

161. Henry C. Whitney, *Life on the Circuit with Lincoln* (Boston: Estes and Lauriat, 1892), 42.

162. The original is housed in the Virginia Historical Society. Most of the detail in the painting is anachronistic and "more in keeping with early nineteenth-century designs on the frontier." Lounsbury, *The Courthouses of Early Virginia*, 152.

163. See McNamara, *From Tavern to Courthouse*, 12.

164. See Lounsbury, *The Courthouses of Early Virginia*, 9 (discussing courthouses "and important private buildings, especially the taverns, that grew up around them").

165. John A. Lupton, "A. Lincoln, Esquire: The Evolution of a Lawyer," in *A. Lincoln, Esquire: A Shrewd, Sophisticated Lawyer in His Time*, ed. Allen D. Spiegel (Macon: Mercer University Press, 2002), 18–19.

On February 24, 1856, Brigham Young delivered a blistering sermon against lawyers and law courts.[166] He began his denunciation by describing the performance of a lawyer that he had observed the day before. "[H]e was so serious, so religious, so pious, and so honest, that he appealed to high heaven to witness his honesty before the jury," said Young, but "[w]hen he had induced the jury to believe that he was honest, he stood there and misrepresented the merits of the case, for half an hour at a stretch, in regular lawyer style."[167] Such conduct, he insisted, was particularly objectionable when done by Mormon lawyers at the instigation of Mormon clients. "Does the Lord love your conduct when you drag each other before the ungodly? . . . Do you think He has fellowship with your conduct in such things? No, you do not."[168] However, while Young's remarks were "severe upon the lawyers"[169] (and their clients), he spent the bulk of the sermon castigating the spectators at the trial.

> It is a shame for men to be found loafing about in such places, where there is contention, and quarrelling, and every stratagem that can be used to deceive juries and witnesses, and lying before them with all the grace and sanctity of a Saint, pretending to be one. Such a place is darker to me than midnight darkness.[170]

In part, he was appalled at the idleness of the spectators. Such men, he said, ought to be "raising grain, potatoes, and other articles of food,

---

166. Young's remarks came as the confrontation between local Mormons and Gentile federal appointees over control of the Territorial government heated up prior to President Buchanan's decision to launch the so-called "Utah War." See Dale D. Goble, "Theocracy vs. Diversity: Local vs. National in Territorial Utah," in *Law in the Western United States*, ed. Gordon Morris Bakken (Norman: University of Oklahoma Press, 2000), 293, 296 (noting that in the wake of Young's remarks "[m]obs sacked the offices of non-Mormon lawyers; federally appointed judges were threatened"). While Goble is correct to locate Young's remarks in the context of pre-Utah War tensions, the mob attack he refers to actually took place some ten months later in December 1856, after Justice George P. Stiles, an apostate Mormon appointed to the Territorial bench, sought to displace the Mormon Territorial Marshall with the non-Mormon US Marshall, thus eroding Mormon influence on the judiciary. See Norman F. Furniss, *The Mormon Conflict, 1850–1859* (New Haven: Yale University Press, 1960), 57–58 (discussing the confrontation between the Mormons and Justice Stiles).

167. Brigham Young, February 24, 1856, *Journal of Discoures*, 3:237.

168. Young, 3:238–39.

169. Young, 3:238–39.

170. Young, 3:238.

instead of following after courts and the nonsense, wickedness, and lying associated with them."[171] It was not simply the waste of time, however, that attracted Young's wrath. Rather, he thought that the spectacle itself was degrading. "Elders of Israel . . . throng to such a place, and that too when no spirit reigns there but the devil's spirit. . . . [Y]ou can get nothing from that den but the principles of hell."[172] Even more colorfully, he called the show of litigation "[t]he fog, the froth, and spawn of hell, and they [that is, the spectators] feast upon it."[173]

Young's attack on litigation is reminiscent of puritanical sermons against the theater over the centuries.[174] While Young himself was not opposed to drama,[175] his attack on litigation shares with the religious denunciation of theaters a basic concern for the moral consequences of watching sin and wickedness as entertainment. In Young's view, litigation was a battle of wits between amoral lawyers, an exciting spectacle but ultimately a degrading one. It was not simply the contentiousness of litigation or the dishonesty of the lawyers themselves that was objectionable. It was the moral impact on the community of placing such a spectacle at the center of civic life. Seen in these terms, the move to bring litigation within the Church was a move to transform the public meaning of dispute resolution.

To be sure, prior to the arrival of the first Gentile appointees to the Utah Territorial bench, the Mormons had their own muted version of court day. In 1852, shortly after the Territory of Utah was organized, Zerubabbel Snow, a Mormon attorney who had been appointed Chief Justice of the new Territorial Supreme Court, rode circuit through the far-flung settlements inaugurating the first district courts. However, he did not enter town as the head of a judicial entourage with lawyers in tow. Rather, he came as a small part of a much larger party led by Brigham

---

171. Young, 3:239.

172. Young, 3:238.

173. Young, 3:239.

174. See Givens, *People of Paradox*, 143–45 (discussing religious denunciations of the theater).

175. See Givens, 145–49 (discussing Young's support for the theater in pioneer Utah); Richard Cracroft, "'Cows to Milk Instead of Novels to Read': Brigham Young, Novel Reading, and Kingdom Building," *Brigham Young University Studies* 40, no. 2 (2001): 112–13 (he quotes Brigham Young: "It is pleasing and instructing to see certain characters personified upon the boards of a theatre . . . [that] is managed upon righteous principles").

Young, who spoke to the citizens as territorial governor and—far more important from their point of view—preached to them as a living prophet and the leader of their church.[176] In this theopolitical pageant, Justice Snow was a decidedly small player.

In place of the secular ritual of court day, the Church courts offered their own set of public symbols. In at least some cases, adjudication was open to the public, and local newspapers sometimes even announced Church trials in advance.[177] For example, during the 1850s, the Salt Lake High Council heard cases each Saturday in the Salt Lake Social Hall before large groups of spectators who were occasionally called upon to participate in the proceedings. Men in the audience might be asked to replace a high councilor who was absent or who recused himself from a particular case.[178] Likewise, in one 1859 case, the minutes record, "The Persons present in the room were called upon and also unanimously sustained the decision about fifty persons present besides the authorities and council."[179] While parties occasionally retained attorneys to represent them before a high council—particularly when resorting to the Church court was one move in protracted litigation spanning both secular and ecclesiastical tribunals—generally speaking, lawyers were excluded from the proceedings.[180] In accordance with rules laid down by Joseph Smith, however, an equal number of high councilors was assigned to speak on either side of

---

176. See William Clayton, *An Intimate Chronicle: The Journals of William Clayton*, ed. George D. Smith (Salt Lake City: Signature Books, 1995), 411–12 (recounting Justice Snow's inaugurating circuit court sittings while touring the territory with Brigham Young); see also Leonard J. Arrington, *Brigham Young: American Moses*, 2nd ed. (Urbana: University of Illinois Press, 1991), 306–10 (discussing Brigham Young's tours through Utah Territory as governor).

177. Salt Lake High Council minutes report that in early cases when members were absent, "[t]he vacancies were filled from bystanders." See, e.g., Morgan, *The Old Fort: Historic Mormon Bastion, the Plymouth Rock of the West*, 76, 79; "Bountiful Briefs," *Davis County Clipper*, Jan. 27, 1899, 1 ("The Bishop's court is trying the Smedley-Goodfellow case this week").

178. See Morgan, 76, 79.

179. Ecclesiastical Court Cases Collection, Disfellowshipment Records, 1839–1965, CR 355, 2, 1858, n.2, Church Archives, The Family and Church History Department, The Church of Jesus Christ of Latter-day Saints, Salt Lake City, Utah (transcript in author's possession).

180. Brooks, *On the Mormon Frontier*, 2:366 (noting that Hosea Stout, an early Utah attorney, served as counsel to a victorious party in a suit before a bishop's court).

a case when the council deliberated.[181] The rule was less of a surrogate for representation than a device to ensure the appearance (and hopefully the reality) of even-handed deliberation. Likewise, the absence of technical rules of evidence was supposed to ensure that Church courts could reach the truth of the matter.[182] In contrast, said Young, "juries are liable to be deceived."[183] Perhaps most dramatically, decisions by Church courts frequently required erring parties to publicly confess their sins before their congregations, and quarrelling members were often required to engage in acts of public reconciliation.[184] In short, ecclesiastical courts transformed adjudication from a spectacle of amoral attorneys engaged in a battle of wits into an essentially Christian drama of sin, confession, reconciliation, and public redemption, a fact not lost on contemporary observers. For example, one diarist recorded the deliberations in an 1843 case using the language of Christian atonement, noting "Hyrum plead for mercy, Joseph for Justice, [and] the Twelve decided according to testimony . . . ."[185] The goal, as the minutes of one early meeting put it, was for "[a]ll differences [to be] settled [and] hearts of all [to be] run together in love."[186]

---

181. See "Kirtland High Council Minutes (Dec. 1834–Nov. 1837)"; see also Doctrine & Covenants, 102:1–3, 5–6, 8–16, 22–30.

182. See Firmage and Mangrum, *Zion in the Courts*, 283 (discussing the treatment of evidence in Mormon courts).

183. Brigham Young, February 24, 1856, *Journal of Discoures*, 3:239.

184. See, e.g., Cannon and Cook, *Far West Record*, 9 ("Confession of br. Ziba Peterson of his transgression which was satisfactory to the Church as approved by unanimous vote").

185. Wilford Woodruff, "Diary of Wilford Woodruff (May 27, 1843)," in *Waiting for World's End: The Diaries of Wilford Woodruff*, ed. Susan Staker (Salt Lake City: Signature Books, 1993), 58–59. Woodruff's language here tracks Mormon scripture's understanding of Jesus Christ's death as a reconciliation of both divine justice of sin and divine mercy toward the sinner:

> [T]hat great and last sacrifice will be the Son of God, yea, infinite and eternal. And thus he shall bring salvation to all those who shall believe on his name; this being the intent of this last sacrifice, to bring about the bowels of mercy, which overpowereth justice, and bringeth about means unto men that they may have faith unto repentance. And thus mercy can satisfy the demands of justice, and encircles them in the arms of safety, while he that exercises no faith unto repentance is exposed to the whole law of the demands of justice . . . (Alma 34:14–16).

186. Cannon and Cook, *Far West Record*, 45.

In nineteenth-century Mormon culture, the displacing of the civic spectacle of litigation with religious spectacle shows up in other ways. In many county seats in nineteenth-century America, the central public building around which the community was physically organized was the courthouse.[187] The physical location of the building reinforced the ritual primacy of adjudication of civic life. Indeed, in some towns the courthouse was the only public building, and religious services were held there.[188] In contrast, when the Mormons laid out their settlements in the Great Basin, they sought to impose a very different symbolic order on their civic landscape. The central public building was not the courthouse, but rather the stake "tabernacle." All roads in a town, for example, were numbered in relation to this religious building, which served as both meeting hall and administrative headquarters for the stake presidency and high council. The link to religious adjudication was not left implicit. For example, when the tabernacle in Salt Lake City, in many ways the symbolic template for literally hundreds of Mormon villages, was dedicated in 1875, the prayer pled:

> Bless the High Council of this and other stakes of Zion, may they be full of the spirit of wisdom, justice and judgment, and, under the inspiration of the Most High, be quick to discern the right, wise to admonish the wrong doer, free from all bias; and with integrity, truth, lowliness, patience, and fidelity, administer impartial justice to all.[189]

---

187. For example, one author described the villages of antebellum Illinois from which the Mormons emigrated in 1846: "The settlement almost invariably clustered around a public square of generous dimensions, in the center of which stood the court-house, a substantial building of brick or stone." Frederick Trevor Hill, *Lincoln the Lawyer* (New York: Century Co., 1906), 171.

188. See Lounsbury, *The Courthouses of Early Virginia: An Architectural History*, 317 ("Because many of these rural communities were devoid of a public place of worship, citizens gathered in the courthouse for divine services"). John Phillip Reid, "The Layers of Western Legal History," in *Law in the Western United States*, ed. Gordon Morris Bakken (Norman: University of Oklahoma Press, 2000), 7 ("As Americans moved westward down the Ohio and Tennessee Rivers, and from the Georgia backcountry across the Mississippi, many of their important centers for commercial, social, and economic life grew up around courthouses. The courthouse square was often the center of town or county, stores and trade shops located about it, and often the better residences were in the vicinity").

189. John Taylor, "Dedicatory Prayer for the Salt Lake Tabernacle," October 9, 1875, Journal History of the Church, Church History Library, Salt Lake City, Utah.

Moreover, while some attacked the actual outcomes in Church court cases,[190] criticism of the system tended to emphasize the symbolic affront of displacing the secular law rather than the actual workings of the Mormon judiciary. For example, in April 1838 Seymour Brunson filed a complaint against Oliver Cowdery, one of Joseph Smith's closest early associates and a leading elder of the Church, charging him with a long list of spiritual and civil lapses, including "dishonestly [r]etaining notes after they had been paid."[191] Cowdery responded with a lengthy letter to the high council in which he denied their jurisdiction, invoking secular myths of noble Anglo-Saxon legality and the symbolic power of the Constitution. "My venerable ancestor was among that little band, who landed on the rocks of Plymouth in 1620," he wrote.[192] "[W]ith him he brought those maxims, and a body of those laws which were the result and experience of many centuries, on the basis of which now stands our great and happy Government."[193] He went on, "This attempt to control me in my temporal interests, I conceive to be a disposition to take from me a portion of my Constitutional privileges and inherent rights."[194] A short time later, Lyman Johnson, another high-ranking elder, refused to submit to the jurisdiction of the high council in a case involving a civil lawsuit, responding with similar imagery. "I should not condescend," he wrote, "to put my constitutional rights at issue upon so disrespectful a point."[195] The rhetoric testifies to the way that the Mormon courts displaced the secular symbols and rituals of litigation with a distinctively religious set of symbols and rituals.

---

190. For example, the Salt Lake Tribune claimed that Church courts were a means by which a Church member could "use his power in the church to oppress and rob a brother member." "Church Robbery," *Salt Lake Tribune*, January 1, 1891, 4. More sinisterly, it insisted that even when the Church excommunicated a member for serious misconduct (in this case, incest) "the secret priestly court, as they always do, kept the crime a secret." "A Sorry Defense," *Salt Lake Tribune*, October 25, 1890, 4.

191. Cannon and Cook, *Far West Record*, 163.

192. Cannon and Cook, 165.

193. Cannon and Cook, 165.

194. Cannon and Cook, 165.

195. Cannon and Cook, 173.

III. "Lawyers of their Own" and the Decline of the Mormon Courts

After seventy years or more of practice, the Mormons ultimately abandoned the resolution of civil disputes in ecclesiastical courts, reserving Church tribunals for more traditional questions of church discipline. The end of the expansive jurisdiction of the Church courts was a ragged affair that involved both an official retreat from certain classes of disputes by Church leaders and a gradual abandonment of the Church courts by rank-and-file members. Ultimately, a variety of causes account for the shift. First, Mormon attitudes toward lawyers and litigation changed as a result of both the attempts by Mormon lawyers to craft legitimating religious narratives for their work and the dramatic changes in the nature of the legal profession itself. Second, as Mormon country integrated into the national economy in the late nineteenth century, ecclesiastical courts increasingly faced disputes that they had neither the technical expertise nor the remedial machinery to handle effectively. Both of these causes, in turn, were part of the accommodation of Mormonism to American culture at the end of the nineteenth century. This process involved the abandonment of distinctive Mormon practices—most notably, polygamy—and an implicit agreement that Mormonism would henceforth conduct itself more in the manner of a Protestant sect rather than a theocratic kingdom. Previous historians have noted that Mormonism was forced to accommodate itself to a Protestant view of the Constitution.[196] The end of the civil jurisdiction of Church courts marked a similar accommodation to a late nineteenth century Protestantism that insisted on the separation of the private law from religious and (non–Anglo-Saxon) ethic allegiances. In short, part of becoming fully American meant fully embracing the secular common law.

From the beginning, Mormon attorneys sought to create an ecclesiastical identity for themselves other than that of lying tricksters bent on stirring up litigation. For example, in 1850 one Mormon lawyer noted in his diary that his client's case was resolved by an "Elders meeting," a method that he praised for "sav[ing] the time, expense & hard feelings of a long and tedious lawsuit" and which he commended to the assembled

196. See, e.g., Gordon, *The Mormon Question*, 82 ("Reformers [hostile to Mormon polygamy] were committed to the release of fetters of human progress, to the onward march of civilization through the purification of marriage to protect and promote freedom, democracy, and equality—all in a constitutional system that integrated Christianity and political liberty").

people.[197] Brigham Young eventually came to adopt this self-conception of Mormon attorneys as working in the spirit of the Church courts. Despite his hellfire and damnation sermons against lawyers in the 1850s, his opposition to attorneys was never absolute. As early as 1852, he said, after acknowledging the law as an educational pursuit, "[w]e want every branch of science taught in this place that is taught in the world."[198] An 1872 sermon shows a further softening. While insisting that he did not "want any lawyers in our society," he went on to say:

> There are many lawyers who are very excellent men. What is the advice of an honorable gentleman in the profession of the law? "Do not go to law with your neighbor. . . ." Why not . . . say we will arbitrate this case, and we will have no lawsuit, and no difficulty with our neighbor, to alienate our feelings one with another? This is the way we should do as a community.[199]

From the amoral tricksters of his earlier sermons, Young's thinking developed to a point in which he envisioned wise and learned men who acted in the spirit of church-based reconciliation rather than court-based litigation.

Young's rapprochement with the legal profession went beyond mere rhetoric. In 1868, Young spoke with Franklin S. Richards, the son of a close associate, about Richards's future plans. Richards replied that he was studying medicine. Young insisted that it would be better if Richards were to take up the study of law, "because the time will come when the Latter-day Saints will need lawyers of their own to defend them in the Courts and strive with fearless inspiration to maintain their constitutional rights."[200] Richards went on to become an attorney, eventually serving as general counsel to the Church. An 1883 sketch of Richards presented him as the incarnation of Young's later vision of learned lawyers embedded within the context of Church courts. "As a churchman and High Councilor [Richards's] advice has uniformly been to litigants to settle

---

197. Brooks, *On the Mormon Frontier*, 370. The diary records: "President Young recommended this method & for brethren to try their difficulties first in the church and not go to law untill [*sic*] a man will not abide the decisions of the church tribunals. I also made a short address recommending the same measures." Brooks, 370.

198. Brigham Young, April 7, 1852, *Journal of Discoures*, 6:317.

199. Brigham Young, October 9, 1872, *Journal of Discoures*, 15:224–25.

200. Ken Driggs, "'Lawyers of Their Own to Defend Them': The Legal Career of Franklin Snyder Richards," *Journal of Mormon History* 21, no. 2 (October 1, 1995): 84, 88.

their difficulties themselves or by arbitration, in the modes prescribed by Church discipline; that only such cases should go to the courts as could not be adjusted by these methods."[201]

As the nineteenth century progressed, Mormons continued to treat the legal profession with suspicion, but they simultaneously sought to sanctify it by embedding Mormon lawyers in the narratives of priesthood authority and revelation that stood at the core of the Church judiciary. Hence, one Latter-day Saint attorney recorded that in the early 1880s he and his law partner were rebuked from the pulpit by their local bishop for having "blossomed out as full-fledged lawyers."[202] At about the same time, the stake president of another young man who was considering law school told him, "You will go to Hell!" and urged him to consult with Brigham Young's successor as president of the Church, John Taylor.[203] The young man met with Taylor, who attempted to dissuade him. When he was unconvinced, Taylor laid hands on his head and gave him a blessing that cautiously sanctified his legal education. "Brother Moyle, in the name of the Lord Jesus Christ, and by the virtue of the Holy Priesthood, we lay our hands upon thy head to seal upon thee a blessing," Taylor began.[204] He continued, "we say unto thee that [law] is a dangerous profession, one that leads many people down to destruction."[205] The blessing, however, went on to affirm the young man's choice. "[I]f thou wilt abstain from arguing falsely and on false principles maintaining only the things that can be honorably sustained by honorable men . . . the Lord God will bless thee in this calling . . . with wisdom and intelligence, and with the light of revelation."[206] Using language normally reserved for men chosen as missionaries or for other Church positions, the blessing concluded, "We set thee apart . . . to go forth as thou hast desired to study and become acquainted with all the principles of law and equity."[207] The trend continued when a decade later, Taylor's successor Wilford Woodruff issued a "call"

201. Edward W. Tullidge, "Franklin S. Richards," *Tullidge's Quarterly Magazine* 2 (1883): 456, 466.

202. John R. Alley, Jr., "Utah State Supreme Court Justice Samuel R. Thurman," *Utah Historical Quarterly* 61 (1993): 233, 237.

203. Gene A. Sessions, ed., *Mormon Democrat: The Religious and Political Memoirs of James Henry Moyle* (Salt Lake City: Signature Books, 1998), 108–9.

204. Sessions, 109–10.

205. Sessions, 110.

206. Sessions, 110.

207. Sessions, 110–11.

to one young school teacher to travel east to Cornell to study law.[208] In doing so, he fused the study of law with the mechanism—a call from the prophet—through which earlier generations of Mormons had been sent forth to proclaim Joseph Smith's message of restoration or to found distant settlements as part of establishing Zion in the Great Basin.

Changing Mormon attitudes toward lawyers, not surprisingly, mirrored changes within the legal profession itself. Developments that occurred early in the metropolitan centers of the East often happened much later on the frontier inhabited by the Latter-day Saints. In the 1750s, incensed at "Pettyfoggers," John Adams recommended that Suffolk County create a bar association.[209] His complaints with what he regarded as the dishonest antics of lawyers bent on deceiving juries and taking advantage of clients might have been penned by Brigham Young a century later. Adams and his associates, however, responded to the failings that they perceived in the legal profession very differently. Their solution was to exclude irregular practitioners from the courts and increase the level of training required to become a licensed attorney, a process of professionalization largely complete in Massachusetts by the third or fourth decade of the nineteenth century.[210]

On the frontier, the professional standards were much more lax. In contrast to the increasingly well-educated professionals in the East, "[w]estern lawyers, as a rule, were the sons of poor or middle-class people and seldom had a college education."[211] Indeed, there was even a process of formal de-professionalization on the frontier. Prior to 1830, most state and territorial statutes required an apprenticeship of two to three years before a man could be admitted to the bar. A widespread movement abolished such requirements during the Jacksonian period, and then the ten-

---

208. "Justin David Call: Biographical Notes," n.d., (unpulished manuscript in the author's possession) ("Father was called to be a missionary to New York and to study law at Cornell University. The call received was from the First Presidency of the L.D.S. Church and signed by President Wilford Woodruff, George Q. Cannon and Joseph F. Smith—Sept. 16, 1895").

209. See Gerard W. Gawalt, *The Promise of Power: The Emergence of the Legal Profession in Massachusetts 1760–1840* (Westport: Greenwood Press, 1979), 13.

210. Gawalt, 168 ("By 1840 the profession's real power had reached a level that was almost immune to front attacks").

211. Anton-Hermann Chroust, *The Rise of the Legal Profession in America*, vol. 2 (Norman: University of Oklahoma Press, 1965), 106.

dency on the frontier was "to allow a young man to practice law as soon as he could convince any judge that he knew 'some law.'"[212]

Initially, Utah Territory adopted this relaxed attitude toward the profession. An 1852 "Act for the Regulation of Attorneys" stated that "it shall be the duty of all Judges of courts in this Territory, to grant a hearing as counsel to any person of good moral character, chosen by any person or persons to prosecute or defend a case."[213] Many otherwise untrained advocates took advantage of this law, relying on their rhetorical powers to sway the jury rather than any specialized legal knowledge. For example, one newly minted attorney defending a man who killed his wife's lover, argued brazenly for jury nullification, insisting that the man's actions were justified by the "mountain common law."[214] Indeed, even Brigham Young appeared as counsel in another 1851 case.[215] Early Utah lawyers did attempt to raise the standards among members of the bar by founding a short-lived "law school" taught by the territory's first chief justice "who tender[ed] his sirvis [*sic*] as a teacher gratis for the benefit of all those who wish to inter [*sic*] into the Study of Law."[216] The "law school," however, does not seem to have survived beyond the winter of 1851–1852.[217]

As conditions on the Mormon frontier became more settled, the leaders of the bar sought to recreate the closed and learned profession they imagined in the East by imposing additional requirements on the practice of law. By 1876, the Supreme Court of the Territory required "the favorable report of an examining Committee appointed for that purpose" before admitting a person to practice in "this Court . . . [and] in all Courts

---

212. Chroust, 2:106.

213. An Act for the Regulation of Attorneys § 1 in 1852 Acts.

214. See Kenneth L. Cannon, "'Mountain Common Law': The Extralegal Punishment of Seducers in Early Utah," *Utah Historical Quarterly* 51 (1983): 309, 310–14.

215. Cannon, 310. In this case, Young also represented a man accused of killing the seducer of his wife. The case was tried before the Territorial Supreme Court and Young's opponent was the Mormon attorney Hosea Stout. The man was acquitted.

216. Brooks, *On the Mormon Frontier*, 2:410. Stout reports the content of instruction thus: "the Judge [Zararubbel Snow] gave us a short lecture on the nature and origin of government & law, after which it was agreed to establish the school." Brooks, 410.

217. Brooks, *On the Mormon Frontier*, 2:411–12 (recording meetings of the "law school" during the winter of 1851–52).

in this Territory."[218] Perhaps most importantly, in 1869, the Union Pacific and Central Pacific Railroads met at Promontory Point, Utah. Retracing the steps of their parents in reverse, young men from Mormon country began riding the trains east to study in the law schools that, following the example of Langdell's Harvard, were emerging as the gatekeepers of the legal profession.[219] Those who returned west after studying at Michigan and at other eastern schools felt that they had been socialized into an entirely different legal profession than the half-educated courtroom brawlers Young had denounced in the 1850s. "[O]ur people generally," wrote one such Mormon lawyer, "were not familiar with the ethics and high ideals that college law students have instilled in them by their teachers and the leaders of the legal profession."[220]

The railroad also set in motion economic changes that would transform the nature of litigation. Brigham Young enthusiastically supported the coming of the railroad, which he saw as a means of hastening Latter-day Saint immigrants from overseas to the Mormon Zion in the Great Basin.[221] However, it also marked the beginning of the integration of Mormon country into the national economy, a trend that the Mormons initially fought with a renewed emphasis on home manufactures, cooperative economic endeavors, and a boycott of Gentile merchants.[222] In the end, these efforts could not succeed against the massive forces of economic integration in the wake of the Civil War.

Not surprisingly, these forces changed the nature of litigation among Latter-day Saints, presenting problems that the Church courts were ultimately ill-equipped to handle. The economic depression that swept the nation in 1893 provides an illustration. Beginning with panics in the distant financial centers of London and New York, the depression spread rapidly

---

218. Rules of the Supreme Court of the Territory of Utah, Rule 21, 1 Utah 1, 7 (1876).

219. See, e.g., Joel Francis Paschal, *Mr. Justice Sutherland: A Man Against the State* (Princeton: Princeton University Press, 1951), 15–21 (discussing George Sutherland's move from Provo, Utah, to Ann Arbor, Michigan, to study law and his return to Utah to practice); Sessions, *Mormon Democrat*, 107–8 (discussing Utahns who traveled east to study law prior to 1882); see also Jonathan Lurie, *Law and the Nation: 1865–1912* (New York: Alfred A. Knopf, 1983), 43–54 (discussing Langdell and the rise of American law schools).

220. Sessions, *Mormon Democrat*, 109.

221. See Arrington, *Great Basin Kingdom*, 236.

222. Arrington, 240.

through the nation's increasingly integrated economy, throwing thousands out of work and drying up credit for troubled enterprises. Mormon businessmen in Utah found themselves scrambling to secure payment of debts in a falling market that was pushing many into bankruptcy. The natural move in such a situation would be for the creditor to obtain a lien on a debtor's property as quickly as possible so as to secure repayment, regardless of how the debtor's assets were distributed. The Church courts, however, could only apply personal pressure to litigants before them. They lacked the ability to provide the kind of *in rem* remedies needed in the context of a race for the courthouse. The result was a Hobson's choice for many Mormon businessmen, who found themselves at a ruinous disadvantage vis-à-vis Gentiles who could pursue actions without impediment in the civil courts.[223] These forces ultimately pushed Mormons to abandon the Church courts. One Mormon lawyer later explained:

> For a good illustration, my bishop, an exceptionally splendid man, was in the mercantile business in Salt Lake City. All ward bishops presided over a bishop's court. But he came to me and said, "I have never sued a brother. And it greatly disturbs me to do so, but I must or go into bankruptcy and let the property of my debtors be taken by strangers who have recently come among us." The conclusion was inevitable, and suits at law rapidly became common.[224]

Other forces were at work as well. After the Civil War, the first truly national capital markets emerged, and with them the corporation became the dominant form of business organization. In 1870, the territorial legislature adopted a general incorporation statute that allowed any group of people who were "desirous of associating themselves together for establishing and conducting any mining, manufacturing, commercial or other industrial pursuit in this Territory" to create a corporation.[225] While Church courts initially did not hesitate to take jurisdiction over disputes involving Mormon-dominated corporations (particularly corporations that were part of communal Mormon economic efforts), Church leaders eventually decided to disclaim jurisdiction over corporations.[226] The separation of ownership and the control inherent in the corporate form

---

223. Sessions, *Mormon Democrat*, 10–11.

224. Sessions, 11.

225. An Act Providing for Incorporating Associations, for Mining, Manufacturing, Commercial and Other Industrial Pursuits § 1, in Acts, Resolutions and Memorials, Passed and Adopted During the Nineteenth Annual Session of the Legislative Assembly of the Territory of Utah (1870).

226. Sessions, *Mormon Democrat*, 110.

necessarily created legal duties on the part of directors and officers. Did a Mormon corporate officer with a fiduciary duty to bring suit on behalf of a corporation violate his religious duties if the corporation sued another Mormon?[227]

Ironically, the First Presidency found itself in the position of seeking legal advice from its general counsel on the fiduciary duties of members in order to resolve cases appealed to it, injecting lawyers into the very apex of a system designed to exclude them from adjudication.[228] Church leaders ultimately decided that rather than wading into these difficulties, Church courts should simply avoid resolving such disputes. "In applying [the rule that Mormons should resolve their disputes in Church courts]," wrote *The Deseret Evening News*, "corporations whose stock holders may be Church members are not included, and have no standing in Church courts, which are for the benefit and discipline of members individually."[229]

---

227. James Henry Moyle, a Mormon attorney active in Utah from the 1880s on, records one such case:

> It was in the early 1890s that I was put on trial in the Twelfth Ward before the bishop with all of the leading officers of a corporation for suing a brother in court. It was my only offense in a Church court but in this case I was only the attorney. The case was promptly dismissed when the corporate offense of the defendants became apparent, which it very soon did.

Sessions, 137.

228. For example, in an 1896 case, the First Presidency was faced with a Church suit against a woman who had sued another Mormon on behalf of an estate for which she was the administrator. The secretary to the First Presidency wrote to the stake president in the case:

> Brother Richards [Franklin S. Richards, general counsel to the Church] is of the opinion that the court will not permit her to waive any of her legal rights in this matter, and that she should be free to wind up the estate as the law directs. The first presidency see this matter in the light in which Brother Richards presents it, and they request that you write the parties (Sister Bouton and the Brothers Harris) to this effect, which will leave Sister Bouton free to act in this matter as she may be legally advised; and this will leave her in the position as though no arbitration proceedings had been taken.

Smoot Hearings, 3:16 (reproducing a letter from George F. Gibbs to President E. D. Wooley).

229. "Lawsuits Between Church Members," *Deseret Evening News*, February 1, 1896, 1.

Another force at work was the growth of the legal profession. In the late nineteenth century, the number of lawyers in America skyrocketed. For example, in 1880 there were roughly 64,000 lawyers in the country, but thirty years later the number had nearly doubled to 122,000.[230] The expansion of the legal profession in the West, however, was even more rapid. Nationally, there was roughly one lawyer per thousand people in 1850. By 1890 that number had risen to nearly 1.5 lawyers per thousand.[231] In the West, however, there were less than 0.5 lawyers per thousand people in 1850, while by 1890 the region was well ahead of the national average with over 2.5 lawyers per thousand.[232] The explosion of the profession in the West was largely the result of legal uncertainty created by Congress. In the years after the Civil War, Congress passed a series of laws designed to encourage farming, ranching, mining, and railroading in the Far West. They did this by granting huge amounts of federally owned land to those willing to develop it. The result was a legal bonanza, as those involved in the land grabs litigated over title to property and the meaning of complex and newly minted federal statutes.[233] These economic forces, changed the nature of civil litigation. No longer was it a generally accessible ritual in which lawyers tried to sway juries with their rhetorical skills while the local crowd looked on. Rather, litigation in the 1870s, 1880s, and 1890s

---

230. Lurie, *Law and the Nation: 1865–1912*, 43.

231. See Kelly Paulson, "Lawyers and the American West: An Empirical Investigation into the Components of Demand for Legal Services from 1850 to 1930" (unpublished master's thesis, Stanford University, 2005), 8 graph 1, http://www-econ.stanford.edu/academics/Honors_Theses/Theses_2005/Paulson.pdf. The regional definitions are those used by the Census Bureau. Paulson, 9 ("The Western region mirrors the Census classification").

232. Paulson, "Lawyers and the American West," 9 graph 2.

233. See generally William M. Landes and Richard A. Posner, "Legal Precedent: A Theoretical and Empirical Analysis," *Journal of Law and Economics* 19, no. 2 (1976): 249–307 (arguing that litigation and the demand for lawyers is driven by legal uncertainty). Kelly Paulson provides empirical support for this conclusion by running regression analysis of the number of lawyers against indicia of railroad and mining activity. He concludes, "given the lingering significance of the Western dummy in 1860, 1870, 1890, and 1900, it seems that the railroad and mining variables, while explaining most of the Western effect, do not account for all of it." Paulson, "Lawyers and the American West," 25. Paulson's conclusion is also supported by a qualitative analysis of the (very limited) surviving Utah Territorial Court records for civil cases, the vast bulk of which are from after the Civil War and involve litigation over property rights conferred under federal statutes.

became a specialized affair involving increasingly well-trained attorneys arguing over the implications of arcane federal statutes. The public spectacle of litigation that had so concerned Brigham Young in the 1850s and 1860s was mostly dead a generation later.

Litigation over the ownership of land illustrates the complexity of the legal environment as the nineteenth century progressed. When the Mormons arrived in the Great Basin in the summer of 1847, the region was still nominally Mexican territory, part of the province of Upper California. Under the Treaty of Guadalupe Hidalgo, the entire region transferred to the United States.[234] Neither Mexican nor American authorities, however, granted formal title to the Mormons, who were, legally speaking, squatters. Rather, the Church allocated land first on a communal basis and then to individual settlers.[235] The uncertain legal status of these ecclesiastical land grants led to contradictory Mormon attitudes toward federal land law. On one hand, they repeatedly petitioned Congress for a territorial land office to regularize title to their land. At the same time, they feared that new settlers would take advantage of federal legislation to appropriate communally or privately held Mormon lands. Nor were their fears entirely unfounded, as federal officials regarded land policy as a tool for diluting Mormon power in Utah Territory. "There can be no doubt," wrote the federal surveyor general of Colorado and Utah in 1864, "that the true policy of the government in regard to Utah is to encourage the emigration to that Territory of a population less hostile to the United States than the present."[236] He went on to write, "[t]o do this, Gentile emigration must have the chance of acquiring title to the land, and must be protected in that title."[237]

The result in Utah was sporadic hostility toward federal surveyors in the 1850s, violence toward Gentile claim jumpers in the 1860s, and

234. See Treaty of Peace, Friendship, Limits, and Settlement, U.S.–Mexico, art. V, Feb. 2, 1848, 9 Stat. 922 (setting forth the new border between the United States and Mexico, ceding all of the Great Basin to the United States).

235. See Lawrence L. Linford, "Establishing and Maintaining Land Ownership in Utah Prior to 1869," *Utah Historical Quarterly* 42, no. 2 (1974): 127–28 (tracing the history of land ownership in early Utah); see also Robert C. Ellickson, "Property in Land," *Yale Law Journal* 102, no. 6 (1993): 1315, 1342–44 (providing an economic theory of why Mormons shifted from communal to private ownership of land in early Utah).

236. Linford, "Establishing and Maintaining Land Ownership in Utah Prior to 1869," 137.

237. Linford, 137.

gradual regularization of title to land beginning in 1870.[238] Throughout Mormon country, however, the title of Mormon settlers to land remained uncertain. Virtually all of the settlements began as Church-sponsored "missions" directed by the Mormon hierarchy in Salt Lake City, and most Mormon settlers acquired land initially via an ecclesiastical grant. The situation was further complicated in the decades after the Civil War as Congress passed a slew of statutes multiplying the methods by which ownership of public land could be moved into private hands.

The case of *Birdsall v. Leavitt* illustrates these problems.[239] The Birdsall family moved from Nebraska to Utah in 1881, eventually settling in Sevier County, located in the central part of the Territory.[240] Three years later, the family converted to Mormonism. Members of the Birdsall family began trying to acquire land under various federal statutes. They purchased land from the Rio Grande railroad, which had been given huge tracts by Congress as a subsidy.[241] They also claimed land under the Timber Culture Act, which granted "ten acres of timber on any quarter section" of public land to any person "who shall plant, protect, and keep in a healthy, growing condition for eight years."[242] However, the land the Birdsalls claimed had long before been claimed by an earlier settler, who had sold the property to a James Leavitt in 1883.[243] Leavitt, who had "owned" the land for a decade in 1893 when the Birdsalls first claimed it, insisted later that they

238. Linford, 134–43.

239. See generally Ardis E. Parshall, "'Church Hounds Woman to Madness': The Trials of Cora Birdsall" (unpublished paper, Sunstone Symposium, Salt Lake City, Utah, August 2002). I am extremely grateful to Ms. Parshall for sharing her extensive research with me.

240. See Smoot Hearings, 2:321 (testimony of Isaac Birdsall).

241. See Deed, Sevier County, Utah, Book 28 Entry 5289 (11 June 1904) (Birdsall deed to the disputed land).

242. An Act to Amend an Act Entitled "An Act to Encourage the Growth of Timber on the Western Prairies" § 1, 20 Stat. 113 (1878). See also Minutes of a Special Session of the High Council of Sevier Stake of Zion Held at the Tabernacle, Richfield, Utah, Tabernacle (Oct. 21, 1902), reprinted in Smoot Hearings, 2:331 ("Isaac Birdsall first took the land under the timber culture act").

243. Smoot Hearings, 2:326 (reproducing a statement by William A. Warnock). Sevier County was not settled by Mormons formally called to pioneer in the area. Rather, as the Mormon population filled up more hospitable valleys to the east, Mormons moved into the area on their own. Their efforts ultimately received substantial encouragement and economic support from the Church. See generally Leonard J. Arrington, "Taming the Turbulent Sevier: A Story of Mormon Desert

agreed to sell to him the portion he occupied, thus quieting title.[244] The Panic of 1893, however, kept Leavitt from obtaining financing, although he apparently gave the Birdsalls some cows in partial payment.[245] In doing so, Leavitt seems to have been trying to follow the established Mormon policy for dealing with title conflicts between older settlers and claims based on federal statutes. As the First Presidency explained in a 1903 letter to one bishop:

> With President Young we hold that when any person secures title from the Government to land, part of which has been occupied and cultivated by others, he or she should respect the rights of such persons by being willing to deed to them the land they have improved, provided that they pay their share of the expenses incurred in securing the Government title, and also a fair remuneration to the pre-emptor or homesteader for the loss of his or her preemption or homestead right in proportion to the amount of land to which they are benefited.[246]

Without successfully finalizing his claim to the land, Isaac Birdsall conveyed it to his daughter Cora, who eventually gained title under the Timber Culture Act.[247] Leavitt continued to press his claims based on the rights of the earlier settler as well as the 1893 agreement with Birdsall. In 1901, he "prefer[red] a charge of unchristianlike conduct against Isaac Birdsall and Sister Cora Birdsall" before their bishop.[248] All parties appeared and presented evidence. The bishop issued a decision "[t]hat Cora Birdsall shall deed unto James E. Leavitt [the disputed land]."[249] Cora wrote the First Presidency asking for permission to proceed at law, and received a letter instructing her to appeal to the Sevier Stake High Council if she was dissatisfied with the bishop's decision.[250] She did so, the case was

---

Conquest," *Western Humanities Review* 21, no. 1 (1951): 393–406 (discussing the settlement of Sevier County).

244. See "Smoot Hearings," 2:331–32.

245. Smoot Hearings," 2:331–32.

246. Smoot Hearings, 3:18 (reproducing a letter from the First Presidency to Bishop O. B. Andersen).

247. Smoot Hearings, 2:333.

248. Smoot Hearings, 2:326 (reproducing a letter from James E. Leavitt to Cora Birdsall).

249. Smoot Hearings, 2:327 (reproducing a letter from Bishop Samuel W. Goold and his counselors to Cora Birdsall).

250. Smoot Hearings, 2:328 (reproducing a letter from the First Presidency to Cora Birdsall).

retried, and the high council affirmed the decision of the bishop's court.[251] The high council seemed to regard the Birdsalls' actions as an underhanded attempt to use the federal statutes to rob Leavitt of his property. "If you were placed in Leavitt's place and paid for the land and possessed it," one of the high councilors asked Cora during the trial, "would you feel right if you were treated as he is?"[252] Cora appealed to the First Presidency, and in 1903 received a letter affirming the high council's decision.[253] She refused to deed the land to Leavitt and was subsequently excommunicated.[254]

At this point, the litigation took an unexpected turn. After her excommunication, Cora began acting increasingly distraught and erratic. In February 1904 a doctor from the state mental hospital judged her insane, insisting that she suffered from hereditary madness. In June 1904 Cora was visited by local priesthood leaders who gave her a blessing and insisted that she could be rebaptized if she would comply with the decision of the Church courts and deed the disputed land to Leavitt. She did so and was rebaptized, but her mental condition continued to deteriorate.[255] By this time, Utah had chosen Mormon apostle Reed Smoot to become its new US Senator, sparking a national drive to unseat him, a movement Cora's father was willing to support. The Senate Committee on Privileges and Elections launched a massive investigation of the economic, legal, and political affairs of the Mormon Church,[256] and in December 1904, Isaac Birdsall traveled east to testify before the Senators. For a brief moment, the case became national news, providing evidence of Mormon dominance in Utah.[257]

---

251. Smoot Hearings, 2:336 (reproducing a letter from the Sevier Stake Presidency to Cora Birdsall).

252. Smoot Hearings, 2:335.

253. Smoot Hearings, 2:337 (reproducing a letter from the First Presidency to Cora Birdsall).

254. Smoot Hearings, 2:339 (reproducing a letter from J. M. Lauritzen to Cora Birdsall).

255. Smoot Hearings, 2:339–41.

256. See generally Kathleen Flake, *The Politics of American Religious Identity: The Seating of Senator Reed Smoot, Mormon Apostle* (Chapel Hill: University of North Carolina Press, 2004) (recounting Smoot's election and the congressional investigation that it precipitated).

257. See generally "Apostle Again Takes the Stand: Story of a Bishop's Court: How One Case Was Decided in Utah," *Salt Lake Herald*, December 20, 1904, 1; "Apostle Smith on the Stand: Strange Case of Isaac Birdsall, His Daughter, His Land, and Why He Left Church," *Salt Lake Tribune*, December 20, 1904, 7;

The case did not stop with the newspapers. Upon his return to Utah, Isaac Birdsall, acting as guardian for his daughter, sued Leavitt for the disputed land, arguing that the deed Cora had executed was invalid. The district court rejected his claim that she was mentally incompetent and that the elders who "labored" with her to comply with the Church court's decision exercised undue influence, writing:

> All churches . . . have a right to discipline their members and . . . they have a right to handle such person so far as their fellowship in such . . . church is concerned. The members, however, are under no legal obligations to obey such regulation or decision of their . . . church . . .[258]

On appeal to the Utah Supreme Court, Birdsall prevailed.[259] The Court held that "[Cora], at the time she executed the deed, was mentally incapacitated and therefore incompetent to make the same."[260] The justices went on to signal their concerns with the Church courts: "While courts do not interfere in disputes between churches and their members in respect to church or spiritual affairs, the property rights of the members will be protected as readily from church interference as from any other."[261]

The perennially pugnacious *Salt Lake Tribune*, always anxious to attack the Mormon majority, hailed the court's decision with glee. "The

---

"John Henry Smith Denies Idaho Story: Isaac Birdsall Testifies to Alleged Forcing of Property from Members of the Church," *Morning Examiner*, December 20, 1904, 1; "Mormonism Taught in School Buildings: Girl Deprived of Property: Excommunicated Until She Gave It to the Church, Her Father Testifies at Smoot Inquiry," *New York Times*, December 20, 1904, 6; "Mormons in Schools: Testimony Shows That Religions Classes Exist," *Washington Post*, December 20, 1904, 4; "Plural Marriages Not Authorized: Apostle John Henry Smith Says He Found No Evidence That Any Had Been Performed in Mexico, as Said," *Salt Lake Telegram*, December 19, 1904, 2; "Public Against Apostle Smoot: Opposed by Sentiment of Country," *Salt Lake Tribune*, December 25, 1904, 5; "Smith Concludes His Testimony: Birdsall Land Case," *Idaho Daily Statesman*, December 20, 1904, 2; "The Birdsall Land Case," *Salt Lake Tribune*, December 22, 1904, 4; "Woman Banned by the Church: Excommunicated Because She Wouldn't Obey Mormon Chief: Bishop's Court Deprived Her of Property to Which She Held Lawful Title, and When She Defied Court She Was Put Under Arrest," *Atlanta Constitution*, December 20, 1904, 3.

258. "Court Findings in Birdsall Case," *Deseret Evening News*, September 30, 1905, 7.

259. Birdsall v. Leavitt, 89 P. 397, 399 (Utah 1907).

260. Birdsall v. Leavitt, 89 P. 397.

261. Birdsall v. Leavitt, 89 P. 399.

opinion of the Supreme Court," wrote the paper, "is a stinging castigation of the methods brought to bear by the Mormon elders. It is a ringing denunciation of the methods of the 'church courts . . .'"[262] Elsewhere, the *Tribune* insisted that "[t]he decision made by the Supreme Court . . . will excite the admiration and win the support of all mankind." As for the Church courts,

> [t]he attention of the civilized world is called anew to the horrors of the hierarchical rule in Utah. . . . [This case] illustrates perfectly the treasonable autocracy with which the hierarchs dominate over the civil government; it demonstrates their intention to maintain themselves as superior to earthly law . . .[263]

All of these developments took place against a background of decades of legal hostility to Mormon institutions and practices. The most dramatic manifestation of this hostility, of course, was the massive federal legal crusade against polygamy, but the Mormon antipathy toward the common law did not go unnoticed. Rather than seeing Mormon practice as the afterlife of a Protestant tradition of civil dispute resolution in Church courts, Mormonism's mainly Protestant critics in the last half of the nineteenth century saw it as further evidence of Mormonism's sinister and un-American power in Utah. For example, Robert N. Baskin, the chief legal strategist against the Church in Utah in the nineteenth century, strikingly begins his memoirs of conflict with the Mormons by noting their hostility to the common law:

> All the states except Louisiana, and territories except Utah, had by statute adopted the common law so far as applicable to the new conditions. That law was and is indispensably necessary for the proper government of any American community. It was, therefore, the imperative duty of the Utah legislature to adopt it at the first territorial session. Instead of doing so the foregoing absurd section of the judiciary act excluding it was passed.[264]

Note the way in which Baskin identified the common law with the "American community," marking Mormon antipathy toward that law as evidence of their status as un-American outsiders. As Gentiles penetrated Utah, the Church courts became one of the flash points in the increas-

262. "Birdsall Triumphs in Supreme Court: Great Outrage Perpetrated by Church Tribunals Thoroughly Put Right," *Salt Lake Tribune*, March 9, 1907, 3.

263. "The Supreme Court Decides Against the Tyrant," *Salt Lake Tribune*, March 10, 1907, 6.

264. R. N. Baskin, *Reminiscences of Early Utah*, ed. Brigham D. Madsen, Signature Mormon Classics (Salt Lake City: Signature Books, 2006), 6.

ingly bitter battles between Mormons and non-Mormons for political, economic, and social power in Utah. For example, the first "Gentile" newspaper in Utah—*The Valley Tan*, named for a locally brewed whiskey of the same name—claimed that Brigham Young's denunciations of lawyers were part of a plot to "throw obloquy upon the character of law courts and drive the people into their ecclesiastical courts, for the adjustment of all grievances."[265] The ultimate goal was "suppressing the Judiciary, and depriving men of their Constitutional rights of trial, by *due process of law* . . ."[266] Likewise, in the eyes of the anti-Mormon *Salt Lake Tribune*, Mormons who refused to comply with the edicts of Church courts were praised for preserving their "manhood," while those who accepted ecclesiastical decisions, the newspaper insisted, "are not men who are fit to exercise the more sacred rights of American citizenship."[267]

The rhetoric surrounding the *Birdsall* case powerfully illustrates the way in which allegiance to the secular courts became a condition for full entry into the American community. The *Washington Post* reported that the bishop's court had deprived Cora of "property to which she held the lawful title,"[268] while the *Washington Times* noted that "[p]robably there is not another organization in the United States with the gall to set itself up as a judicial authority and apply its own code, regardless of statutory law."[269] The *Times* went on to compare the Mormons to the "Chinese highbinders of San Francisco," writing:

> [The Chinese] are reckoned to be living in heathen darkness. They scorn utterly the duly constituted courts, even in relation to such serious acts as murder. However, there is not involved in their demeanor any threat to society. They are aliens, in no manner concerned with the affairs of the land. They . . . could no more appreciate what we think is civilization than they

---

265. Kirk Anderson, Esq., *Valley Tan*, December 24, 1858, 3.

266. Anderson, Esq., 3.

267. "Church Robbery," 4. Similarly, when a Mormon witness stated before Congress that "the judiciary are the judges" of whether people are protected in their inherent rights, the *Salt Lake Tribune* insisted that his words had an esoteric and treasonable meaning. "He meant the chiefs of the Church when sitting as a Church court, and nothing else, and he would obey an edict of that court if it was in direct violation of the laws of the land, after being upheld, unanimously, by the court of last resort in this Republic." "A Little More of Richards," *Salt Lake Tribune*, March 9, 1888, 2.

268. "Mormons in Schools: Testimony Shows That Religions Classes Exist," 4.

269. "Public Against Apostle Smoot," 5 (citing the *Washington Times*).

could fly. They do not think in terms that can be grasped by any but the Oriental mind.[270]

The racial status of the Mormons, however, made their courts much more threatening. "The Mormon is in our midst . . ." the paper wrote. "His defiance is brazen, deliberate, and the climax of arrogance."[271] The editorial closed darkly, "If any banded bigots can rise superior to the United States, it is interesting to watch them rise, and speculate as to the character of the meat on which they feed."[272] In short, the hostility of Mormons to the common law was evidence that they—like the Chinese—were dangerous outsiders.

In an era when the Mormon Church was aggressively seeking the shelter of respectability after decades of intense hostility, it is not surprising that Church leaders had actually been trying to disentangle the Church courts from disputes over land for some time by 1900. In 1896, the *Deseret News* published an article instructing that "in cases involving title to lands . . . the Church courts could not consider them if requested to do so, as the Church discipline is such that it will not attempt the adjustment of any controversy where there might be a possibility of conflict with the laws of the land."[273] Likewise, during the 1890s, the First Presidency sent a number of letters instructing lower Church courts not to try cases "when matters relating to the boundary of lands and kindred subjects are in dispute."[274] The First Presidency's pronouncements, however, were ambivalent. Another 1896 letter reads:

> We can not, as a church, put ourselves in the position of using our church courts to enforce the laws or to set aside the laws or the decisions of the courts. With a little reflection you can readily see that this would be dangerous. But if men who are members of the church act unjustly and trespass upon their neighbor's rights by the misuse of the law or by taking advantage we can deal with them.[275]

---

270. "Public Against Apostle Smoot," 5.

271. "Public Against Apostle Smoot," 5.

272. "Public Against Apostle Smoot," 5.

273. "Lawsuits Between Church Members," 8.

274. Smoot Hearings, 3:14 (reproducing a letter from the First Presidency to the president and high council of the Bannock Stake). For a reproduction of a number of letters from the First Presidency regarding land disputes in Church courts, see Smoot Hearings, vol. 3.

275. Smoot Hearings, 3:15 (reproducing a letter from the First Presidency to Elder John A. Kidman).

Church leaders wished both to avoid the perception of hostility to the common law, but also desired to discipline members for conduct that, while technically legal, violated religious standards. Elsewhere, the First Presidency seemed to draw the jurisdictional line for Church courts between *in personam* complaints against individuals and *in rem* attempts to settle title to land.[276] Not surprisingly, the precise limits of ecclesiastical jurisdiction in cases like *Birdsall v. Leavitt*, which involved claims based on both the title of earlier settlers and personal contracts, was unclear.[277] The

276. The First Presidency explained the policy thus in a 1903 letter:

> Before our lands were surveyed by the Government settlements had been formed and boundaries clearly established. After the survey was made it was found that, as a general thing, the lines of a quarter section would run through the lands of more than one settler; and in order that every man might have title to that which belonged to him, one of the interested parties would comply with the provisions of the law and obtain title, and after doing this he would deed to others such portions of the homestead entry as belonged to them; and it was not an uncommon thing for our church courts to settle disputes arising under those circumstances. But since the Government survey it has not been customary for church courts to entertain complaints involving the title to lands, and the same may be said with respect to water. All disputes involving legal titles must be adjudicated by courts of competent jurisdiction. The point we wish to make clear is this, that church courts must not undertake to deprive any of its members of their legal rights.

Smoot Hearings, 3:18. The letter, however, went on to insist that members had an obligation to accommodate the claims of earlier settlers whose rights conflicted with government surveys.

277. The *Birdsall* case was probably further complicated by the fact that in 1896, just five years before Leavitt preferred charges to Cora's bishop, the First Presidency had sent a letter to the Sevier Stake President specifically encouraging him to promote the arbitration of title disputes among his flock. Smoot Hearings, 3:17 (reproducing a letter from the First Presidency to President W. H. Seegmiller stating that they "heartily approve" arbitration of a dispute over title to "22 acres of school land"). In context, the First Presidency seems to have endorsed arbitration as a process separate from Church courts whereby "[t]here is a method which can be adopted under the law by which the decision of arbitrators can be entered on the court records and made legal." Smoot Hearings, 3:17. It is possible, however, that when the *Birdsall* case came before his high council, President Seegmiller did not make a distinction between arbitration and Church courts, taking the previous letter as permission for Church courts to hear land disputes. In any case, none of the First Presidency correspondence in the *Birdsall* case suggests that they regarded the dispute as being improper for Church courts.

resulting confusion exposed the Church to widespread charges of duplicity, as Church leaders had claimed during the Smoot hearings that Church courts did not adjudicate cases involving land.

In the years after the Utah Supreme Court's decision in *Birdsall v. Leavitt*, high Church leaders resolved to further limit the jurisdiction of Church courts. In October 1908, a committee of apostles authored a report to the First Presidency suggesting that Church courts "be not used as agencies for the collection of ordinary debts."[278] The report went on to suggest that "Church Courts shall not be used to enforce compliance with [the] moral obligation" to pay debts discharged in bankruptcy or otherwise unenforceable at law.[279] The report, however, reveals the same ambivalent attitude seen in the First Presidency letters on land disputes a decade earlier. The Church was unwilling to say that questions of church discipline were disposed of by resolving questions of legality. Hence, the report stated:

> [B]ut if a member of the church shall unjustly, and in an unchristianlike manner, bring his brother before the civil courts, or if there be an element of fraud or dishonesty on the part of a member who owes a debt, which he refused to pay, either would be liable to trial for his fellowship in the church by the Bishops Court or High Council.[280]

Likewise, while Church courts were not to be used to enforce debts discharged by bankruptcy, "every consistent effort should be made to persuade [debtors financially able to pay discharged debts] to settle with their former creditors."[281]

The reality was that the Mormon judiciary was already in decline by 1908. Indeed, in urban areas Mormons seemed to have largely abandoned the Church courts for civil disputes by the turn of the century. In 1904, Mormon attorney James Henry Moyle was called to the high council of the newly organized Ensign Stake in Salt Lake City, where he continued to serve for more than twenty years. During that time, the high council did not consider a single civil dispute. "So ended," he wrote, "a salient feature of pioneer times when pretty much all were of one faith."[282] Ecclesiastical disputes in outlying settlements where the legal culture was simpler con-

278. Firmage and Mangrum, *Zion in the Courts*, 343 (quoting the report).
279. Firmage and Mangrum, 343–44 (quoting the report).
280. Firmage and Mangrum, 343.
281. Firmage and Mangrum, 344.
282. Sessions, *Mormon Democrat*, 136.

tinued for longer, as illustrated by the *Birdsall* case. As late as 1919, an article in the Church-published *Improvement Era* stated that:

> We hold that in matters of difference between brethren, in which no specific infraction of the secular law is involved, and in offenses called "civil" as distinguished from "criminal", it is truly unworthy of members of the Church today as it was in Paul's time that "brother goeth to law with brother" and that it stands to our shame if righteous judgment cannot be rendered among ourselves.[283]

Despite this plea, Mormons continued to take their civil disputes to the secular courts. The forces of a modernizing economy, the quest of Mormon lawyers for religious legitimacy within their community, and the importance of allegiance to the common law as a condition for Mormon entry into the American community had combined to end the judging of civil cases within the temple of the Church.

IV. Conclusion

The inheritors of a strong Protestant tradition of church discipline, early Mormons took it for granted that adjudication was a central religious practice, and as Joseph Smith developed his increasingly radical theology in the 1830s and 1840s, he found ways of embedding the emerging Mormon judiciary within its narratives. This chapter began with two contrasting stories: one about Mormon elders preaching to a court-day crowd, and the other about Mormon elders adjudicating a civil dispute in their temple. The arc connecting these events illustrates the relationship between religion and litigation for nineteenth-century Latter-day Saints. The Mormons wished to preach to the courthouse, denouncing its divisiveness, chicanery, and corrosive moral spectacle. At the same time, they wished to domesticate civil disputes, forcing litigious Church members to embed their arguments within the theological narratives and institutional settings of the Church. Suing before the ungodly was to be replaced by lawsuits in the temple.

In a world where most disputes were relatively simple and could be resolved without specialized legal knowledge, such a system was tenable. Indeed, given the frequent legal illiteracy of frontier judges, Church courts were not necessarily even at a comparative disadvantage vis-à-vis secular

---

283. James E. Talmage, "Judiciary System of the Church of Jesus Christ of Latter-Day Saints, Improvement Era (April 1919)," in *The Essential James E. Talmage*, ed. James P. Harris (Salt Lake City: Signature Books, 1997), 198, 200.

courts with regard to legal knowledge. With the economic integration that came in the wake of the Civil War, and more importantly, the completion of the transcontinental railroad in 1869, the disputes Church courts were called upon to resolve became increasingly complicated. In addition, the nature of civil litigation itself changed in ways that made it less religiously objectionable. Given these forces, the decline of the Mormon court system is less surprising than the fact that it continued to aggressively operate for decades after the coming of the railroad.

An important part of this transition was the creation of a religiously sanctioned persona for Latter-day Saint lawyers. This not only facilitated the softening of Mormon attitudes toward recourse to secular courts but also provided a bridge that allowed Mormons to maintain continuity with the older tradition of the Church judiciary. In 1856, Brigham Young referred to litigation as a Satanic froth that right-thinking Latter-day Saints should avoid.[284] In 1872, however, he insisted that "[f]or a man to understand the law is very excellent."[285] He went on to explain the proper Mormon understanding of the law: "They that [understand the law]," he insisted, "are peacemakers, they are legitimate lawyers."[286] This vision of law properly understood could continue even in the absence of Church courts deciding civil cases. It also facilitated Mormon acceptance of the common law by providing continuity with the older tradition of Church courts, even as these tribunals were abandoned as part of Mormonism's accommodation with American Protestantism.

Indeed, this vision of law properly understood continues to be echoed in modern Mormon sermons. For example, in 1986, former law professor and judge Dallin H. Oaks, then a Mormon apostle, gave a sermon to the Church's semiannual general conference denouncing sharp dealing and frivolous litigation:

> We live in a world where many look on the marketplace as a ruthless arena where the buyer must beware, where no one is obligated to do more than the law requires, and where fraud isn't fraud unless you can prove it in court.
>
> Members of the Church of Jesus Christ have a higher standard.[287]

He went on to denounce "[s]cheming promoters with glib tongues and ingratiating manners [who] deceive their neighbors into investments.

---

284. Brigham Young, February 24, 1856, *Journal of Discoures*, 3:237.
285. Brigham Young, October 9, 1872, *Journal of Discoures*, 15:224.
286. Young, 15:224.
287. Young, 15:224.

. . . Difficulties of proof make fraud a hard crime to enforce. But the inadequacies of the laws of man provide no license for transgressions under the laws of God."[288] Likewise, he condemned "[p]ersons who prosecute frivolous lawsuits."[289] In the same sermon, however, he praised an "idealistic young professional," presumably an attorney, who denounced the illegal and unchristian treatment of migrant farm workers.[290] The themes of supra-legal religious obligations, the denunciation of litigation, and the role of the religiously informed professional mark the afterlife of the ideals that both gave rise to the expansive jurisdiction of the Mormon courts in the nineteenth century and negotiated its eventual decline.

Likewise, something of the First Presidency's ambivalence in the 1890s remains in the current procedures governing Mormon courts, which continue to operate, albeit on a smaller scale. Today, the justification for the Mormon judiciary is couched almost entirely in pastoral terms. According to modern guidelines promulgated by the Church, ecclesiastical discipline exists to "facilitate repentance by helping transgressors recognize and forsake sin, seek forgiveness, make restitution, and demonstrate a renewed commitment to keep the commandments."[291] Consonant with Oaks' sermon, however, the Church refuses to concede its prerogative to inquire into misconduct related to civil litigation: "Disciplinary councils should not attempt to resolve disputes over property rights or other civil controversies. However, if such a dispute involves accusations that a member has committed acts that would justify church discipline, the accusations should be treated like any other accusations of transgressions."[292]

In a similar vein, the modern rules state that "[n]ormally a disciplinary council is not held to consider conduct being examined by a criminal trial until the court has reached a final judgment" but clearly reserve the right to inquire into matters resolved in secular courts.[293] Indeed, the rules even contemplate that Church leaders might be asked by members to arbitrate disputes, but insist that in such a case "they should act as unofficial,

288. Dallin H. Oaks, "Brother's Keeper," *Ensign*, November 1986, 20.

289. Oaks, 21.

290. Oaks, 21.

291. The Church of Jesus Christ of Latter-day Saints, *Church Handbook of Instructions: Book 1, Stake Presidencies and Bishoprics* (Salt Lake City: The Church of Jesus Christ of Latter-day Saints, 2006), 105.

292. The Church of Jesus Christ of Latter-day Saints, 111.

293. The Church of Jesus Christ of Latter-day Saints, 116.

private advisers and should not involve the Church."[294] In short, while the Mormon courts have abandoned the expansive jurisdiction that they once claimed, preaching continues to the courthouse, and judging continues apace within the temple.

294. The Church of Jesus Christ of Latter-day Saints, 111.

CHAPTER 3

"Established Agreeable to the Laws of Our Country": Mormonism, Church Corporations, and the Long Legacy of America's First Disestablishment

I. Introduction

The early Republic saw the disestablishment of government-supported churches in the original colonies. This was a decentralized, local process, and one that in the ordinary telling began during the American Revolution and was completed by the early 1830s. According to the traditional story, the body of law produced by this so-called "first disestablishment" fostered freedom and religious pluralism in the new Republic. In this view, the first disestablishment ended just as the Second Great Awakening, a religious upheaval that produced a welter of new sects and established various forms of evangelical Protestantism as the dominant religion in the United States, reached its height.[1] Among the new religious movements that emerged from the Second Great Awakening, perhaps none has proven as successful as Mormonism. Indeed, one might point toward the rise of The Church of Jesus Christ of Latter-day Saints as one of the fruits of the religious freedom vouched safe by the first disestablishment. This article, however, tells a different story, one that recasts both the timing and the substance of America's first disestablishment.

The scriptures of the Church mark its beginning with a legal event. They speak of "The rise of the Church of Christ in these last days . . . it being regularly organized and established agreeable to the laws of our country; by the will and commandments of God" (D&C 20:1) "The laws of our country" in this case refers to *An Act to Provide for the Incorporation of Religious Societies* passed by the New York legislature in 1813.[2] From its legal beginnings in April 1830, the Church struggled to find a legal personality. In the lifetime of Church founder Joseph Smith, it was in-

1. See generally Roger Finke and Rodney Stark, "How the Upstart Sects Won America: 1776–1850," *Journal for the Scientific Study of Religion* 28, no. 1 (1989): 27–44.

2. Act of Apr. 5, 1813, ch. 60, 1813 N.Y. Laws 212.

corporated under the laws of two states—and perhaps a third—in an unsuccessful effort to find a legal model that would accommodate its ecclesiastical ambitions. After the murder of Joseph Smith in 1844, the Latter-day Saints emigrated en mass beyond the borders of the United States to what was then Mexican territory. Once there, they organized a government that provided a more congenial legal existence for the Church. However, with the integration of Mormon country into the United States, these legal structures drew the ire of Congress which wished to impose the legal model of the first disestablishment on the Latter-day Saints. This launched a three-decade-long battle between the federal government and the Latter-day Saints over the nature of their legal personality. The final skirmishes in this legal war were not completed until the opening decade of the twentieth century. At the heart of these battles was a fundamental disagreement between the Latter-day Saints and the broader currents of American law over what it meant to be a church.

This chapter provides a history of The Church of Jesus Christ of Latter-day Saints as a legal entity.[3] In so doing, it makes two contributions to our understanding of legal history. First, it recasts the story of the first disestablishment, revealing it as longer-lasting and more contentious than has often been assumed. The first disestablishment produced a body of law governing churches encoded with profoundly Protestant assumptions about church government and the role of religion in society. Unsurprisingly, these assumptions created problems for the Latter-day Saints, who did not share the law's theological commitments. The story of the Church's corporate existence is thus a useful corrective to whiggish stories of American disestablishment, revealing the iron fist that often lay beneath the velvet glove of religious freedom and pluralism in the United States. It also illustrates the ways in which being far from settled in the early 1830s, the legal structures of the first disestablishment continued to spawn hard-fought battles into the late-nineteenth and early twentieth centuries. The Latter-day Saints weren't the only religious group that struggled against the Protestantism of nineteenth-century church law. The Roman Catholic Church found American law uncongenial as well. However, controversies involving Catholics tended to center on questions of internal church governance, whereas the Latter-day Saints found restrictions of property and corporate

3. This is not the first effort to take the approach of a case study of a church corporation as a lens for examining disestablishment and its legacies. See generally Elizabeth Mensch, "Religion, Revival, and the Ruling Class: A Critical History of Trinity Church," *Buffalo Law Review* 36 (1987): 427–571.

purposes more irksome.[4] Second, this chapter contributes to our understanding of Mormon history by providing the first comprehensive history of the Church as a legal institution. This story reveals legal personality as one of the key points of legal conflict between the Latter-day Saints and American society. This insight, in turn, is a useful corrective to the dominant narratives in Mormon historiography which emphasize polygamy and theocracy as the points of legal contention. An understanding of the history of the Church as a legal entity, however, supplements these stories by revealing how the hard-fought legal battles of the late nineteenth century can be seen as an extension of the process of legal disestablishment that began during the American Revolution.

This chapter is organized chronologically and proceeds as follows. Part II examines the legacy of America's first disestablishment, which provided the legal context for the founding of the Latter-day Saint movement. Part III examines the quest for legal personality during the lifetime of Church founder Joseph Smith. Part IV recounts the grueling battle between the federal government and the Latter-day Saints in the second half of the nineteenth century through the lens of the Church's legal personality. Part V discusses the reconciliation between the Latter-day Saints and American society in the twentieth century and the ultimate legal form that their church took. Part VI concludes.

II. The Legacy of America's First Disestablishment

In 1774, on the eve of the American Revolution, nine of the thirteen colonies had established churches.[5] What precisely establishment meant as a legal matter varied from colony to colony. In all of the colonies, established churches benefited from tax revenues, grants of valuable land, or both. In some colonies the established church had a monopoly on certain

---

4. See generally Patrick J. Dignan, *A History of the Legal Incorporation of Catholic Church Property in the United States (1784–1932)* (Washington, DC: Catholic University of America Press, 1933) (recounting the legal controversies surrounding Catholic property and organizations in the United States during the nineteenth century); See also Sarah Barringer Gordon, "The First Disestablishment: Limits on Church Power and Property Before the Civil War," *University of Pennsylvania Law Review* 162 (2014): 319–20 (recounting legal conflicts between lay Catholics and bishops over the control of parishes).

5. See Mark D. McGarvie, *One Nation Under Law: America's Early National Struggles to Separate Church and State* (DeKalb: Northern Illinois University Press, 2004), 41.

activities, such as poor relief or the performance of legally valid marriages.[6] The most commonly established denomination was Anglicanism. In New England, Congregationalists dominated, although in theory the principle of local church governance meant that multiple establishments were possible. This structure led to intense legal battles in early nineteenth-century Massachusetts when Unitarianism replaced old-line Congregationalism in churches across New England. In addition to de jure establishments, all colonies regulated religion to some extent in order to support Protestant Christianity. Blasphemy laws restricted religious speech, preaching without a license was an offense in some jurisdictions, and voting and holding public office was often contingent on subscribing to some version of Christianity.[7]

During the Revolution, the states began disestablishing their established churches. This was a long process that took a variety of forms, and it wasn't finally completed until the 1830s. The establishment clause of the First Amendment to the federal constitution provided that "Congress shall make no law respecting an establishment of religion,"[8] but this prohibition applied only to the federal government.[9] Rather, disestablishment was a matter of state corporate law.[10] This is because, in large part, incorporation had been the mechanism for establishment. The corporation didn't become the dominant form of private business organization until after the Civil War, and in the early Republic, corporations were thought of as public institutions whose primary role was to serve the common good. As one Virginia judge put it in the early nineteenth century, a legitimate corporation could not have a purpose that was "merely private or selfish, if it is detrimental to, or not promotive of the public good."[11] Incorporation also required a special act of the legislature. Thus, a church being incorporated marked it out as the recipient of a special favor from the state.

Broadly speaking, there were two approaches to disestablishment. Some states simply disincorporated all churches, while other states threw

---

6. See generally Marcus Wilson Jernegan, "The Development of Poor Relief in Colonial Virginia," *Social Service Review* 3, no. 1 (1929): 1–18.

7. See generally Sarah Barringer Gordon, "Blasphemy and the Law of Religious Liberty in Nineteenth-Century America," *American Quarterly* 52, no. 4 (December 1, 2000): 682–719 (discussing blasphemy laws and restrictions on religious speech).

8. U.S. Const. amend. I.

9. Cf. Permoli v. City of New Orleans, 44 U.S. 589 (1844) (holding that the first amendment did not apply to the states).

10. See generally Gordon, "The First Disestablishment."

11. Quoted in McGarvie, *One Nation under Law*, 131.

the corporate form open to all churches.[12] Both approaches sought to diminish the social power of religious institutions by limiting the amount of property that could be held by or for a church.[13] These so-called "mortmain" provisions assumed that churches were essentially congregational structures and needed no more than a meetinghouse, a parsonage, and a small glebe (an income-producing parcel of land with which to pay the minister).[14] In addition, general incorporation statutes created mandatory governance structures for churches.[15] These rules followed the strongly Protestant and congregational assumptions about church government. Each incorporated congregation was legally independent of any denominational or supra-congregational structure. Ultimate power was conferred on the laity rather than on the clergy who were to be treated as employees of the corporation and as subject to the control of a lay board of trustees.[16] The result was a legal structure that represented very strong ecclesiological assumptions, assumptions that were congenial to Calvinists and Evangelical Protestants but were more difficult for hierarchical churches such as the Roman Catholics and the Episcopalians to navigate.[17] This preference was not accidental. In the early Republic, both Catholicism and Anglicanism were seen as threats to republican government that should be either suppressed or sharply limited. Indeed, in 1779 the New York legislature went so far as to adopt a bill of attainder sentencing the royalist Anglican rector of Trinity Church in New York and his wife to death.[18]

III. Joseph Smith and the Search for Legal Personality

The Church was thus born into a world in which the corporate personality of churches was both a chief site of legal conflict over disestablishment and the primary mechanism by which the state regulated religious

---

12. See McGarvie, 67–96 (recounting the story of disestablishment in New York); Thomas E. Buckley, *Church and State in Revolutionary Virginia, 1776–1787* (Charlottesville: University of Virginia Press, 1977) (discussing disestablishment in Virginia).

13. See Gordon, "The First Disestablishment," 323.

14. See Paul G. Kauper and Stephen C. Ellis, "Religious Corporations and the Law," *Michigan Law Review* 71, no. 8 (August 1, 1973): 1499–1574.

15. See Gordon, "The First Disestablishment," 330–35.

16. See Gordon, 334–35.

17. See Dignan, *A History of the Legal Incorporation of Catholic Church Property*, 46–66 (discussing the Catholic experience).

18. See McGarvie, *One Nation under Law*, 111.

communities. During the lifetime of Joseph Smith, the Church spanned four different American jurisdictions: New York, Ohio, Missouri, and Illinois. Each of these states took a somewhat different approach to disestablishment, and in all of them the nascent Mormon movement struggled to find a workable legal personality.

A. New York

The New York statute of which Joseph Smith and his associates availed themselves in 1830 was the result of more than a century of conflict over the legal status of churches under New York law.[19] The colony of New Amsterdam was originally founded by the Dutch West India Company in 1625 as a trading entrepot, and the Company consistently subordinated its nominal support for the Dutch Reformed Church to commercial expediency by adopting a tolerant stance toward religion. In 1664, the English acquired the colony in the Second Anglo-Dutch War and renamed it New York. In the late seventeenth and early eighteenth centuries, royal officials sought to create an established Anglican church in the colony. However, their efforts were met with resistance from largely secular commercial interests in New York City and various dissenting sects. Nevertheless, royal charters and provincial legislation granted benefits to the Church of England, including the incorporation of Trinity Church in New York City, the wealthiest and most important Anglican congregation in the colony. Up to the time of the revolution, however, whether or not Anglicanism was in fact the established church of the colony was a hotly contested question.[20] The state's revolutionary constitution of 1777 provided that "the free exercise and enjoyment of religious profession and worship, without discrimination or preference, shall forever hereafter be

19. See generally McGarvie, 97–130; Mensch, "Religion, Revival, and the Ruling Class."

20. The so-called "Duke's Laws" promulgated immediately after the English takeover of New Amsterdam required local parishes to elect overseers who could then choose any ordained Protestant minister for the local church, who was paid from taxes collected by the local courts. This system was later codified in the 1693 Ministry Act, which decreed that in each parish "there shall be called, inducted, and established, a good sufficient Protestant Ministry." Quoted in Mensch, "Religion, Revival, and the Ruling Class," 444. The dispute over whether there was a single established church in the colony centered on whether this law, which was silent on the question, required that the minister be Anglican.

allowed within this State to all mankind"[21] and the state constitutional convention published a statement that with the new constitution "all such . . . statutes and acts . . . as may be construed to establish or maintain any particular denomination of Christians or their ministers . . . be and they are . . . rejected."[22] In 1784, the legislature abrogated the provisions in previously granted corporate charters giving churches taxing authority.[23] The New York legislature also took the radical step of allowing any religious society to incorporate without legislative action merely by electing trustees and filing a certificate containing their names and the name of the church with the local court.[24] This law was repeatedly amended in the succeeding decades, but it provided the basic framework under which Joseph Smith organized his new church in 1830.

The traditional date and place for the incorporation of the Church of Christ, later renamed The Church of Jesus Christ of Latter-day Saints, is April 6, 1830, in Fayette, New York. Because no documents from 1830 attesting this event have survived, some writers have suggested that no such legal organization ever occurred.[25] A revelation purportedly given to Joseph Smith on April 6, 1830, declares that the Church was organized "agreeable

---

21. N.Y. Const. of 1777, art. XXXVIII.

22. Quoted in McGarvie, *One Nation under Law*, 111.

23. See Act of Mar. 17, 1784, ch. 9, 1784 N.Y. Laws 597, 598 (removing taxing power from the Reformed Protestant Dutch Church of the city of New York); Act of Apr. 17, 1784, ch. 33, 1784 N.Y. Laws 646, 646 (removing taxing power from Trinity Church).

24. See Act of Apr. 6, 1784, ch. 18, 1784 N.Y. Laws 613 ("An Act to enable all religious denominations in this State to appoint trustees who shall be a body corporate, for the purpose for taking care of the temporalities of their respective congregations, and for other purposes therein mentioned").

25. See, e.g., David Keith Stott, "Organizing the Church as a Religious Association in 1830," in *Sustaining the Law: Joseph Smith's Legal Encounters*, ed. Gordon A. Madsen, Jeffrey N. Walker, and John W. Welch (Provo: BYU Studies, 2014), 113–40; H. Michael Marquardt, "An Appraisal of Manchester as Location for the Organization of the Church," *Sunstone*, February 1992. According to Marquardt, no legal organization was attempted in New York and the alleged incorporation was a later invention designed to fool creditors in Ohio. However, Marquardt, who is not a lawyer, fails to explain how an earlier Church incorporation would have frustrated collection efforts against the Church or Church officers in Ohio. Nor does his article point to any legal proceedings in Ohio in which the New York incorporation was invoked to shield Latter-day Saint debtors, although there were numerous collection actions brought against Joseph Smith in the wake of the failure of the Kirtland Safety Society.

to the laws of our country," (D&C 20:1) but the original document has not survived and the earliest extant copy of the revelation dates from March 1831.[26] Most tellingly, the 1813 New York law required those organizing a religious corporation to file a certificate with the county clerk. Despite extensive searches by multiple researchers, however, such a document has never been located in New York for Joseph Smith's Church of Christ.[27] It is possible that the certificate was filed and then subsequently lost or destroyed. It is also possible that Smith sought to incorporate his church but through ignorance or oversight never filed the required paperwork. Nevertheless, there is evidence that at least an attempt at incorporation was made in New York. The records of the event insist that there were six original "members" of the Church, despite the fact that more than six people had been previously baptized into the movement.[28] The number, however, makes sense if it refers not to "members of the church" but rather to the trustees required by New York law.[29] It's entirely possible that Smith and his associates failed to comply with New York law, but the best evidence

---

26. See Robin Scott Jensen, Robert J. Woodford, and Steven C. Harper, eds., *Manuscript Revelation Books*, facsimile edition, first volume of the Revelations and Translations series of *The Joseph Smith Papers*, ed. Dean C. Jessee, Ronald K. Esplin, and Richard Lyman Bushman (Salt Lake City: Church Historian's Press, 2009), 75–87 [hereafter cited as *JSP*, MBR] for a reproduction of the earliest extant version of what became D&C 20.

27. See Larry C. Porter, *A Study of the Origins of the Church of Jesus Christ of Latter-Day Saints in the States of New York and Pennsylvania*, reprint edition (Provo: Joseph Fielding Smith Institute for Latter-day Saint History and BYU Studies, 2000), 155–60 (recounting an exhaustive archival search for the document).

28. See Karen Lynn Davidson, David J. Whittaker, Mark Ashurst-McGee, and Richard L. Jensen, eds., *Histories, Volume 1: Joseph Smith Histories, 1832–1844*, vol. 1 of the Histories series of *The Joseph Smith Papers*, ed. Dean C. Jessee, Ronald K. Esplin, and Richard Lyman Bushman (Salt Lake City: Church Historian's Press, 2012), 197: ("<We> made known also to the <those> members who had already been baptized, that we had received commandment to organize the Church: and according to accordingly <we> met to together, <(being about 30 <six> in number) besides a number who were beleiving—met with us> on Tuesday the Sixth day of Aprile in the year of our A.D. A thousand & One thousand, Eight hundred and thirty").

29. See Act of Apr. 5, 1813, ch. 60, sec. III, 1813 N.Y. Laws 212, 214 (stating that any church or religious society may "elect any number of discreet persons of their church, congregation or society, not less than three, nor exceeding nine in number, as trustees"). Notice that the number chosen by Smith—six—exactly splits the statutory range of three and nine.

suggests that they were attempting to do so.[30] David Whitmer, who was present, insisted that, "On the 6th of April, 1830, the church was called together and the elders acknowledged according to the laws of New York."[31]

In 1830, incorporation conferred three concrete legal benefits on New York churches. The first was legal personality, which simplified the process of obtaining property and incurring debts. The second was the clear segregation of the church's assets from those of its members and officers. The third was perpetual succession, which avoided conflicts with heirs and creditors upon the death of a trustee.[32] In 1830, however, Joseph Smith's nascent church held no property. Its only real economic activity was the effort to publish the Book of Mormon, which legally took the form of a written business partnership between Joseph Smith and his associate Martin Harris.[33]

---

30. David Keith Stott suggests that rather than trying to incorporate, Smith and his associates were deliberately creating an unincorporated association. However, it is anachronistic to imagine that an unincorporated association was a particular legal status that would have been aimed at in the April 6, 1830, meeting. Unincorporated association was simply the default legal treatment for any religious group. Thus, the nascent Mormon movement was already an unincorporated association prior to April 6, 1830. Stott reads subsequent references to being organized under New York law as referring to the deliberate invoking of unincorporated association as a distinct legal status, but all of the sources he cites that discuss unincorporated association in this way are from the second half of the nineteenth century when ideas of corporate law were far more developed. The concept was not used this way in New York in the 1820s and 1830s.

31. David Whitmer, "Mormonism," *Kansas City Journal*, June 5, 1881, 1. It's worth noting that Whitmer was hostile to the retroactive alteration of earlier sources. A close early supporter of Joseph Smith, he objected to the increasing institutionalization of the Mormon movement and later broke with Joseph Smith in part over this issue. He was also scathing in his criticisms of retroactive editing of Smith's revelations. Nevertheless, in later reminiscences he insisted that a legal incorporation occurred on April 6, 1830. He is also the scribe who recorded the earliest extant copy of D&C 20, containing the "agreeable to the laws of our country" language. See *JSP*, MRB:3–391.

32. In addition, ordinary trusts could run afoul of the rule against perpetuities, which would make it impossible for a trust to survive for the benefit of later Church members. This problem, however, could be circumvented through a so-called charitable trust, which lacks specific beneficiaries.

33. Under the terms of the agreement, Harris mortgaged his farm to finance the publication of the Book of Mormon and was then entitled to sell the Book of Mormon, to which Joseph Smith held the copyright, until the debt was repaid. Ultimately, Harris lost his farm, although he insisted that he eventually recouped

The New York organization of the Church thus presents a puzzle. What were the movement's problems for which incorporation was a solution? Why did the Church seek a legal existence rather than simply operate as an unincorporated religious society? Indeed, prior to April 6, 1830, this is precisely what Smith and his followers had been doing. As early as March 1829, his revelations speak of "my church" (D&C 5:14). Smith began performing baptisms by May 1829, and the next month his associate Oliver Cowdrey drew up "Articles of the Church of Christ,"[34] providing a governing structure for the Church that says nothing about "the laws of our country." As David Whitmer later wrote, "we were as fully *organized*—spiritually—before April 6th as we were on that day."[35] Why then incorporate?

The most likely reason is that the attempted incorporation was expressive. Gaining legal status was less a matter of solving concrete problems than using the law to define the place of the new Church in the minds of both believers and outsiders. When Joseph Smith first began receiving revelations about "the church," they spoke of an entity that was already in existence and employed the term in ways that suggest they referred to the universal Christian church rather than a particular denomination or institution.[36] These earliest revelations, however, predated the translation and 1830 publication of the Book of Mormon, which contains a more concrete vision of an institutionalized church. As early as Oliver Cowdery's 1829 "Articles," the Book of Mormon was taken as an ecclesiological model. Indeed, large portions of Cowdrey's "Articles" consist of verbatim quotations from the Book of Mormon. Between 1828 and 1830, what had begun as a diffuse,

---

his money through later sales of the Book of Mormon. See "Agreement with Martin Harris, 16 January 1830," in Michael Hubbard MacKay et al, eds., *Documents, Volume 1: July 1828–June 1831*, vol. 1 of the Documents series of *The Joseph Smith Papers,* ed. Dean C. Jessee, Ronald K. Esplin, Richard Lyman Bushman, and Matthew J. Grow (Salt Lake City: Church Historian's Press, 2013), 104–8 [hereafter cited as *JSP*, D1].

34. *JSP*, D1:368–377. See Scott H. Faulring, "An Examination of the 1829 'Articles of the Church of Christ' in Relation to Section 20 of the Doctrine and Covenants," *Brigham Young University Studies* 43, no. 4 (Winter 2004): 57–91.

35. David Whitmer, *An Address to All Believers in Christ* (Richmond: David Whitmer, 1887), 33.

36. See Terryl L. Givens, *Wrestling the Angel: The Foundations of Mormon Thought: Cosmos, God, Humanity* (New York: Oxford University Press, 2014), 34–37; Terryl L. Givens, *Feeding the Flock: The Foundations of Mormon Thought: Church and Praxis* (New York: Oxford University Press, 2017), 22–23 (discussing the development of the idea of a church and its link to Joseph Smith's evolving covenant theology).

prophetic movement centered on Joseph Smith increasingly defined itself as an institutionalized church. The act of incorporation in 1830 would have signaled to believers this shift. This, for example, is how David Whitmer, who ultimately came to regard the increasing institutionalization of the Church as a spiritual disaster, saw the April 6, 1830, organization.[37]

Mormonism began life as a legally disfavored variety of religion. Joseph Smith, his family, and his closest earliest associates were all deeply involved in "folk magic."[38] While in his later life Smith tried to publicly distance himself from these practices, the reality is that they were integrated into a spiritual life that also included his earliest visions and the translation of the Book of Mormon. In 1826, Smith had been tried for fraud as a result of his magical activities, although he was found not guilty.[39] While the use of seer stones and the like drew scorn as well as possible legal censure from elites, for many believers it marked the return of spiritual gifts and revelation.[40] Nevertheless, Joseph Smith was in search of religious respectability, and this is part of what incorporation provided. Prior to the Revolution, the corporate form had

---

37. See Whitmer, *An Address to All Believers in Christ*, 33.

38. The seminal scholarly studies are D. Michael Quinn, *Early Mormonism and the Magic World View*, revised 2nd ed. (Salt Lake City: Signature Books, 1998) and Richard Lyman Bushman, *Joseph Smith and the Beginnings of Mormonism* (Urbana: University of Illinois Press, 1984). While I use the term "folk magic" in the text, the term is deeply problematic as it lacks any clear meaning and has generally been used as a derogatory term for disfavored spiritual practices. See generally Randall Styers, *Making Magic: Religion, Magic, and Science in the Modern World*, Reflection and Theory in the Study of Religion (New York: Oxford University Press, 2004). I choose to use the term because in the context of Joseph Smith's use of legal formalities, it is precisely the elite disdain and hostility conveyed by the term "magic" that is important. Other writers on Mormon history, however, have used alternative terms such as "cunning-folk traditions." See Jonathan A. Stapley, *The Power of Godliness: Mormon Liturgy and Cosmology* (New York: Oxford University Press, 2018), 105; see also Samuel M. Brown, *Joseph Smith's Translation: The Words and Worlds of Early Mormonism* (New York: Oxford University Press, 2020), 25 (discussing the terminological difficulties with "magic" in the Mormon context).

39. See Gordon A. Madsen, "Joseph Smith's 1826 Trial: The Legal Setting," *Brigham Young University Studies* 30, no. 2 (1990): 91–108; Marvin S. Hill, "Joseph Smith and the 1826 Trial: New Evidence and New Difficulties," *Brigham Young University Studies* 12, no. 2 (1972): 223–33.

40. Indeed, David Whitmer became increasingly disillusioned with Joseph Smith's revelations in part because he ceased to use his seer stone and simply spoke the revelations as a "mouthpiece." See Whitmer, *An Address to All Believers in Christ*, 36.

been a mark of religious establishment in New York. In 1784, the New York legislature had in effect thrown open the doors of "establishment" to all religious societies. Incorporation thus offered Joseph Smith's nascent movement a way of signaling its respectability by claiming legal recognition.

Finally, the Church of Christ was contemplating the use of legal benefits conferred by the state of New York. David Whitmer wrote that "the world had been telling us that we were not a regularly organized church, and we had no right to officiate in the ordinances of marriage, hold church property, etc., and that we should organize according to the laws of the land."[41] However, under New York law, property could be held in trust without a corporation, and marriages could be performed by "ministers of the gospel and priests of every denomination."[42] While the marriage statute was silent about incorporation, what precisely was necessary to be recognized as a "minister of the gospel" was left unclear. Formal incorporation would have provided at least some evidence that one was a bona fide minister. Efforts to claim legal benefits were not entirely hypothetical. On July 7, 1830, the *Palmyra Reflector* reported:

> A disciple of the "Gold Bible," lately called on an assessor and demanded an exemption from taxation, to the amount of $1500—alleging that he was a Minister of the Gospel, at the same time producing a certificate, signed by Jo. Smith, and Oliver Cowdry, by way of proof—the course to be taken in this matter has not as yet transpired.[43]

New York exempted the property of "every minister of the gospel, or priest, of any denomination" from taxation up to the value of $1,500.[44] Again, the statute is silent on incorporation, but legal formality would have strengthened the claim to be a minister or priest. Tellingly, on June 9, 1830, Joseph Smith and Oliver Cowdry issued written licenses "signifying & proveing that [the holder] is a Priest of this Church of Christ established & regularly Organized in these last days AD 1830 on the 6th. day of April."[45] These seem to be the documents referred to by the *Palmyra Reflector*.[46]

---

41. Whitmer, 33.

42. N.Y. Dom. Rel. Law § 8(1) (1829) (amended 1888).

43. Dan Vogel, ed., *Early Mormon Documents: Volume 2* (Salt Lake City: Signature Books, 1998), 237 (reproducing the article from the *Palmyra Reflector*, July 7, 1830).

44. N.Y. Tax Law § 4(8) (1829) (amended 1884).

45. *JSP*, D1:146–148. See Donald Q. Cannon, "Licensing in the Early Church," *Brigham Young University Studies* 22, no. 1 (Winter 1982): 96–105.

46. Three licenses from the June 1830 conference survive. They belong to Joseph Smith Sr., John Whitmer, and Christian Whitmer. Each references a different

B. Ohio

Early in 1831 Joseph Smith relocated the headquarters of the Church to Kirtland, Ohio, where missionaries had baptized a large number of converts the previous year. The Church's legal affairs became far more complicated in Ohio than in New York. Latter-day Saint religious practice both conformed with Protestant models in some ways and, more importantly, began to depart dramatically from them. This resulted in a series of unstable legal entities, none of which used the corporate model that Smith and his associates had used in New York. For the first time in Ohio, the Church engaged in the prototypical legal transaction for a church: the purchase of real property and the construction of a meetinghouse, namely the Kirtland Temple. The Latter-day Saints acquired the property on which the temple was to be built from a local landowner named Peter French through a confused series of transactions that clouded title to the building for decades. In May 1834, John and Elsey Johnson, a Latter-day Saint couple who had purchased a portion of the French property, executed a deed conveying the temple site to "Joseph Smith Junior President of the Church of Christ organized on the 6th of April, in the year of our Lord, on thousand eight hundred and thirty, in the Township of Fayette, Seneca County and State of New York."[47] In 1819, Ohio had passed a general incorporation statute for churches modeled on New York's law.[48] There is no evidence that the Church sought to avail itself of this law. In 1824, however, Ohio passed a second law providing that any property deeded to "any person as trustee

---

office. John Whitmer is an "an Apostle of Jesus Christ, an Elder of this Church of Christ"; Christian Whitmer is "a Teacher"; and Joseph Smith Sr. is a "priest." It is possible that the designation of a "priest" was done in part so that licenses would use the title contained in the New York tax statute. Other licenses issued at the June 1830 conference did not survive, but surviving documents suggest that a license as a "priest" was issued to Hyrum Smith, Joseph Smith's brother, who at the time had been assessed for taxes on a shop that he was renting. It is possible that he was the person who applied for tax exemption. Mark Staker, Historical Department, The Church of Jesus Christ of Latter-day Saints, email message to the author, August 28, 2019. Unfortunately, other than the notice in the *Palmyra Reflector*, no other documents regarding this petition seem to have survived.

47. Kim L. Loving, "Ownership of the Kirtland Temple: Legends, Lies, and Misunderstandings," *Journal of Mormon History* 30, no. 2 (2004): 5.

48. Act of Feb. 5, 1819, ch. 54, 1818 Ohio Laws 120 ("An act for the incorporation of religious societies").

or trustee in trust for any religious society"[49] should be held in perpetual succession by the religious society and that the trustee "shall have the same power to defend and prosecute suits . . . and do all other acts . . . as individuals may do in relation to their individual property."[50] In effect, this law meant that property held in trust for an otherwise unincorporated religious society would be treated as though it were held by a corporation. In 1834, the Ohio Supreme Court treated the conveyance of property under this law to a Baptist congregation in Dayton as creating a corporation.[51] The meaning of the deed to Joseph Smith as "President of the Church of Christ" was never ultimately decided in court.[52] In all likelihood the deed created a corporation under Ohio law at the time.[53]

Kirtland also saw the divergence of Joseph Smith's religious vision from that which was encoded within the law of religious corporations. With the doctrine of gathering and the proclamation that Zion was to be built in Jackson County, Missouri, the Church's conception of its own mission spilled beyond congregational structures devoted merely to the

---

49. Act of Jan. 3, 1825, §1, 1824 Ohio Laws 9, 9 ("securing to religious societies a perpetuity of title to lands and tenements, conveyed in trust for meetinghouses, burying grounds of residence for preachers").

50. Act of Jan. 3, 1825, § 2.

51. See Keyser v. Stansifer, 6 Ohio 363 (1834).

52. Years after Smith's death, the Reorganized Church of Jesus Christ of Latter-day Saints unsuccessfully brought suit to quiet title to the temple in an effort to establish itself as the legitimate successor to Smith's church. In the end, the court, after adopting a proposed finding of fact by the Reorganized Church's counsel as *obitur dicta*, denied relief on the grounds that the plaintiff was not in possession of the property. Eventually, the Reorganized Church quieted title by adverse possession. For many years, the leaders of the Reorganized Church claimed that the court in the Kirtland Temple Suit had declared the Reorganized Church of Jesus Christ of Latter-day Saints to be the legitimate successor to the Church of Jesus Christ of Latter-day Saints founded by Joseph Smith Jr., although ultimately the Ohio court made no such holding. The litigation is recounted in detail in Loving, "Ownership of the Kirtland Temple." While the Church of Jesus Christ of Latter-day Saints did not participate in the litigation over the Kirtland Temple, members of the Church eventually became aware of the Reorganized Church's legal claims and produced their own rebuttal. See Paul E. Reimann, *The Reorganized Church and the Civil Courts* (Salt Lake City: Utah Printing Company, 1961).

53. The 1824 statute was not raised in the litigation by the Reorganized Church. It's applicability to the Church was first suggested by Jesse St. Cyr, "A Brief Corporate History of The Church of Jesus Christ of Latter-Day Saints, 1829–1901" (paper delivered at the Mormon History Association, May 24, 2008).

maintenance of houses of worship.[54] Rather, it became involved in the project of defining a new people and creating economically viable communities in which to build the city of God. Thus, the most important manifestations of the Church's legal personality in Ohio were not religious corporations but rather a business partnership and a bank.

The business partnership was called the United Firm.[55] In New York, Joseph Smith had already revealed a preference for pursuing religious missions outside of religious corporate law, forming a business partnership with Martin Harris to publish the Book of Mormon. He massively expanded this model in Ohio, forming a partnership with the leaders of the nascent Church that encompassed three "firms." The first of these was centered on the Newel K. Whitney store in Kirtland and focused on the economic development of the town for the benefit of the Latter-day Saints gathering to Church headquarters. The second firm was located in Jackson County, Missouri, and served similar purposes to the Newel K. Whitney store. Finally, the so-called "literary firm" was devoted to the publication of Church newspapers and a collection of Joseph Smith's revelations. At the time, neither Ohio nor Missouri law allowed for the general incorporation of business enterprises, so as a legal matter these "firms" were part of a single general partnership. The partners drew up a "bond" (contract) to govern the business.[56] By 1834, however, in large part because of the violent expulsion of the Saints from Jackson County, Missouri, the United Firm had failed as a business entity. It was dissolved, internal debts between the partners cancelled—mainly to the detriment of Newel K. Whitney and Frederick G. Williams, who had contributed the bulk of the capital—and the remaining property distributed to its members.

This business partnership found its way into Latter-day Saint scripture in a way that was to have lasting effects on the movement. During his time in Kirtland, Joseph Smith received a number of revelations relating to the

54. For more insight into the Latter-day Saints' efforts to create ideal communities, what they called Zion, see generally Leonard J. Arrington, Feramorz Y. Fox, and Dean L. May, *Building the City of God: Community and Cooperation Among the Mormons*, 2nd ed. (Urbana: University of Illinois Press, 1992).

55. The most extensive treatment of the United Firm can be found in Max H. Parkin, "Joseph Smith and the United Firm: The Growth and Decline of the Church's First Master Plan of Business and Finance, Ohio and Missouri, 1832–1834," *Brigham Young University Studies* 46, no. 3 (2007): 5–62.

56. See Parkin, 13–14. Unfortunately, this document does not seem to have survived.

affairs of the United Firm (see D&C 78, D&C 82, D&C 92, and D&C 104).[57] When these revelations were subsequently published, however, they were edited. The term "United Firm" was replaced with the term "united order," and references to the firm's "mercantile and publishing establishments" were changed to "the affairs of the storehouse of the poor."[58] Thus, what began as a series of revelations on a business partnership was transformed into a set of texts about a more cosmic and utopian scheme. Drawing on these texts a generation later, Brigham Young would use the term "united orders" for Latter-day Saint cooperatives aimed at establishing the autarky of Zion in the Great Basin against the integrating force of American capitalism after the Civil War. From there, the term "united order" has passed into Mormon thought and language as a shorthand reference to an ideal community marked by righteousness, economic egalitarianism, and cooperation for the common good. What began as a religiously directed business firm became central to Mormonism's utopian imagination.

In Kirtland, the Church also sought to organize a bank—the Kirtland Safety Society.[59] Its purpose was to assist with the gathering of the Latter-day Saints in Kirtland by providing credit and liquidity to the local economy and by assisting in financing the construction of the Kirtland Temple. Ohio law required that banks receive a charter of incorporation from the state legislature in order to issues notes, and this was the initial route taken by Joseph Smith and his associates. They drew up a "constitution" for their bank and petitioned the legislature for a charter.[60] When this effort proved unsuccessful, they pursued two other routes. First, Latter-day Saint leaders organized the Kirtland Safety Society as a joint stock company, drawing up a new set of "articles of agreement."[61] This was an unincorporated

57. See Mark Lyman Staker, *Hearken, O Ye People: The Historical Setting of Joseph Smith's Ohio Revelations* (Salt Lake City: Greg Kofford Books, 2010), 230–37 (discussing the context for some of these revelations).

58. See Parkin, "Joseph Smith and the United Firm," 37–53.

59. See generally Staker, *Hearken, O Ye People*, 391–548; Marvin S. Hill, C. Keith Rooker, and Larry T. Wimmer, "The Kirtland Economy Revisited: A Market Critique of Sectarian Economics," *Brigham Young University Studies* 17, no. 4 (1977): 391–475.

60. Brent M. Rogers et al, eds. *Documents, Volume 5: October 1835–January 1838*, vol. 5 of the Documents series of *The Joseph Smith Papers,* ed. Ronald K. Esplin, Matthew J. Grow, and Matthew C. Godfrey (Salt Lake City: Church Historian's Press, 2017), 299–306 [hereafter cited as *JSP*, D5].

61. See *JSP*, D5:324–31. This was also when the "Kirtland Safety Society" was renamed the "Kirtland Safety Society Anti-Banking Company."

entity that functioned much like a partnership, with unlimited liability for the stockholders and no separate legal personality for the bank.[62] Second, the Latter-day Saints acquired a controlling interest in the Bank of Monroe, which was incorporated under Michigan law. They then set up the Kirtland Safety Society as a branch of the Michigan bank.[63] Ohio law allowed "foreign" banks to operate branches in the state. This effort to circumvent Ohio's anti-banking laws, however, proved ineffective when the Bank of Monroe was forced to close its doors in the Panic of 1837.[64] Michigan also enacted a "free banking" law, which allowed unincorporated joint stock companies to operate banks, throwing into doubt Ohio's recognition of the Ohio branches of Michigan banks.[65] While it initially sold stock and issued notes backed by the resulting capital and loans, the Safety Society rapidly ran into trouble. In part, the bank was built on the expectation of increasing land prices, an expectation that was disappointed during the Panic of 1837 when land prices became depressed. More importantly, as a joint stock company, the legal enforceability of the notes that the bank issued was questionable under Ohio law.[66] The

---

62. See Jeffrey N. Walker, "The Kirtland Safety Society and the Fraud of Grandison Newell: A Legal Examination," *BYU Studies Quarterly* 54, no. 3 (2015): 44–49.

63. See Walker, 50–54.

64. See Walker, 54–55.

65. See Walker, 54–55.

66. In 1816, Ohio passed "an act to prohibit the issuing and circulating of unauthorized bank paper." Act of Jan. 27, 1816, ch. 4, 1815 Ohio Laws 10. Section 9 of the law provided that "all bonds, bills, notes, or contracts" of unincorporated banks "are hereby declared null and void." Act of Jan. 27 at § 9. However, section 11 and section 12 of the act went on to declare that "every stockholder" and "the persons who were interested in such bank" were "jointly and severally answerable, in their individual capacity, for the whole amount of the bonds, bills, notes, and contracts of such bank." See Act of Jan. 27 at §§ 11–12. The contradiction between these two sections left the enforceability of the Kirtland Safety Society notes in doubt. The uncertainty was further exacerbated by the fact that the validity of the 1816 law itself was open to doubt. In 1824, the Ohio legislature passed a further law that declared, "no action shall be brought upon any notes, or bills hereafter issued by any bank . . . unless such bank. . . . Shall be incorporated and authorized by the laws of this state to issue such bills and notes." See Act of Jan. 28, 1824, § 23, 1823 Ohio Laws 358, 365–66; see also Hill, Rooker, and Wimmer, "The Kirtland Economy Revisited," 437–41 (discussing the effect of legal uncertainty on the value of Kirtland Safety Society paper).

result was that the notes rapidly traded at a steep discount, which made it difficult for the Safety Society to build up its asset book by issuing loans.

An 1816 Ohio law provided that the officer of any unincorporated bank issuing notes "shall, for every such offence, forfeit and pay the sum of one thousand dollars."[67] The law also contained a qui tam provision that allowed a private party to sue on behalf of the state and keep one half of the recovery as bounty.[68] In 1837, a Samuel Rounds brought suit against Joseph Smith and other promoters of the Kirtland Safety Society.[69] Rounds, however, was a strawman paid $200 by Grandison Newell, an anti-Mormon agitator in Ohio, to bring the suit.[70] The suits against most of the other defendants were dropped, but those against Joseph Smith and his counselor Sydney Rigdon proceeded to trial. In 1824, the Ohio State legislature amended the 1816 law invoked in the Round's suit, and Smith and Rigdon likely could have successfully argued that the 1816 law was no longer in force. The Ohio Supreme Court later ruled this way in another case.[71] However, their counsel at trial never made this argument, and a judgment was entered against them. A short time later, fearing violence, Smith and Rigdon fled Ohio for Missouri. Until the end of his life, Smith made efforts to repay his Ohio debts, and both the judgments in the Rounds case were collected upon.[72] After Smith's death, Grandison Newell fraudulently persuaded the Ohio legislature to revive the judgments against Smith in a special act passed in 1859.[73] Newell then had an administrator appointed for the Smith estate in Ohio and sought to sell the Kirtland Temple to "satisfy" the already paid judgments, further clouding the already murky chain of title to the property.[74]

---

67. Act of Jan. 27, 1816, ch. 4, § 1, 1815 Ohio Laws 10, 10.

68. See Act of Jan. 27 at § 5.

69. See Walker, "The Kirtland Safety Society and the Fraud of Grandison Newell," 60–98 (recounting the Rounds litigation against Smith and Rigdon).

70. At common law, paying another to bring a lawsuit is the crime of maintenance.

71. See Johnson v. Benjamin Bentley et al., 16 Ohio 97 (1847).

72. See Gordon A. Madsen, "Tabulating the Impact of Litigation on the Kirtland Economy," in *Sustaining the Law: Joseph Smith's Legal Encounters*, ed. Gordon A. Madsen, Jeffrey N. Walker, and John W. Welch (Provo: BYU Studies, 2014), 233–42.

73. See Walker, "The Kirtland Safety Society and the Fraud of Grandison Newell," 100.

74. See Walker, 105, 127–39.

C. Missouri and Illinois

In Missouri, the Church had no legal personality for the simple reason that the Missouri Constitution explicitly provided that "no religious corporation can ever be established in this state."[75] As we have seen in New York, disestablishment after the Revolution took the form of opening the corporate form to all comers. In Virginia, however, disestablishment had taken a different form. Virginia's 1776 Declaration of Rights declared "[t]hat religion . . . can be directed only by reason and conviction, not by force or violence[.]"[76] In 1786, the Virginia Statute for Religious Freedom, authored by Thomas Jefferson, abolished tax support for churches.[77] The following decade, the Virginia legislature repealed laws that "establish any religious sect; and have incorporated religious sects, all of which is inconsistent with the principles of the constitution, and of religious freedom, and manifestly tends to the re-establishment of a national church."[78] For Virginia, disestablishment meant that churches had to be organized as a trust and lack any distinct legal personality, with all church property held by trustees. Missouri followed Virgina's model rather than New York's. It would be an oversimplification to call this a "southern" model of disestablishment, as some southern states allowed churches to incorporate.[79] It does, however, mark the difference in the legal culture between New York, where the Church emerged, and Missouri. The goal of Missouri law, following Virginia, was to keep churches even more institutionally weak than they were under the New York legal model. Coupled with the experience in Ohio, this meant that for most of Joseph Smith's career—from 1831 on—there was no effort to create a legal entity for the Church as such. As a legal matter, the temporal affairs of the Church were either managed by leaders acting in an individual capacity or through business partnerships. That changed when the Latter-day Saints founded their city of Nauvoo in Illinois.

The Latter-day Saints arrived in Illinois as refugees from Missouri in 1839. Eventually the Saints settled on the tiny village of Commerce,

75. Mo. Const. of 1820, art. XIII, § 5.

76. Va. Decl. of Rts. of 1776, art. XVI.

77. See generally Merrill D. Peterson and Robert C. Vaughan, eds., *The Virginia Statute for Religious Freedom: Its Evolution and Consequences in American History*, Cambridge Studies in Religion and American Public Life (New York: Cambridge University Press, 1988).

78. Act of Jan. 24, 1799, ch. 9, 1798 Va. Laws 8.

79. See, e.g., McGarvie, *One Nation under Law*, 131–51 (discussing general incorporation statutes for churches in South Carolina).

Illinois, as their gathering place. Renamed Nauvoo, it would be the headquarters of the Church—until the city was abandoned by the Saints in 1846. During the final stages of their Missouri sojourn, the Latter-day Saints sought to acquire title to land by settling on public land and making improvements. Technically, they were squatters, but following a well-established American pattern by that time, they anticipated that the federal government would enact a pre-emption statute. This would allow them to purchase the public land at favorable prices, based on their improvements. Indeed, one of the factors motivating those who drove the Saints from northern Missouri was a desire to take possession of improved Latter-day Saint land and thereby acquire the favorable pre-emption rights, something that the leaders of the Missouri mob were ultimately able to do.[80] In contrast, the Mormons acquired their right to real property in Illinois by purchase. Most of the large tracts of land on and near the future site of Nauvoo were purchased on credit, mainly from land speculators.[81] These large lots of land were then subdivided into small lots and sold to the gathering Saints so that the original debt could be repaid.

These purchases were made through "agents" acting on behalf of "the Church."[82] The Church, however, lacked any legal existence under Illinois law, and eventually much of this property was titled in the name of Joseph Smith, who found himself exposed to massive liability on the debt used to purchase the land. Beginning in 1840, the leaders of the Church made efforts to create a more formal legal existence for the Church. That year, the state legislature considered a slew of bills related to the Latter-day Saints, including the passage of the Nauvoo charter incorporating the Mormon city rising on the banks of the Mississippi.[83] On December 14, State

80. This story is recounted in detail in Jeffrey N. Walker, "Losing Land Claims and the Missouri Conflict of 1838," in *Sustaining the Law: Joseph Smith's Legal Encounters*, ed. Gordon A. Madsen, Jeffrey N. Walker, and John W. Welch (Provo: BYU Studies, 2014), 247–70.

81. See Glen M. Leonard, *Nauvoo: A Place of Peace, a People of Promise* (Salt Lake City: Deseret Book Co., 2002), 47–61.

82. See Matthew C. Godfrey, Spencer W. McBride, Alex D. Smith, and Christopher James Blythe, eds., *Documents, Volume 7: September 1839–January 1841*, vol. 7 of the Documents series of *The Joseph Smith Papers*, ed. Ronald K. Esplin, Matthew J. Grow, and Matthew C. Godfrey. Salt Lake City: Church Historian's Press, 2018), 534–38 [hereafter cited as *JSP*, D7]; Leonard, *Nauvoo*, 58–59.

83. See *JSP*, D7: 472–88; James L. Kimball Jr., "The Nauvoo Charter: A Reinterpretation," *Journal of the Illinois State Historical Society (1908–1984)* 64, no. 1 (April 1, 1971): 66–78; James L. Kimball Jr., "Protecting Nauvoo by

Senator Sidney Little, who represented Hancock County where Nauvoo was located, introduced "A Bill to Incorporate the Church of Jesus Christ of Latter-Day Saints."[84] The bill listed the names of Smith and a number of other Church leaders and declared that they and "members of the Church of Jesus Christ of Latter Day Saints, commonly called Mormons, are hereby created, constituted, and declared to be a body corporate and politic."[85] The law would have made the First Presidency "in conjunction with the General Assembly of said church, or the general Conference of said church . . . the law-making department of such corporation for all secular purposes."[86] The First Presidency were to be "trustees in trust for the church, for the acquisition, regulation, and disposal of" Church property. The corporation was given "full power and authority to do all such acts as they may consider necessary for the welfare and prosperity of said church" with the proviso that "no act shall be done repugnant to, or inconsistent with, the Constitution of the United States, or the constitution and laws of this state."[87]

The bill was never passed, and the absence of any documents discussing the proposal makes it difficult to interpret its significance.[88] In 1835, Illinois passed a general incorporation statute for churches, and some historians have speculated that the bill was dropped when this fact was brought to its sponsors' attention.[89] This explanation, however, overlooks the importance of the distinctions between the 1840 bill and the kind of corporation permitted by the 1835 law. Under the 1835 law, religious corporations could own no more than five acres of property, and the property had to be used "for the purposes of religious worship."[90] In contrast, the

---

Illinois Charter in 1840," in *Sustaining the Law: Joseph Smith's Legal Encounters*, ed. Gordon A. Madsen, Jeffrey N. Walker, and John W. Welch (Provo: BYU Studies, 2014), 297–308.

84. See *JSP*, D7: 450–55.

85. *JSP*, D7: 454.

86. *JSP*, D7: 454

87. *JSP*, D7: 454.

88. Procedurally, the state senate approved an amendment that completely deleted the content of the bill, replacing it with a proposal stating that the governor could appoint a notary public for Nauvoo. This amended bill was then passed. *JSP*, D7: 452.

89. This is the explanation offered by the Joseph Smith Papers Project, which first published the bill. See *JSP*, D7: 453–54.

90. Act of Feb. 6, 1835, 1834 Ill. Laws 147, 147 ("An Act Concerning Religious Societies"). Earlier scholars have suggested that during his lifetime, Joseph Smith

proposed incorporation of the Church would have allowed it to hold unlimited amounts of property for any purpose not otherwise prohibited by law. It is worth noting that under Illinois law the uses to which religious corporations could put their property were sufficiently restricted that, a few years later in 1845, the legislature felt that it was necessary to explicitly authorize religious societies to lease their property if the church found "it more convenient to occupy for worship some other lot or building."[91] It is possible, of course, that the very broad powers that would have been granted to the Church by the proposed incorporation were accidental, arising from the legal ignorance of those who drafted the bill.[92] However, it is striking that at the time, Joseph Smith and the Church were involved in what amounted to a massive real estate development of Nauvoo. Such a project would have been clearly beyond the legal power of a corporation created under the 1835 act, but the proposed law provided the Church with the precise legal powers it needed at the time.

The proposed incorporation also raises another intriguing possibility. Prior to the passage of the 1835 act, the Illinois legislature had not granted a special act of incorporation to any church. However, such special acts were not unknown under New York law, even after the passage of the first general incorporation statute for churches in 1784. Thus in 1830, when Smith first attempted to avail his movement of legal incorporation, there continued to be a de facto legal hierarchy among the state's churches.

---

and his associates were unaware of the restrictions on the ability of church corporations to own more than five acres (later increased to ten acres) under Illinois law. See Dallin H. Oaks and Joseph I. Bentley, "Joseph Smith and Legal Process: In the Wake of the Steamboat Nauvoo," *Brigham Young University Law Review* 1976 (1976): 776 ("There is no evidence that Joseph Smith or other Church leaders were ever aware of this 10-acre limitation on Church ownership of land"). However, Oaks and Bentley wrote prior to the discovery of the proposed incorporation by special statute. If one assumes that this statute was deliberately drafted, then it suggests that as early as 1840, Joseph Smith and his associates were likely aware of the mortmain provision in the Illinois general incorporation statute.

91. Act of Feb. 28, 1845, 1844 Ill. Laws 272, 272. This act had to be further amended in 1847 to allow churches to sell certain real property. See Act of Feb. 26, 1847, 1846 Ill. Laws 25, 25. While not directly applicable to all property that a church might own, these laws illustrate the assumption that the power of religious corporations to use or dispose of real property was limited.

92. This seems to be the position of the Joseph Smith Papers Project, which does not discuss the exceptional nature of the broad powers that the proposed incorporation would have granted to the Church. See *JSP*, D7: 453–54.

Most religious corporations, for example, were limited to holding $3,000 worth of property.[93] Nevertheless, a number of powerful congregations had obtained special statutes which allowed them to hold as much as three times that amount of property.[94] Likewise, an 1813 act for religious incorporation contained special procedures to accommodate the operations of the powerful Episcopal and Dutch Reformed churches.[95] It is possible that by seeking a special act of incorporation in 1840, rather than using Illinois's general incorporation statute, Smith and his followers were trying to signal Mormonism's status as a specially preferred religion, at least in Nauvoo. This might also explain why the state legislature refused to pass the law. The preamble to the 1835 law suggests that the Illinois legislature was sensitive to the kind of special privileges that were common in New York. Were the legislature to grant pleas for special incorporation, the preamble said, "it would lead to an endless system of partial legislation; and . . . all religious societies, of every denomination, should receive equal protection and encouragement from the legislature, and no one society be

93. Act of Mar. 27, 1801, ch. 79, 1801 N.Y. Laws 161, 164 (comprehensive "act to provide for the incorporation of religious societies" establishing a $3,000 maximum annual income for all churches except the Reformed Protestant Dutch Church in New York City and the First Presbyterian Church in New York City); Act of Apr. 5, 1813, ch. 60, 1813 N.Y. Laws 212, 215 (revised "act to provide for the Incorporation of Religious Societies" reiterating $3,000 maximum annual income for all churches except the two exempted by the 1801 act and further exempting St. George's Episcopal Church of New York and the Reformed Protestant Dutch Church of Albany from the limit).

94. See Act of Mar. 27, 1801, ch. 79, 1801 N.Y. Laws 161, 164 (the Reformed Protestant Dutch Church in New York City could lease property up to $9,000 in value and the First Presbyterian Church in New York City, up to $6,000); Act of Apr. 5, 1813, ch. 60, 1813 N.Y. Laws 212, 215 (same exceptions as the 1801 act, as well as allowances for St. George's Episcopal Church of New York to hold up to $6,000 worth of property and the Reformed Protestant Dutch Church of Albany to hold up to $10,000). See also Act of Mar. 5, 1819, ch. 33, § 3, 1819 N.Y. Laws 34, 34 (all churches in New York City were permitted an annual income of $6,000).

95. By the early nineteenth century, much of the Revolutionary era hostility to Episcopal tension in New York had dissipated, in part because of Alexander Hamilton's successful attack on anti-Tory confiscation statutes, which among other things were aimed at Trinity Church, before the state courts immediately after the Revolution. See Mensch, "Religion, Revival, and the Ruling Class: A Critical History of Trinity Church," 475–76.

granted exclusive privileges."[96] Exclusive privileges, however, are precisely what the proposed incorporation would have granted to the Church.

After the failure of these efforts, the Church availed itself of the Illinois general incorporation statute. At a special conference of the Church held on January 30, 1841, the membership voted to elect Joseph Smith as sole trustee for the Church. A week later, Joseph Smith filed a certificate of incorporation with the Hancock County clerk. In the document, Smith declared, "I was elected Sole Trustee for Said Church to hold my office during life (my successors to be the first Presidency of Said Church) and vested with Plenary Powers as sole Trustee in Trust for the Church of Jesus Christ of Latter Day Saints."[97]

Illinois law, following New York and that of most other jurisdictions, sought to enshrine the principle of lay control over ecclesiastical government. To a certain extent, Latter-day Saint ecclesiology, as it developed in the lifetime of Joseph Smith, contained echoes of this assumption. In particular, the authority of the general conference of the Church to ratify, and at times veto, actions taken by the hierarchy was largely consistent with this Protestant approach to church government. But by the Nauvoo period, Joseph Smith and his inner circle were developing a vision of ecclesiastical power increasingly centered on priestly authority rather than lay supremacy. At the heart of this ecclesiology were the Latter-day Saint temple rituals and the developing idea of "priesthood keys," both of which tended to centralize authority within the highest councils of the Church rather than in the membership as a body.[98] The 1835 act provided that "every society . . . shall have the power to provide for filling vacancies which may happen in the office of trustee and also to remove trustees from office."[99] The certificate filed by Joseph Smith, however, purported to remove this power from the general membership, insuring that succession as trustee was to be confined to the first presidency. More impor-

---

96. Act of Feb. 6, 1835, 1834 Ill. Laws 147, 147 ("act concerning Religious Societies").

97. Brent M. Rogers, Mason K. Allred, Gerrit J. Dirkmaat, and Brett D. Dowdle, eds., *Documents, Volume 8: February–November 1841*, vol. 8 of the Documents series of *The Joseph Smith Papers,* ed. Ronald K. Esplin, Matthew J. Grow, Matthew C. Godfrey, and R. Eric Smith. Salt Lake City: Church Historian's Press, 2019, 4–6.

98. See, e.g., Stapley, *The Power of Godliness*, 34–56 (discussing the development of Mormon ideas of priesthood and the liturgy associated with the temple).

99. Act of Feb. 6, 1835, 1834 Ill. Laws 147, 149.

tantly, Joseph and Emma Smith began executing deeds to transfer real property that he had held as an individual to himself as trustee for the Church. Emma's signature was likely required in order to extinguish her dower rights to the property. (Dower is a common-law doctrine that gave a widow the right during her lifetime to occupy some portion of the real property owned by her husband upon his death. Traditionally, the common law did not allow the husband to extinguish these rights unilaterally.) As a result, the Church soon purported to own real property far in excess of the five-acre limit contained in the 1835 statute. Furthermore, this property was being held for sale rather than "for the purposes of religious worship" as provided for by the statute.

The 1841 incorporation also seems to have given birth to a quasi-religious office that was retained thereafter in the Mormon movement: the trustee-in-trust. At common law it is unexceptional to convey property to "A as trustee, in trust for B." Such a deed splits legal and equitable ownership of the property, creating a trust in which A has title to the property but is required to manage it exclusively for B's benefit. General incorporation statutes borrowed concepts from trust law. Thus the 1835 Illinois statute explicitly referred to the agents of a religious corporation as "trustees." However, the idea of "trustee-in-trust" as a distinct office was a Latter-day Saint neologism, a truncating of the traditional conveyancing language of trusts into something new.[100] The trustee-in-trust became a quasi-ecclesiastical office designating the person with ultimate control over Church assets. This can be seen, for example, in the fact that the term "trustee-in-trust" as an office or legal status never appears in American case law except in reference to the Latter-day Saints.[101] Half a century later, the laws of Utah and surrounding states in the west with large Mormon populations would treat the term as referring to a religious rather than a legal office.[102]

---

100. See Samuel D. Brunson, "Mormon Profit: Brigham Young, Tithing, and the Bureau of Internal Revenue," *Brigham Young University Law Review* 2019, no. 1 (2019): 43 n.7 ("The term 'trustee-in-trust' seems to have been unique to Mormonism").

101. Interestingly, the term is used by both The Church of Jesus Christ of Latter-day Saints and the Community of Christ, formerly the Reorganized Church of Jesus Christ of Latter-day Saints. No non-Mormon denominations use the term.

102. See, e.g., Incorporation of Churches and Religious Societies, ch. 73, 1903 Utah Laws 62, 62 (allowing a "bishop, president, trustee in trust, [or] president of stake" to organize as a corporation sole). See also text accompanying infra notes 156–58.

In the succession crisis after Joseph Smith's murder in 1844, the office of trustee-in-trust proved important. At the time of his death, there were a half dozen or more different theories of who was to succeed him as leader of the Church.[103] Ultimately, Brigham Young and the Quorum of the Twelve Apostles persuaded the bulk of the Latter-day Saints to accept their claim to be carrying forward Smith's work. However, while Brigham Young and the Twelve succeeded in defeating the claims of Smith's counselor Sydney Rigdon at a conference in August 1844, it wasn't until December 27, 1847, that the First Presidency was formally reorganized.[104] While Brigham Young was signing letters as "Prest of the Church of L.D.S." as early as December 1844, his precise ecclesiastical authority beyond his undoubted title as president of the Quorum of the Twelve remained ambiguous for over three years.[105] However, the office of trustee-in-trust allowed Young and the Quorum of the Twelve to gain control of Church assets without resolving the question of their precise theological status. Likely based on the certificate of incorporation filed by Joseph Smith, many Latter-day Saints—including his widow Emma Smith—assumed that only the president of the Church could act as trustee-in-trust after Joseph Smith's death. Young and his associates rejected this position, and they succeeded in having a series of loyal, lesser Church officials appointed to this office. Brigham Young was thus able to control Church assets prior to settling the precise nature of the succession to the presidency.

The legal structure created in 1841 ultimately proved ineffective. Matters came to a head when a Nauvoo-based steamboat sank.[106] Joseph Smith had guaranteed a loan that the promoters of the steamboat had used to finance its purchase, and Joseph was left liable on the guarantee after it sank. In 1842, Congress passed one of its recurrent nineteenth-century bankruptcy laws, and Smith sought to take advantage of the law while it

103. See generally D. Michael Quinn, "The Mormon Succession Crisis of 1844," *Brigham Young University Studies* 16, no. 2 (1976): 187–233.

104. See Ronald W. Walker, "Six Days in August: Brigham Young and the Sucession Crisis of 1844," in *A Firm Foundation: Church Organization and Administration*, ed. David J. Whittaker and Arnold K. Garr (Provo: Religious Studies Center, Brigham Young University & Deseret Book, 2011), 161–96; Quinn, "The Mormon Succession Crisis of 1844."

105. Quinn, "The Mormon Succession Crisis of 1844," 216.

106. See Oaks and Bentley, "Joseph Smith and Legal Process."

was in force.[107] At the time of his death, Joseph's bankruptcy petition was languishing in federal court and would not be finally resolved until the 1850s. The court ultimately found that the efforts to segregate Smith's personal property from the property of the Church had been unsuccessful because of the mortmain provision in the 1835 statute. The chief beneficiary of this failure was his widow, Emma Smith. Because the conveyances from Joseph Smith as an individual to Joseph Smith as trustee for the Church were found to be invalid, Emma was able to assert her dower rights against the subsequent occupiers of the property. Had Smith not been murdered in 1844, it is unlikely that the legal structure under which the Church sought to promote the gathering to Nauvoo by selling real estate to new immigrants could have continued. Ultimately, Illinois law simply would not permit a church to engage in such expansive activity. Churches were to confine their activities to Sunday worship rather than dream of Zion and build new cities of God in the wilderness.

Legal uncertainty over the nature of the Church's property holdings also created conflicts with Joseph Smith's heirs after his death. Emma Smith was anxious to provide assets for her children, particularly as Smith's estate was likely to be depleted by the claims of his creditors.[108] This led to a series of negotiations between Brigham Young and Emma Smith over disputed property. The relationship between the two was already strained by their differing responses to Joseph Smith's plural marriages—Brigham accepted the doctrine, and Emma, after some initial prevarication, rejected it—and disputes about succession to the presidency. She saw Brigham's efforts to appoint a new trustee-in-trust as a move to deprive her and her children of their inheritance. For his part, Brigham believed that Emma was making

107. Prior to 1898, the United States had no permanent bankruptcy legislation. Rather, Congress periodically passed bankruptcy laws in response to financial downturns only to repeal them a few years later. See David A. Skeel, *Debt's Dominion: A History of Bankruptcy Law in America* (Princeton: Princeton University Press, 2004).

108. Emma Smith's biographers suggest that Emma inherited Joseph's debts and became liable on them, writing that on his death "Emma inherited a debt that would plague her for years." Linda King Newell and Valeen Tippetts Avery, *Mormon Enigma: Emma Hale Smith*, 2nd ed. (Urbana: University of Illinois Press, 1994), 200. This, however, is a misunderstanding of how the law worked. Debts are not transmitted to the heirs of the debtor. However, creditors of the deceased are entitled to be paid before heirs, which means that without substantial assets in the estate, Emma and her children were unlikely to receive anything after the creditors were satisfied.

unwarranted claims to Church property, particularly to Smith's papers. In the end, Brigham arranged for a series of cash payments to be made to Emma, and the bulk of the Saints abandoned Nauvoo with him before any kind of comprehensive settlement of the issues was reached.

IV. Legal Personality and the Battle with the Federal Government

In 1851 the legislature of the State of Deseret, the de facto government created by the Latter-day Saints upon their arrival in the Great Basin in 1847, granted the Church a corporate charter that eliminated the issues that had bedeviled the Church for the previous two decades.[109] It gave the Church the unlimited ability to hold property but did not break completely with American church law of the time. It conceptualized the Church as the corporate expression of the Church's members. It also contemplated ultimate lay control. Church officers in control of Church property were required to post bonds, and "said trustee and assistant trustees shall continue in office during the pleasure of said church."[110] At the same time, the statute was unique. It provided that the Church could "solemnize marriages compatible with the revelations of Jesus Christ," a sly way of providing legal recognition to polygamous unions.[111] It went on to provide that the Church's power for:

> [T]he pursuit of bliss, and the enjoyment of life, in every capacity of public association, and domestic happiness; temporal expansion; or spiritual increase upon the earth, may not legally be questioned: provided, however, that each and every act, or practice so established, or adopted for law, or custom, shall relate to solemnities, sacraments, ceremonies, consecrations, endowments, tithings, marriages, fellowship, or the religious duties of man to his Maker, insasmuch as the doctrines, principles, or performances, support virtue, and increase morality and are not inconsistent with, or repugnant to, the Constitution of the United State of this State and are founded in the revelations of the Lord.[112]

This exuberantly broad grant of powers seems to have carried forward and expanded the vision of the Church's legal capacity first sketched out in the failed 1840 proposal to the Illinois state senate. After Congress organized

109. See Dale Morgan, *The State of Deseret* (Logan: Utah State University Press, 1987), 185–87 (reproducing the statute).

110. Morgan, 186.

111. Morgan, 186.

112. Morgan, 186.

Utah Territory, the territorial legislature adopted the previous statutes of the now defunct State of Deseret, thus incorporating the Church under American law.[113]

In 1860 the Republican Party, which was founded to rid the territories of the twin relics of barbarism—slavery and polygamy—came to power. In 1862, Congress passed the Morrill Anti-Bigamy Act.[114] The centerpiece of the act was section 1, which made bigamy a crime in the territories.[115] However, the law contained two other provisions aimed at the Church's legal personality. Section 2 of the act invalidated the charter issued by the territorial legislature.[116] However, the law stated that "this act shall be so limited . . . as not to affect or interfere with the right property legally acquired under [the Church's charter] . . . but only annul such acts and laws which establish, maintain, protect, or countenance the practice of polygamy."[117] Section 3 went on to state that "it shall not be lawful for any corporation . . . for religious purposes to acquire or hold real estate . . . of a greater value than fifty thousand dollars."[118] Property "acquired or held" in violation of the act was to escheat to the United States, however "existing vested rights in real estate shall not be impaired by the provisions of this section." As was explained by the bill's manager in the Senate, "the third section . . . is in the nature of a mortmain law."[119] He went on to explain:

> The object is to prevent the accumulation of real estate in the hands of ecclesiastical corporations in Utah. Though the Territory is large, the value of real estate is not of large amount; and the object of the section is to prevent the accumulation of that property and wealth of the community in the hands what may be called theocratic institutions, inconsistent with our form of government.[120]

Interestingly, the House sponsor was careful to note that while the law applied to all territories, it would have no impact on the large Catholic establishments in New Mexico, as those religious institutions were pro-

---

113. Joint Resolution Legalizing the Laws of the Provisional Government of the State of Deseret, 1851 Utah Laws 205.

114. Morill Anti-Bigamy Act, ch. 126, 12 Stat. 501 (1862).

115. Morill Anti-Bigamy Act, ch. 126, 12 Stat. 501, § 1.

116. Morill Anti-Bigamy Act, ch. 126, 12 Stat. 501, § 2.

117. Morill Anti-Bigamy Act, ch. 126, 12 Stat. 501, § 2.

118. Morill Anti-Bigamy Act, ch. 126, 12 Stat. 501, § 3.

119. Cong. Globe, 37th Cong., 2d. Sess. 2506 (1862) (statement of Sen. Bayard).

120. Cong. Globe, 37th Cong., 2d. Sess. 2506 (1862) (statement of Sen. Bayard).

tected under the 1848 Treaty of Guadalupe Hidalgo which had ceded northern Mexico to the United States.[121] (Left unexplained is why the Church, not incorporated at the time but settled in Mexican territory in 1847, didn't receive protection under the Treaty.)

The effect of the Morrill Act was unclear. The property holdings of the Church as of its passage were unaffected. Whether the Church continued to have a legal existence seemed open to doubt, as the law could be construed to repeal only those portions of its charter that directly supported polygamy, leaving unaffected those provisions conferring legal personality. Given this ambiguity and the nation's immediate focus on the Civil War and Reconstruction, the law unsurprisingly remained a dead letter in Utah for more than a decade. Brigham Young responded to this uncertainty by claiming to hold Church property as trustee-in-trust regardless of the status of the Church as a legal entity. This meant that property was titled in Brigham Young's name but held on behalf of the Church. The precise nature of this holding, however, was uncertain. It was not clear that there was a common-law trust—in which case Young would have held "bare legal title" while "equitable title" would have been held by Church members as a whole—or if the property was owned outright by Brigham Young.[122] Upon Young's death in 1877, another bitter dispute between the Church and his heirs took place in the courts.[123]

Successive presidents of the Church continued to hold Church property personally as trustee-in-trust. In the early 1880s, Franklin S. Richards, the Church's legal counsel, foresaw that Congress was likely to pass further laws to escheat Church property and urged the creation of stake and ward corporations to which Church President John Taylor, as trustee-in-trust, could transfer Church property, thus shielding it from federal confisca-

---

121. Cong. Globe, 37th Cong., 2d. Sess. 2906 (1862) (statement of Rep. Morrill).

122. Brigham Young might also have held the property as a charitable trust, meaning that there was no identifiable group for whose benefit the property was held. In this case the property would simply have been held for a particular purpose, like advancing religion. Strictly speaking, the property couldn't be held in trust for the Church as an entity because, as a matter of law, no such entity existed.

123. See Leonard J. Arrington, "The Settlement of the Brigham Young Estate, 1877–1879," *Pacific Historical Review* 21, no. 1 (1952): 1–20.

tion.[124] It was difficult for the Church's lawyer to persuade Taylor and other leaders, but this was finally done around 1884. The law used was an 1878 territorial statute that allowed for the creation of corporations consisting of "persons associated together for religious, social, scientific, benevolent or other purposes"[125] but limited their ability to hold property. "[N]o such corporation," the statute read, "must own or hold more real estate than may be necessary for the business and objects of the association."[126] The resulting corporations were also cumbersome, requiring multiple trustees and the authoring of elaborate bylaws.

This structure created a variety of risks. First, relatively complex corporate formalities had to be maintained, or else the wards and stakes risked losing their corporate charters. Second, the acquisition and transfer of property required that the complex internal governance procedures of the corporations be followed exactly at the risk of invalidating the transfers. Third, upon the death or release of ward or stake officers serving as corporate trustees, relatively complex legal formalities had to be observed to replace them. Finally, because the corporations were self-governing entities, there was a risk that the Church hierarchy could lose control over Church property if enough local congregants wished to go their own way. All of these factors likely contributed to John Taylor's hesitancy in forming such corporations in the early 1880s, and his insistence that the governing board of trustees be as large as possible under the then-existing Utah law likely reflected concern about concentrating power over Church property in the hands of local leaders.

As Richards had predicted, Congress moved decisively against the Church in 1887 with the passage of the Edmunds-Tucker Act.[127] Beginning in 1874 with the passage of the Poland Act, which facilitated prosecutions under federal anti-bigamy laws, Congress had been steadily increasing legal pressure on the Latter-day Saints over the practice of plural marriage.

---

124. See Ken Driggs, "'Lawyers of Their Own to Defend Them': The Legal Career of Franklin Snyder Richards," *Journal of Mormon History* 21, no. 2 (October 1, 1995): 104. "Stakes" refer to regional collections of Latter-day Saint congregations analogous to a Catholic diocese. "Wards" refer to individual Latter-day Saint congregations.

125. Act of Feb. 22, 1878, ch. 18, § 1, 1878 Utah Laws 46, 46 ("act supplemental to An Act providing for Incorporating Associations for Mining, Manufacturing, Commercial and other Industrial Pursuits").

126. Act of Feb. 22, 1878, ch. 18, § 3.

127. Edmunds-Tucker Act, ch. 397, 24 Stat. 635 (1887) (repealed 1978).

This pressure intensified after the Supreme Court upheld the constitutionality of the Morrill Act in the 1879 case of *Reynolds v. United States.*[128] The Edmunds-Tucker Act represented the federal government's final move to escalate the conflict. The act's primary aim was to strike at the institutional basis of Latter-day Saint power in Utah and the surrounding territories. The centerpiece of the bill was a provision revoking the 1851 corporate charter granted to the Church and dissolving the corporation that the territorial legislature had created based on that charter. Proponents of the bill insisted that the purpose of the law was "to amend the incorporation of the church, so as to divorce it from the state."[129]

The House sponsor of the bill, John Randolph Tucker, was the scion of an important Virginia political family.[130] He served as attorney general of Virginia under the Confederacy, and later became a professor of constitutional law at Washington & Lee Law School.[131] For Tucker, the disincorporation of the Church was simply the final chapter in the process of disestablishment begun by "the immortal Thomas Jefferson in the immortal act for religious freedom of the people of the State of Virginia."[132] Furthermore, Tucker argued that unlike states, territories governed by Congress were subject to the full force of the Establishment Clause of the First Amendment.[133] For Tucker, disincorporation was a way to "disestablish the civil establishment" of the Church. He said, "I have in reality attempted to engraft the polity of old Virginia upon the polity of Utah. In old Virginia we do not allow the church to have any property except the property upon which the church building stands and that upon which

---

128. 98 U.S. 145, 166 (1879). For background on the *Reynolds* litigation and its aftermath, see Nathan B. Oman, "Natural Law and the Rhetoric of Empire: Reynolds v. United States, Polygamy, and Imperialism," *Washington University Law Review* 88, no. 3 (2011): 661–706.

129. 49 Cong. Rec. 584 (1887) (statement of Rep. Taylor).

130. He was the grandson of St. George Tucker, professor of law at the College of William & Mary and the author of a highly influential edition of Blackstone's Commentaries, and the nephew of John Randolph of Roanoke, Henry Clay's chief antagonist in Congress for much of his career. See John W. Davis, "John Randolph Tucker: The Man and His Work," in *The John Randolph Tucker Lectures Delivered Before the School of Law of Washington and Lee University* (Lexington: Journalism Laboratory Press of Washington and Lee University, 1949), 11–36.

131. See Davis, 11–12.

132. 49 Cong. Rec. 593 (1887) (statement of Rep. Tucker).

133. See 49 Cong. Rec. 595 (1887)(statement of Rep. Tucker).

the personage for its pastor is erected."[134] In his posthumously published treatise on constitutional law, Tucker characterized the act in terms of disestablishment, stating that it repealed "[a]ll laws giving special privileges to the Mormon Church."[135]

By the 1880s, however, Tucker's approach to disestablishment was increasingly anachronistic. The Jeffersonian attack on religious corporations in Virginia took place in a world where the creation of corporate entities was cumbersome and the idea of incorporation was closely tied to the agency of the state. New York began chipping away at this idea with its 1784 general incorporation statute, and a century later the legal landscape had shifted dramatically. In particular, in the decades after the Civil War the corporate form had been thrown open not only to churches but to private businesses and other enterprises.[136] Tucker insisted that the Church as an "ecclesiastical organism is a menace to the civil power" because of "the influence which concentrated and corporate wealth always acquires."[137] By 1887, however, it was relatively easy for Franklin S. Richards to fragment the legal personality of the Church and scatter the bulk of its property across dozens of corporate entities. As a result, by the time that the Edmunds-Tucker Act was passed, the corporate entity that it dissolved owned, ironically enough, comparatively little property.

Richards' strategy paid off when the Solicitor General of the United States ruled that property held by stake corporations was not subject to the Edmunds-Tucker Act.[138] Accordingly, federal officials made no effort to move against property held by those entities. The federal receiver, however, did take control of property not held by stake or ward corporations, including the Salt Lake Temple for a brief period.[139] Richards challenged the constitutionality of the Edmunds-Tucker Act in court, arguing that it violated the Contracts Clause of the US constitution under the *Dartmouth*

---

134. 49 Cong. Rec. 594 (1887)(statement of Rep. Tucker).

135. John Randolph Tucker, *Constitution of the United States: A Critical Discussion of Its Genesis, Development, and Interpretation*, ed. Henry St. George Tucker (n.p.: n.p., 1899), 668.

136. See generally Herbert Hovenkamp, *Enterprise and American Law, 1836–1937* (Cambridge: Harvard University Press, 2013), 11–67.

137. 49 Cong. Rec. 594 (1887) (statement of Rep. Tucker).

138. See Franklin S. Richards, "Reminiscences," Church History Library, Salt Lake City, Utah.

139. See Richards, "Reminiscences."

College Case.[140] In addition, a group of Church tithe payers intervened in the case, arguing that if the Church was to be dissolved, its property ought to revert to the original donors, instead of being allocated to the territorial schools as provided by the act.[141] During the debates over the act, its supporters in Congress had claimed that church property should be returned to the original donors if possible and that only the residue would be escheated for the benefit of public schools.[142]

Both the Utah Territorial Supreme Court and the US Supreme Court rejected all of these arguments, affirming the federal government's plenary authority over the territories and its ability to direct the Church assets to public purposes if it so chose.[143] Three members of the US Supreme Court dissented in a brief opinion by Chief Justice Fuller. While acknowledging Congress's power to criminalize polygamy in Utah despite the Latter-day Saints' plea of religious freedom, they insisted that Congress "is not authorized, under the cover of that power, to seize and confiscate the property of persons, individuals, and corporations, without office found, because may have been guilty of criminal practices."[144] Shortly after the constitutionality of the Edmunds-Tucker Act was upheld by the US Supreme Court in 1890, President Wilford Woodruff issued the Manifesto, which stated that the Church would no longer perform plural marriages.[145] In response, the Utah Territorial Supreme Court, which was administering the case, ruled that property should be returned to the trustee-in-trust to advance the legal, non-polygamous goals of the Church.[146]

---

140. See United States v. Church of Jesus Christ of Latter-day Saints, 5 Utah 361, 369 (Utah) (rejecting the argument based on *Dartmouth College*); see also Richards, "Reminiscences."

141. See Richards, "Reminiscences."

142. 49 Cong. Rec. 1898 (1887) (statement of Sen. Edmunds).

143. See United States v. Church of Jesus Christ of Latter-day Saints, 15 Pac. 473 (Utah 1887); Late Corporation of the Church of Jesus Christ of Latter-day Saints v. United States, 136 U.S. 1 (1890).

144. *Late Corporation*, 136 U.S. at 267 (Fuller, C. J. dissenting).

145. See Late Corporation of the Church of Jesus Christ of Latter-day Saints v. United States, 136 U.S. 1 (1890). See also Driggs, "Lawyers of Their Own to Defend Them" (discussing the relationship between the Supreme Court's decision and the Manifesto).

146. See United States v. Late Corporation of the Church of Jesus Christ of Latter-day Saints, 8 Utah 310 (1892).

V. Legal Personality in the Twentieth Century

Utah became a state in 1896, and the legislature adopted a law allowing for the incorporation of religious societies.[147] However, the Church chose not to avail itself of this law. Most local meetinghouses continued to be held by stake and ward corporations. The remainder of Church property was held by the president of the Church as trustee-in-trust. By this time, the Church had become heavily involved in the economic life of the Intermountain West.[148] This arose in part from the cooperative movement of the 1870s. By the time of statehood, the United Orders of Brigham Young's time had largely ceased to function, but many of the businesses that they spawned continued to live on as Church-owned enterprises. In addition, the Church had invested in a variety of businesses from the Union Pacific Railroad to the Utah salt industry as a way of fostering economic growth and a diversified economy. By the turn of the century, however, Latter-day Saint dreams of autarky were dead and Church-owned businesses were increasingly run along the lines of mainstream American capitalism.

By 1901, Richards had hit upon a new mechanism for holding Church property.[149] Borrowing the strategy adopted by the Catholic hierarchy in the United States, he proposed that stake and ward corporations be reorganized as corporations sole. Most corporations are fictitious persons who are the legal representative of some collective of natural persons, such as members of a church or shareholders in a company. A corporation sole, however, is the legal instantiation of an office—such as the King of England or the Bishop of Canterbury—that has but a single occupant.[150] The corporation sole is distinct from the natural person who occupies the office and thus persists when this person dies or when a new person takes office. Under the Utah law, a corporation sole could consist of a single

---

147. See Utah Rev. Stat. §§ 343–46 (1898).

148. See Leonard Arrington, *Great Basin Kingdom: An Economic History of the Latter-Day Saints, 1830–1900* (Cambridge: Harvard University Press, 1958); Arrington, Fox, and May, *Building the City of God.*

149. See generally Franklin S. Richards, "Corporations and Land Titles," Memorandum to the Presiding Bishop and the First Presidency, Nov. 2, 1931, Church History Library.

150. See generally F. W. Maitland, "Corporation Sole," *Law Quarterly Review* 16, no. 4 (1900): 335–54; M. W. S., "The Corporation Sole," *Michigan Law Review* 26, no. 5 (1928): 545–51.

person—either the stake president or bishop.[151] Furthermore, the identity of this person would be defined in terms of their ecclesiastical status. In other words, a bishop who died or was released would automatically cease to be the occupant of the corporation, which would continue to exist until his successor was chosen by the Church hierarchy. This eliminated the risk of title to Church property passing by operation of law to the heirs of Church leaders or of rogue leaders taking control of Church assets. Richards later wrote:

> It occurred to me that this system was admirably adapted to our condition, and after giving the matter careful consideration, I suggested it . . . to the First Presidency. After much deliberation they decided to adopt this plan, which involved the necessity of getting the legislatures of states where our wards and stakes were located to enact laws providing for the creation of corporations sole to hold title to church property. We finally succeeded, after much effort and persuasion in getting laws passed in Idaho, Utah, Nevada, Arizona, and Wyoming providing for corporations sole.[152]

In 1901, Rulon S. Wells, a member of the First Council of the Seventy then serving in the Utah House of Representatives, introduced a bill providing for the creation of corporations' sole, which passed unanimously.[153] Originally this statute was intended only for the use of wards and stakes. Thus, while only an "arch-bishop, bishop, overseer, presiding elder, rabbi or clergyman"[154] could formally be a member of the corporation, the corporation could not dispose of property without "the consent of the majority of the members of the church or religious society present at a meeting duly called for that purpose."[155] Such a procedure would clearly be too cumbersome for use by the president of the Church.

However, Richards's thinking on this topic continued to develop. In 1903, almost certainly at the discrete request of the Church, the Utah legislature replaced the 1901 statute with a new law governing corporations

---

151. Church and Charitable Incorporations § 2.

152. Franklin S. Richards, "Corporations and Land Titles," Memorandum to the Presiding Bishop and the First Presidency, Nov. 2, 1931, Church History Library.

153. See Church and Charitable Incorporations, ch. 80, 1901 Utah Laws 78. See also Andrew Jenson, "Wells, Rulon Seymour," in *Latter-Day Saint Biographical Encyclopedia* (Salt Lake City: Andrew Jenson History Co., 1901).

154. Church and Charitable Incorporations § 2.

155. Church and Charitable Incorporations § 4.

sole.[156] By this point, Richards seems to have been thinking of providing a corporate existence above the stake and ward level. The religious officials allowed to incorporate as a corporation sole now included "bishop, president, trustee in trust, [and] president of stake."[157] The inclusion of the term "trustee in trust" is particularly telling, because as we have seen, this term was a Mormon neologism coined in Nauvoo. However, it is also clear that the Church hierarchy had not yet decided to avail itself of incorporation. The evidence for this can be seen in the statute. Incorporating the trustee-in-trust as a corporation sole would eliminate the possibility of a dispute between the Church and the heirs of a deceased president of the kind that had broken out upon the deaths of Joseph Smith and Brigham Young. Richards, however, inserted a provision in the law providing that:

> [In the case of a] trustee in trust . . . who at the time of his death . . . was holding the title to trust property for the use or benefit of any church . . . and not incorporated as a corporation sole, the title to any and all such property . . . shall not revert to the donor, nor vest in the heirs of such deceased person, but shall . . . vest in the person appointed to fill such vacancy.[158]

In other words, the statute solved this problem without requiring the hierarchy to decide on whether to incorporate. Likewise, the 1901 provision that required a vote by Church members prior to the conveyancing of Church property was eliminated from the 1903 version of the law.

---

156. See Incorporation of Churches and Religious Societies, ch. 73, 1903 Utah Laws 62. While Richards did not explicitly claim authorship of the 1903 law, he did claim authorship of the 1901 law. See Franklin S. Richards, "Corporations and Land Titles," Memorandum to the Presiding Bishop and the First Presidency, Nov. 2, 1931, Church History Library. There is, however, very good reason to suppose that the 1903 law was authored and introduced in the state legislature at his request. The law was introduced by William Newjent Williams, an English convert to the Church who was married to Clarissa W. Smith, a daughter of apostle and counselor to Brigham Young, George A. Smith. Williams served as a missionary in Australia, and at the time he introduced the law, he was a high priest. Clarissa was the treasurer of the Church-wide Relief Society organization. In short, he was precisely the kind of loyal and well-connected Latter-day Saint that the Church would have used to get the law introduced. It was passed unanimously by the legislature. See Utah Senate Journal, 1903; *Biographical Record of Salt Lake City and Vicinity* (Chicago: National Historical Record Co., 1902), 279–81.

157. Incorporation of Churches and Religious Societies § 2.

158. Incorporation of Churches and Religious Societies § 9.

Issues came to a head in 1906 when Charles Smurthwaite, a disgruntled Latter-day Saint, sued the then-Church president, Joseph F. Smith.[159] Smurthwaite was joined in his suit by Don Carlos Musser, the scion of a prominent Mormon family who had previously served as the president of the Church's mission in the Middle East. The origin of Smurthwaite's and Musser's disaffection was complicated. They objected to the Church's political and economic influence, as well the practice of polygamists continuing to live with plural families after the Manifesto.[160] In addition, Smurthwaite's salt business was in direct competition with a Church-owned enterprise. Their suit came as national controversy over the election and the seating of apostle Reed Smoot to the US Senate was heating up.[161] Represented by Charles Zane, the former territorial chief justice who had presided over the proceedings against the Church under the Edmunds-Tucker Act, the plaintiffs alleged that Joseph F. Smith was misappropriating tithing funds by investing them in for-profit enterprises.[162] Zane's original argument was that the Church had been incorporated under Utah's religious corporations statute and that its actions were ultra vires.[163] The problem with this argument was that no such incorporation had actually occurred. Zane then argued that Smith received all tithing as a trustee for individual Church members.[164] Representing the Church, Franklin S. Richards argued that Zane needed to prove the individual intentions of tithe payers to establish the scope of any trust-based obliga-

---

159. See Nathan B. Oman, "Salt, Smurthwaite, and Smith: The Origins of the Legal Identity of the Church of Jesus Christ of Latter-day Saints," paper prepared for the 2020 Mormon History Association meeting (copy in the author's possession).

160. During this period some Church leaders also continued to perform new plural marriages in defiance of the Manifesto and the federal government, although this does not seem to have been an issue driving the Smurthwaite case. See generally D. Michael Quinn, "LDS Church Authority and the New Plural Marriages, 1890–1904," *Dialogue: A Journal of Mormon Thought* 18, no. 1 (Spring 1985): 9–105.

161. See generally Kathleen Flake, *The Politics of American Religious Identity: The Seating of Senator Reed Smoot, Mormon Apostle* (Chapel Hill: University of North Carolina Press, 2004).

162. For a brief biography of Zane, see Thomas G. Alexander, "Charles S. Zane: Apostle of a New Era," *Utah Historical Quarterly* 34, no. 3 (Fall 1966): 290–314.

163. Oman, "Salt, Smurthwaite, and Smith."

164. Oman.

tions applying to Smith as trustee-in-trust.[165] Finally, Zane argued that there was a public policy against churches investing in for-profit businesses.[166] As Richards pointed out, however, Zane was unable to point toward any authority supporting his position and, as Richards argued, it was quite common for churches to hold for-profit investments in support of their religious activities.[167] Ultimately, the non-Mormon judge in the case dismissed Smurthwaite's lawsuit.[168]

Richards did not explicitly link the *Smurthwaite* case to his accounts of the legal structure of the Church.[169] However, the case illustrated the problems created when the top hierarchy of the Church was left without any formal legal existence. Joseph F. Smith was styled as a trustee-in-trust, but in *Smurthwaite* Richards clearly wanted to resist the idea that the president of the Church was a trustee in the ordinary common-law sense. He could not be a trustee on behalf of the Church as a legal beneficiary because the Church did not exist as a legal entity. At the same time, to say that the president of the Church held Church property as a trustee for every Church member exposed him to enormous potential liability and thus created an opportunity for ecclesiastical disputes with disgruntled members to spill over into the courts. At the same time, as it had developed in the nineteenth century, the traditional assumptions of corporate law that applied to churches were essentially hostile to the hierarchical priesthood structure of Latter-day Saint ecclesiology. In particular, the emphasis on congregational structure worked awkwardly at best for holding denominational—rather than congregational—buildings such as the temples or mission homes. Likewise, the law's emphasis on lay control created a system in which ecclesiastical disputes could be refought in the courts, as happened repeatedly in other denominations during the nineteenth century.[170] The *Smurthwaite* case was an effort to apply this basic

165. Oman.

166. Oman.

167. Oman.

168. Oman.

169. See Franklin S. Richards, "Corporations and Land Titles," Memorandum to the Presiding Bishop and the First Presidency, Nov. 2, 1931, Church History Library; Franklin S. Richards, "Address Delivered by President Franklin S. Richards to the High Priests Quorum of the Ensign Stake, Sunday November 13, 1932," Church History Library.

170. See generally Gordon, "The First Disestablishment: Limits on Church Power and Property Before the Civil War"; Kellen Funk, "Church Corporations

approach to the Church, and in winning the case, Richards provided the Church hierarchy with the time to develop an alternative.

Ten years after the *Smurthwaite* case, the solution that had been latent in Utah law since 1903 was adopted when the Corporation of the Presiding Bishop of the Church of Jesus Christ of Latter-day Saints was organized.[171] Seven years after that, in 1923, Richards organized the Corporation of the President of the Church of Jesus Christ of Latter-day Saints, which finally created a formal legal structure for the Church completely independent of the personal identity of the hierarchy.[172] For most of the twentieth century, this dual structure of corporations sole provided the legal framework for the Church.[173]

The policy of widespread local incorporations begun in the 1880s, however, persisted for nearly a century. In 1903, Church headquarters began instructing bishops to avail themselves of the new law to incorporate as corporations sole.[174] These corporations would hold title to ward property, but all conveyancing of real property was centralized in the Church's counsel's office "as complications may arise that will be difficult to overcome."[175] In 1909, property held by local Relief Societies, the

---

and the Conflict of Laws in Antebellum America," *Journal of Law and Religion* 32, no. 2 (2017): 263–84.

171. See Franklin S. Richards, "Corporations and Land Titles," Memorandum to the Presiding Bishop and the First Presidency, Nov. 2, 1931, Church History Library.

172. See Franklin S. Richards, "Corporations and Land Titles."

173. In 2019, after more than a century, the Corporation of the Presiding Bishop was merged into the Corporation of the President, which has been renamed The Church of Jesus Christ of Latter-day Saints. See Human Resources Department, The Church of Jesus Christ of Latter-day Saints, "Further Changes to Emphasize the Correct Name of the Church of Jesus Christ," June 19, 2019 (email in the author's possession). Thus, for the first time since 1862, there is a legal entity bearing that name. However, The Church of Jesus Christ of Latter-day Saints as a legal matter remains a corporation sole, meaning that as of 2019 it has but a single member, Church President Russell M. Nelson. This odd structure is a legacy of Mormonism's effort to find a legal structure less infected with Protestant ecclesiology than that which was on offer in the legal world when it was born.

174. See The Church of Jesus Christ of Latter-day Saints, *Annual Instructions to Presidents of Stakes and Counselors, High Counselors, Bishops and Counselors and Stake Tithing Clerks of Zion* (Salt Lake City: The Church of Jesus Christ of Latter-day Saints, 1903), 10–12.

175. The Church of Jesus Christ of Latter-day Saints, *Annual Instructions to Presidents of Stakes and Counselors, Bishops and Counselors Stake Clerks and General*

Latter-day Saints' women's organization, was transferred to the bishop's corporations sole.[176] During this period the incorporation of stake presidents as corporations sole was left to the discretion of local leaders.[177] By the 1920s, however, the Church was organizing wards and stakes beyond the Mormon heartland of the Great Basin.[178] In California, for example, Latter-day Saints lacked the political power to pass the kind of bespoke legislation that the Church had obtained in Utah and the surrounding states. Accordingly, other legal mechanisms for holding Church property had to be found. However, by the mid-twentieth century the relaxation of the ultra vires doctrine and the increasing flexibility of the corporate form had rendered earlier difficulties the Church had faced anachronistic. Property could be held directly by the Corporation of the Presiding Bishop and the Corporation of the President, and the legal management of property had passed into the hands of the general counsel's office decades earlier.[179] By the late 1960s, except where required by local law, the Church had dispensed with ward and stake corporations, the final legal vestige of the Latter-day Saints' long conflict with the legacy of America's first disestablishment.[180]

Authorities of Zion (Salt Lake City: The Church of Jesus Christ of Latter-day Saints, 1906), 14–15.

176. See The Church of Jesus Christ of Latter-day Saints, *Annual Instructions, 1909* (Salt Lake City: The Church of Jesus Christ of Latter-day Saints, 1909), 28.

177. See The Church of Jesus Christ of Latter-day Saints, *Annual Instructions to Presidents of Stakes and Counselors, Bishops and Counselors Stake Clerks and General Authorities of Zion* (Salt Lake City: The Church of Jesus Christ of Latter-day Saints, 1910), 33.

178. See The Church of Jesus Christ of Latter-day Saints, *Handbook of Instructions for Bishops and Counselors Stake and Ward Clerks* (Salt Lake City: The Church of Jesus Christ of Latter-day Saints, 1928), 57–58.

179. See The Church of Jesus Christ of Latter-day Saints, *Handbook of Instructions for Bishops and Counselors Stake and Ward Clerks* (Salt Lake City: The Church of Jesus Christ of Latter-day Saints, 1928), 57 ("In some states, such as California, Colorado, New Mexico, Oregon, Montana, and a number of others, titles may be held by the 'Corporation of the Presiding Bishop' under varying conditions").

180. The 1963 edition of the handbook issued to bishops and stake presidents is the last one to include specific instructions about local church corporations sole. See The Church of Jesus Christ of Latter-day Saints, *General Handbook of Instructions* (Salt Lake City: The Church of Jesus Christ of Latter-day Saints, 1963), 93.

VII. Conclusion

Since its formal organization in April 1830, the Church has sought a legal personality, both as a way of solving concrete legal problems, such as the disposition of Church property upon the death of Church leaders, and as an expressive mechanism for gaining public legitimacy. However, the law created by America's first disestablishment was encoded with very definite ideas about what constituted legitimate activity for religious organizations. It took aggressively Protestant positions on church structure and government, insisting that church corporations should limit their activity to weekly worship services and remain firmly under lay control. The Latter-day Saints, in contrast, saw their church primarily as a mechanism for establishing Zion. In concrete terms, this meant that they needed mechanisms that would allow their Church to foster the creation of religiously inspired settlements on the American frontier under the hierarchical control of Mormon priesthood leaders. The conflict between these differing visions of a church provided grist for legal conflicts throughout the nineteenth century, long after we traditionally assume that the battles of the first disestablishment were over.

Ultimately, Mormon conflicts over the legacy of the first disestablishment point to a deeper issue in the relationship between religion and the state. Governments will always have their own vision of the proper role for religious institutions, and that vision does not often coincide with believers' own conceptions of their mission in the world. The result is legal conflict. Ironically, at the very moment the Church had finally found a congenial form under American law, it faced new versions of its old problems as it expanded beyond the borders of the United States. As early as 1913, the Church had run into difficulties in pursuing its nineteenth-century strategy of having property outside the United States held by the president of the Church as "Trustee-in-Trust."[181] Mexico, for example, has long placed legal restrictions on the ability of foreigners to own land.[182] Furthermore, succes-

181. See The Church of Jesus Christ of Latter-day Saints, *Circular of Instructions* (Salt Lake City: The Church of Jesus Christ of Latter-day Saints, 1913), 44 ("Title to mission property should be vested in the name of Joseph F. Smith, Trustee-in-Trust for the Church of Jesus Christ of Latter-day Saints, except in countries where a foreign trustee is barred by statute").

182. See Constitución Política de los Estados Unidos Mexicanos art. 27(I), Diario Oficial de la Federación [DOF] 05-02-1917, últimas reformas DOF 20-12-2019 (Mex.) ("For no reason may foreigners acquire the direct ownership of

sive waves of Mexican reform in the nineteenth and early twentieth centuries, aimed directly at the land holdings of the Catholic Church, resulted in mortmain provisions complicating the ecclesiastical ownership of land.[183] Again and again over the course of the Church's international expansion in the second half of the twentieth century, the Latter-day Saints found themselves facing the same issue that bedeviled them from the Church's legal beginnings in 1830: how to accommodate law and religious practice to one another when they have conflicting visions of what it is proper for a church to do.

---

lands or waters within a zone of one hundred kilometers along the frontiers and of fifty along the shores . . .").

183. William D. Signet, "Grading a Revolution: 100 Years of Mexican Land Reform," *Law & Business Review of the Americas* 16, no. Summer, 2010 (2010): 487–93.

CHAPTER 4

"We the People of the Kingdom of God": Mormon Constitution-Making and the Council of Fifty

In the spring of 1844, Joseph Smith created a secret organization called the Council of Fifty, which consisted of high Church officials and civic leaders, and tasked it with establishing the Kingdom of God, a political organization to be set up by the Latter-day Saints someplace on the North American continent in expectation of the imminent end times. This grandiose and abstract goal came amid very concrete concerns about the deteriorating political situation in Illinois and the felt need by the Mormons to look elsewhere for a place of refuge. Once operating, the Council of Fifty spent the lion's share of its efforts on the practical question of where to locate the projected Mormon commonwealth and how to escape from hostile neighbors and governments in Illinois and Washington, DC. On March 11, 1844, the Council appointed a committee of John Taylor, Willard Richards, W. W. Phelps, and Parley P. Pratt "to draft a constitution which should be perfect, and embrace those principles of which the constitution of the United States lacked."[1] Slightly more than a month later, on April 18, the committee reported a draft constitution to the entire Council. The authors, however, expressed their dissatisfaction with what they had produced, and it was returned to committee.[2] A week later, Joseph Smith announced to the Council a revelation abandoning the effort to draft a written constitution for the Kingdom of God, and the Council devoted the rest of its efforts to the more immediate problems facing the Saints, which ultimately culminated in the abandonment of Nauvoo after Joseph Smith's murder and the relocation en masse of the Saints to the Great Basin.[3]

---

1. Matthew J. Grow et al., eds., *Administrative Records: Council of Fifty Minutes, March 1844–January 1846*, The Joseph Smith Papers (Salt Lake City: Church Historian's Press, 2016), 54.

2. See Grow et al., 110–15.

3. See Grow et al., 134–35.

This bare statement of events casts the Latter-day Saints as radicals, operating scandalously outside the American political tradition.[4] The Treaty of Paris, which ended the American Revolution, placed the western border of the United States on the Mississippi River. Beginning with the Northwest Ordinance of 1785, Congress organized the area west of the Appalachian Mountains into discrete territories, with local governments under federal supervision. In time, these territories became states. With the exception of the unsuccessful effort to conquer Canada in the War of 1812, this orderly process of expansion continued as the United States government transformed the Louisiana Purchase and the cession of land from Mexico into territories and then states. Thus, the United States established itself as single polity occupying the center of North America. Within this narrative of unified national expansion at the expense of native tribes, Spain, France, and Mexico, the Mormon dream of an independent commonwealth and an alternative constitution is a jarring aberration.

The problem is that the narrative of smooth national expansion through a system of settlement, territorial government, and finally statehood is false. In the nineteenth century, North America was littered with abortive republics seeking varying levels of independence from the federal government and the other competing powers on the continent. Very early in the history of the United States, settlers formed breakaway polities on the borders of existing states. Vermont, for example, declared itself an independent republic before being incorporated as a state in 1791. The abortive State of Franklin, which would have sat athwart the Blue Ridge and Appalachian Mountains, was less successful.[5] In 1804 Aaron Burr, Thomas Jefferson's disgruntled vice president, began hatching plans to detach the western territories of the United States to form a new nation with himself at its head. Those efforts ended in failure when a coconspirator betrayed him to Jefferson in 1806.[6] Then in 1810, American settlers in

4. See, e.g., Grant H. Palmer, "Did Joseph Smith Commit Treason in His Quest for Political Empire in 1844?," *The John Whitmer Historical Association Journal* 32, no. 2 (2012): 52–58.

5. Echoes of the lost State of Franklin continued to reverberate as late as the Civil War, when east Tennessee continued to support the Union and attempted to secede from the Confederacy. See Eric Foner, *Reconstruction: America's Unfinished Revolution, 1863–1877*, 1st ed. (New York: Harper & Row, 1988), 62 (discussing the link between the State of Franklin and mountain separatism in Tennessee).

6. In fairness, Burr said so many different things to so many different people about his plans that it is difficult to determine his ultimate goals. See Gordon S.

Spanish territory declared the Republic of West Florida, raising the lone star flag that would be adopted by Texas revolutionaries a few decades later. In the 1830s, as the Mormon movement gathered steam, settlers in the disputed borderlands between Canada and the United States declared the tiny Indian Stream Republic.[7] More spectacularly, American filibusters in Mexico managed to detach the territory north and east of the Rio Grande to form the Republic of Texas, which operated as an independent nation for a decade from 1836 to 1846.[8] Shortly after the Council of Fifty adjourned its meetings in Nauvoo for the last time, American settlers in the Mexican province of Upper California declared the short-lived Bear Flag Republic.[9] As late as 1894, American businessmen in the Sandwich Islands formed the Republic of Hawaii, which operated as an independent nation for four years. Most dramatically, the Confederate States of America made a bid for political independence from 1861 to 1865.

In this welter of imagined states, drafting a written constitution was far from being a radical gesture: it was a well-established political ritual.[10] Most of these would-be constitution writers self-consciously modeled their work on the Constitution of the United States or on state constitutions. Hence, for example, the republics of Texas and Hawaii both had presidents and congresses, and the constitution of the Confederate States of the America copied much of the federal constitution verbatim. This is not to say that these documents didn't self-consciously seek to correct the perceived failures present in their models. Nineteenth-century Americans were frequently critical of the constitution of 1787 and willing to experiment. Likewise, the apparently stable and well-established route from territory to statehood was in fact ad hoc and anything but legally clear or

---

Wood, *Empire of Liberty: A History of the Early Republic, 1789–1815*, The Oxford History of the United States (New York: Oxford University Press, 2009), 384–85.

7. See Robert L. Tsai, *America's Forgotten Constitutions* (Cambridge: Harvard University Press, 2014), 18–48.

8. See generally Michael Van Wagenen, *The Texas Republic and the Mormon Kingdom of God*, 1st ed, South Texas Regional Studies, no. 2 (College Station: Texas A&M University Press, 2002).

9. See John A. Hawgood, "John C. Frémont and the Bear Flag Revolution: A Reappraisal," *Southern California Quarterly* 44, no. 2 (1962): 67–96; George Tays, "California Never Was an Independent Republic," *California Historical Society Quarterly* 15, no. 3 (1936): 242–43.

10. See Tsai, *America's Forgotten Constitutions*, 1–15.

well-established.[11] Thomas Jefferson, for example, called the 1820 controversy over the admission of Missouri a "fire bell in the night, [that] awakened and filled me with terror." He went on, "I considered it at once the knell of the Union."[12] Even more spectacularly, the controversy over the Taney Court's territorial jurisprudence in *Dred Scott v. Sandford*[13] galvanized the nascent Republican Party and helped bring on the Civil War.

It is only against this far messier background of American political history that we can see what was unique in the abortive constitution making of the Council of Fifty in March and April of 1844. The urge to establish a new republic in the liminal spaces of the continent and author a new constitution for it was not unique. Rather, in this Mormons stood firmly within an American tradition running from Aaron Burr to Sam Houston. What was unique was their effort to cast these structures in religious terms. Even in this, however, they were not entirely unique. John Brown's proposed constitution for a redeemed America spoke in apocalyptic religious terms and "We the People of the Confederate States" invoked "the favor and guidance of Almighty God" in their constitution.[14] Even more striking, the Mormons ultimately turned away from written constitutionalism in their process of constitution-making.

The Constitution in Joseph Smith's Revelations and Early Mormon Experience

Mormon political theology began with Joseph Smith's revelation commanding the Saints to gather for the formation of the New Jerusalem.[15] Mormonism emerged from the welter of competing millenarian sects. As

11. See generally J. W. Smurr, *Territorial Jurisprudence: What Judges Said About Frontier Government in the United States of America During the Years 1787–1900* (Ann Arbor: University Microfilms, 1970).

12. Thomas Jefferson, "Thomas Jefferson to John Holmes," April 22, 1820, series: Series 1: General Correspondence. 1651–1827 Microfilm Reel: 051, Library of Congress, https://www.loc.gov/item/mtjbib023795/.

13. 60 U.S. 393 (1857).

14. See Tsai, *America's Forgotten Constitutions*, 83–117; "Constitution of the Confederate States, March 11, 1861," The Avalon Project, Yale Law School, accessed August 22, 2016, http://avalon.law.yale.edu/19th_century/csa_csa.asp.

15. For works on LDS political theology, see Patrick Q. Mason, "God and the People: Theodemocracy in Nineteenth-Century Mormonism," *Journal of Church and State* 55, no. 3 (Summer 2013): 349–75; Jeremiah John, "The Site of Mormon Political Theology," *Perspectives on Political Science* 40 (2011): 87–96.

their name affirmed, the Latter-day Saints believed that they were living in the end times. However, despite their sense of Christ's imminent return, Mormons ultimately located the millennium in space rather than in time.[16] The question was less precisely *when* the *parousia* would occur than *where* the Saints should begin establishing Zion to meet it. As a result of the gathering, Latter-day Saints formed concrete Mormon communities, which in the democratic context of Jacksonian America meant that they inevitably found themselves wielding political power and influence—to the horror of their non-Mormon neighbors. This local political power became especially explosive because of Joseph Smith's claim to receive direct revelation from God and the authority with which Mormons invested Smith's direction.[17] The gathering thus imposed two imperatives on Mormon thought. The first was to imagine the shape of the Zion to be built by the Saints. The second was to cope with the practical and cognitive problems created by Gentile hostility to their efforts to realize that Zion. It was this second issue that gave rise to Joseph Smith's revelations about the constitution.

Contemporary Mormons often affirm that their scriptures teach about "the divinely inspired constitution" of the United States.[18] However, the revelations of Joseph Smith do not contain this phrase. The constitution makes its first appearance in those revelations in August 1833.[19] Earlier, Joseph Smith had received revelations commanding the Saints to gather in Jackson County, Missouri, and promising that they would receive the law of the Lord. In 1831 that promised law had been received in a revelation that set forth communal property arrangements and claimed at least quasi-sovereign authority for Mormon revelations.[20] In July 1833,

16. See Nathan B. Oman, "A Local Faith," *Brigham Young University Studies* 49, no. 2 (2010): 163–72.

17. See Steven C. Harper, "'Dictated by Christ': Joseph Smith and the Politics of Revelation," *Journal of the Early Republic* 26, no. 2 (2006): 275–304.

18. See Dallin H. Oaks, "The Divinely Inspired Constitution," *Ensign*, February 1992, https://www.lds.org/ensign/1992/02/the-divinely-inspired-constitution.

19. See Mark Ashurst-McGee, "Zion in America: The Origins of Mormon Constitutionalism," *Journal of Mormon History* 38, no. 3 (2012): 90–101 (discussing the context of these revelations).

20. This "law," given over two days, is now canonized as Doctrine & Covenants 42 and evidences a schizophrenic attitude toward its own legal authority, both claiming absolute sovereignty for divine law and also retreating from those claims in the face of conflict with secular law. See generally Nathan B. Oman, "'I Will Give Unto You My Law': Section 42 as a Legal Text and the Paradoxes of Divine Law," in *Embracing*

Mormon leaders in Missouri were forced to agree to abandon their Zion in Jackson County. However, Joseph Smith was located in Kirtland, Ohio, at the time and was unaware of the expulsion of the Saints.[21] Nevertheless, the worsening affairs in Missouri seem to have been on his mind when he dictated a revelation in which the Lord stated:

> And that law of the land which is constitutional, supporting that principle of freedom in maintaining rights and privileges, belongs to all mankind, and is justifiable before me. Therefore, I, the Lord, justify you, and your brethren of my church, in befriending that law which is the constitutional law of the land; and as pertaining to the law of man, whatsoever is more or less than this, cometh of evil. I, the Lord God, make you free, therefore ye are free indeed; and the law also maketh you free. Nevertheless, when the wicked rule the people mourn. Wherefore, honest men and wise men should be sought for diligently, and good men and wise men ye should observe to uphold; otherwise whatsoever is less than these cometh of evil. (D&C 98:4–10)

A few months later, having heard the details of the increasingly intense pressure on Mormons in Missouri, Joseph dictated a second revelation in which the Lord said:

> Therefore, it is not right that any man should be in bondage one to another. And for this purpose have I established the Constitution of this land, by the hands of wise men whom I raised up unto this very purpose, and redeemed the land by the shedding of blood. (D&C 101:79–80)

Even as late as 1836, Joseph Smith pleaded in the Kirtland Temple dedication with the Lord, "have mercy upon the rulers of our land; may those principles, which were so honorably and nobly defended, namely, the Constitution of our land, by our fathers, be established forever" (D&C 109:54). These revelations represent the appearance of the US Constitution in the revelations of Joseph Smith, which had previously spoken only of God's law. As Mark Ashurst-McGee notes, "Formerly disengaged from outside politics and politicians, the Saints were now to support those Gentile officials who were willing to uphold laws consistent with the principles of freedom articulated in the US Constitution."[22]

---

the Law: Reading Doctrine and Covenants 42, ed. Jeremiah John and Joseph M. Spencer (Provo: Neal A. Maxwell Institute for Religious Scholarship, 2017).

21. See David Grua, "Waiting for the Word of the Lord," Church History, The Church of Jesus Christ of Latter-Day Saints, April 18, 2016, https://history.lds.org/article/waiting-for-the-word-of-the-lord?lang=eng.

22. Ashurst-McGee, "Zion in America: The Origins of Mormon Constitutionalism," 94.

From a constitutional perspective, the most striking thing about these passages is how ordinary they are by the standards of the time. The idea that the US Constitution in part embodied general principles of freedom and justice was widely accepted. Likewise, the providential role of God in the founding of America was commonplace. Furthermore, the passages presented a conservative and even anachronistic vision of politics. Modern political scientists have identified contemporary American politics with what they call the procedural republic, a system where the public interest is supposed to emerge from competition between interest groups that are pursuing narrow agendas within the context of a supposedly neutral constitutional order.[23] Joseph Smith's revelations, however, did not present the US constitution in these familiar modern terms. Rather, they present politics as essentially adjudicative, with "honest men and wise men" (D&C 98:10) and "wise men whom I raised up unto this very purpose" (D&C 101:80), applying the "principle of freedom in maintaining rights and privileges" (D&C 98:5) as "rulers of our land" (D&C 109:54). This vision is republican and aristocratic, focusing on wise statesmen above party or faction. Absent is any valorization of democracy or the common man. In the voice of Joseph Smith's God, vox populi is not vox dei. Rather, the ideal is of virtuous leaders, what John Adams called a "natural Aristocracy of 'Virtues and Talents,'"[24] disinterestedly applying timeless principles. In this, Joseph Smith's early constitutional revelations hearken back to the republican tradition that animated early American politics.[25] Crucially, this adjudicative model of statesmanship made the emergence of organized political parties and mass political movements disconcert-

---

23. See V. O. Key, *Politics, Parties, & Pressure Groups*, 5th edition (New York: Crowell, 1964); Richard Hofstadter, *The American Political Tradition: And the Men Who Made It*, reissue edition (New York: Vintage, 1989). Louis Menand identifies the intellectual origins of this vision in the American pragmatist tradition, which emerged only after the Civil War. See Louis Menand, *The Metaphysical Club: A Story of Ideas in America*, reprint edition (New York: Farrar, Straus and Giroux, 2002). However, one can find intimations of it, if one is so inclined, as early as "Federalist No. 10." See Alexander Hamilton, John Jay, and James Madison, "Federalist No. 10" in *The Federalist: A Commentary on the Constitution of the United States*, ed. Robert Scigliano (New York: Modern Library, 2001).

24. Thomas Jefferson and John Adams, *The Adams-Jefferson Letters*, ed. Lester J. Cappon (Chapel Hill: University of North Carolina Press and the Omohundro Institute of Early American History and Culture, 1988), 400.

25. See Gordon S. Wood, *The Creation of the American Republic, 1776–1787* (Chapel Hill: University of North Carolina Press, 1998).

ing for many nineteenth-century Americans.[26] It was difficult to see such politics as anything other than a fall from a more noble past into a grubby and amoral tourney of selfish factions.[27]

By 1840, Mormon faith in this constitutional model had been shattered. Events in Missouri had played themselves out to their bitter conclusion, with the expulsion first from Jackson County and then from the entire state. Mormon property had been seized, Mormons had been massacred by mobs, Mormon women had been raped, and Governor Lilburn Boggs had issued his extermination order. Efforts at relief before the courts of Missouri were futile. Finally, in obedience to an 1834 revelation commanding him to seek redress, Joseph Smith traveled to Washington, DC, to petition the nation's statesmen for relief. There he ran up against the realities of antebellum federalism and the electoral needs of Martin Van Buren's embattled Democratic Party.[28] Indeed, there is an almost perfect symmetry in the fact that Joseph Smith came to Washington based on a vision of adjudicative politics by a natural aristocracy to meet Van Buren, who wrote and posthumously published one of the first analyses and defenses of mass political parties in American history.[29] That disjunction proved decisive for the political development of Mormonism. In the end the federal constitution was wholly inadequate as a mechanism for

26. Compare Wood, *Empire of Liberty*, 34–35. While dated, see also Richard Hofstadter, *The Idea of a Party System: The Rise of Legitimate Opposition in the United States, 1780–1840* (Berkeley: University of California Press, 1970).

27. Consider, for example, how John Taylor presented the pursuit of private interests in politics in 1852:

> Those private, jarring interests have kept the world in one continual ferment and commotion from the commencement until the present time; and the history of the world is a history of the rise and fall of nations—of wars, commotions, and bloodshed—of nations depopulated, and cities laid waste. Carnage, destruction, and death, have stalked through the earth, exhibiting their horrible forms in all their cadaverous shapes, as though they were the only rightful possessors.

John Taylor, *The Government of God* (Liverpool: S. W. Richards, 1852), 8.

28. See Ronald O. Barney, "Joseph Smith Goes to Washington," in *Joseph Smith, the Prophet and Seer*, by Richard Neitzel Holzapfel and Kent P. Jackson (Provo: Religious Studies Center, Brigham Young University, 2010), 391–420.

29. See Martin Van Buren, *Inquiry into the Origin and Course of Political Parties in the United States*, ed. Abraham Van Buren and John Van Buren (New York: Hurd and Houghton, 1867).

protecting Mormon rights, and in Mormon eyes "honest men and wise men" were nowhere to be seen in high office. This sense of betrayal and alienation only deepened with the murders of Joseph and Hyrum Smith. In the spring of 1845, W. W. Phelps said before the Council of Fifty, "[W]hat is the patriotism of these United States—fifteen thousand souls driven from their homes in Missouri and no means made use of to restore them to us, or redress our wrongs and to finish off with, they have spilt our best blood."[30] More poignantly, during the same period, Heber C. Kimball made a motion before the Council "that we declare ourselves an independent nation," to which Orson Pratt replied "he did not think it necessary inasmuch as the nation has already made us independent."[31] It was in this context of deepening disillusionment toward the United States and its legal institutions that the Council of Fifty embarked on its constitution-making project.

The Written Constitution of the Kingdom of God

There are two features of the text presented by Taylor, Richards, Phelps, and Pratt that are immediately apparent. The first is that unlike most efforts at American constitution-making, the document was written without copying from an existing constitution. To be sure, there are echoes of the federal constitution in its very basic structure. The document begins with a preamble announcing its authors as "We the people of the people of the Kingdom of God,"[32] and it is divided into articles like the constitution of 1787. However, there is no copying of governing structure or text from that constitution or any other. As the committee explained, in writing the document "They cant refer to any constitution of the world because they are corrupt."[33] The second feature is that the constitution is in no sense a practical document. Only in the final article is there any effort to articulate procedures or institutions for governing a community, and then only in the most skeletal form. In this sense, it is perhaps closer in genre to the Declaration of Independence, which propounded a theory of just government, as opposed to the constitution of 1787, which contained elaborate rules on such eminently practical subjects as taxation and the spending of

30. Grow et al., *Administrative Records: Council of Fifty Minutes, March 1844–January 1846*, 288.

31. Grow et al., 454.

32. Grow et al., 110.

33. Grow et al., 114.

government money. As written, the constitution of the Kingdom of God was less an effort to construct a working legal system than to set forth a theory of government.

Roughly half of the document consisted of a prolonged preamble condemning all contemporary political arrangements. The preamble concludes:

> We have supplicated the great I am, that he would make known his will unto his servants, concerning this, his last kingdom, and the law by which his people shall be governed: And the voice of the Lord unto us was,—Verily thus saith the Lord, this the name by which you shall be called, the kingdom of God and his Laws, with the keys and power thereof, and Judgement in the hands of his servants Ahman Christ . . .[34]

The second half of the document consists of three articles in which "I . . . the Lord thy God" rather than "We the People of the Kingdom of God" speaks in the first person. The constitution thus aspires to be a direct revelation from God, consistent with the claim in the preamble that "the supreme law of the land shall be the word of Jehovah,"[35] a stark and perhaps deliberate contrast to Article VI of the US Constitution, which declares that the "supreme law of the law" shall be the constitution, laws, and treaties of the United States.[36]

The critique of existing governments begins with the assertion of the sovereignty of God.[37] "[A]ll power emanates from God . . . and he alone

---

34. Grow et al., 112. Joseph Smith had announced this name earlier to the Council of Fifty, and the name referred not only to the commonwealth to be established but to the Council itself, which was conceptualized as the commonwealth in embryo. See Andrew F. Ehat, "'It Seems Like Heaven Began on Earth': Joseph Smith and the Constitution of the Kingdom of God," *Brigham Young University Studies* 20, no. 3 (1980): 253–79.

35. Grow et al., *Administrative Records: Council of Fifty Minutes*, 111.

36. See U.S. Const. art. vii, cl. 2 ("This Constitution, and the Laws of the United States which shall be made in Pursuance thereof; and all Treaties made, or which shall be made in Pursuance thereof; and all Treaties made, or which shall be made, under the Authority of the United States, shall be the supreme Law of the Land; and the Judges in every State shall be bound thereby, any Thing in the Constitution or Laws of any State to the Contrary notwithstanding").

37. The structure and language of the argument of the preamble is strikingly similar to the arguments that John Taylor was to lay out in an 1852 pamphlet. It's possible, of course, that both were simply influenced by the ideas promulgated or discussed in the Council of Fifty or that the constitution of the kingdom of God influenced Taylor's later writings. I suspect, however, that John Taylor was

has the right to govern the nations and set in order the kingdoms of this world."[38] The "We the people" of this document is thus fundamentally different than the "We the people" of the constitution of 1787 which claimed itself as a sufficient font of sovereignty.[39] Mormon political thinking on the nature of sovereignty had already begun moving in this direction nearly a decade earlier, when the Church's 1835 declaration of beliefs regarding governments stated:

> We believe that governments were instituted of God for the benefit of man; and that he holds men accountable for their acts in relation to them, both in making laws and administering them, for the good and safety of society. (D&C 134:1)[40]

However, by 1844 Taylor, Richards, Phelps, and Pratt were prepared to state categorically that all existing governments were illegitimate because "none of the nations, kingdoms or governments of the earth do acknowledge the creator of the Universe as their Priest, Lawgiver, King and Sovereign, neither have they sought unto him for laws by which to govern themselves."[41] Rather, they believed that "all nations have obtained their power, rule and authority by usurpation, rebellion, bloodshed, tyranny and fraud."[42] This is a Hobbesian vision of the state unredeemed even by Hobbes's contractual

the author of at least the preamble. Compare Taylor, *The Government of God*, chs. 1 and 2.

38. Grow et al., *Administrative Records: Council of Fifty Minutes*, 110.

39. Compare U.S. const. preamble ("We the people of the United States, in order to form a more perfect union, establish justice, insure domestic tranquility, provide for the common defense, promote the general welfare, and secure the blessings of liberty to ourselves and our posterity, do ordain and establish this Constitution for the United States of America").

40. While it has been argued that the political theory behind section 134 comes out of the political theory of the Scottish Enlightenment as filtered through the founding generation, Fred Gedicks has persuasively argued that its account of political sovereignty differs markedly from the standard account of American constitutional law. Compare Rodney K. Smith, "James Madison, John Witherspoon, and Oliver Cowdery: The First Amendment and the 134th Section of the Doctrine and Covenants," *Brigham Young University Law Review* 2003, no. Spring (2003): 891–940; Frederick Mark Gedicks, "The Embarrassing Section 134," *Brigham Young University Law Review* 2003, no. Spring (2003): 959–72.

41. Grow et al., *Administrative Records: Council of Fifty Minutes*, 111.

42. Grow et al., 111.

justification for Leviathan.[43] Indeed, in its uncompromising insistence on the exclusive sovereignty of God, the preamble bears a more striking resemblance to classical Islamic legal theories than to the liberal and republican traditions from which the US Constitution emerged.[44]

Despite the stark theocentrism of this theory of political legitimacy, the preamble also invoked two ideas familiar to liberal democratic theory: the rights of man and utility. Because existing governments arise from "usurpation, rebellion, bloodshed, tyranny and fraud," they lack "the disposition and power to grant the protection of the persons and rights of man, viz life, liberty, possession of property, and pursuit of happiness, which was designed by the creator of all men."[45] The debt to the Declaration of Independence's vision of men "endowed by their Creator with certain unalienable Rights, that among these are Life, Liberty and the pursuit of Happiness" is clear. The usurpations of human governments also result in human suffering. The preamble declares, "the natural results of these illegitimate governments" are "cruelty, oppression, bondage, slavery, rapine, bloodshed, murder, carnage, desolation, and all the evils that blast the peace, exaltation, and glory of the universe."[46] From the cosmic "glory of the universe," the preamble descends to what was no doubt a descrip-

---

43. Compare Thomas Hobbes, *The Leviathan* (New York: Barnes & Noble Books, 2004), 77 (claiming that in the state of nature there is "continuall feare, and danger of violent death; And the life of man, solitary poor, nasty, brutish, and short").

44. As one historian of Islamic law summed up the classical theory:

> Western jurisprudence has provided a number of different answers to the question of the nature of law, variously finding its sources to lie in the orders of a political superior, in the breasts of the judiciary, in the "silent, anonymous forces" of evolving society, or in the very nature of the universe itself. For Islam, however, this same question admits of only one answer which the religious faith supplies. Law is the command of God; and the acknowledged function of Muslim jurisprudence, from the beginning, was simply the discovery of the terms of that command.

Noel J. Coulson, *A History of Islamic Law* (Edinburgh: Edinburgh University Press, 1964), 75. See also Nathan B. Oman, "Preaching to the Court House and Judging in the Temple," *Brigham Young University Law Review* 2009, no. 1 (2009): 185–87 (comparing decision-making in Mormon courts to Islamic jurisprudence and discussing reasons for the divergent approaches to divine law).

45. Grow et al., *Administrative Records: Council of Fifty Minutes*, 111.

46. Grow et al., 112.

tion of contemporary American politics from the Mormon point of view, insisting that by ignoring God governments have bred "pride, corruption, impurity, intrigue, spiritual wickedness in high places, party spirit, faction, perplexity and distress of nations."[47] This is the voice of someone whose hopes of a political order in the "hands of wise men whom [the Lord] raised up unto this very purpose" (D&C 101:80) had been dashed on the realities of party and regional politics in democratic America. In response to this disappointment, the voice of the Lord in the three articles of the constitution presents an even more extreme version of this vision of adjudicative politics.

In article 1, the Lord announces that he rules "the armies of heaven above, and among the nations of the earth beneath."[48] He goes on to insist that "I alone am the rightful law giver of man."[49] Intentionally or unintentionally, this claim mirrors the structure of the US Constitution, where Article I also begins with the law-making power, declaring in contrast that "[a]ll legislative powers herein granted shall be vested in a Congress of the United States, which shall consist of a Senate and House of Representatives."[50] In article 2 of the Mormon document, "wise men raised up for this very purpose" are replaced with even more inspired agents of God's providence:

> I the Lord will do nothing but what I have revealed or shall reveal unto my servants the prophets and I have appointed one man, holding the keys and authority, pertaining to my holy priesthood, to whom I will reveal my laws, my statutes, my ordinances, my Judgements, my will and pleasure concerning my kingdom on the earth.[51]

Wise statesmen adjudicating the public good have been replaced by an inspired prophet announcing God's designs.[52] Both sit above the "pride,

---

47. Grow et al., 111.
48. Grow et al., 114.
49. Grow et al., 114.
50. U.S. const. art I §1.
51. Grow et al., *Administrative Records: Council of Fifty Minutes*, 114.
52. Compare the statement of an anonymous editorial in the *Times & Seasons* supporting Joseph Smith's bid for the US presidency in February 1844:

> Executive power, when correctly wielded, is a great blessing to the people of this great commonwealth, and forms one of the firmest pillars of our confederation. It watches the interests of the whole community with a fatherly care; it wisely balances the other legislative powers when over-heated by party spirit or sectional feelings; . . . The President stands at the head of

corruption, impurity, intrigue, spiritual wickedness in high places, party spirit, faction" of a corrupt democracy. In the Council of Fifty, however, the aristocracy of republican virtue is transformed into the spiritual aristocracy of priestly and prophetic authority. Only in article 3, which is literally the single, final sentence of the document, do we find anything that resembles the ordinary subject of written constitutions, namely governing procedures. "My Servant and Prophet whom I have called and chosen shall have power to appoint Judges and officers in my kingdom, and my people shall have the right to choose or refuse those officers by common consent . . . and if the judges or officers transgress, they shall be punished according to my laws."[53] This is also the only place in which the will of the people is given any play in the vision of the Kingdom of God. It is an attempt to find a place for democracy in a political vision that ultimately rejects the idea of popular sovereignty. Three days before the committee reported their draft constitution to the Council, Joseph Smith had published an article in the *Times & Season* as part of his presidential campaign, writing, "I go emphatically, virtuously, and humanely, for a theodemocracy, where God and the people hold the power to conduct the affairs of men in righteousness."[54] Theodemocracy, however, was not merely a religious synonym for the democratic elections of the 1840s, where the voice of the expanding electorate was taken to be supreme. As a constitutional matter, the mechanism in the Constitution of the Kingdom of God looks rather more like the assemblies of the Roman Republic, copied during the French Revolution, in which voters were allowed only to approve or veto the proposals of magistrates. The Mormon model, however, was clearly the emerging ecclesiology of the Church, in which members were asked to give their assent and support to the revelations of the leadership.[55]

> these United States, and is the mouth-piece of this vast republic. If he be a man of an enlightened mind and a capacious soul,—if he be a virtuous man, a statesman, a patriot, a man of unflinching integrity,—if he possesses the same spirit that fired the souls of our venerable sires, who founded this great commonwealth, and wishes to promote the good of the whole republic, he may indeed be made a blessing to the community.

"Who Shall Be Our Next President," *Times & Seasons*, February 15, 1844.

53. Grow et al., *Administrative Records: Council of Fifty Minutes*, 114.

54. Joseph Smith, Jr., "The Globe," *Times & Seasons*, April 15, 1844.

55. Compare Richard Lyman Bushman, "The Theology of Councils," in *In Revelation, Reason, and Faith: Essays in Honor of Truman G. Madsen*, ed. Donald W. Parry, Daniel C. Peterson, and Stephen D. Ricks (Provo: Foundation for

Taken as a whole, the Constitution of the Kingdom of God is less a blueprint for a functioning government than an effort to state a philosophy of government. At its center is the absolute sovereignty of God. Acknowledging that sovereignty and following God's laws will lead to the protection of rights to life, liberty, property, and the pursuit of happiness. Disregarding God's sovereignty leads to misery and suffering. In a properly functioning polity, the community is led by benevolent and inspired leaders endowed with divine authority and upheld by the common consent of the people. As a revelation, however, the authors of the Constitution of the Kingdom of God expressed their doubts. Upon reporting the committee's work to the Council, John Taylor said, "If they can get intelligence from God they can write correct principles, if not, they cannot."[56] He did not, however, claim that the committee had in fact found that inspiration. They were sent back to work, presumably to search for more "intelligence from God." Parley P. Pratt later gave a hint as to the problem faced by the committee: "[I]f we made a constitution it would be a man made thing, and he considered that if God gave us laws to govern us and we received those laws God must also give us a constitution."[57] It wasn't enough to state a proper theory of government or to announce wise legal mechanisms. As the first-person voice of the Lord in articles 1 through 3 testified, the committee believed that they must produce a revelation, something that they did not seem to feel they had done.[58]

Ancient Research and Mormon Studies, Brigham Young University, 2002), 433–46 (discussing the emergence of Mormon ideas of revelation, councils, and consent in church government).

56. Grow et al., *Administrative Records: Council of Fifty Minutes*, 115.

57. Grow et al., 467.

58. The process here is instructive of how revealed texts within Mormonism were produced. While the constitution has the Lord speaking in the first person, the document itself was the product of a committee and contained clear instances of borrowing from other texts. They seem to have understood the voice of the Lord to have been less a matter of writing down divine dictation than of producing a text that they felt confident expressed divine intentions. Compare Scott H. Faulring, "An Examination of the 1829 'Articles of the Church of Christ' in Relation to Section 20 of the Doctrine and Covenants," *Brigham Young University Studies* 43, no. 4 (Winter 2004): 57–91 (recounting the production of the uncanonized "Articles of the Church of Christ," which also have God speaking in the first person).

Joseph Smith's Final Constitutional Revelation

They were never allowed to complete their work. Rather, in late April Joseph Smith "advised that we let the constitution alone."[59] He summed up the "whole matter about the constitution" in a three-sentence revelation:

> Verily thus saith the Lord, ye are my constitution, and I am your God, and ye are my spokesmen. From henceforth do as I shall command you. Saith the Lord.[60]

The revelation ended any further discussion of a written constitution for the Kingdom of God. Writing without the benefit of full access to the minutes of the Council of Fifty, Andrew F. Ehat claimed, "[g]iven the unwritten nature of the Constitution of the Kingdom" after Joseph Smith's revelation, the internal parliamentary procedures of the Council took on "constitutional proportions."[61] However, there isn't much evidence in the minutes that the members of the Council regarded these parliamentary rules as somehow foundational. Rather, with this revelation, the Council simply abandoned the constitution-writing project and focused its attention on the immediate practical concerns facing the Saints, including their ongoing legal difficulties of one kind or another. They certainly did not abandon the ideal of a political Kingdom of God; they often pursued fanciful plans, such as massive military alliances with native American tribes. In that sense, the revelation did not represent any abandonment of theocratic ambitions. It did, however, represent an important turning point in Mormon legal thought and experience in two ways. First, it represented the final resting place of the constitution as a concept in the revelations of Joseph Smith. Second, it helped to set the course for later developments in Mormon legal thinking and action.

Almost exactly two months after reporting his revelation to the Council of Fifty, Joseph Smith was murdered in the Carthage Jail. This document thus represents the final statement on the constitution in Joseph Smith's

59. Grow et al., *Administrative Records: Council of Fifty Minutes*, 135.

60. Grow et al., 137. It is interesting to note that while the written constitution produced by Taylor, Richards, Phelps, and Pratt lodged virtually all power in a single "Prophet whom I have called and chosen," Joseph Smith's revelation addresses a plural audience who collectively made the constitution. This is consistent with the tendency that Richard Bushman has noted of Joseph Smith to disperse prophetic authority into councils. See Bushman, "The Theology of Councils."

61. Ehat, "'It Seems Like Heaven Began on Earth': Joseph Smith and the Constitution of the Kingdom of God," 6.

revelatory oeuvre, albeit one that was never canonized. As noted above, Joseph's revelations on the constitution, given a decade earlier, present a thoroughly conventional political theology in which the constitution embodies principles of justice and freedom to be upheld by wise and honest rulers. It is an aristocratic and republican vision rather than a liberal or a democratic one, but it very much fits within the mainstream of American political thought, albeit in a way that was anachronistic even when the revelation was given. By the 1840s, the adjudicative ideal of republican politics was giving way to mass political parties and a politics based on a balancing of sectional interests.[62] Joseph's revelation to the Council of Fifty seems to have finally escaped the gravitational force of American constitutional models. In place of a written document setting forth the formal procedures of government—the sine qua non of American constitution-making—the revelation offered an existing body of men endowed with divine authority as all the constitutional structure necessary for the Kingdom of God.

This does not mean that the ideas expressed in the written constitution of the Kingdom of God became irrelevant. The theodemocratic vision that Taylor, Richards, Phelps, and Pratt sought to articulate in their draft continued to dominate Mormon thinking, and even public Mormon political discourse. As the Twelve put it in a proclamation issued in 1845:

> The city of Zion, with its sanctuary and priesthood, and the glorious fullness of the gospel will constitute the standard which will put an end to jarring creeds and political wranglings, by uniting the republics, states, provinces, territories, nations, tribes, kindred, tongues, people and sects of North and South America in one great common bond of brotherhood; while truth and knowledge shall make them free and cement their union.
>
> The Lord also shall be their king, and their law-giver, while wars shall cease and peace prevail for a thousand years. Thus shall American rulers, statesmen, citizens, and savage know "*this once*" that there is a God in Israel, who can utter his voice and it shall be fulfilled.[63]

Members of the Council of Fifty continued to speak of themselves as legal actors in some cosmic sense, implementing the laws of God. However, their actions did not involve casting those laws in the forms

62. This is not to claim that such elements weren't also present earlier in American politics. Certainly, the early republic's politics involved much sectional bickering and balancing.

63. Quoting M. H. Cannon, "The Mormon Declaration of Rights," *The Harvard Theological Review* 35, no. 3 (1942): 191.

familiar to American politics, namely as written rules and procedures. In this, the Kingdom of God differed from the other imagined republics of nineteenth-century North America. Even the tiny Indian Stream Republic, for example, was legislatively loquacious, producing constitutions and legal codes in great abundance.

This is not to say that as the Mormons sought to create the Kingdom of God in the decades after 1844, they did not also produce law in great abundance. They did. The State of Deseret and the Territory of Utah, under the direction of ecclesiastical leaders, produced multiple constitutions and volumes of legislation. Ironically, the character of this legislation was decisively influenced by Joseph Smith's revelation in its very ordinariness. One of the striking things about subsequent Mormon history is the relative lack of Mormon legal innovation. The effort to create the Kingdom of God on earth was by no means abandoned after Joseph Smith's murder. If anything, it intensified with the mass migration to the Great Basin. Furthermore, the Council of Fifty continued to regard itself as a law giving body, and its minutes were filled with discussions of law, both in the cosmic sense of God's law and in the consideration of the endless and often technical legal challenges that the Mormons faced. (For example, at one point members of the Council debated the arcane question of whether the US Constitution allowed Congress to appoint an officer in the US Army.[64]) However, for all of their self-conception as law-givers and their constant interest in legal matters, Mormon leaders in Nauvoo—and later in Utah—produced very little law that strongly reflected their theocratic ambitions.[65] Most strikingly, never again would Mormons seek to author a unique constitution for their commonwealth, even when they adopted unorthodox procedures for promulgating proposed constitutions.[66] Rather,

64. Grow et al., *Administrative Records: Council of Fifty Minutes.*

65. This isn't entirely true, of course. The Utah Territorial Legislature, for example, passed a number of laws designed to make the decisions of Church courts in civil cases legally binding, although the statutes never seem to have operated as intended. See Oman, "Preaching to the Court House and Judging in the Temple," 181–91. Likewise, the State of Deseret adopted a criminal code in 1851 that provided for execution by beheading for murder, which may have been a nod to Brigham Young's doctrine of blood atonement. See Dale Morgan, *The State of Deseret* (Logan: Utah State University Press, 1987), 177 (reproducing the ordinance).

66. See Peter Crawley, *The Constitution of the State of Deseret* (Provo: Friends of the Harold B. Lee Library, 1982) (arguing that the published minutes of the first constitutional convention of the proposed State of Deseret is a record of an

in the series of constitutions drafted by the Mormons between 1847 and 1896, they uniformly chose to copy the constitution of an existing state.[67]

It is also striking that the Mormons never developed a legal hermeneutic of their own scriptures. Here the example of Islam is instructive. The absolute and exclusive vision of divine sovereignty articulated in the written constitution for the Kingdom of God is remarkably similar to the approach taken by classical Muslim jurists. It was precisely because God alone could be the fount of legitimate law that they labored so intensely to wring the last ounce of legal meaning out of every verse of the Qur'an or the example of the Prophet Mohammed. They even developed a unique word for this hermeneutic struggle—*ijtihad*. This necessity existed, however, precisely because Muslim jurists denied that additional revelation was possible because Mohammed had been the final "seal of the prophets."[68] Because ultimate religious authority within Mormonism centered on living prophets rather than prophetic texts, no such religious jurisprudence developed among the Latter-day Saints. This is despite the fact that throughout the nineteenth century, Church courts exercised extensive jurisdiction over civil cases and could easily have used such religious law had it been developed.[69] By foreclosing the creation of a written constitution for the Kingdom of God, Joseph Smith's April 1844 revelation eliminated a possible textual competitor with Mormonism's "living oracles."[70]

---

event that never actually occurred, the records being a modification of minutes from Church meetings).

67. See Jean Bickmore White, *Charter for Statehood: The Story of Utah's State Constitution* (Salt Lake City: University of Utah Press, 1996).

68. Modern scholars have questioned the traditional Islamic narrative in which authority after the death of the Prophet shifted decisively to the religious scholars, arguing instead that the early caliphs wielded for more creative authority than later jurists claimed. See Patricia Crone and Martin Hinds, *God's Caliph: Religious Authority in the First Centuries of Islam*, revised ed. (New York: Cambridge University Press, 2003).

69. See Oman, "Preaching to the Court House and Judging in the Temple"; Raymond T. Swenson, "Resolution of Civil Disputes by Mormon Ecclesiastical Courts Note," *Utah Law Review* 1978, no. 2 (1978): 573–96; C. Paul Dredge, "Dispute Settlement in the Mormon Community: The Operation of Ecclesiastical Courts in Utah," in *Access to Justice: The Anthropological Perspective: Patterns of Conflict Management: Essays in the Ethnography of Law*, ed. Klaus-Friedrich Koch, vol. 4 (n.p.: Giuffrè Editore/Sijthoff/Noordhoff, 1979).

70. See also Nathan B. Oman, "'The Living Oracles': Legal Interpretation and Mormon Thought," *Dialogue: A Journal of Mormon Thought* 42, no. 2 (Spring

It is dangerous, of course, to imagine that the revelation had great influence on later events. It was produced in a particular time and place amidst a myriad of other concerns. Furthermore, the Council of Fifty itself became a less important factor in Mormon governance after 1846.[71] For the rest of the century, Mormon leaders were constantly responding to particular circumstances in their legal maneuverings, and they generally exhibited great pragmatism in grasping at whatever legal theory would suit their needs. Nevertheless, a half-century later John Taylor continued to think of the revelation. Speaking to a reconstituted Council of Fifty in the 1880s, he said:

> These words are pregnant with meaning & full of intelligence & point out our position in regard of these matters – it is expected of us that [we] can act right—that our interests [are] bound up in the the K[ingdom] of God. That we should consider we are not acting for ourselves, but we are the Spokesmen of God selected for that purpose in the interest of God & to bless & exalt all humanity. We acknowledge him as our God and all men who enter this body must acknowledge him here. There is peculiary [*sic*] significance in these things which needs some consideration.[72]

More important than any conscious reliance on the revelation, however, was the brute fact that in 1844, Mormon leaders abandoned any effort to express their political Kingdom of God in the lingua franca of American government, namely via a written constitution. They might have done so. Indeed, in March 1844 that is precisely what they set out to do. Brigham Young and the Mormons are often presented as supremely practical,[73] and it is tempting to see simple pragmatism in the conventional constitution-

---

2009): 1–19 (arguing that one may apply a legal hermeneutic to Mormon practices, even if such a hermeneutic was never applied to Mormon texts).

71. See D. Michael Quinn, "The Council of Fifty and Its Members, 1844 to 1945," *Brigham Young University Studies* 20, no. 3 (1980): 163–97.

72. Taylor made this statement at a meeting of the Council of Fifty held on April 8, 1881. Quoted in Ehat, "'It Seems Like Heaven Began on Earth': Joseph Smith and the Constitution of the Kingdom of God," 5–6. Others spoke publicly of the revelation in this period. In 1870, Erastus Snow referenced it in a sermon before a stake conference. See Jedediah Smart Rogers and Klaus J. Hansen, eds., *The Council of Fifty: A Documentary History* (Salt Lake City: Signature Books, 2014), 46 (quoting Charles Walker's diary entry for June 5, 1870).

73. See, e.g., Leonard J. Arrington, *Brigham Young: American Moses*, 2nd ed. (Urbana: University of Illinois Press, 1991), 195 ("Brigham Young was generally considered to be a practical genius but, like Don Quixote, he was also capable of tilting at windmills").

copying after 1847. But it is important to remember that the successors of Joseph Smith were anything but practical on many things. Plural marriage was not practical. The gathering to the Great Basin was not practical. The period of the United Orders of the Utah was not practical. All of these projects involved vast expenditures of effort, and they often created intense conflict within and outside the Church. Had the Council of Fifty produced an elaborate written constitution in 1844, it's plausible to imagine the Mormons of later decades doggedly struggling to implement it. Instead, Mormon theocracy in the nineteenth century used thoroughly conventional legal mechanisms to pursue its ends, relying on ecclesiastical structures and a religiously infused political culture rather than formal constitutional institutions. It was set on this course by Joseph Smith's revelation on the constitution of the Kingdom of God in late April 1844.

Conclusion

In September 1897, George Q. Cannon, then an aging counselor in the First Presidency of the Church, traveled to Paris, Idaho, to speak at a Church conference. Less than a decade earlier in 1890, President Wilford Woodruff had issued the Manifesto, publicly abandoning plural marriage and bringing the federal government's legal crusade against the Mormons to an end. Just the year before Cannon's sermon, Utah had been formally admitted to the Union. While the Mormon conflict with the nation would dramatically flare up one final time a few years later during the Smoot hearings, Mormonism's theocratic ambitions were at an end, and the political Kingdom of God had been postponed to an ever-delayed millennium.[74] Strikingly, Cannon chose to preach on Joseph Smith's April 1844 revelation to the Council of Fifty:

> There was an attempt made . . . during the life of Joseph Smith by some of the priesthood at the prophet's request to write a constitution for the kingdom of God. A committee was appointed of the most capable men. They tried and tried to draft it and so did the prophet himself but all in vain. Joseph sought the Lord and he told them: "Ye are the constitution of my church." And so

---

74. See Kathleen Flake, *The Politics of American Religious Identity: The Seating of Senator Reed Smoot, Mormon Apostle* (Chapel Hill: University of North Carolina Press, 2004) (discussing the controversy over the Smoot hearings).

> it is. The priesthood the living oracles are the word of God unto us and this constitutes the growth and strength of the kingdom of God.[75]

Cannon's subtle recasting of the precise language of the revelation is telling. Joseph Smith's original "Ye are my constitution" becomes "Ye are the constitution of my church." It is a shift that marks the final afterlife of the prophet's final revelation on the constitution.

In a fine essay on Mormon political thought in the nineteenth century, Patrick Mason notes the way in which the ideas of theodemocracy were cabined after 1890 into an vision of church government where, ideally, righteous and inspired leaders upheld by the consent of members would lead the community in its religious—if not its political—life.[76] The ability of Mormon thinkers in the early twentieth century, such as Orson F. Whitney and James E. Talmage, to make this move was important in creating continuity within Mormon religious discourse even as Mormon political, social, and religious ambitions were radically transformed. This flexibility, which somehow managed to treasure the Mormon experience even as much of it was being repudiated, helped Mormonism survive, and in many ways, thrive in the modern world. In some sense, this is also a legacy of Joseph Smith's April 1844 revelation. Had the Kingdom of God been poured into an inspired written constitution, as originally envisioned by Taylor, Richards, Phelps, and Pratt, it would almost certainly have shattered amidst the post–Civil War battles over the "Mormon Question." The fluid, unwritten structure bequeathed to the Kingdom of God by Joseph Smith proved more resilient. To be sure, nineteenth-century Mormon theologians drew careful—if not always consistent—distinctions between

---

75. "Cannon on Politics," *Salt Lake Herald*, September 16, 1897. There is no contemporary evidence, of which I am aware, that Joseph Smith participated in the effort to draft the written constitution for the Kingdom of God. Cannon was not a member of the Council of Fifty at the time, although he was later close to men who were. Strikingly, Cannon's remarks allude to the then-recent decision to drop Moses Thatcher from the Quorum of the Twelve as a result of conflicts with the First Presidency over the role of church leaders in partisan politics. The controversy was one of the first steps towards defining the more limited political role of the Church in the post-Manifesto era. See Kenneth W. Godfrey, "Moses Thatcher in the Dock: His Trials, The Aftermath, and His Last Days," *Journal of Mormon History* 24, no. 1 (1998): 54–88; Edward Leo Lyman, "The Alienation of an Apostle from His Quorum: The Moses Thatcher Case," *Dialogue: A Journal of Mormon Thought* 18 (Spring 1985): 67–91.

76. Mason, "God and the People."

church and kingdom, the Council of Fifty and The Church of Jesus Christ of Latter-day Saints.[77] Still, "ye are my constitution, and I am your God, and ye are my spokesmen" is a constitutional ideal easily taken up in a church populated by prophets and apostles. By shifting theodemocracy from the political Kingdom of God to the ecclesiastical structure of the Church, Cannon and those who followed him could reach back to Joseph Smith's earliest revelations on the constitution without the later constitutional complications of the Council of Fifty.[78] It is a constitutional vision that allows contemporary Latter-day Saints to make their peace with human governments and to continue building up the Kingdom of God, albeit in radically different ways than their nineteenth-century forbearers.

---

77. For example, in his autobiography Benjamin F. Johnson described the Council of Fifty thus:

> About this time was organized his private council of Fifty,—the embryo kingdom of God upon the earth—an organization distinct from the Church, a nucleus of popular government which will exist for all people when heather are given [up] for inheritance, and the uttermost parts of the earth as a possession "to Him whose right it is to reign . . ."

Quoted in Rogers and Hansen, *The Council of Fifty*, 32.

78. Kathleen Flake has documented a similar dynamic in this period, during which Joseph Smith's accounts of the First Vision first gained wide prominence and the early efforts to preserve Mormon historic sites were made, allowing Joseph F. Smith and other turn-of-the-century Mormons to claim the history of the Restoration, even as they abandoned polygamy and dramatically transformed the meaning of Latter-day Saint Zion building. See Flake, *The Politics of American Religious Identity*, 109–37.

CHAPTER 5

Natural Law and the Rhetoric of Empire: *Reynolds v. United States*, Polygamy, and Imperialism

Introduction

On January 6, 1879, the US Supreme Court handed down its decision in *Reynolds v. United States*.[1] The decision affirmed the bigamy conviction of George Reynolds, a Mormon polygamist. In doing so, the court construed the meaning of the free exercise clause of the First Amendment for the first time, earning *Reynolds* a place in the constitutional law canon. Reading the case in a historical context, however, reveals it as far more than a hoary chestnut from the birth of free exercise jurisprudence. Legal historians have tended to place *Reynolds* in the context of what came immediately before it.[2] Sarah Barringer Gordon, for example, has persuasively demonstrated the deep affinities between the anti-polygamy ju-

1. 98 U.S. 145 (1879).

2. See Edwin Brown Firmage and Richard Collin Mangrum, *Zion in the Courts: A Legal History of the Church of Jesus Christ of Latter-Day Saints, 1830–1900* (Urbana: University of Illinois Press, 1988), 151–59 (discussing Reynolds v. United States within the context of Mormon legal history); Sarah Barringer Gordon, *The Mormon Question: Polygamy and Constitutional Conflict in Nineteenth-Century America* (Chapel Hill: University of North Carolina Press, 2002), 119–45 (discussing Reynolds v. United States within the context of nineteenth-century legal thought); Mary K. Campbell, "Mr. Peay's Horses: The Federal Response to Mormon Polygamy," *Yale Journal of Law and Feminism* 13, no. 1 (2001): 29–70 (discussing the history of anti-polygamy laws and the Reynolds case); Ray Jay Davis, "Plural Marriage and Religious Freedom: The Impact of Reynolds v. United States," *Arizona Law Review* 15, no. 2 (1973): 287–306; Sarah Barringer Gordon, "'Our National Hearthstone': Anti-Polygamy Fiction and the Sentimental Campaign Against Moral Diversity in Antebellum America," *Yale Journal of Law & the Humanities* 8, no. 2 (1996): 295–350 (discussing the anti-polygamy politics leading to Reynolds); Orma Lindford, "The Mormons and the Law: The Polygamy Cases," *Utah Law Review* 9, no. 2 (1964): 308–71 (discussing the history of Reynolds and the other anti-polygamy cases).

risprudence[3] midwifed by *Reynolds* and the anti-slavery movement.[4] In her telling, *Reynolds* is an extension of the constitutional debates sparked by abolitionism, debates dominated by domestic narratives of federal versus local power and the social preconditions for American democracy. The decision in *Reynolds*, however, also drew on international narratives, using analogies to British imperial law to interpret the scope of the First Amendment. This chapter unravels the work done by these international analogies, revealing how the legal debates in *Reynolds* reached back to natural law theorists of the seventeenth century, such as Samuel Pufendorf and Hugo Grotius, and forward to *fin de siècle* imperialists, such as Henry Cabot Lodge and Theodore Roosevelt. At the center of this debate lay the Mormons, who were defined by nineteenth-century Americans as not only religious but also racial—and thus imperial—outsiders.

The Supreme Court heard oral arguments in *Reynolds* in November 1878. Reconstructing the now-forgotten theory of the First Amendment advanced by the Mormons' lawyers shows that the Latter-day Saints had a nuanced account of religious freedom quite different than the caricature attributed to them by the Court's opinion. Contrary to the common perception, they did not claim that the free exercise clause was a trump card exempting any religiously motivated action—regardless of its nature—from the criminal law. Rather, they sought to provide a workable theory of religious freedom that defined those religious actions entitled to constitutional protection and those actions that could be criminalized regardless of their religious motivation. Their argument hinged on the distinction between actions that are *mala in se* versus merely *mala prohibita*. The First Amendment, they claimed, protected only criminalized religious acts that were *mala prohibita* but did not extend to acts that were *mala in se*. Acts could be sorted into one category rather than the other by appeal to a

3. See United States v. Late Corp. of the Church of Jesus Christ of Latter-day Saints, 150 U.S. 145 (1893); Late Corp. of the Church of Jesus Christ of Latter-day Saints v. United States, 140 U.S. 665 (1891); Late Corp. of the Church of Jesus Christ of Latter-day Saints v. United States, 136 U.S.1 (1890); Davis v. Beason, 133 U.S. 333 (1890); Ex Parte Snow, 120 U.S. 274 (1887); Cannon v. United States, 116 U.S. 55 (1885); Clawson v. United States, 114 U.S. 477 (1885); Murphy v. Ramsey, 114 U.S. 15 (1885); Clawson v. United States, 113 U.S. 143 (1885); Miles v. United States, 103 U.S. 304 (1880).

4. See Gordon, *The Mormon Question*, 55–83 (discussing the relationship between anti-polygamy jurisprudence and the anti-slavery movement).

series of arguments drawn from the natural law tradition, arguments that depended on analogies to non-Western legal systems.

The court's implicit response to the natural law reasoning of the Mormons' lawyers in *Reynolds* was an appeal to the nineteenth-century ideals of progress and imperialism that were displacing the earlier, eighteenth-century ideals of universal reason and natural law. The justices analogized Mormons to "the Asiatic and African races"[5] that, at the time, were being subjected to the supposedly benign and progressive influence of imperial legal systems. They went on to implicitly liken the federal government to the British Raj, bringing civilization through law to a benighted race. It is well known that in the wake of the Spanish-American War in 1898, American legal thinkers turned to imperial models abroad for analogies with which to interpret the US Constitution, culminating in the Supreme Court's 1901 decisions in the *Insular Cases*.[6] Historians have also increasingly rejected an exceptionalist interpretation of the United States' expansion across North America, seeing it instead as a local manifestation of the international spread of imperial ambitions in the nineteenth century. A fuller understanding of *Reynolds* reveals how the apparently domestic battles over polygamy from the 1860s to the 1880s were also part of this international story of American imperial expansion, forming a legal prelude to its constitutional denouement in the *Insular Cases*.

The court's racial analogy also foreshadowed the aggressive legal tactics employed against the Mormons in the wake of *Reynolds*. Originally, anti-polygamy politics was associated with anti-slavery Republicanism. By the late 1870s, however, the federal government had abandoned African Americans to the tender mercies of newly resurgent state governments in the South in return for national reconciliation and an end to the bitter sectional politics surrounding the Civil War. In *Reynolds*, the court adopted the rhetorical roadmap that allowed Republicans, in the decade after the

5. See Reynolds v. United States, 98 U.S. 145, 150 (1879).

6. See generally Christina Duffy Burnett and Burke Marshall, eds., *Foreign in a Domestic Sense: Puerto Rico, American Expansion, and the Constitution*, American Encounters/Global Interactions (Durham: Duke University Press, 2001) (discussing the legal debates over imperialism sparked by the Spanish-American War); James Edward Kerr, *The Insular Cases: The Role of the Judiciary in American Expansionism* (Port Washington: Kennikat Press, 1982) (discussing the constitutional debates over the status of the territory acquired from Spain in the Spanish-American War); Bartholomew H. Sparrow, *The Insular Cases and the Emergence of American Empire* (Lawrence: University Press of Kansas, 2006) (same as previous).

decision, to employ the tactics of Reconstruction against the Mormons without reopening the bitter political battles of the late 1860s. It did this by associating the suppression of polygamy with the control—rather than the liberation—of racial minorities, a stance that allowed the condemnation of polygamy without an implicit condemnation of the emerging system of post-emancipation racial subordination in the South. While historians rightly tend to interpret the federal government's anti-polygamy crusade in the 1880s as an extension of Reconstruction into the West, the interplay of natural law and imperialism in *Reynolds* reveals the way that crusade also acted as a prelude to imperial adventures at the turn of the century. Indeed, the rhetorical association of anti-polygamy with imperialism abroad rather than Reconstruction at home was part of what made employing the unpopular legal tactics of Reconstruction in Utah palatable to national politicians in the 1880s.

All of these rhetorical moves were part of a much deeper intellectual shift that occurred over the course of the nineteenth century. Writing a generation ago, Christopher Lasch captured that shift in terms of the fault line running through the debates over American expansion after the Spanish-American War of 1898:

> [American imperialists] substituted for the Jeffersonian proposition that the right to liberty is "natural"—hence universal—the proposition that rights depend on environment: on "civilization," of which there were now seen to be many stages of development; on race; even on climate. A pseudo-Darwinian hierarchy of cultural stages, unequal in the capacity for enjoyment of the rights associated with self-government, replaced the simpler and more liberal theory of the Enlightenment, which recognized only the distinction between society and nature. "Rights," as absolutes, lost their meaning by becoming relative to time and place. Rights now depended on a people's "readiness" to enjoy them.[7]

A recovery of the lost debates over natural law and imperialism in *Reynolds* shows this shift from Enlightenment reason to nineteenth-century progress playing out in the hard-fought anti-polygamy battles of the 1860s, 1870s, and 1880s.

---

7. Christopher Lasch, *The World of Nations: Reflections on American History, Politics, and Culture* (New York: Alfred A. Knopf, 1973), 73. Interestingly, in the chapter immediately preceding his discussion of the arguments over imperialism and anti-imperialism in the wake of the Spanish-American War, Lasch has a prolonged discussion of Mormonism in which he fails to recognize the connection between the anti-Mormon crusades of the 1880s and the debates over imperialism a decade later. See Lasch, 56–69 (discussing the place of Mormonism in American history).

This chapter proceeds as follows: part I recounts the birth of the *Reynolds* litigation and the natural law arguments that the Mormons' lawyers offered before the Supreme Court. Part II shows how the court used the rhetoric of imperialism to reject those arguments, tapping into international narratives of racial hierarchy and the progress of civilization. Part III reconstructs the afterlife of the imperial analogies in *Reynolds*, showing first how they formed a bridge between the decline of Radical Reconstruction and the anti-polygamy crusade of the 1880s, and showing second how *Reynolds* prefigured the constitutional analogies to British imperialism in the debates over American expansion at the end of the 1890s which ultimately culminated in the 1901 *Insular Cases*.

I. Mormon Polygamy and Natural Law at the Supreme Court

To see how a fuller understanding of *Reynolds* recasts standard narratives about the politics of polygamy and the role of imperialism in late nineteenth-century constitutional interpretation, we must first reconstruct the litigation that led to the decision. This allows us to recover the now-forgotten theory of religious freedom put before the court in 1878, a theory grounded in the natural law tradition and based on a series of analogies to non-Western legal systems.

A. The Origins of the Reynolds *Litigation*

In 1847, Mormon refugees under Church leader Brigham Young arrived in the wastes of the Great Basin, fleeing more than a decade of intermittent mob violence in the East. At the time, what would become Utah was beyond the borders of the United States, in Mexico. In 1848, however, Mexico ceded the entire region to the United States under the Treaty of Guadalupe Hidalgo, and in 1850, Congress created the territory of Utah to govern the newly conquered community. By 1852, Mormon leaders felt confident enough in their independence to publicly announce the doctrine of plural marriage, which had been practiced clandestinely by elite Mormons for over a decade, and went so far as to send a high Church leader to Washington, DC, to preach the doctrine.[8]

8. See Breck England, *The Life and Thought of Orson Pratt* (Salt Lake City: University of Utah Press, 1985), 175–76 (discussing Orson Pratt's mission to Washington, DC, after the announcement of polygamy).

Four years later, during the 1856 presidential election, the Republican Party burst on the national scene, dedicated to the eradication of "the twin relics of barbarism" in the territories: slavery and polygamy. By 1862 the Republicans were in control of Congress and had passed their first anti-polygamy law, the Morrill Act. The law proved ineffective, and an attempt to prosecute Brigham Young ended in failure when the US Supreme Court ruled that federal officials had exceeded their authority in order to bring the case to the court.[9] Congress responded in 1874 with the Poland Act, which firmly placed criminal prosecution in Utah in the hands of non-Mormons.[10] However, both the willingness of Utah jurors to find Mormons guilty of a crime for "living their religion" and the constitutionality of the Morrill Act's prohibition on polygamy under the free exercise clause remained in doubt.

Both federal officials and Mormon leaders wanted to test the validity of the Morrill Act. The Mormons wished to vindicate their belief that the law was unconstitutional, and federal officials, jaded by years of unsuccessful legal wrangling against Church leaders, were eager to grasp any opportunity to prosecute a high-profile polygamy case and lay Mormon arguments to rest. In addition, George Q. Cannon, one of Young's counselors and the political mastermind of Mormon resistance, turned to the law as part of a high-stakes political game in Congress. As Utah's non-voting territorial delegate, Cannon fought in Washington, DC, to delay new proposals dealing with "the Mormon question" and hoped to create a favorable Supreme Court precedent.[11] For their part, federal officials in Utah despaired of ever enforcing the anti-polygamy laws because, as one Utah lawyer put it in a letter to the attorney general, "[t]he sympathy of the great mass of the people here is with the parties to be prosecuted."[12]

---

9. See generally Clinton v. Englebrecht, 80 U.S. 434 (1872) (declaring that grand juries in the Utah Territory had been illegally impaneled using the procedure for Article III courts rather than the procedure for territorial courts); Firmage and Mangrum, *Zion in the Courts*, 138 (discussing how Englebrecht ended the prosecution of Brigham Young).

10. See Firmage and Mangrum, 148–49. The Poland Act did this by giving control over juries to the federally appointed (and non-Mormon) US marshal rather than the locally appointed (and Mormon) Territorial marshal.

11. See Davis Bitton, *George Q. Cannon: A Biography* (Salt Lake City: Deseret Book Co., 1999), 169–96 (detailing Cannon's political activities in the early 1870s).

12. "Letter from J. S. Wiekizer to A. J. Ackerman, U.S. Attorney General," October 9, 1971, National Archives, College Park, Maryland.

A deal was struck: Mormon leaders would provide a defendant for a test case.[13] Cannon picked a loyal English convert—and a recently married polygamist—named George Reynolds, and the Mormons provided the federal prosecutors with a list of witnesses.[14]

---

13. Orson F. Whitney, *History of Utah*, vol. 3, 1893, 46–47. According to Whitney, a partisan Mormon, the terms of the deal were as follows: "It was stipulated that the defendant in the case should produce the evidence for his own indictment and conviction, and it was generally understood that the infliction of punishment in this instance would be waived. Only the first half of the arrangement was realized." Whitney, 3:46–47. However, Robert N. Baskin, who consulted with the US attorney in the case, denied that any such deal was struck. See Robert N. Baskin, *Reminiscences of Early Utah* (Salt Lake City, 1914), 61–62. Baskin's blanket denial cannot be correct in light of the overwhelming contemporary evidence that Reynolds was a preselected and (initially, at least) willing defendant. See Bitton, *George Q. Cannon: A Biography*, 218–24 (discussing Cannon's conversation with Reynolds and the initial stages of the litigation); Bruce A. Van Orden, *Prisoner for Conscience' Sake: The Life of George Reynolds* (Salt Lake City: Deseret Book Co., 1992), 61–62 (same as previous). One likely explanation, in light of the rapid breakdown of relations, is that an agreement was made but its precise terms were left vague. Cannon and the other Mormon leaders do not seem to have had any legal counsel in their negotiations with the US attorney. Very likely, the Mormons did not play out the "end game" with sufficient detail ahead of time in order to nail down specifics with the federal officials. As the full implications of the deal became apparent, they understood the ambiguity in the terms outlined by Whitney; namely, that Reynolds would not be punished if he was found guilty. This theory is also consistent with Whitney's equivocal language—"it was generally understood that"—about the precise contours of the deal. See Whitney, *History of Utah*, 3:47. However, there is at least some semi-contemporaneous evidence to suggest that, as part of the deal, federal officials affirmatively agreed that Reynolds would not be punished. In 1878, while Reynolds's case was pending before the US Supreme Court, James Horrocks, one of the members of the grand jury that indicted Reynolds, told a journalist that there was an agreement not to inflict punishment. C. C. Goodwin, ed., *History of the Bench and Bar of Utah* (Salt Lake City: Interstate Press Association, 1913), 48. According to the journalist, "'he said without equivocation that the jurors were instructed, or at least advised, that there was no disposition to inflict punishment, but merely a design on the part of the Government's representatives to make sure of their ground before going further.'" Goodwin, 48 (quoting journalist S. A. Kenner). James Horrocks was a Mormon who was born in England in 1835 and had immigrated to Utah with his father and mother. See "Mormon Family History Records," on file with author, accessed January 3, 2011, FamilySearch.

14. See Van Orden, *Prisoner for Conscience' Sakes*, 61–62.

On October 23, 1874, Reynolds was indicted for bigamy under the Morrill Act.[15] The US attorney explained the deal to the grand jury. He later wrote the attorney general:

> I told them my plan of operations, that crime must be punished &c and that there were questions here that had divided the people and caused bitter animosities for many years: that the sooner these questions were settled the better, and that I purposed to make some test cases and let the highest tribunal of the country settle them, if all parties felt disposed so to do.[16]

Reynolds was found guilty, and after an initially successful appeal to the Territorial Supreme Court and a retrial,[17] he ultimately appealed to the US Supreme Court, where his case was argued in November 1878.[18]

B. The Natural Law Argument in Reynolds

Reynolds's lawyers defended polygamy by situating the free exercise clause within the natural law tradition. The bare bones of their position can be seen in the *U.S. Reports*' summary of the arguments presented before the Supreme Court. According to that truncated report, they argued that:

> The offence prohibited by [the anti-polygamy laws] is not *malum in se*; it is not prohibited by the decalogue [i.e. the Ten Commandments]; and, if it be said that its prohibition is to be found in the teachings of the New Testament, we know that a majority of the people of [the Territory of Utah] deny that the Christian law contains any such prohibition.[19]

By invoking the distinction between actions that are *mala in se* and those that are *mala prohibita*, Reynolds's lawyers built on a theory that saw cer-

---

15. Van Orden, 62.

16. "Letter from William Carey, U.S. Dist. Attorney, to George H. Williams, U.S. Attorney General," December 29, 1874, National Archives, College Park, Maryland.

17. See generally United States v. Reynolds, 1 Utah 226 (1875) (Reynolds's first, successful appeal to the Territorial Supreme Court); United States v. Reynolds, 1 Utah 319 (1876) (Reynolds's second, unsuccessful appeal to the Territorial Supreme Court). The Territorial Supreme Court dismissed Reynolds's First Amendment claim without argument: "The Appellant assigns as error the rejection of evidence offered by him to show that plural or polygamous marriage was part of his religion. This objection of the Appellant, is, as we conceive, based upon neither reason, justice nor law, and therefore we dismiss it without further notice." Reynolds, 1 Utah 226, at 227.

18. See "The Utah Polygamy Case," *The New York Times*, November 16, 1878, 2 (describing oral arguments in the case).

19. Reynolds v. United States, 98 U.S. 145, 152–53 (1879).

tain actions as inherently subject to prohibition. Furthermore, by turning to the Bible and the opinions of the majority of the people, they were adopting two forms of argument with deep roots in Blackstone, Grotius, and the natural law tradition.

A key source for understanding the natural law theory presented to the Court in *Reynolds* is *A Review of the Decision of the Supreme Court of the United States, in the Case of George Reynolds vs. the United States*, a short book responding to the decision that was penned by George Q. Cannon, the moving force behind the Mormon legal strategy, shortly after the opinion came down.[20] Cannon had no legal training, and Reynolds's lawyers—George Biddle, a former attorney general in the Buchanan administration, and Benjamin Sheeks, the local trial counsel in the case—almost certainly assisted in preparing the pamphlet. In their brief to the court, Reynolds's lawyers focused overwhelmingly on technical objections unrelated to his First Amendment claim.[21] At oral argument, however, the justices were more interested in the Free Exercise Clause.[22] Biddle, who argued the case, was clearly prepared with a theory of the amendment, but because there is no transcript of the oral argument, we must piece the argument together from a variety of sources. The arguments in Cannon's *Review* expand on the truncated descriptions of the oral arguments that have survived, and it likely reflects the theory offered to the court by Biddle in detail.

---

20. See Bitton, *George Q. Cannon: A Biography*, 226. Cannon's *Review* is, in many ways, a remarkable document. Coming out as it did between the time of the Reynolds decision and the court's disposition of the petition for rehearing, Cannon prepared it in a relatively short period—no more than a few months—during which time he was busy with other duties. Nevertheless, it evidences a great deal of research and careful thought. Cannon's sources range from Blackstone (three separate American editions were consulted) to Justinian and St. Ambrose. In short, of the contemporary Mormon writings on the *Reynolds* decision, Cannon's *Review* is by far the most legally and philosophically sophisticated. See generally George Q. Cannon, *A Review of the Decision of the Supreme Court of the United States, in the Case of George Reynolds vs. The United States* (Salt Lake City: Deseret News Printing and Publishing Establishment, 1879).

21. See generally Brief of the Plaintiff in Error, Reynolds v. United States, 98 U.S. 145 (1978) (No. 108) [hereinafter Reynolds Brief] (focusing on the admissibility of transcripts of prior oral testimony in lieu of live testimony by absent witnesses and on the proper number of grand jurors under federal statutes governing the territorial judiciary).

22. "The Utah Polygamy Case" (describing oral arguments in the case).

The problem of creating a workable regime of religious freedom is ultimately one of baselines. If any religiously motivated action forbidden by the law is *ipso facto* unprotected because it is a "crime," then there are no meaningful restrictions on the state's ability to criminalize religious practices. Such prohibitions will tautologically justify themselves. On the other hand, if any religious claim can vitiate the requirements of any criminal statute, then the law would be fully exposed to the anarchic claims of religious conscience. In order to create a workable system of religious freedom, we need some baseline of acceptable regulation from which deviations—while perhaps normally tolerable—will not be permitted in the case of religious objections. The court in *Reynolds* ultimately resolved the issue by finding a baseline in the definition of religion. "Congress cannot pass a law . . . which shall prohibit the free exercise of religion,"[23] it argued, but religiously inspired conduct (as opposed to religious belief) did not count as "religion" within the meaning of the First Amendment.[24] Such a regime provided a coherent and workable solution to the baseline problem of religious liberty by separating protected "religion" (belief) from unprotected "religion" (action).

In effect, Reynolds's lawyers resolved the baseline issue by giving a natural-law gloss to the free exercise clause's use of the word "law." The natural law tradition on which they drew did not deny that the legal enactments of human governments are always law in some sense. What it affirmed was that some laws are qualitatively different than others because they conform to the eternal law of nature. Blackstone gave a crude and absolutist version of this position when he wrote, "no human laws are of any validity, if contrary to [natural law]; and such of them as are valid derive all their force, and all their authority, mediately or immediately, from this original."[25] Biddle and Sheeks, however, did not take this extreme position. Rather, by invoking the distinction between actions that

---

23. Reynolds, 98 U.S. at 162.

24. Reynolds, 98 U.S. at 164 (Thomas Jefferson is quoted: "'[T]he legislative powers of the government reach actions only, and not opinions . . .'").

25. William Blackstone, *Commentaries on the Laws of England*, ed. Wilfrid R. Prest (New York: Oxford University Press, 2016), 1:42 (pagination in original edition). It is important to note that Blackstone did not believe that natural law justified judicial review and invalidation of legislation.

> Contrary to the perceptions of modern critics . . . Blackstone did not believe that judges or legislators could use the principles of natural law to derive appropriate answers to all or even most legal questions. . . . As Blackstone

are *mala in se* and those that are merely *mala prohibita*, they played on the discontinuous character of law in the natural law perspective. Even if one did not believe that natural law exempted one from positive law by its own force, some laws were still more truly "law" than others. Cannon and the lawyers who advised Reynolds did not maintain any illusions that—as the Supreme Court caricatured their argument—"the professed doctrines of religious belief [should be] superior to the law of the land, and every citizen [should be permitted] to become a law unto himself."[26] Rather, they offered a carefully worked-out limiting principle to their claim, implicitly appealing to natural law for a baseline that could arbitrate the claims of both church and state.[27]

According to Reynolds's brief, the Bill of Rights limited congressional authority over the territories.[28] Although it did not explicitly cite the First Amendment, it effectively argued that Congress could not forbid religious behavior that was not *malum in se*. Thus, the key question was whether polygamy was *malum in se*. The brief argued:

> Bigamy is not prohibited by the general moral code. There is no command against it in the decalogue. Its prohibition may, perhaps, be said to be found in the teachings of the New Testament. Granted, for the purpose of the argument. But a majority of the inhabitants might be persons not recognizing the binding force of this dispensation. In point of fact, we know that a majority of the people of this particular Territory deny that the Christian law makes any such prohibition. We are therefore led to the assertion that as to the people of this Territory the supposed offence is a creature of positive enactment.[29]

---

observed, God was not concerned with whether English law forbade or permitted the export of wool.

Albert Alschuler, "Rediscovering Blackstone," *University of Pennsylvania Law Review* 145, no. 1 (1996): 24–25.

26. Reynolds v. United States, 98 U.S. 145, 167 (1879).

27. It was a move with antecedents in earlier American legal thought. For example, a review in an 1830 American law journal asked rhetorically, "How else than by principles of the natural law, are we to discuss the questions of religious toleration [and] the obligation of mere positive laws, with the distinction between mala prohibita and malum in se . . . ?" Quoted in Charles M. Haar, ed., *The Golden Age of American Law* (New York: George Braziller, Inc., 1965), 490.

28. Reynolds Brief, at 53–55. Interestingly, the only provision of the Bill of Rights that Reynolds did explicitly cite in this part of his argument was the Second Amendment. See Reynolds Brief, supra note 46, at 53.

29. Reynolds Brief, at 54–55.

In oral argument, Biddle hammered away at this point, claiming that polygamy "is an artificial crime, created by legislative enactment, and involving, when practiced as a religious duty, no moral guilt."[30] In his *Review*, Cannon amplified on the argument. He claimed that polygamy as a crime was merely *malum prohibitum*.[31] Unlike crimes that are *mala in se*, which he argued "cannot be committed under the name of religion without exposing the perpetrator to the just punishment of the laws," a crime that "depends entirely for its existence upon statute" is different when the underlying activity is motivated by religion.[32]

> When it is a religious belief and ordinance, and men and women believe their future salvation and happiness are intimately interwoven with and dependent upon its correct and virtuous observance, it is beyond the reach of the legislative arm. . . . The first amendment of the Constitution protects it.[33]

The concept of *malum in se* was linked—as the brief's reference to "the general moral code" suggests[34]—to natural law. Blackstone provides a useful elaboration on the distinction used by Reynolds's lawyers. He spoke of "crimes that are *malum in se* [*sic*] and prohibited by the law of nature, such as murder and the like."[35] He also distinguished acts that are *mala in se* (contrary to natural law) from those that were *mala prohibita*. He wrote that "things in themselves indifferent become either right or wrong, just or unjust, duties or misdemeanors according as the municipal legislator sees proper for promoting the welfare of the society and more effectually carrying on the purposes of civil life."[36] The distinction thus drew the line between rules rooted in the law of nature and those that resulted from decisions of mere convenience or expedience by lawmakers.

---

30. "The Utah Polygamy Case" (quoting Biddle in oral argument).

31. See Cannon, *A Review of the Decision of the Supreme Court of the United States, in the Case of George Reynolds vs. The United States*, 33 (referring to polygamy as a crime created entirely by statute).

32. Cannon, 33.

33. Cannon, 33–34.

34. Reynolds Brief, at 54.

35. Blackstone, *Commentaries on the Laws of England*, 1:55. Blackstone was speaking here of the rule of criminal law that a woman who committed a crime in the presence of her husband was presumed to have acted under coercion, except in the cases that were *mala in se*. See Blackstone, 1:55. The rule was followed in the United States at the time of the *Reynolds* decision. See, e.g., Hensly v. State, 52 Ala. 10 (1875); State v. Williams, 65 N.C. 398 (1871).

36. Alschuler, "Rediscovering Blackstone," 25 (internal citations omitted).

By invoking the Bible and the opinions of the people of the territory, Cannon and the brief were making two independent arguments about how one discovers natural law. First, natural law was thought to coincide with divine law. Quoting Grotius, Cannon argued that "[w]hen God permits a thing in certain cases, and to certain persons, or in regard to certain nations, it may be inferred, that the thing is not evil in its own nature."[37] Although Grotius argued that natural law would be valid "even if we should concede that which cannot be conceded without the utmost wickedness, that there is no God, or that the affairs of men are of no concern to him," he insisted that "the law of nature . . . can nevertheless rightly be attributed to God."[38] The link between divine and natural law also emerges in Blackstone, who argued that the fallen state of man's reason

> has given manifold occasion for the benign interposition of divine providence; which, in compassion to the frailty, the imperfection, and the blindness of human reason, hath been pleased, at sundry times and in divers manners, to discover and enforce its laws by an immediate and direct revelation. The doctrines thus delivered we call the revealed or divine law, and they are to be found only in the holy scriptures. These precepts, when revealed, are found upon comparison to be really a part of the original law of nature, as they tend in all their consequences to man's felicity.[39]

The claim put forward by Grotius and Blackstone was not that the Bible could be applied as a source of law in and of itself. Rather, it was that the revealed word of God provided evidence as to the content of natural law, although there were other admitted sources of evidence for such law. Following this tradition, nineteenth-century American courts routinely referred to the Decalogue as a standard for discovering natural law.[40] These judges did not claim that the Ten Commandments were legally binding in themselves. Rather, they used the Ten Commandments as one of several

---

37. Cannon, *A Review of the Decision of the Supreme Court of the United States, in the Case of George Reynolds vs. The United States*, 37 (quoting Hugo Grotius, On the Law of War and Peace bk. I, ch. 2 § 17 [1625]).

38. See Hugo Grotius, *Prolegomena to the Law of War and Peace (1625)*, trans. Francis W. Kelsey (Macmillian Publishing Company, 1957), 10–11.

39. Blackstone, *Commentaries*, 1:41–42.

40. See, e.g., Stramler v. Coe, 15 Tex. 211, 215 (1855) ("'Honor thy father and mother' is a command not only of the decalogue, but of nature . . ."); Caldwell v. Hennen, 5 Rob. 20, 26 (La. 1843) (same as previous); State v. Foreman, 16 Tenn. 256, 284 (1835) (referring to "the law of God and nature contained in the decalogue").

baselines from which natural law might be deduced.[41] In pointing to the absence of a prohibition against polygamy in the scriptures, Reynolds's defenders were explicitly invoking this conventional legal argument. Because polygamy was not forbidden by revelation in the Bible, they argued with Grotius that "it cannot be inferred that the thing [polygamy] is evil in itself, according to the law of nature."[42]

The second line of reasoning implicitly invoked by Cannon and the brief was what was called the *consensus gentium*. According to this argument, things such as murder, which are universally forbidden by all legal systems, violate natural law. On the other hand, things that are not universally forbidden, such as polygamy, do not violate natural law. The appeal to comparative law had deep roots in natural law theory. Grotius regularly cited "scores of examples and arguments taken from the writings of ancient philosophers, historians, poets, rhetoricians, and theologians, as well as from the Bible."[43] Such examples constituted proof of a principle of natural law. "[W]hen so many learned and wise men, who also happen to represent different nations . . . affirm the same principles as being true or certain," he argued, "it must be due to the operation of a 'universal cause.'"[44]

The concept of *consensus gentium* also found its way to Blackstone, although he did not use the term. Rather, he constantly invoked historical and comparative analogies to defend and justify English law. For example, Blackstone described the way that English judicial power flowed from the king as the highest judge into a myriad of lower courts.[45] He then explicitly linked this process of delegating authority with natural law, citing the laws of different nations as a justification. Such an arrangement, he said, is:

> An institution that seems highly agreeable to the dictates of natural reason, as well as of more enlightened policy; being equally familiar to that which prevailed in Mexico and Peru before they were discovered by the Spaniards; and that which was established in the Jewish republic of Moses.[46]

---

41. See, e.g., Foreman, 16 Tenn. at 284 (referring to "the law of God and nature contained in the decalogue").

42. Cannon, *A Review of the Decision of the Supreme Court of the United States*, 37 (quoting Hugo Grotius, On the Law of War and Peace bk. II, ch. 5, § 9 [1625]).

43. Richard H. Cox, "Hugo Grotius," in *A History of Political Philosophy*, ed. Leo Strauss and Joseph Cropsey, 3rd ed. (Chicago: University of Chicago Press, 1987), 389.

44. Cox, 389.

45. Blackstone, *Commentaries*, 1:30–31.

46. Blackstone, 1:31.

Agreement across cultures and times—including Biblical history—suggested "the dictates of natural reason." This mode of comparative argument is ubiquitous in the *Commentaries*. For example, on the subject of testamentary succession, Blackstone argued that "the universal law of almost every nation (which is a kind of secondary law of nature) has . . . given the dying person a power of continuing his property, by disposing of his possessions by will."[47] Note the link between "the universal law of almost every nation" and the "law of nature."

To be sure, it is easy to overstate the respect accorded to non-Western legal systems by natural law writers. These authors generally appealed to the *consensus gentium* as a way of bolstering the claim that their own legal systems corresponded to natural law. Blackstone's appeals to non-Western legal systems, for example, always take the form of an apologetic for the common law, showing its conformity with universal reason.[48] He never uses the conflict between common-law rules and non-Western legal practices as evidence that English law did not emanate from the law of nature. Indeed, the usual absence of any critical bite to the *consensus gentium* might lead to the conclusion that, in practice, it was more of a *consensus occidentorum* with a few exotic examples thrown in as rhetorical window dressing. It would be a mistake, however, to dismiss the argument as entirely ephemeral. For example, Hugo Grotius, operating in the firmly monogamous context of early seventeenth-century Holland, nevertheless concluded that the natural law permitted polygamy, in part on the basis of the laws of the ancient Hebrews.[49]

---

47. Blackstone, 2:10.

48. Daniel Boorstin summed up the approach, writing that for Blackstone:

> From the uniformity of man's nature and the constancy of God's purposes arises the uniformity of the laws of nature which makes relevant all information about the past of English law and the analogous institutions of ancient Rome and the distant kingdom of Widdah. It would be impossible to conceive of a country or an epoch whose experience could not illuminate these eternal, universal laws.

Daniel J. Boorstin, *The Mysterious Science of the Law: An Essay on Blackstone's Commentaries* (Chicago: University of Chicago Press, 1996), 47.

49. Hugo Grotius, *The Rights of War and Peace*, ed. Richard Tuck, Natural Law and Enlightenment Classics (Indianapolis: Liberty Fund, 2005), 195 ("And those, who are of that Opinion, are strangely embarrassed to prove, that certain Things which are forbid by the Gospel, as Concubinage, Divorce, Polygamy, are likewise condemned by the Law of Nature. Indeed these are such that Reason

Seen in this light, the Mormon reference to the Decalogue fits into a familiar pattern of comparative argument. The absence of a prohibition on polygamy in ancient Israel, in the New Testament, or among the Mormons themselves suggested that—unlike murder—there is no universal consensus against polygamy. In support of this claim, Cannon marshaled not only the support of the Bible and the Mormon legal experience, but also early Church Fathers and non-Western legal systems.[50] For example, he acknowledged that traditional bigamy, in which a husband abandoned or deceived his wife and married a second woman without informing her of the previous marriage, "is a wrong of the most grave and damning character."[51] However, he argued that the universal condemnation of this crime did not extend to "the patriarchal marriage of the Latter-day Saints, or even the marriages of Mohammedans and other Asiatics," because in such cases there is no deception or abandonment.[52] If this sort of polygamy was *malum in se*, Reynolds's defenders argued, there should be a universal consensus against it. The absence of such a consensus suggested that it was merely *malum prohibitum* and therefore protected by the First Amendment when done as a religious ordinance.[53]

The natural law authorities and the style of argument used by Biddle before the court in 1878 was a common part of American legal discourse in the first half of the nineteenth century. For most of the nineteenth century, apprenticeship and an informal program of "reading law" in an established attorney's office was the dominant model of legal education. Of the books available to nineteenth-century American lawyers, Blackstone was by far the most widely read. However, the classic natural law treatises

---

itself informs us it is more Decent to refrain from them, but yet not such, as [without the Divine Law] would be criminal. The Christian Religion commands, that we should lay down our Lives one for another; but who will pretend to say, that we are obliged to this by the Law of Nature. Justin Martyr says, To live only according to the Law of Nature, is to live like an Infidel"). Grotius's argument over polygamy, however, is also thoroughly embedded in debates over the relationship between divine law and natural law. He uses the example of polygamy mainly to drive a wedge between the notion that the commands of natural law are identical with the commands of the Christian gospel. Hence, his argument has as much to do with biblical interpretation as with the *consensus gentium*.

50. See Cannon, *A Review of the Decision of the Supreme Court of the United States*, 37–38.

51. Cannon, 31.

52. See Cannon, 29.

53. See Cannon, 34.

of the seventeenth and eighteenth centuries—Grotius, Pufendorf, and Vattel—remained an important part of the standard law books that an aspiring lawyer might study. In addition, writers such as James Kent and St. George Tucker produced treatises on American law with a natural law bent which became standard works for several generations. For example, Kent opens his 1826 *Commentaries on American Law* with a discussion of the relationship between natural law and the law of nations, insisting that

> it would be improper to separate this law entirely from natural jurisprudence, and not to consider it as deriving much of its force, and dignity, and sanction, from the same principles of right reason, and the same view of the nature and constitution of man, from which the science of morality is deduced.[54]

He likewise identifies the foundations of the common law with "the application of the dictates of natural justice, and of cultivated reason, to particular cases."[55] Perhaps more importantly, throughout the nineteenth century, the American courts regularly referred to "natural law" or "natural justice" either as a source of law or, more frequently, as a justification for a particular rule or interpretation.[56]

By the time Biddle invoked this style of argument in November 1878, newer narratives of race, progress, and imperialism were replacing the earlier ideal of natural reason based on a universal human nature. It was these narratives that the court turned toward in rejecting the arguments put forth by the Mormons' lawyers.

II. Imperialism and the Rejection of Natural Law in *Reynolds*

The court's opinion was silent with respect to Reynolds's natural law arguments. It implicitly responded to them, however, by noting that "[p]olygamy has always been odious among the northern and western na-

54. James Kent, *Commentaries on American Law*, 1st ed. (New York: O. Halstead, 1826), 2.

55. Kent, 439.

56. See, e.g., Windsor v. McVeigh, 93 U.S. 274, 277 (1876) (describing the right to defense of person and property as "a principle of natural justice"); Ex parte Robinson, 86 U.S. 505, 512 (1873) (describing an attorney's right to receive notice of the grounds for disbarment and an ample opportunity for defense as "a rule of natural justice"); Ogden v. Saunders, 25 U.S. 213, 221 (1827) (describing retroactive laws as "contrary to the first principles of natural justice"); Vowles v. Craig, 12 U.S. (8 Cranch) 371, 376 (1814) (appealing to the writers of "natural law" as a source of law).

tions of Europe, and, until the establishment of the Mormon Church, was almost exclusively a feature of the life of Asiatic and of African people."[57] In contrast to the argument from a *consensus gentium*, with its essentially positive attitude toward non-Western legal systems, in the court's reasoning this comparative link became a damning indictment of the Mormon legal claim. The reasons for this shift lie, at least in part, in the different jurisprudential universe in which the court's opinion moves, a universe animated by Victorian ideas of civilization, barbarism, and progress, rather than seventeenth- and eighteenth-century ideas of natural reason.

If the discussion of religious freedom in the brief for *Reynolds* was truncated, the discussion of the same issue in the brief for the United States was virtually nonexistent. The attorney general's only reference to the issue of whether "the circumstance that polygamy was a *matter of religion* with the church to which the defendant belonged, was a defense"[58] was a curt dismissal. "None of these last mentioned exceptions," he wrote, "call for any remark."[59] Nevertheless, in oral argument, the government did deal with the issue of religious freedom by presenting a parade of horrible things that would ensue if the Mormon position was adopted. The attorney general argued that "under this rigid interpretation of the Constitution, a sect of East Indian Thugs who should settle in the Territories might commit murder with impunity, on the ground that it was sanctioned and enjoined by their system of religious belief."[60] He amplified on the Indian parallel, citing "the burning of widows in India as [a crime] committed in the name of religion, to which he compared plural marriage."[61] By invoking examples from India, the government implicitly responded to the natural law arguments of the Mormons by inviting the court to equate federal suppression of polygamy with the British Raj's suppression of similar barbarisms in India.

---

57. Reynolds v. United States, 98 U.S. 145, 164 (1879).

58. Brief for the United States at 8, Reynolds v. United States, 98 U.S. 145 (1879) (No. 180).

59. Brief for the United States at 8.

60. "Is Polygamy a Crime?," *New York Times*, November 15, 1878, 4.

61. See Cannon, *A Review of the Decision of the Supreme Court of the United States*, 34. In his review, Cannon vents his exasperation with this exceedingly common comparison, writing: "Respect for his position as Attorney-General of the United States, prevents me from characterizing this argument as it deserves." Cannon, 34–35. He also notes the surprise "that lawyers and men of sense would use it." Cannon, 35.

The court accepted this invitation, writing that "[l]aws are made for the government of actions, and while they cannot interfere with mere religious belief and opinions, they may with practices."[62] It went on to ask rhetorically, "if a wife religiously believed it was her duty to burn herself upon the funeral pile of her dead husband, would it be beyond the power of the civil government to prevent her carrying her belief into practice?"[63] The court's reference was more than a simply unflattering comparison of Mormon polygamy to the Hindu practice of "suttee." It was a jurisprudential reference with a long history in the anti-polygamy battles. At the heart of this reference was a two-step move. First, the Mormons were conceptualized as a foreign race akin to the inhabitants of the Indian subcontinent, and second, the federal rule in territorial Utah was likened to the British Raj in India, bringing civilization through law to the benighted masses over whom it ruled.

After the Mormon exodus to the Great Basin, Americans came to see Mormons—the majority of whom were either displaced Yankees or converts from Northern Europe—as a foreign race. For example, in 1858 Roberts Barthelow, an assistant surgeon attached to the US Army, wrote a report for the War Department on conditions in Utah. After discussing the exotic flora and fauna of the remote territory, he wrote, "The Mormon, of all human animals now walking this globe, is the most curious in every relation."[64] According to Barthelow, the practice of polygamy had given rise to a physiologically distinct race.

> Isolated in the narrow valleys of Utah, and practising the rites of a religion grossly material, of which polygamy is the main element and cohesive force, the Mormon people have arrived at a physical and mental condition, in a few years of growth, such as densely-populated communities in the older parts of the world, hereditary victims of all the vices of civilization, have been ages in reaching. This condition is shown by the preponderance of female births, by the mortality in infantine life, by the large proportion of the albuminous and gelatinous types of constitution, and by the striking uniformity in facial expression and in physical conformation of the younger portion of the community.[65]

According to Barthelow, the rise of this new race resulted from two causes. First, he claimed that the insatiable lust of Mormon patriarchs interfered

62. Reynolds, 98 U.S. at 166.

63. Reynolds, 98 U.S. at 166.

64. U.S. War Dep't, Statistical Report on the Sickness and Mortality in the Army of the United States, S. Exec. Doc. No. 36–52, at 301 (1860).

65. U.S. War Dep't, 301.

with the ordinary sexual development of girls, resulting in racial degradation.[66] "To sustain the system," he wrote, "girls are 'sealed' at the earliest manifestations of puberty, and I am credibly informed, that means are not unfrequently made use of to hasten the period."[67] This interference with the proper course of nature resulted in an anemic offspring. In particular, he noted that "[o]ne of the most deplorable effects of polygamy is shown in the genital weakness of the boys and young men, the progeny of the 'peculiar institution.'"[68] This "sexual debility" was compounded by the fact that, among the Mormons, "[t]he sexual desires are stimulated to an unnatural degree at a very early age, and as female virtue is easy, opportunities are not wanting for their gratification."[69]

The accuracy of Barthelow's claims regarding Mormon sexual habits, organs, and general anatomy is doubtful. He was an army surgeon in a camp located some distance from any of the major Mormon settlements.[70] His report, however, is a striking example of how the nineteenth-century American imagination racialized Mormons using Asian stereotypes. The image of the indolent Oriental, descended from an anemic racial stock and made effete by sexual excess was a standard trope in contemporary treatments of Asians ranging from the Turks to the Chinese. Likewise, according to Barthelow:

> [The Mormon expression is] compounded of sensuality, cunning, suspicion, and a smirking self-conceit. The yellow, sunken, cadaverous visage; the greenish-colored eyes; the thick, protuberant lips; the low forehead; the light, yellowish hair; and the lank, angular person, constitute an appearance so characteristic of the new race, the production of polygamy, as to distinguish them at a glance.[71]

Tellingly, it was precisely its proximity to Christian civilization that made the degradation of the new Mormon race especially acute:

---

66. U.S. War Dep't, 301.
67. U.S. War Dep't, 301.
68. U.S. War Dep't, 301.
69. U.S. War Dep't, 302.
70. See Eugene E. Campbell, "Governmental Beginnings," in *Utah's History*, ed. Richard D. Poll et al. (Provo: Brigham Young University Press, 1978), 153, 170 ("The army moved quietly through abandoned and silent Great Salt Lake City on June 26 and soon established itself forty miles to the southwest in Cedar Valley; the post was named Camp Floyd").
71. U.S. War Dep't, 302.

> In eastern life, where [polygamy] has been a recognized domestic institution for ages, women are prepared for its continuance, and do not feel degraded by their association with it. The women of this Territory, how fanatical and ignorant soever, recognize their wide departure from the normal standard in all Christian countries; and from the degradation of the mother follows that of the child, and physical degeneracy is not a remote consequence of moral depravity.[72]

While to modern racial sensibilities it may seem odd that a group as Yankee and European as nineteenth-century Mormons should be considered a race distinct from white Americans, but at the time it was common for ethnic groups that we now think of as prototypically white to be classified as non-white. Noel Ignatiev, for example, has shown how the Irish were classified by nineteenth-century Anglo-Americans as non-white.[73] Rather, they were members of the separate Celtic race, with their own characteristic propensities toward drunkenness, crime, indolence, and stupidity. The logic of Mormon racial identity was slightly different. According to the standard racial logic, behavior resulted from racial identity. Orientals were indolent and sensual because indolence and sensuality were the natural condition of the Oriental race. For Mormons, however, the logic moved in the opposite direction. A new race arose precisely because of the unnatural behaviors of the Latter-day Saints. For example, Barthelow's description of the new race in Utah became the subject of debate before the New Orleans Academy of Science in 1860.[74] According to one member of the academy, "the whole of Mohammedan polygamy" differs from Mormonism because "[i]t is not a violation of natural law, where the natural instincts of the normal condition of the race do not forbid it."[75] In contrast, polygamy was "contrary to his nature and his instincts" for a white man.[76] The unnatural polygamy of the Mormons thus led to degradation similar to miscegenation, another supposedly unnatural practice. "[T]he Mormon type, is . . . the violation of natural law, which all men read in the instinctive aversion of *different* races, [and] degrades the offspring and commences the process of a certain extinction."[77] Thus,

72. U.S. War Dep't, 302.

73. See generally Noel Ignatiev, *How the Irish Became White* (New York: Routledge, 1995).

74. See C. G. Forshey, "Hereditary Descent; or Depravity of the Offspring of Polygamy Among the Mormons," *De Bow's Review* 30 (1861): 210.

75. Forshey, 211.

76. Forshey, 210.

77. Forshey, 211.

the Mormon racial identity, rather than arising from "natural or second causes,"[78] was defined by what Martha Ertman has aptly described as "race treason."[79] Whatever the complexities of racial theorizing in the popular imagination, Mormons were associated with Asians and Africans.[80]

While Barthelow thought of himself as a "medical philosopher,"[81] the creation of a Mormon race had legal implications. Their status as a degenerate people justified imperial control, hence the common equation of federal rule in Utah with the British Empire in India. For example, the court in *Reynolds* used virtually the same arguments that Grant's vice president, Schulyer Colfax, had advanced nine years earlier in a widely reported speech and newspaper article in the *New York Independent.*[82] In those materials, Colfax made the comparison between the federal government and the British Raj explicit. "The Brahmins claimed," he wrote, "as the Mormons do now in regard to their institution, that it [i.e. "suttee"] was taught in their sacred books, and conferred the highest merit on both husband and wife."[83] He went on to laud the English imperial authorities for disregarding Indian objections to their efforts to suppress "suttee."

> This, history tells us, created much excitement in Bengal, and, indeed, all over India, the Brahmins denouncing it with great violence (as the Mormons denounce our anti-polygamy law of 1862) as an "interference with their religion." . . . But England disregarded their "religious" arguments, and stood

---

78. Forshey, 213.

79. See generally Martha M. Ertman, "Race Treason: The Untold Story of America's Ban on Polygamy," *Columbia Journal of Gender and Law* 19, no. 2 (2010): 287–366.

80. Ertman powerfully illustrates this popular perception through an analysis of Mormons in nineteenth-century political cartoons. Her research reveals that Mormon polygamists were routinely associated visually with Blacks and Asians. The implication was that Mormons constituted a foreign agent of miscegenation within the American polity. See Ertman, 304–6 (discussing the presentation of Mormon polygamists in nineteenth-century cartoons); see also Nathan B. Oman, "Preaching to the Court House and Judging in the Temple," *Brigham Young University Law Review* 2009, no. 1 (2009): 213–14 (discussing the analogy made between Mormon ecclesiastical courts and private dispute resolution among Chinese immigrants).

81. Forshey, "Hereditary Descent," 208.

82. See generally John Taylor and Schulyer Colfax, *The Mormon Question* (Salt Lake City: Deseret News, 1870); see also Willard H. Smith, *Schuyler Colfax: The Changing Fortunes of a Political Idol* (Indianapolis: Indiana Historical Bureau, 1952), 219–31 (discussing Colfax's newspaper debate with Taylor).

83. Taylor and Colfax, *The Mormon Question*, 15.

> as one man, with the whole power of the kingdom . . . and wherever English power is recognized, there, this so-called religious rite is now sternly forbidden and prevented. England, with united voice, said "Stop!" and India obeyed.[84]

In the wake of Colfax's attacks on Mormon polygamy, the Church-owned *Deseret News* immediately picked up on the allusion, writing that "Mr. Colfax and his ilk . . . insist that the United States government should extirpate the marriage sacrament of the 'Mormons,' as the British government abolished the religious widow-burning of the Hindoos."[85] Although it does not appear in the court's discussion of the issue, during Reynolds's second trial, the judge, in charging the jury, also compared the suppression of polygamy to the suppression of "suttee."[86] Not surprisingly, Cannon wrote in the wake of *Reynolds*, "For thirty years the people of Utah have been forced to think upon and argue this subject [i.e. "suttee"] in all its bearings."[87] Thus, the court's opinion drew on a well-worn rhetorical image that explicitly linked the suppression of polygamy to British legal policy in India.

"Suttee" is the nineteenth-century Anglicization of the Sanskrit word *sati*, which refers to the ritual suicide of a Hindu widow. Victorian British were horrified by the practice.[88] Lurid pamphlets sold in England described "suttee" and called for its abolition.[89] However, decisive legal action was slow to come. During the eighteenth century, British legal influence in India was weak, extending only to disputes involving Englishmen in a few narrowly circumscribed port towns. As conquest and intrigue carried British authority into the interior of the subcontinent, they expanded

---

84. Taylor and Colfax, *The Mormon Question*, 15.

85. A. M. M., "Suttee and Polygamy," *Deseret News* (undated reprint, L. Tom Perry Special Collections, Brigham Young University) (on file with author).

86. See Van Orden, *Prisoner for Conscience' Sake*, 78 (discussing the Mormon newspaper response to the judge's comments).

87. Cannon, *A Review of the Decision of the Supreme Court of the United States, in the Case of George Reynolds vs. The United States*, 35.

88. See Niall Ferguson, *Empire: The Rise and Demise of the British World Order and the Lessons for Global Power* (London: Allen Lane, 2002), 117–20 (briefly recounting the Victorian movement against sati).

89. See, e.g., James Peggs, *India's Cries to British Humanity* (n.p: 1832) (a pamphlet containing thoughts "relative to the Suttee, infanticide, British connection with idolatry, ghaut murders, and slavery in India: to which is added humane hints for the melioration of the state of society in British India").

their legal jurisdiction.[90] Initially, the English adopted a positive attitude toward indigenous law and made little attempt to use imperial law to impose their cultural norms on Indians.[91] Rather, they left existing legal structures intact as much as possible.[92]

Strikingly, the vestiges of this more relaxed, eighteenth-century attitude toward imperial government in India also made a brief appearance in the anti-polygamy battles. In 1872, Representative James Blair, a Liberal Republican from Missouri, made a quixotic attempt to repeal the Morrill Act, thus legalizing polygamy in the territories.[93] In India, he noted, the British Raj had taken a tolerant attitude toward polygamy, with English missionaries in India going so far as to argue that polygamy did not contravene divine law.[94] "Shall England be more regardful of the obligations imposed upon her by the law of nations and public policy than the United States," he asked rhetorically, "or shall England be more generous and indulgent to her polygamous citizens in India than the United States to her polygamous citizens in Utah?"[95]

---

90. See M. Rama Jois, *Legal and Constitutional History of India*, vol. 2 (Littleton: Fred B. Rothman, 1984), 245.

91. See Jois, 2:31 ("[T]he whole of Hindu Law and Mohamedan Law concerning family and religious usages was fully respected by the Courts"); see also Ferguson, *Empire*, 118 (describing the relatively laissez-faire attitude that the British initially took toward sati).

92. See Jois, *Legal and Constitutional History of India*, 2:31 ("[T]he whole of Hindu Law and Mohamedan Law concerning family and religious usages was fully respected by the Courts").

93. Cong. Globe, 42d Cong., 2d Sess. 1096–1100 (1872); see Kelly Elizabeth Phipps, "Marriage and Redemption: Mormon Polygamy in the Congressional Imagination, 1862–1887," *Virginia Law Review* 95, no. 2 (2009): 483 (discussing Blair's political background).

94. See Cong. Globe, 42d Cong., 2d Sess. 1097 (1872) (Rep. Blair) (discussing British imperial policy in India toward polygamy).

95. Cong. Globe, 42d Cong., 2d Sess. 1097 (1872). British missionaries in India were eager to baptize Indians into Christianity. See Ferguson, *Empire*, 112–15 (recounting the genesis of missionary work by British Protestants in India). They seemed to realize, however, that given the widespread practice of polygamy on the subcontinent, requiring monogamy of all Indian Christians would reduce their pool of potential converts. Accordingly, they concluded on the basis of the Bible that polygamy was not inconsistent with Christianity. See Cong. Globe, 42d Cong., 2d Sess. 1097 (1872) (discussing a meeting of Protestant ministers in Calcutta that concluded that polygamy did not violate the Bible or Christianity).

Blair bolstered his argument by appealing to American cases that had looked to the treatment of marriage by non-Western legal systems as evidence of a natural law unopposed to polygamy.[96] In the years before the Civil War, a number of state courts had grappled with the legal status of Native American marriages, which courts regarded as potentially polygamous.[97] While Indian tribes were sovereign nations in theory, the judges concluded that Native American marriages were entered into in "a state of nature," and the civil law would recognize them so long as they did not violate natural law.[98] Faced with a claim that the ease of divorce among Native Americans meant that their unions could not be recognized as binding as a matter of natural law, the Missouri Supreme Court asked rhetorically, "To what quarter shall we look for proofs of the law of nature, if we exclude the manners and customs of the American aborigines?"[99] To be sure, these cases take a disparaging tone toward Native American customs, but in their willingness to see in them an instantiation of natural law, they hark back to the older tradition on which Reynolds's lawyers relied. Such arguments, however, proved to have little traction in the Mormon context, and Blair's bill attracted so little attention that no one even bothered to speak in opposition to it.[100] It died without ever coming to a vote.[101]

The more tolerant legal sensibility invoked by Blair was already anachronistic when he referenced it in 1872. From the early nineteenth century on, the English approach to the polyglot legal environment of India bore

---

96. See Cong. Globe, 42d Cong., 2d Sess. 1098 (1872) (citing state court cases dealing with Native American weddings).

97. See Johnson v. Johnson's Adm'r, 30 Mo. 72, 86 (1860) ("[An Indian marriage] is also disannulled and the wife dismissed from the wigwam whenever the husband pleases, or the marital state is continued under the evils of discord or a state of polygamy" (emphasis omitted) (quoting William Robertson, The History of America bk. 4 [1777]); Wall v. Williams, 11 Ala. 826, 828 (1847) ("The [Choctaw] tribe had no written laws. They married and unmarried at pleasure—a man frequently having several wives").

98. See Wall, 11 Ala. at 839 ("Marriages among the Indian tribes must be regarded as taking place in a state of nature . . ."); Morgan v. M'Ghee, 24 Tenn. (5 Hum.) 13, note (1844) ("The contract of marriage is a stable and sacred contract of natural, as well as municipal, law").

99. Johnson, 30 Mo. at 88.

100. See Cong. Globe, 42d Cong., 2d Sess. 1097 (1872) (reproducing Blair's speech in support of his bill with no response from other members of Congress).

101. See Phipps, "Marriage and Redemption," 484–87 (discussing the failure of Blair's bill).

the stamp of progressive, reform-minded thinkers in England who saw law as an instrument through which they could "civilize" Indian society.[102] In 1833, Thomas Babington Macaulay was appointed as the Law Member of the Governor-General's Council and given the task of preparing a criminal code for India.[103] The military chaos of the Great Mutiny delayed its final passage, but the code was adopted in 1860.[104] It played a key part in the campaign to eliminate "suttee" and other forms of Indian "barbarism."[105]

In comparing "suttee" to polygamy and the Mormons to Indians, the court cast the federal government as an agent of civilization against barbarism, akin to the civilizing British imperialism under Macaulay in India. Within this imperialist jurisprudence, Reynolds's natural law arguments became incoherent and invisible—"exceptions [not calling] for any remark."[106] The arguments from the *consensus gentium*, on which his lawyers rested their claim that polygamy was not *malum in se*, looked to non-Western societies and legal systems as evidence of natural laws or their absence. In this sense, they took an optimistic and universalist view of human reason in which all societies, regardless of their cultural differences,

---

102. V. D. Kulshreshtha, *Landmarks in Indian Legal and Constitutional History*, ed. B. M. Gandhi, 7th ed. (Lucknow: Eastern Book Co., 1995), 226; see also, e.g., A. C. Banerjee, *English Law in India* (Humanities Press, 1984), 169–70 (discussing Macaulay's complex relationship with Bentham and other English reformers).

103. See Kulshreshtha, *Landmarks in Indian Legal and Constitutional History*, 226 (discussing the consolidation of British rule in India and the appointment of Macaulay). Prior to Macaulay's work, the criminal law administered in India was mainly of Muslim origin. Kulshreshtha, 215–16. There were some areas of India that were not governed by Muslim law. See Kulshreshtha, 217–19. Prior to Macaulay's code, the British had made piecemeal reforms of various aspects of the existing Muslim criminal law, generally by choosing to enforce rules espoused by minority Muslim jurisprudential schools rather than through outright legislation. See Kulshreshtha, 221–24.

104. See Pen. Code, No. 45 of 1860 (India).

105. According to one Indian commentator:

> [I]t . . . abated, if not extirpated, the crimes peculiar to India, such as *thuggee*, professional sodomy, dedicating girls to a life of temple-harlotry, human sacrifices, exposing infants, *burning widows*, burying lepers alive, gang robbery, torturing peasants and witnesses and sitting *dharna*.

Kulshreshtha, *Landmarks in Indian Legal and Constitutional History*, 227 (emphasis added).

106. Cf. Brief for the United States at 8.

would converge on eternal moral laws.[107] In contrast to these earlier arguments, the court laid emphasis on the concept of "civilization," understood in terms of the particular cultural apogee reached by the "the northern and western nations of Europe," instead of "African and Asiatic" practices.[108]

This racially charged rhetoric was typical of an age where "progress" had replaced "reason" as an ideological talisman and where imperialism was in full swing. It is not that the court rejected the universalist aspirations of the earlier natural law tradition. Rather, those aspirations were transferred from a static vision of natural law to a more dynamic and aggressive vision of progressive civilization pitted against the forces of barbarism. In this narrative of violent evolution from barbarism to civilization, Mormons were cast—along with "Asiatic and African"[109] peoples—as a benighted race in need of civilizing imperial masters.

III. The Afterlife of the Imperial Rhetoric in *Reynolds*

Understanding the shift to imperial rhetoric in response to the natural law arguments in *Reynolds* sheds light on two major legal debates in the last quarter of the nineteenth century. Historians have long recognized that *Reynolds* ushered in successive rounds of increasingly harsh anti-polygamy legislation in the 1880s, which ultimately culminated in the Mormon Church's public abandonment of polygamy in 1890.[110] This story has been told most powerfully by Sarah Barringer Gordon, who interprets it as a final extension of the politics of anti-slavery and Reconstruction into the American West.[111] The imperialist rhetoric in *Reynolds*, however, represented a strand of anti-polygamy rhetoric largely divorced from the humanitarian politics of anti-slavery. It was this rhetoric that allowed anti-polygamy activists in the 1880s to negotiate the ultimate exhaustion of

---

107. Cf. Clifford Geertz, *The Interpretation of Cultures* (New York: Basic Books, 1973), 38–39 ("The notion of a consensus gentium [a consensus of all mankind]—the notion that there are some things that all men will be found to agree upon as right, real, just, or attractive and that these things are, therefore, in fact right, real, just, or attractive—was present in the Enlightenment and probably has been present in some form or another in all ages and climes").

108. Cf. Reynolds, 98 U.S. at 164.

109. See Reynolds, 98 U.S. at 150.

110. See, e.g., Gordon, *The Mormon Question*, 119–46 (discussing Reynolds and its aftermath); Edward Leo Lyman, *Political Deliverance: The Mormon Quest for Utah Statehood* (Urbana: University of Illinois Press, 1986), 120–26 (same as previous).

111. See generally Gordon, *The Mormon Question*.

anti-slavery politics and the decline of Radical Reconstruction. The prominence of imperial analogies in the anti-polygamy debates of the 1880s suggests that the federal suppression of polygamy can be seen not only as an extension of Reconstruction, but also as a harbinger of American imperial adventures in the final decade of the century. When America conquered Cuba, Puerto Rico, and the Philippines from Spain in 1898, legal intellectuals grappled with the constitutional questions presented by the new territories by using analogies to British imperialism. In this debate, *Reynolds* and its progeny emerged as important precedents illustrating the extent of the Republic's imperial power.

A. Imperialism and the Anti-Polygamy Crusade of the 1880s

The court's turn to imperialist imagery reflected shifting attitudes toward race within the Republican Party from which Chief Justice Waite and the other members of the court were drawn.[112] The Republican Party originally formed in the 1850s around the issue of excluding slavery from the territories. After the election of 1860 and the Civil War, Radicals within the party gained the upper hand and passed sweeping amendments to the Constitution, designed to eliminate slavery and to ensure the equal rights of newly freed African Americans. After the war, the Radicals sought to ensure the reality of these goals by using federal power to suppress the political power of ex-Confederates and other whites hostile to racial equality in the South. The central thrust of this movement was humanitarian. The Radical Republicans saw African Americans as victims of oppression to be saved by the federal government. In tandem with the politics of anti-slavery, anti-polygamy was initially another humanitarian mission aimed

112. At the time of *Reynolds*, seven of the nine justices (Swayn, Miller, Strong, Bradley, Hunt, Waite, and Harlan) were Republicans, and of the two Democrats, one (Stephen Field) was a westerner appointed by Lincoln. See Kermit L. Hall, James W. Ely, and Joel B. Grossman, eds., *The Oxford Companion to the Supreme Court of the United States*, 2nd ed. (New York: Oxford University Press, 2005), 81–82, 361–63, 417, 547–48, 845–46, 850–51, 906–7 (providing short biographies of the justices). See generally Peter Charles Hoffer, William James Hull Hoffer, and N. E. H. Hull, *The Supreme Court: An Essential History* (Lawrence: University Press of Kansas, 2007), 131–58 (discussing the political make up of the Waite Court and its place in the politics of the 1870s).

at the rescue of Mormon plural wives from the domineering force of their husbands, perceived as akin to white slave owners.[113]

The initial efforts to suppress polygamy, however, were anemic and ineffective. In 1870, the Radicals sought to give substance to federal anti-polygamy policy through the Cullom Bill, which would have applied the tactics of Reconstruction to Utah.[114] Participants in the debates over the bill explicitly located the issues within domestic narratives of rebellion and Reconstruction. For example, one opponent of the bill worried that "[The Mormons] would regard the passage of this bill as a declaration of war. . . . Of course we could finally conquer them, because we could exterminate them. But it would cost us millions upon millions of treasure; it would cost us thousands upon thousands of lives."[115] He went on:

> The truth is that our system of government is unfit to deal with a problem such as the Mormon question presents. . . . If the people of any county tacitly agree that a particular crime shall not be considered a crime if committed within that county, what is to be done about it? . . . Cases of this character can be reached only by . . . the interposition of military rule. The remedy is expensive, and its frequent use most dangerous to republican government.[116]

Of course, all these arguments were being used at this time to justify the abandonment of Radical Republicanism. With his concern for the local power, the need to respect "republican" practices, and the specter of military law in place of civil law, Representative Fitch might have been condemning Union practices in the defeated Confederacy rather than proposing federal policy in far-off Utah.[117]

Proponents of the bill insisted that Utah deserved such tactics precisely because of the Mormon similarity to the defeated South. Utah, one congressman insisted, was like the territory "south of Mason and Dixon's

---

113. See Gordon, *The Mormon Question*, 55–58 (cataloging political efforts to draw parallels between slavery and polygamy, which Republicans deemed the "twin relics of barbarism").

114. See H.R. Rep. No. 41-21 (1870); Cong. Globe, 41st Cong., 2d Sess. 1367 (1870); see also Phipps, "Marriage and Redemption," 452–54 (discussing the legislative history and politics of the Cullom Bill).

115. Cong. Globe, 41st Cong., 2d Sess. 1517 (1870) (Rep. Fitch).

116. Cong. Globe, 41st Cong., 2d Sess. 1518 (1870).

117. Cf. Eric Foner, *Reconstruction: America's Unfinished Revolution, 1863–1877*, 1st ed. (New York: Harper & Row, 1988), 242–43 (discussing arguments employed by Democrats and moderate Republicans against the reconstruction tactics of the Radical Republicans in the defeated Confederacy).

line" before "slavery was abolished."[118] He went on to insist that reluctance to use harsh measures against Mormon polygamists was part of a more general softening of attitudes toward the defeated South:

> I am sorry to see in this country the signs of a sickly sentimentality which proposes to punish nobody, which proposes to hang nobody, which proposes to let all the unchained passions of the human heart become free to prey upon mankind. We have seen too much of that in this day and generation. Had you hung one hundred traitors you would not have had rebellion in North Carolina and Tennessee to-day.[119]

By 1870, Radical Reconstruction was a waning political force, and the bill failed.[120] Two years later, the Republican Party would split over the politics of Reconstruction, with the so-called Liberal Republicans nominating Horace Greely to run against Grant.[121] While Grant was able to fend off Greely's challenge, "[t]he 1872 campaign spelled the final collapse of Republican radicalism."[122]

Nevertheless, anti-polygamy legislation thrived in the period following the decline of Radical Republicanism, at least in part by abandoning domestic political narratives tied to the debates over slavery in favor of international, imperial analogies. During the campaign of 1872, for example, E. L. Godkin, the editor of *The Nation* and a leading voice of the Liberal Republicans, declared that "'Reconstruction . . . seems to be morally a more disastrous process than rebellion.'"[123] Anti-polygamy legislation managed to escape an analogous indictment of moral disaster, despite employing many of the same legal tactics as Reconstruction.[124] The rhetoric exemplified in Vice President Colfax's speeches and the *Reynolds* decision helped to articulate a new vision of anti-polygamy for these post-

---

118. Cong. Globe, 41st Cong., 2d Sess. 2143 (1870) (Rep. Ward).

119. Cong. Globe, 41st Cong., 2d Sess. 2144 (1870).

120. See Phipps, "Marriage and Redemption," 461–64 (discussing the failure of the Cullom Bill to pass).

121. See Foner, *Reconstruction*, 499–511 (recounting the election of 1872).

122. David W. Blight, *Race and Reunion: The Civil War in American Memory* (Cambridge: Belknap Press of Harvard University Press, 2001), 127.

123. Blight, 123.

124. For the anti-polygamy legislation of the 1880s, see Edmunds Act, ch. 47, 22 Stat. 30 (1882); Edmunds-Tucker Act, ch. 397, 24 Stat. 635 (1887); see also Firmage and Mangrum, *Zion in the Courts*, 161–67 (discussing the passage and effects of the Edmunds Act and the Edmunds-Tucker Act); Gordon, *The Mormon Question*, 151–55, 164–67 (same as previous).

Radical politics. Unlike the humanitarian rhetoric that first galvanized the Republican response to Mormonism, Colfax's narrative of polygamy did not center on the plural wife as a victim.[125] Indeed, in contrast to the earlier vision of women as victims of fraud and kidnapping, Colfax brushed aside the question of whether plural wives consented to polygamy as essentially irrelevant.[126] Rather, he insisted on the analogy to the British Raj where one nation exercised a right to dominate and coerce another nation by virtue of its superior civilization and the barbarism of the subordinate people. By nesting anti-polygamy in the international but nevertheless racialist narrative of imperialism, the Mormons could be subject to legal coercion without reopening the explosive domestic issue of race relations in the South, to say nothing of the delicate issue of the former Confederacy's status as a conquered territory.[127]

---

125. Taylor and Colfax, *The Mormon Question*, 15. ("I pass over the obvious argument that wherever polygamy prevails in the world woman occupies necessarily a degraded and inferior condition . . .").

126. Taylor and Colfax, *The Mormon Question*, 15. ("The Brahmin reasoning that the woman consented (akin as it is to the Mormon argument now) had no effect. For England understood the power of religious fanaticism; of assumed revelation, of a potential public opinion").

127. Accompanying the attack on Radical Reconstruction was a set of racial narratives that replaced the domestic story of enslavement and emancipation with an international conception of barbarism and imperial civilization. In 1874, for example, the *Shreveport Times* attacked the political power that Radical Reconstruction conferred on freed Blacks by appealing to the "negro" tendency to "barbarism." Citing English explorers in the vanguard of Victorian imperialism as authority, the paper argued for white supremacy:

> These plantation negroes, who to-day control the destiny of Louisiana, are fac similes of the natives of Central Africa, as described by Sir Samuel Baker. . . . This Englishman is the special friend of the negro and an advocate for universal emancipation. He informs the world that the negro is incapable of self-government; that he is constantly on the retrograde to barbarism, unless supported and upheld by the white man, and that a certain amount of compulsion is necessary to make him a useful member of society . . .

"Who Shall Deliver Us from the Body of Death?," *Shreveport Times*, Sept. 14, 1874, reprinted in President of the United States, Use of the Army in Certain Southern States, H.R. Exec. Doc. No. 44-30, at 372 (1953). The article goes on to discuss the racial views of Stanley and other famous explorers and agents of the British Empire. See H.R. Exec. Doc No. 44-30, at 372–74.

The debates over the Edmunds Act of 1882[128] illustrate the way that the imperial rhetoric invoked in *Reynolds* helped to midwife a new, harsher anti-polygamy policy. The Edmunds Act was important because it was the first anti-polygamy law that went beyond criminalizing Mormon marital and sexual conduct.[129] Rather, it struck directly at Mormon political power in Utah by placing the territorial elective machinery under the control of a presidentially appointed commission and by excluding all polygamists from voting or holding public office.[130] It thus represented the crossing of a threshold with important connections to the recent past of Reconstruction, when the federal government also aggressively intervened in local elections across the defeated Confederacy.[131] The strength of the imperial analogy, however, proved sufficient to overcome any tainted association with the rejected politics of Radical Reconstruction. The potency of the imperialist rhetoric invoked by the court in *Reynolds* is perhaps best illustrated by Augustus Hill Garland.

In 1866, Garland brought one of the earliest legal challenges to Reconstruction policies.[132] Garland was a former member of the Confederate Senate, and a congressional act designed to exclude ex-Confederates from public life through loyalty oaths kept him from returning to the practice of law.[133] After a pardon by President Johnson in 1865, he fought a case to the US Supreme Court successfully challenging his continued exclusion from the bar.[134] Notwithstanding this experience, sixteen years later, Garland, now the US Senator from Arkansas, took

128. See Edmunds Act, ch. 47, 22 Stat. 30 (1882).

129. Compare Morrill Act, ch. 12, 12 Stat. 501 (1862) (making bigamy a crime in federal territories) with Edmunds Act, ch. 47, 22 Stat. 30 (1882) (defining the crime of unlawful cohabitation).

130. Edmunds Act, ch. 47, 22 Stat. 30 (1882) (restricting the voting and political rights of polygamists).

131. See generally David Buice, "A Stench in the Nostrils of Honest Men: Southern Democrats and the Edmunds Act of 1882," *Dialogue: A Journal of Mormon Thought* 21, no. 3 (1988): 100 (discussing ideological origins of opposition to the Edmunds Act by ex-Confederates and other Southerners).

132. See Ex Parte Garland, 71 U.S. 333 (1866).

133. See Ex Parte Garland, 71 U.S. 336 (1866). ("Having taken part in the Rebellion against the United States . . . Mr. Garland could not take the oath prescribed by the acts of Congress before mentioned, and the rule of the court of March, 1865").

134. See Ex Parte Garland, 71 U.S. 340 (1866). ("The President has fully pardoned him for this offence; and the constitutional effect of that pardon is to restore him to all his rights, civil and political, including the capacity or

to the Senate floor to defend the Edmunds Act, emphatically endorsing complete federal control of the elective machinery in Utah.[135] Senator Call of Florida objected to the bill, using themes drawn from the Southern critique of Reconstruction.[136] Senator Garland's reply is telling. His response to these politically potent post-Reconstruction claims was to explicitly invoke the Supreme Court's reasoning in *Reynolds*, insisting that Congress must suppress "crimes which the civilized world denounces."[137] He went on to bolster his argument with references to "Professor Heeren's Historical Researches."[138] The professor had "published some seven volumes of his own travels and researches in Asia and other countries" that discussed, "under the head of 'Asia,'" the evils of polygamy.[139] In short, he rejected Senator Call's domestic objections based on local self-government by appealing to a global imperial narrative about the superiority of the white race and the depraved practices of Asiatics. This imperial story proved powerful enough to displace his own vivid experience on the receiving end of similar tactics by the federal government.

Interestingly, even those who attacked the Edmunds Bill did so using imperial analogies. For example, in contrast to Senator Call, who implicitly placed "the Mormon question" within a domestic framework of concern over the distribution of local and federal power, Senator Brown of Georgia saw the issue in terms of the dangers of imperial overreach and the need for civilized masters to accommodate the barbaric practices of their subjects, citing sources on how British authorities in India were forced to tolerate polygamy by the limits of imperial power.[140] The response of Senator

---

qualification to hold office, as fully in every respect as though he had never committed the offence").

135. See 13 Cong. Rec. 1159 (1882) (statement of Sen. Garland).

136. 13 Cong. Rec. 1156 (1882). (statement of Sen. Call). ("[The bill] is an act which virtually declares that the President may give the whole political power of elections in the Territory of Utah to five persons nominated by himself and confirmed by the Senate. It seems to me that if there is anything in the institutions of this country and in the idea of self-government, that is a proposition which destroys the whole of it").

137. 13 Cong. Rec. 1159 (1882) (statement of Sen. Garland).

138. 13 Cong. Rec. 1159 (1882).

139. 13 Cong. Rec. 1159 (1882).

140. 13 Cong. Rec. 1202 (1882) (statement of Sen. Brown) ("England has had this same question to deal with. When she assumed the dominion of India she found polygamy there, and it has been there from time immemorial. They did not do what popular sentiment seeks to compel us now to do. The English people

Edmunds, the bill's sponsor, was to note limits to the tolerance of even the over-extended British. "May I ask the Senator," Edmunds interjected, "if the same book contains a statement of the laws of Thibet, where one woman may lawfully marry several husbands, and all of them be bound to the marital relation?"[141] Even the Raj balked at tolerating polyandry, and the United States, he implicitly claimed, ought to have higher standards.

Later, Edmunds expanded on the imperial example by deliberately posing a hypothetical designed to distance the situation in Utah from that in the South:

> Would the Senator really object to a law, supposing it were not unconstitutional, (which is another question,) which said that no man should be entitled to participate in the government of the State of Georgia that was in the practice of having all his father's wives, one or more, burned, Hindoo fashion, when his father died?[142]

Edmunds's rhetoric in this passage was subtle. It drew the sting of objections based on local self-government by raising the exotic hypothetical of "suttee" in Georgia. So outlandish and foreign an image was meant to lay to rest concerns that heavy-handed federal tactics in Utah had anything to do with the now-legitimized concern for local self-government in the South. Utah was akin to India, not Georgia. To be sure, there continued to be some Southern opposition to deploying federal power against the Mormons, but unlike the Cullom Bill of 1870, the anti-Mormon legislation of the 1880s—particularly after the successful passage of the Edmunds Act in 1882—was able to employ the legal tactics of Reconstruction without upsetting the consensus against the politics of Radical Republicanism.[143] *Reynolds* thus represented the triumph of a set of rhetorical moves that situated polygamy in a global narrative of racial superiority which accommodated the rising force of Jim Crow by exoticiz-

---

did not attempt to crush it out by law, but the British Parliament and the British courts recognize it in India on assuming control and recognize it to-day. Indeed they dare not do otherwise. They can enforce no law in India that proposes to exterminate polygamy").

141. 13 Cong. Rec. 1202 (1882) (statement of Sen. Edmunds).

142. 13 Cong. Rec. 1204 (1882) (statement of Sen. Edmunds).

143. See Phipps, "Marriage and Redemption," 480 ("Republicans in the 1880s displaced the sectionalism entrenched in earlier forms of anti-polygamy activism by claiming that a shared tradition of monogamy united the North and South").

ing the problem of Mormon polygamy, portraying its suppression as part of the onward march of the "northern and western nations of Europe."[144]

B. *Reynolds* and *Fin de Siècle* American Imperialism

Historians have traditionally ended the story of the anti-polygamy crusades in 1890, when the Mormon Church publicly abandoned plural marriage.[145] The jurisprudential dialogue with international imperialism at work in *Reynolds* and the subsequent debates over the suppression of polygamy, however, continued in the final decade of the century. On February 15, 1898, the U.S.S. Maine exploded in Havana Harbor. Two months later, Congress declared war on Spain. Within six days, the American Asiatic Squadron under George Dewey engaged a Spanish squadron in Manila Bay. Within a month, American forces had occupied the archipelago, and on August 12, 1898, the United States and Spain agreed to a ceasefire. By that time, American forces had occupied not only the Philippines, but also Guam, Cuba, and Puerto Rico. All of these territories were subsequently ceded to the United States by Spain in the Treaty of Paris.[146]

---

144. Reynolds v. United States, 98 U.S. 145, 164 (1879).

145. As more recent historians have made clear, however, the 1890 cutoff date for battles over Mormon polygamy is not quite correct. The Church of Jesus Christ of Latter-day Saints continued the limited and clandestine practice of plural marriage until the first decade of the twentieth century, when the threat of renewed prosecutions during the controversy over the seating of Senator Reed Smoot, a monogamist Mormon leader, led the Church's leadership to act decisively to end all new plural marriages. See generally Kathleen Flake, *The Politics of American Religious Identity: The Seating of Senator Reed Smoot, Mormon Apostle* (Chapel Hill: University of North Carolina Press, 2004); D. Michael Quinn, "LDS Church Authority and New Plural Marriages, 1890–1904," *Dialogue: A Journal of Mormon Thought*, 1895, 9. Since 1904, the Church has automatically excommunicated any member who enters into a plural marriage. See Danel W. Bachman and Ronald K. Esplin, "Plural Marriage," in *Encyclopedia of Mormonism*, ed. Daniel H. Ludlow, vol. 3 (Macmillian Co., 1992), 1091, 1095. Even thereafter, schismatic groups that repudiated the Church's stance on plural marriage continued to practice polygamy. These schismatic groups, often referred to as "Mormon fundamentalists," continue today, over a century after the Mormon Church itself rejected the practice. See generally B. Carmon Hardy, *Solemn Covenant: The Mormon Polygamous Passage* (Urbana and Chicago: University of Illinois Press, 1992) (discussing the roots and development of twentieth-century polygamy in the western United States).

146. See Treaty of Peace Between the United States and Spain, U.S.–Spain, Dec. 10, 1898, S. Exec. Doc. No. 55-62, pt. 1 (1899); see also Paolo E. Coletta,

Just as American victory over a Spanish-speaking power had sparked an intense round of constitutional debate in the wake of the Mexican-American War, the Spanish-American War launched an intense conversation over the nature of American expansion.[147] The Treaty of Guadalupe Hidalgo had left the United States with sovereignty over a community—the Mormons—enmeshed in barbaric and "Asiatic" practices that rendered them unfit for democratic self-government. The result was the transnational dialogue reflected in *Reynolds*. In the Mormon case, the "Asiatic" practice of polygamy had to be shed as a precondition for full integration into the American Union.[148] The Spanish-American War confronted American law with a similar question but on a much larger scale.[149] What was to be the status of the newly conquered Spanish colonies? Were they to be governed by the territorial model begun with the Northwest Ordinance of 1787, granted limited self-government, and admitted to the Union as states at some future point? Were they colonies of the American Republic, subject to the plenary authority of Congress for as long as it wished to exercise it? Did the Constitution "follow the flag" into Cuba, Puerto Rico, Guam, and the Philippines? Once again, American legal intellectuals looked to British imperial models.[150]

"McKinley, the Peace Negotiations, and the Acquisition of the Philippines," *Pacific Historical Review* 30, no. 4 (1961): 348 (discussing the negotiations over the Treaty of Paris of 1898).

147. See Burnett and Marshall, *Foreign in a Domestic Sense*, 3–17 (recounting the constitutional debate in the wake of the Spanish-American War).

148. Utah was admitted to the Union in 1896, decades after it had reached the level of population at which other territories were admitted as states. The reason for the delay, of course, was federal hostility to polygamy and other distinctive Mormon practices. See generally Lyman, *Political Deliverance*.

149. For a succinct summary of the debates, see Burnett and Marshall, *Foreign in a Domestic Sense*. See generally Kerr, *The Insular Cases* (discussing the constitutional debates over the status of the territory acquired from Spain in the Spanish-American War); Sparrow, *The Insular Cases and the Emergence of American Empire* (same as previous).

150. See, e.g., Lebbeus R. Wilfley, "How Great Britain Governs Her Colonies," *Yale Law Journal* 9, no. 5 (1900): 207–14 (examining the administration of the British Empire as a model for American law). According to Wilfley:

> The peculiar interest which attaches to the study of the Colonial Empire of Great Britain at the present time arises . . . because the United States have recently acquired possessions, some of which are so far removed from our shores and are surrounded by such climatic, social, racial and religious condi-

The debate first began in the pages of the recently launched *Harvard Law Review*.[151] Christopher Columbus Langdell and James Bradley Thayer argued that Congress could rule the new territories as subject colonies.[152] They were opposed by Simeon Baldwin and Carman F. Randolph, who insisted that annexing Spanish possessions would entitle their inhabitants to all the rights of United States citizens.[153] Finally, Abbot Lawrence Lowell proposed an intermediate position in which territories enjoyed more rights than those bestowed on European colonies but not the full protection of the US Constitution.[154] All of the protagonists examined the issues through the lens of British imperialism, and both sides invoked the legal suppression of polygamy in Utah as a precedent revealing the true nature of American power over conquered peoples.

For example, Randolph insisted that plenary congressional authority over territories not incorporated into a state would unacceptably leave American "'colonists . . . in a state of the most complete subordination, and as dependent upon the will of Congress as the people of this country would have been upon the king and parliament of Great Britain, if they could have sustained their claim to bind us in all cases whatsoever.'"[155] Thayer's argument was equally nested in imperial narratives. he argued that the nation could "govern these islands as colonies, substantially as England might

---

> tions that they will have to be treated, for a time at least, as dependencies, before they can be incorporated into the Federal Union.

Wilfley, 207. He went on to gush that "[t]he record of the Colonial Empire of Great Britain is a wonderful record; a tale of peace and war, of change, of enlargement, of unparalleled growth." Wilfley, 207.

151. See Burnett and Marshall, *Foreign in a Domestic Sense*, 5–7 (discussing the debates in *Harvard Law Review* prior to the decision of the Court in the Insular Cases).

152. See generally C. C. Langdell, "The Status of Our New Territories," *Harvard Law Review* 12, no. 6 (1899): 365–92; James Bradley Thayer, "Our New Possessions," *Harvard Law Review* 12, no. 7 (1899): 464–85.

153. See generally Simeon E. Baldwin, "The Constitutional Questions Incident to the Acquisition and Government by the United States of Island Territory," *Harvard Law Review* 12, no. 6 (1899): 393–416; Carman F. Randolph, "Constitutional Aspects of Annexation," *Harvard Law Review* 12, no. 5 (1898): 191–315.

154. See generally Abbott Lawrence Lowell, "Abbott Lawrence Lowell, The Status of Our New Possessions—A Third View, 13 Harv. L. Rev. 155 (1899)," *Harvard Law Review* 13, no. 3 (1899): 155–76.

155. Randolph, "Constitutional Aspects of Annexation," 303 (quoting James Kent, *Commentaries on American Law*, 1:360–61 [1826]).

govern them; that we have the same power that other nations have."[156] He went on to pair "the entire recent history of England and of the United States" as examples of benevolent imperial administration.[157] Strikingly, Thayer gave an example of the "wise and free colonial administration"[158] of the United States: its control of the territory conquered from Mexico.[159] Here, he noted that "[w]hatever restraints may be imposed on our congress and executive by the Constitution of the United States, they have not made impossible a firm and vigorous administration of government in the territories. Witness especially the case of . . . the Territory of Utah."[160]

Lowell also conceptualized the nineteenth-century expansion of the United States across the continent in imperial terms. Writing in *The Atlantic Monthly*, he argued, "there has never been a time, since the adoption of the first ordinance for the government of the Northwest Territory in 1787, when the United States has not had colonies."[161] This fact was obscured for some, he went on to argue, because America's control over her colonies had been smooth and benign, "[w]ith the exception of . . . the disturbances in Utah, where polygamy was a rock of offense."[162] Like Thayer, he saw America's westward expansion as a local species of the global genus of imperialism, with the Mormons serving as one of the points of contention that revealed the true relationship between the metropolitan center and its colonial periphery. The shift in anti-polygamy politics midwifed by the imperial rhetoric in *Reynolds* lay just below the surface of these allusions. Thus, notably absent from this imperial conceptualization of the history of federal power was any discussion of Reconstruction. The exercise of federal authority in Utah was a form of benign imperialism, while the exercise of federal authority in the defeated South was passed over in discreet silence.

Eventually, the argument shifted to the judiciary. In 1901, a series of disputes collectively dubbed the *Insular Cases* reached the US Supreme Court.[163] Although the facts and issues in the cases varied, they forced the

---

156. Thayer, "Our New Possessions," 467.

157. Thayer, 475.

158. Thayer, 475.

159. Thayer, 476.

160. Thayer, 478.

161. A. Lawrence Lowell, "The Colonial Expansion of the United States," *Atlantic Monthly*, February 1899, 145.

162. Lowell, 146.

163. See Fourteen Diamond Rings v. United States, 183 U.S. 176 (1901); Dooley v. United States, 183 U.S. 151 (1901); Huus v. New York, 182 U.S. 392

court to address the constitutional status of the new possessions conquered from Spain. The intricacies of the court's reasoning and holding are beyond the scope of this chapter.[164] Suffice it to say that the intermediate position of Lowell triumphed in the court's confused formulation that Puerto Rico and the other territories were "foreign in a domestic sense."[165] Tellingly, *Reynolds v. United States* made an appearance in the arguments to the court, where it was seen not as a precedent over the scope of religious freedom but rather as a case defining the scope of American imperial power.[166]

Proponents of the theory that the Constitution applies fully and of its own force in all American territories looked to *Reynolds* as an example of the Bill of Rights's control, even over Congress's authority, beyond the territory of the organized states.[167] In contrast, the attorney general insisted that the Constitution had applied in *Reynolds* only because Congress had, in the exercise of its plenary power over conquered territories, chosen to extend its protections by statute in 1850.[168] Relying on language from one of *Reynolds*'s progeny, the attorney general told the court in oral argument:

> We plant ourselves squarely on the statement of this court in the Mormon Church case . . . that in legislating for Territories, Congress would be subject

---

(1901); Downes v. Bidwell, 182 U.S. 244 (1901); Armstrong v. United States, 182 U.S. 243 (1901); Goetze v. United States, 182 U.S. 221 (1901); De Lima v. Bidwell, 182 U.S. 1 (1901).

164. For a fuller discussion of the cases, see sources cited supra note 6.

165. Downes, 182 U.S. at 341.

166. See Brief for Appellant, Armstrong v. United States, 182 U.S. 143 (1900) (No. 509), in The Insular Cases, Comprising The Records, Briefs, and Arguments of Counsel in the Insular Cases of the October Term, 1900, in the Supreme Court of the United States, Including the Appendixes Thereto, H.R. Doc. No. 56-4171, at 890 (1901) ("Congress is not omnipotent as to the Territories, We have in the Reynolds case, 98 U.S., 162, a decision of the Supreme Court that it is not omnipotent"); see also Brief for the United States, Goetze v United States, 182 U.S. 221 (1900) (No. 340), in The Insular Cases, Comprising The Records, Briefs, and Arguments of Counsel in the Insular Cases of the October Term, 1900, in the Supreme Court of the United States, Including the Appendixes Thereto, H.R. Doc. 56-4171, at 220 (1901) ("[In *Reynolds v. United States*], Chief Justice Waite said: 'By the Constitution of the United States (amendment 6), the accused was entitled to a trial by an impartial jury.' This was correct, in view of the fact that in 1850 the Constitution and laws of the United States, so far as applicable, were extended to the Territory of Utah").

167. See Brief for Appellant, supra note 222, at 890.

168. See Brief for the United States, supra note 222, at 220.

> . . . [rather] by . . . the general spirit of the Constitution than by any express and direct application of its provisions."[169]

To be sure, *Reynolds* and the other cases spawned by the anti-polygamy battles were not a major, let alone causal, force in resolving the constitutional debates precipitated by the Spanish-American War. Their cameo appearance, however, shows the continuity between the earlier battles over polygamy and *fin de siècle* arguments over imperialism.

The invocation of imperial models in both *Reynolds* and the *Insular Cases* was part of a much broader shift in late nineteenth-century thinking, in which eighteenth-century narratives of universal rights were replaced by imperial narratives centered on potent ideas of race and progress. Early nineteenth-century statesmen such as Thomas Jefferson and John Quincy Adams had contrasted the virtue of republican America with the grasping European empires while aggressively pushing the territorial expansion of the United States at the expense of Indian tribes and rival powers such as Spain, France, Britain, and Mexico.[170] However, late nineteenth-century Americans were more willing to explicitly identify with Great Power imperialism.[171] As the United States' commercial and military power expanded outward in the years after the Civil War, Americans increasingly found themselves in a world dominated by British imperialism.[172] In the liminal spaces of empire such as the Philippines (a nominally Spanish colony dominated by English commercial interests) or Burma (a newly acquired frontier of the Indian Raj where American engineers successfully bid for

---

169. Argument of the Attorney General, De Lima v. Bidwell, 182 U.S. 1 (1900) (No. 456), in The Insular Cases, Comprising The Records, Briefs, and Arguments of Counsel in the Insular Cases of the October Term, 1900, in the Supreme Court of the United States, Including the Appendixes Thereto, H.R. Doc. 56-4171, at 345 (1901).

170. See, e.g., Daniel Howe, *What Hath God Wrought: The Transformation of America, 1815–1848* (New York: Oxford University Press, 2007), 111–16 (discussing John Quincy Adams's role in the acquisition of Florida and the promulgation of the Monroe Doctrine).

171. See generally Paul A. Kramer, "Empires, Exceptions, and Anglo-Saxons: Race and Rule between the British and United States Empires, 1880–1910," *The Journal of American History* 88, no. 4 (2002): 1315–53 (discussing American encounters with the British Empire and the effect on American understanding of American experience).

172. Kramer.

government contracts), Americans abroad began identifying themselves with the triumphant Britons.[173]

At home, many Americans came to see their own expansion as an expression of the wider story of European—and especially Anglo-Saxon—migration to, and benign domination of, foreign territories and peoples.[174] For example, in his 1889 book *The Winning of the West*, Theodore Roosevelt told the story of westward expansion in the context of global Anglo-Saxon colonization.[175] His book literally opens with the expansion of English legal models:

> During the past three centuries the spread of the English-speaking peoples over the world's waste spaces has been not only the most striking feature in the world's history, but also the event of all others most far-reaching in its effects and its importance.
>
> . . . The Common Law which Coke jealously upheld in the southern half of a single European island, is now the law of the land throughout the vast regions of Australasia, and of America north of the Rio Grande.[176]

To be sure, Roosevelt insisted on a certain amount of American exceptionalism, but it was defined in relation to other imperial adventures.[177] Likewise, under the influence of Harvard historian Henry Adams and European scholars like Henry Maine, Roosevelt's chief ally—Senator Henry Cabot Lodge—came to believe that the origins of American constitutionalism could be traced back through the story of the Anglo-Saxons to

---

173. Kramer.

174. Kramer, 1315 ("Along different timelines, pursuing varied agendas, and mobilizing diverse discourses to defend them, Americans from varied political backgrounds came to recognize that the United States' new colonial empire—part of its much vaster commercial, territorial, and military empires—operated within a larger network of imperial thought and practice").

175. See generally Theodore Roosevelt, *The Winning of the West*, vol. 1 (New York: Putnam, 1889), 1–31. See also Kramer, "Empires, Exceptions, and Anglo-Saxons," 1325 (discussing the Winning of the West in the context of a broader stream of transatlantic borrowing of imperialist ideologies).

176. Roosevelt, *The Winning of the West*, 1:1.

177. For example, he noted with a touch of national pride that the Native Americans were "the most formidable savage foes ever encountered by colonists of European stock. Relatively to their numbers, they have shown themselves far more to be dreaded than the Zulus or even the Maoris." Roosevelt, 1:17.

the tribes of ancient Germania.[178] According to Lodge, the unique talent of the Anglo-Saxon race was their aptitude for law and self-government.[179]

A corollary of this theory was that races unblessed with the Teutonic gift for administration were in need of benign Anglo-Saxon domination. Indeed, they were congenitally unfit for self-government without a long period of tutelage. Lodge insisted:

> You can not change race tendencies in a moment. . . . [The] theory, that you could make a Hottentot into a European if you only took possession of him in infancy and gave him a European education among suitable surroundings, has been abandoned alike by science and history as grotesquely false. . . . We know what sort of government the Malay makes when he is left to himself.[180]

His conclusion was that the United States should exercise imperial control over "lower" peoples without legal or constitutional scruple.[181] Such control was nothing more than the working out of America's destined part in the global and historical process of applying the Anglo-Saxon genius for government to a benighted world, a genius embodied in the United States Constitution.[182] Nevertheless, in this racially and historically charged vision of the Constitution, Mormons, Filipinos, and others who stood outside the story of Anglo-Saxon progress occupied a decidedly second-class status.[183]

---

178. See Mark S. Weiner, "Teutonic Constitutionalism: The Role of Ethno-Juridical Discourse in the Spanish-American War," in *Foreign in a Domestic Sense: Puerto Rico, American Expansionism, and the Constitution*, ed. Christina Duffy Burnett and Burke Marshall (Durham: Duke University Press, 2001), 48 (discussing Lodge's constitutional views).

179. Weiner, 57 ("'[T]he laws and institutions of the ancient German tribes flourished and waxed strong on the soil of England. . . . Strong enough to resist the power of the church in infancy, stronger still to resist the shock of the Norman invasion, crushed then, but not destroyed, by foreign influence, the great principles of Anglo-Saxon law, ever changing and assimilating, have survived in the noblest work of the race—the English common law.'" [quoting Wai-Chee Dimock, Empire for Liberty: Melville and the Poetics of Individualism 9 (1989)]).

180. Weiner, 62 (internal quotation marks omitted) (quoting 33 Cong. Rec. 2621 [1900]).

181. Weiner, 63–75 (discussing the "Progressive Anglo-Saxon Interpretation of the Insular Cases").

182. Weiner, 63–75.

183. In this regard, it is worth noting that one of the "bones of contention" between the Mormons and the federal government was the Latter-day Saints' hostility to the common-law courts. Nineteenth-century Mormons sought to

Conclusion

As the *Insular Cases* were making their way to the Supreme Court, the popular *McClure's Magazine* published an appeal by the poet laureate of British imperialism.[184] Lest anyone mistake the topic of his poem, Rudyard Kipling subtitled it, "The United States in the Philippine's Islands."[185] "Take up the White Man's burden," he implored Americans, "To wait, in heavy harness, / On fluttered folk and wild—/ Your new-caught sullen peoples, / Half devil and half child."[186] The rhetorical invitation of the poem was clear. America, Kipling argued, needed to see itself in modern imperial terms and adopt the "dear-bought wisdom" of its international peers.[187] The poetic appeal, however, had already been foreshadowed in a legal appeal more than twenty years earlier, when Reynolds's lawyers rose before the court armed with arguments about natural law, only to be defeated by the more powerful, progressive myth that Kipling ultimately set to verse. Where Reynolds's lawyers had seen an organon for discover-

---

bypass these courts by resolving their civil disputes in ecclesiastical courts. See generally Oman, "Preaching to the Court House and Judging in the Temple," 212–14. One anti-Mormon critic writing in 1904 compared the Mormons to the "Chinese highbinders of San Francisco" who similarly eschewed the common-law courts because "[t]hey . . . could not more appreciate what we think is civilization than they could fly." See Oman, 218 (internal quotation marks omitted) (quoting Public Against Apostle Smoot: Opposed by Sentiment of Country, Salt Lake Trib., Dec. 20, 1904, at 2).

184. See Rudyard Kipling, "The White Man's Burden: The United States and the Philippines Islands," *McClure's Magazine*, February 1899, 4; see also Rudyard Kipling, *The Collected Poems of Rudyard Kipling* (Ware: Wordsworth Editions, 1994), 334 (containing Kipling's subtitle to the work).

185. *The Collected Poems of Rudyard Kipling*, 334.

186. *The Collected Poems of Rudyard Kipling*, 334.

187. The final stanza of the poem reads:

> Take up the White Man's burden!
> Have done with childish days—
> The lightly-proffered laurel,
> The easy ungrudged praise:
> Comes now, to search your manhood
> Through all the thankless years,
> Cold, edged with dear-bought wisdom,
> The judgment of your peers.

The Collected Poems of Rudyard Kipling, 334.

ing immutable natural laws in the diversity and unity of human laws, the court saw barbarism. In the justices' vision, the Mormons were among the "sullen peoples, / Half Devil and half child," who were like "African and Asiatic"[188] populations and needed a firm imperial hand. The appeal to non-Western culture had gone from defense to indictment.

As the voice of the losers in the case, it is fitting to close this chapter by returning to George Q. Cannon. While the arguments that he penned in his *Review* almost certainly had their genesis with the decidedly non-Mormon George Biddle, Cannon adopted them into a narrative which he directed inward, toward the Mormon community that would shortly reap the whirlwind of their 1879 defeat in *Reynolds*. He wrote:

> Not the least of the considerations which prompt me in this review, is that I desire that all the people of my faith may know that we have not been deceived in our ideas respecting the Constitution and our rights under it; that if we are to be stricken down . . . it shall not be in ignorance nor in doubt as to the wrongfulness of the blows from which we suffer; that our children may know that we fell contending for constitutional rights, liberty of conscience for ourselves and all others. . . .[189]

The court's appeal to imperial models did not go unnoticed. Cannon was born an Englishman. He immigrated to America after joining the Mormon Church, and, at one point, his political opponents dogged him with the accusation that he was never naturalized as a US citizen and remained a British subject, making him ineligible for his office as territorial delegate.[190] There is thus a biographical irony in his response to the court's invocation of the British Raj. After recounting the court's reliance on analogies to "suttee" and "thugee," Cannon turned to a different story about British imperial power:

> I was taught to look upon the experience which the [American] colonies underwent in the suffering of wrongs, in the endurance of oppression, in the struggles for religious and political liberty, as a preparatory training to enable them to value, contend for and achieve independence. I was taught that the firmness, valor and undaunted cheerfulness, hope and confidence of Washington, and . . . the Adamses, Franklin, Jefferson, and Madison . . . were due to the direct blessing and inspiration of Heaven bestowed upon them.[191]

---

188. Reynolds v. United States, 98 U.S. 145, 164 (1879).

189. Cannon, *A Review of the Decision of the Supreme Court of the United States*, 6.

190. See Bitton, *George Q. Cannon: A Biography*, 241–50 (recounting the controversy regarding Cannon's citizenship).

191. Cannon, *A Review of the Decision of the Supreme Court of the United States*, 5.

Against the court's admiring analogy to nineteenth-century British imperialism, Cannon thus responded with the story of eighteenth-century British imperialism and the divine sanction for its defeat. As the court's opinion in *Reynolds* itself demonstrates, Jefferson and Madison were names to conjure with, but in Cannon's argument they proved insufficient. The eighteenth-century imperialism, on whose opprobrium he traded, lacked a connection to the potent contemporary rhetoric of race and barbarism. Universal reason had been replaced by progress and the white man's burden.

CHAPTER 6

Salt, Smurthwaite, and Smith: The Origins of the Modern Legal Identity of The Church of Jesus Christ of Latter-day Saints

In 2019 there existed a legal entity known as The Church of Jesus Christ of Latter-day Saints.[1] This fact will likely strike most readers as unexceptional. More interesting, however, is the fact that before 2019 there had been no such legal entity as The Church of Jesus Christ of Latter-day Saints for over 150 years, the last of that name likely having been disincorporated in 1862. Even more strange, although there were millions of people around the globe who identified themselves as Latter-day Saints, in 2019 the only member of the legal entity known as The Church of Jesus Christ of Latter-day Saints was Russell M. Nelson. This somewhat surprising state of affairs resulted from the effort to disestablish the established colonial churches in the wake of the American Revolution that created a body of corporate law in the United States with a distinctly Protestant inflection; it is also a result of how The Church of Jesus Christ of Latter-day Saints, with its hierarchical emphasis on prophetic authority and its massive ecclesiastical ambitions, became entangled with and ultimately resisted that body of law. It may also have been the result of a bitter dispute over salt, now long forgotten but famous at the time, between Joseph F. Smith, president of the Church from 1901 to 1918, and Charles Smurthwaite, a Utah entrepreneur.[2]

Beginning in 1830, the Church struggled to define the nature of its legal personality. During the lifetime of Joseph Smith, it attempted to for-

1. See Human Resources Department, The Church of Jesus Christ of Latter-day Saints, "Further Chances to Emphasize the Correct Name of the Church of Jesus Christ," email message to author, June 19, 2019 (explaining that the Corporation of the Presiding Bishop of the Church of Jesus Christ of Latter-day Saints has been merged with the Corporation of the President of the Church of Jesus Christ of Latter-day Saints and has been renamed).

2. Evidence of the dispute's notoriety at the time can be seen in the fact that in his 1911 exposé of Mormon affairs in Utah, Frank Cannon devoted considerable space to the case. See Frank J. Cannon and Harvey J. O'Higgins, *Under the Prophet in Utah: The National Menace of a Political Priestcraft* (Boston: The C. M. Clark Publishing Co., 1911), 323–26.

mally incorporate under the laws of two states. No American jurisdiction at the time, however, provided a legal form that meshed harmoniously with the ecclesiastical structure and government of the Church, contributing to the chaos that marked its legal affairs at the time of Smith's murder. The Latter-day Saints took advantage of the comparative legal independence of early territorial Utah to incorporate the Church in a way that allowed it to pursue its ecclesiastical ambitions, but this legal structure soon drew the ire of Congress. In the late 1880s, as the federal government's crusade against polygamy reached its height, the corporate structure of the Church became a key legal battleground. In the aftermath of those battles, the Church chose to eschew any centralized legal entity for its affairs, despite its hierarchal ecclesiology. Unresolved questions came to a head when controversies over post-Manifesto polygamy and church business enterprises boiled over into litigation during Joseph F. Smith's administration. Smurthwaite, an excommunicated Mormon businessman, and Don Carlos Musser, the scion of a prominent Latter-day Saint family, sued Smith over the use of tithing funds. The case drew national media attention and pitted two of the most prominent and talented members of the Utah Bar—Church general counsel Franklin S. Richards and former Utah Supreme Court justice Charles Zane—against one another. Ultimately Richards prevailed, but the case vividly illustrated the precarious nature of the Church's ambigious legal structure and likely contributed to the creation of the corporate entity that continues to legally embody the Church today.

A Brief History of the Church as a Legal Entity to 1905

The Church of Jesus Christ of Latter-day Saints was born into a legal system defined by the legacy of America's first disestablishment. In 1774, nine of the thirteen colonies had established churches, all of which had been abandoned by the end of the 1830s. The New York law that Joseph Smith tried to use to organize his new church in 1830 was the result of more than a century of conflict over the legal status of New York's established church.[3] The colony of New Amsterdam was founded by the Dutch West India Company in 1625. While nominally committed to the Dutch Reformed Church, the company consistently subordinated Calvinist or-

3. See Mark D. McGarvie, *One Nation Under Law: America's Early National Struggles to Separate Church and State* (DeKalb: Northern Illinois University Press, 2004), 97–130; Elizabeth Mensch, "Religion, Revival, and the Ruling Class: A Critical History of Trinity Church," *Buffalo Law Review* 36 (1987): 427–571.

thodoxy to commercial expediency by adopting a tolerant stance toward religion. After the English takeover of New Amsterdam in 1664, royal officials sought to create an established Anglican Church by granting special benefits to the Church of England and incorporating Trinity Church in New York City, the wealthiest and most important Anglican congregation in the colony. By the time of the American Revolution, however, Trinity Church was widely hated, and dissenting sects continued to dispute whether Anglicanism was actually the established church.[4] The state's revolutionary constitution of 1777 provided that "the free exercise and enjoyment of religious profession and worship, without discrimination or preference, shall forever hereafter be allowed within this State to all mankind."[5] The state constitutional convention published a statement that with the new constitution "all such . . . statutes and acts . . . as may be construed to establish or maintain any particular denomination of Christians or their ministers . . . be and they are, abrogated and rejected."[6] But shortly after the Revolution, parishioner Alexander Hamilton fought off an effort to disincorporate Trinity, the approach taken to disestablishment in Virginia.[7] In 1784, the legislature responded by abrogating the provisions in previously granted corporate charters that gave churches taxing authority.[8] Before this time, corporations had been formed by some special act of the legislature. However, with the new law, the New York legislature took the radical step of allowing any religious society to incor-

4. The so-called "Duke's Laws" promulgated immediately after the English takeover of New Amsterdam required local parishes to elect overseers who could then choose any ordained Protestant minister for the local church, who was paid from taxes collected by the local courts. This system was later codified in the 1693 Ministry Act, which decreed that in each parish "there shall be called, inducted, and established, a good sufficient Protestant Ministry." Quoted in Mensch, "Religion, Revival, and the Ruling Class," 444. The dispute over whether there was a single established church in the colony centered on whether this law, which was silent on the question, required that the minister be Anglican.

5. New York Const. art. XXXVIII (1777).

6. Quoted McGarvie, *One Nation Under Law*, 111.

7. See Mensch, "Religion, Revival, and the Ruling Class," 475–76.

8. See "An Act to remove doubts which may have arisen respecting the charter rights of the minister, elders and deacons of the Reformed Protestant Dutch Church of the city of New York, in consequence of the late invasion of this State," in *Laws of New York* 597 (1784); "An Act for making such alterations in the charter of the Corporation of Trinity Church, as to render it more conformable to the Constitution of the State," in *Laws of New York* 646 (1784).

porate without legislative action. This could be done simply by electing trustees and filing papers with the local court.[9] This 1784 law and its descendants provided the basic framework for Joseph Smith in 1830.

New York provided a model for many of the new states of the expanding republic, including Ohio and Illinois, where the Church relocated.[10] At the heart of this legal regime were three core assumptions.[11] The first was that, as a legal entity, a church consisted of the aggregation of its individual members. A church corporation was not an independent institution providing religious services and instruction to congregants. Rather, it was a legal representation of the congregants themselves. The second key assumption flowed from the first: ecclesiastical control was to reside with the laity rather than the clergy. During the mid-nineteenth century, this produced a series of conflicts within the Catholic Church with the bishops on one side, insisting on the right to control parish property and choose parish priests, and dissident church members on the other, eager to use the power conferred on them by state corporate law to control their own parishes.[12] The third assumption was that the amount of property that a church could hold must be sharply limited. These so-called "mortmain" provisions had their origins in the Tudor Reformation as the mechanism by which the crown seized church property.[13] In the United States, they reflected congregational Protestant assumptions about church government and hostility toward the concentration of economic power in ecclesiastical hands.

---

9. See "An Act to enable all religious denominations in this State to appoint trustees who shall be a body corporate, for the purpose for taking care of the temporalities of their respective congregations, and for other purposes therein mentioned," in *Laws of New York* 613 (1784).

10. Missouri was an exception. Its 1820 Declaration of Rights provided that "no religious corporation can ever be established in this state." Missouri Const. art. XIII, § 5 (1820). In this, it followed the example of Virginia, where disestablishment took the form of a blanket prohibition on incorporation by churches.

11. For an excellent summary of this legal regime prior to the Civil War, see Sarah Barringer Gordon, "The First Disestablishment: Limits on Church Power and Property Before the Civil War," *University of Pennsylvania Law Review* 162 (2014): 307–72.

12. Patrick J. Dignan, *A History of the Legal Incorporation of Catholic Church Property in the United States (1784–1932)* (Washington, DC: Catholic University of America Press, 1933), 46–93.

13. See Paul G. Kauper and Stephen C. Ellis, "Religious Corporations and the Law," *Michigan Law Review* 71, no. 8 (August 1, 1973): 1499–1574.

For most of its history before the move to Utah, the Church was an unincorprated religious society. Church members likely failed to comply with the formalities required to organize under New York law. Missouri law prohibited religious corporations, and it seems that no effort was made to incorporate the Church as opposed to various Church-related entities in Ohio.[14] This changed in Nauvoo. Joseph Smith borrowed large sums of money on the credit of the Church to purchase the land on which to build the city.[15] However, because the Church lacked legal existence, this meant that the status of these debts was ambiguous. Matters came to a head when a Nauvoo-based steamboat sank.[16] Joseph Smith had guaranteed the loan that the steamboat's promoters had used to finance its purchase and after it sank, Smith became liable on the guarantee. In 1842, Congress passed one of its recurrent nineteenth-century bankruptcy laws, and Smith sought to take advantage of the law while it was in force.[17] The statute made Smith's personal assets available to his creditors as a condition of discharge. In order to preserve church assets, he sought to incorporate the Church under Illinois law and transfer church assets to this new legal entity prior to filing for bankruptcy. An 1839 Illinois law, however, limited religious corporations to owning, at most, forty acres of land "for the purpose of camp-meeting ground."[18] Thus, at the time

---

14. See David Keith Stott, "Organizing the Church as a Religious Association in 1830," in *Sustaining the Law: Joseph Smith's Legal Encounters*, ed. Gordon A. Madsen, Jeffrey N. Walker, and John W. Welch (Provo: BYU Studies, 2014), 113–40; Max H. Parkin, "Joseph Smith and the United Firm: The Growth and Decline of the Church's First Master Plan of Business and Finance, Ohio and Missouri, 1832–1834," *Brigham Young University Studies* 46, no. 3 (2007): 5–62; Jeffrey N. Walker, "The Kirtland Safety Society and the Fraud of Grandison Newell: A Legal Examination," *BYU Studies Quarterly* 54, no. 3 (2015): 32–148. See also Missouri Const. art. XIII, § 5 (1820).

15. Glen M. Leonard, *Nauvoo: Place of Peace People of Promise* (Salt Lake City: Deseret Book Co., 2002), 47–61.

16. Dallin H. Oaks and Joseph I. Bentley, "Joseph Smith and Legal Process: In the Wake of the Steamboat Nauvoo," *Brigham Young University Law Review* 1976 (1976): 735–82.

17. Prior to 1898, the United States had no permanent bankruptcy legislation. Rather, Congress periodically passed bankruptcy laws in response to financial downturns, only to repeal them a few years later. See David A. Skeel, *Debt's Dominion: A History of Bankruptcy Law in America* (Princeton: Princeton University Press, 2004).

18. Act of March 2, 1839, 1838 Ill. Laws 267.

of Joseph Smith's murder, the legal status of the Church was hopelessly complicated, contributing to the bitter disputes between Brigham Young, as representative of the Church, and Emma Smith, who was the residual claimant on Smith's estate.[19]

In 1851, the legislature of the State of Deseret sought to solve these problems by granting the Church a corporate charter. It eliminated the issues that had bedeviled it for the previous two decades.[20] The law gave the Church the unlimited ability to hold property but did not break completely with American church law of the time. It conceptualized the Church as the corporate expression of the members. It also contemplated ultimate lay control. Church officers in control of church property were required to post bonds, and "said trustee and assistant trustees shall continue in office during the pleasure of said church." At the same time, the statute was unique. It provided that the Church could "solemnize marriages compatible with the revelations of Jesus Christ," a sly way of providing legal recognition for plural marriages.[21] It went on to provide the Church with the power to govern itself using language that envisioned a broad competence and jurisdiction:

> Said church . . . shall possess . . . the power and authority, in and of itself, to originate, make, pass, and establish rules, regulations, ordinances, laws, customs, and criterions, for the good order, safety, government, conveniences, comfort, and control of said church, and for the punishment or forgiveness of all offenses, relative to fellowship, according to church covenants: that the pursuit of bliss, and the enjoyment of life, in every capacity of public association, and domestic happiness; temporal expansion; or spiritual increase upon the earth, may not legally be questioned: provided, however, that each and every act, or practice so established, or adopted for law, or custom, shall relate to solemnities, sacraments, ceremonies, consecrations, endowments, tithings, marriages, fellowship, or the religious duties of man to his Maker, inasmuch as the doctrines, principles, or performances, support virtue, and increase morality and are not inconsistent with, or repugnant to, the Constitution of the United States, or of this State, and are founded in the revelations of the Lord.[22]

---

19. See Linda King Newell and Valeen Tippetts Avery, *Mormon Enigma: Emma Hale Smith*, 2nd ed. (Urbana: University of Illinois Press, 1994), 200.

20. See Dale Morgan, *The State of Deseret* (Logan: Utah State University Press, 1987), 185–87.

21. Morgan, 186.

22. Morgan, 186.

After Congress organized the Utah Territory, the territorial legislature adopted the previous statutes of the now-defunct State of Deseret, thus incorporating the Church under American law.[23]

By 1860, the Republican party—founded to rid the territories of the "twin relics of barbarism" (slavery and polygamy)—was in power, and in 1862, the Morrill Anti-Bigamy Act repealed the Utah statute incorporating the Church and went on to limit its property holdings to $50,000.[24] The Morrill Act, however, remained a dead letter in Utah for more than a decade, making the legal status of the Church uncertain once again. Brigham Young responded by holding church property as "trustee in trust" (a legal neologism invented in Nauvoo as part of the effort to untangle Joseph Smith's legal affairs).[25] This meant that the property was titled in Brigham Young's name but held on behalf of the Church. The precise nature of this holding, however, was uncertain. It was not clear that there was a common-law trust—in which case Young would have held "bare legal title" while "equitable title" would have been held by church members as a whole—or if the property was owned outright by Brigham Young.[26] Unsurprisingly,

23. See Joint Resolution Legalizing the Laws of the Provisional Government of the State of Deseret, *Utah Laws* 205 (1851).

24. Technically, there was a legal question as to whether the Morrill Act disincorporated the church because it stated, "this act shall be so limited . . . as not to affect or interfere with the right of property legally acquired under [the church's charter] . . . but only annul such acts and laws which establish, maintain, protect, or countenance the practice of polygamy." Morrill Anti-Bigamy Act, ch. 126 § 3, 12 Stat. 501 (1862). Nevertheless, Church leaders in Utah acted as though the Church lacked a separate legal existence after 1862.

25. See Samuel D. Brunson, "Mormon Profit: Brigham Young, Tithing, and the Bureau of Internal Revenue," *Brigham Young University Law Review* 2019, no. 1 (2019): 43n7.

26. There were serious legal problems with conceptualizing the trustee-in-trust as holding Church property in trust for all Church members. Under the notoriously arcane common-law rule against perpetuities, "No interest subject to a condition precedent is good, unless the condition must be fulfilled, if at all, within twenty-one years after some life in being at the creation of the interest." John Chipman Gray, *The Rule against Perpetuities*, 3rd ed. (Boston: Little, Brown, and Company, 1915), 174. The purpose of the rule is to insure that title to property is not clogged by legal interests that spring into existence many lifetimes after the initial grant is made. A conveyance of property to the trustee-in-trust to be held in trust for all Church members tries to create an interest in the property in favor of Church members. The Church members in question must be born

upon his death in 1877, another bitter dispute between the Church and the heirs took place in the courts.[27]

Successive presidents of the Church continued to hold church property personally as trustee-in-trust. In the early 1880s, Franklin S. Richards, the Church's legal counsel, foresaw that Congress was likely to pass laws to escheat church property and urged the creation of stake and ward corporations. John Taylor, as trustee-in-trust, could then transfer church property to the corporations to shield the property from federal confiscation.[28] It was difficult for Richards to persuade Taylor and other leaders, but this was done around 1884. The law used was an 1878 statute that allowed for the creation of corporations consisting of "persons associated together for religious, social, scientific, benevolent or other purposes"[29] but limited their ability to hold property. "[N]o such corporation," the statute read, "must own or hold more real estate than may be necessary for the business and objects of the association."[30] The resulting corporations were also cumbersome, requiring multiple trustees and the authoring of elaborate bylaws. However, the strategy paid off when the solicitor general of the United States ruled that property held by these corporations

---

for that interest to be considered a condition precedent. However, there are many Church members that would be born in the future outside of the time limits of the rule. Accordingly, the attempted trust would fail. Strictly speaking, the property couldn't be held in trust for the Church as an entity because, as a matter of law, likely no such entity existed. At best, a trust could be created in favor of living Church members and those future church members who would be born within the time limits of the rule. Brigham Young might also have held the property as a charitable trust, meaning that there was no identifiable group for whose benefit the property was held. In this case, the property simply would have been held for a particular purpose, like advancing religion or the like. Such a trust, however, would have exposed Church finances to potential oversight by government officials, who, unlike in the case of ordinary trusts, are given standing to intervene in charitable trust cases.

27. Leonard J. Arrington, "The Settlement of the Brigham Young Estate, 1877–1879," *Pacific Historical Review* 21, no. 1 (1952): 1–20.

28. See Franklin S. Richards, "Reminiscences," Church History Library, The Church of Jesus Christ of Latter-day Saints, Salt Lake City (hereafter Church History Library).

29. An Act supplemental to An Act providing for the Incorporating Associations for Mining, Manufacturing, Commercial and other Industrial Pursuits, approved February 18th, 1870, 1878 Laws of Utah 46, § 1.

30. 1878 Laws of Utah 46, § 3.

was not subject to the Edmunds-Tucker Act passed in 1887.[31] The law did allow a federal receiver to confiscate property not held by stake or ward corporations, briefly including the Salt Lake Temple. Shortly after the constitutionality of the Edmunds-Tucker Act was upheld by the US Supreme Court in 1890, Wilford Woodruff issued the Manifesto, which stated that the Church would no longer perform plural marriages.[32] In response, Charles Zane, chief justice of the Utah Territorial Supreme Court, ruled that property should be returned to the trustee-in-trust to advance the legal, non-polygamous goals of the Church.[33]

Utah became a state in 1896, and the legislature adopted a law allowing for the incorporation of religious societies.[34] However, the Church chose not to avail itself of this law. Most local meetinghouses continued to be held by stake and ward corporations. The remainder of church property was held by the Church president as trustee-in-trust. The Church had become heavily involved in the economic life of the Intermountain West, in part due to the cooperative movement of the 1870s.[35] By the time of statehood, the United Orders of Young's time had largely ceased to function, but many of the businesses they spawned continued as church-owned enterprises. In addition, the Church had invested in a variety of businesses from the Union Pacific Railroad to the Utah salt industry as a way of fostering economic growth and a diversified economy. With the arrival of a new century, however, Latter-day Saint dreams of autarky were dead and church-owned businesses were increasingly run along the lines of mainstream American capitalism. This is how matters stood in 1904 when a dispute over salt helped spur on the transformation of the Church's legal personality.

---

31. See Richards, "Reminiscences."

32. See Late Corporation of the Church of Jesus Christ of Latter-day Saints v. United States, 136 U.S. 1 (1890).

33. See United States v. Late Corporation of the Church of Jesus Christ of Latter-day Saints, 8 Utah 310 (1892).

34. See Rev. Stat. Utah. §§ 343–46 (1897).

35. See Leonard Arrington, *Great Basin Kingdom: An Economic History of the Latter-Day Saints, 1830–1900* (Cambridge: Harvard University Press, 1958); Leonard J. Arrington, Feramorz Y. Fox, and Dean L. May, *Building the City of God: Community and Cooperation Among the Mormons*, 2nd ed. (Urbana: University of Illinois Press, 1992).

Salt and Smurthwaite

Charles Smurthwaite was born in England in 1862. At the age of nineteen, he joined the Church in Manchester and emigrated to Utah, settling ultimately in Ogden.[36] Although he never served a mission for the Church, he was ordained a Seventy and was active in the Church-sponsored People's Party in the 1890s.[37] His estrangement from the Church seems to have begun around this time, when he supported apostle Moses Thatcher in his political campaign and subsequent battle with Church leaders.[38] However, he was still active in his ward in 1904 when, in association with Richard J. Taylor, son of deceased Church President John Taylor, he purchased controlling shares in the Beck Salt Company and began investing to expand its operations.[39] Sometime later, then Church President Joseph F. Smith contacted Smurthwaite through Ogden capitalist David Eccles.[40] At a meeting in Salt Lake with the First Presidency and apostle John Henry Smith, Smurthwaite and his associate learned that the Church controlled the Inland Crystal Salt Company, the Beck Salt Company's chief competitor. Indeed, after its creation via a merger with a competitor in 1898, the Inland Crystal Salt Company had a de facto monopoly on salt manufacture in Utah.[41] Joseph F. Smith said, "I am very surprised . . . that a man of your experience would go into business in opposition to us without first coming to consult us. An hour . . . would have set you brethren right on this matter if you had

---

36. See Proceedings before the Committee on Privileges and Elections of the United States Senate in the Matter of the Protests against the Right of Hon. Reed Smoot, a Senator from the State of Utah, to Hold His Seat (Washington, DC: Government Printing Office, 1906), 4:78 (hereafter Smoot Hearings).

37. "People's County Convention," *Salt Lake Herald-Republican*, October 4, 1890, 6; "Threatened with Ruin in His Salt Business," *Salt Lake Telegram*, March 15, 1905, 8.

38. See "Smurthwaite Is Now Out," *Salt Lake Tribune*, March 26, 1905, 1. See also Edward Leo Lyman, "The Alienation of an Apostle from His Quorum: The Moses Thatcher Case," *Dialogue: A Journal of Mormon Thought* 18 (Spring 1985): 67–91; Kenneth W. Godfrey, "Moses Thatcher in the Dock: His Trials, The Aftermath, and His Last Days," *Journal of Mormon History* 24, no. 1 (1998): 54–88.

39. See Smoot Hearings, 4:78; Cannon and O'Higgins, *Under the Prophet in Utah*, 323.

40. See Smoot Hearings, 4:79.

41. John L. Clark, "History of Utah's Salt Industry 1847–1970" (master's thesis, Provo, Utah, Brigham Young University, 1971).

come to consult us about it."[42] Smith suggested that if Smurthwaite and his associates wished to invest in the salt business, they might be able to purchase shares in the Inland Crystal Salt Company. But if they continued, he said, "we will ruin you" because the Inland Crystal Salt Company would cut prices in the face of increased competition.[43] The Church had been involved in the salt business since the 1880s, and the Inland Crystal Salt Company—due to its more efficient capital investments—was capable of undercutting smaller, less efficient producers such as the Beck Salt Company.[44] The Inland Crystal Salt Company was also allegedly part of the national "salt trust," and thus may have been required to engage in unprofitable price cutting as a way of driving competitors out of business.[45]

The interview with Smith was the final straw in Smurthwaite's mounting religious crisis. Two years earlier, the Utah legislature chose apostle Reed Smoot to fill one of the state's seats in the United States Senate. The choice set off a furor of national protest, and the Senate Committee on Privileges and Elections launched a wide-ranging investigation into Mormon affairs in Utah.[46] Joseph F. Smith was called to testify before the United States Senate, where he admitted to cohabitating with his plural wives after the Manifesto of 1890. For Smurthwaite and many other Latter-day Saints, such conduct not only violated unlawful cohabitation statutes but was also sexually immoral, a violation of what they regarded as the Church's new understanding of marriage. He informed his bishop that he thought Smith was "a bad man" and not a prophet of God. He went on to publish a lengthy letter in the *Salt Lake Tribune* in which he denounced all forms of post-Manifesto polygamy, demanded that church meetings be thrown open to debate on religious questions, and that the Church retire from all political and commercial affairs.[47] He also wrote: "I demand

42. Smoot Hearings, 4:79.

43. Smoot Hearings, 4:79–80.

44. See John L. Clark, "The Mormon Church and Utah Salt Manufacturing 1847–1918," *Arizona and the West* 26, no. 3 (1984): 225–42.

45. Certainly, lower level employees of the Inland Crystal Salt Company had used aggressive tactics against competitors in the 1890s, in one case dynamiting a rival salt works, and in another case, filling in a competitor's canal that crossed company property. See Clark, "History of Utah's Salt Industry," 85–86.

46. See Kathleen Flake, *The Politics of American Religious Identity: The Seating of Senator Reed Smoot, Mormon Apostle* (Chapel Hill: University of North Carolina Press, 2004); Harvard S. Heath, "The Reed Smoot Hearings: A Quest for Legitimacy," *Journal of Mormon History* 33, no. 2 (2007): 1–80.

47. Smoot Hearings, 4:83–90.

that all tithes be accounted for in detail, beginning at the next April conference, twice each year from that time forward at general conferences; that a list of all property holdings of the church and of the leaders of the church, acquired since he [*sic*] became president, be read semiannually at each conference."[48] In response, Smurthwaite's "block teacher" preferred a charge against him before his bishop for "apostasy and unchristianlike conduct" in March 1905.[49]

Smurthwaite's ecclesiastical trial became big news. Each stage of the proceedings before the bishop's court and the high council was reported in the press.[50] He raised the stakes by preferring his own charge against Hyrum Goddard, the block teacher who began the proceedings against him. Goddard was a polygamist who continued to cohabitate with his plural wives, and Smurthwaite asked the bishop to investigate him for "unchristianlike conduct."[51] Smurthwaite was ultimately excommunicated on April 4, 1905.[52]

While the action against him seems to have arisen entirely at the local level in response to his published letter to the *Salt Lake Tribune*, press reports presented it as a vindictive plot instigated by Joseph F. Smith against a business rival.[53] State legislators and other politicians discussed the case.[54] The *Salt Lake Tribune* compared Smurthwaite to the Book of Mormon prophet Abinadi standing before a wicked King Noah in the person of Smith,[55] and *Godwin's Weekly* hinted ominously that the case might require a return to the legal hardball of the 1880s:

---

48. Smoot Hearings, 4:89.

49. Smoot Hearings, 4:92.

50. See "About Mr. Smurthwaite," *Salt Lake Tribune*, March 25, 1905, 1; "Smurthwaite and the Church," *Godwin's Weekly*, March 3, 1905, 3; "Smurthwaite Charges Goddard with Living in Active Polygamy," *Ogden Daily Standard*, March 23, 1905, 6; "Smurthwaite Is Now Out"; "Threatened with Ruin in His Salt Business"; "Threatened with Ruin in His Salt Business."

51. See "Smurthwaite Charges Goddard with Living in Active Polygamy"; "Smurthwaite Counters on Hyrum H. Goddard," *Salt Lake Telegram*, March 23, 1905, 6.

52. See Smoot Hearings, 4:78.

53. See "Smurthwaite Is Now Out."

54. See "Utah Editors Roast Solons," *Salt Lake Tribune*, March 19, 1905, 3.

55. See "A Parallel For Mormons," *Salt Lake Tribune*, April 8, 1905, 4. The *Tribune* was careful to insist it was writing "without assuming that the Book of Mormon knew anything about Charles Smurthwaite or Joseph F. Smith, or

> [I]t will be remembered that no arguments, nor prosecutions in the old days in Utah had the least effect until a bill to disenfranchise the whole organization was introduced into Congress. That brought the manifesto of President Woodruff. He was sincere and so were a few others who surrounded him; they wanted this alien system placed in accord with free institutions. But no such spirit is apparent among the leaders today and a caustic remedy is not only just, but a necessary act of self-defense on the part of the nation. The man who gives unquestioned allegiance to the rule of Joseph F. Smith and believes he has a right to rule, cannot give any but qualified allegiance to the Government of this Republic.[56]

If Church leaders thought that Smurthwaite's excommunication would bring the controversy to an end, they were mistaken. Three days after being expelled from the Church, Smurthwaite filed a complaint in the Third District Court in Salt Lake City in the case of *Smurthwaite et al. v. The Church of Jesus Christ of Latter-day Saints et al.*, and the Salt Lake County sherriff served the papers personally on Joseph F. Smith.[57]

Going to Law

Smurthwaite was joined in his lawsuit by thirty-six-year-old Don Carlos Musser, the son of A. Milton Musser, a prominent Latter-day Saint leader who was serving as assistant Church historian at the time of his son's lawsuit against Joseph F. Smith. Musser had four plural wives; Don Carlos's mother, Mary Elizabeth White, was the second.[58] During the Raid of the 1880s, Musser was convicted in a celebrated unlawful cohabitation case where he refused an offer of leniency by then Territorial Chief Justice Zane, rather than pledge to abandon his relationship with Mary, her children, and his other plural families.[59] In 1891, Don Carlos was called to

---

without assuming that Joseph F.'s uncle, the prophet, made any such discovery as the plates."

56. "Smurthwaite and the Church."

57. See Smurthwaite et al. v. The Church of Jesus Christ of Latter-day Saints et al., 3rd Judicial District Court, Utah, Case No. 7115, Utah State Archives, Series 1622, Reel 171 (hereafter Smurthwaite v. Church). Sometimes the pleadings and motions in the case are styled "Smurthwaite et al. v. The Church of Jesus Christ of Latter-day Saints et al." and sometimes they are styled "Smurthwaite et al. v. Joseph F. Smith et al."

58. See Amos Milton Musser Sr. (1830–1909), FamilySearch.

59. See C. C. Goodwin, *History of the Bench and Bar of Utah* (Salt Lake City: Interstate Press Association, 1913), 60–62.

the Swiss-German Mission where he served for a year. He was then made president of the Turkish Mission from 1892 to 1894.[60] After returning to the United States and working in journalism for a time, he volunteered to serve in the Spanish-American War, eventually becoming editor of an English language newspaper in the Philippines called *Freedom*.[61] By 1905, he had become disillusioned with the Church over a variety of issues, particularly polygamous husbands, including his father, continuing to cohabitate with plural wives after the Manifesto.

As Smurthwaite's excommunication was being finalized, the Church held its April 1905 general conference, and Don Carlos was one of two members who cast a dissenting vote to the sustaining of Church leaders.[62] In an interview with the *Salt Lake Tribune*, he called on common Mormon narratives of apostasy. Drawing on anti-Catholic tropes, he compared Smith to the Pope.[63] "Is it not possible that if the people who make up the Mormon church do not think for themselves and act in accordance with their God-given reason, they, too will fall away and apostatize?" he said. "Indeed, is there a thinking, well informed man in the church, who cannot see that a great change has come over his people; that there is a class distinction in the church today that threatens the spiritual and temporal welfare of the masses?"[64]

Despite Smurthwaite's extended list of complaints against the Church in his published letter and Musser's broad ranging objections to polygamy, Mormon theology, and the conditions in Utah, the legal issues in their lawsuit were fairly narrow. Suing on behalf of themselves and "all other members of the Church of Jesus Christ of Latter-day Saints who may come into the case," they asked the court to order Smith to provide an

60. See "Don Carlos White Musser," The Church of Jesus Christ of Latter-Day Saints, accessed April 30, 2024, https://history.churchofjesuschrist.org/chd/individual/don-carlos-white-musser-1869.

61. See "Light to Be Thrown on Hierarch's Method," *Salt Lake Tribune*, April 8, 1905, 1.

62. "Light to Be Thrown on Hierach's Method."

63. For a discussion on the link between late nineteenth- and early twentieth-century Mormon narratives of the Great Apostasy and anti-Catholicism, see Matthew Bowman, "James Talmage, B. H. Roberts, and Confessional History in a Secular Age," in *Standing Apart: Mormon Historical Consciousness and the Concept of Apostasy*, ed. Miranda Wilcox and John D. Young (New York: Oxford University Press, 2014), 77–92.

64. "Great Work for Utah Doing by the Tribune," *Salt Lake Tribune*, April 8, 1905, 9.

accounting for the investment of all tithing funds and issue an injunction "restraining said defendants from investing said funds . . . in any business or enterprise established or prosecuted for commercial, industrial or business purposes."[65] The case was national news, with journalists embellishing beyond the facts alleged in the lawsuit. The complaint contained no allegation that Smith was appropriating Church funds or profiting from Church investments, but the *New York Herald* reported that he, "has been charged with taking the money paid as an offering to the Lord and using it for speculations to build up his own private wealth."[66]

Given the origins of the dispute in the Inland Crystal Salt Company's monopoly in Utah, one interesting question is why Smurthwaite didn't choose to pursue a case under the antitrust laws. In 1890, Congress had passed the Sherman Antitrust Act, which made "[e]very contract, combination in the form of trust or otherwise, or conspiracy, in restraint of trade . . . illegal."[67] Critics such as Frank Cannon denounced the Church's involvement in the salt industry in antitrust terms, although he suggested that at the time of the suit, the Inland Crystal Salt Company may not yet have formally been part of the national "salt trust."[68] Antitrust suits over salt had recently been brought elsewhere. In 1902, the federal government sued the "Federal Salt Company . . . popularly known as the 'Salt Trust'"[69] in federal court in San Francisco, obtaining a restraining order against price fixing agreements.[70] Furthermore, section 7 of the Sherman

65. Complaint, Smurthwaite v. Church.

66. Reprinted as "Mormon Grip on Fair State," *Salt Lake Tribune*, April 7, 1905, 3; "Mormon Church Row Is Taken Into Court," *San Francisco Call*, April 8, 1905, 4.

67. Sherman Antitrust Act of 1890 § 1, 26 Stat. 209.

68. See Cannon and O'Higgins, *Under the Prophet in Utah*, 323. According to Cannon, all Latter-day Saints "must buy salt from 'the Church's' salt monopoly (Joseph F. Smith, president), which is part of, and pays dividends to, the national salt trust" (365). However, this was written in 1911 and not in 1905 when Smurthwaite filed his suit.

69. "Temporary Injunction Against the 'Salt Trust,'" *American Law Review* 35 (1902): 907–9.

70. See J. H. Benton, "Sherman or Anti-Trust Act," *Yale Law Journal* 18, no. 5 (1909): 318–19. During this period, the "salt trust" in the western United States was consistently associated with the Federal Salt Company. See Theodore Roosevelt, *Works: Presidential Addresses and State Papers, Dec. 3, 1901, June 1910, and European Addresses* (New York: Review of Reviews Publishing Company, 1910), 283–84. However, in his study of the salt industry in Utah, John C. Clark never mentions any relationship between the Inland Crystal Salt Company—or

Act gave victims of monopolies a private cause of action for violations of the act, including the right to treble damages.[71] Under the US Supreme Court's 1894 decision in *United States v. E.C. Knight Company*, however, the Sherman Act did not reach purely intrastate manufacturers of "a necessity of life" such as the Inland Crystal Salt Company.[72] Both the Utah state constitution and an 1896 state statute prohibited "any combination . . . having for its object or effect the controlling of the prices of . . . any article of manufacturing."[73] But it was unclear whether the law provided an aggrieved party such as Smurthwaite a private cause of action.[74] Furthermore, Smith's threat to merely undersell Smurthwaite's company was likely not prohibited by the Utah law unless it could be shown to be part of a broader conspiracy to control prices, as opposed to merely underprice a competitor. Regardless, Smurthwaite chose not to pursue any antitrust related claims against Smith, the Church, or the Inland Crystal Salt Company.

Inevitably with the filing of suit, lawyers became the leading actors in the resulting drama. For their attorney, Smurthwaite and Musser retained Charles Zane, one of the most prominent lawyers in Utah. Zane was born in 1831 and was admitted to the Illinois bar in 1857, becoming a member of the Springfield legal community just as its leading light, Abraham Lincoln, rose to national prominence. Zane had become a judge

---

any other Utah firm—and the Federal Salt Company. See Clark, "History of Utah's Salt Industry 1847–1970." It is very difficult to determine what formal relationship, if any, existed between the Inland Crystal Salt Company and the "salt trust." It is entirely possible that Smurthwaite and his legal team were afflicted with a similar uncertainty, which might also explain the absence of an antitrust suit. Finally, and perhaps most likely, antitrust law was still new in 1904, and it's quite probable Zane and Smurthwaite simply weren't familiar with its possibilities.

71. See Sherman Antitrust Act of 1890 § 7, 26 Stat. 209.

72. See United States v. E. C. Knight Company, 156 U.S. 1 (1894).

73. "To Prevent Pools and Trusts,"§ 1, 1896 Laws of Utah 125, chap. 39. See also Utah Const. art. XII, § 20 (1896). See James May, "The Role of the States in the First Century of the Sherman Act and the Larger Picture of Antitrust History," *Antitrust Law Journal* 59, no. 1 (1990): 93–108; James May, "Antitrust Practice and Procedure In the Formative Era: The Constitutional and Conceptual Reach of State Antitrust Law, 1880–1918," *University of Pennsylvania Law Review* 135, no. 3 (1987): 594–93.

74. See Jonathan A. Dibble and James S. Jardine, "The Utah Antitrust Act of 1979: Getting into the State Antitrust Business," *Utah Law Review* 1980, no. 1 (1980): 75–76.

in Illinois when he was appointed chief justice of the Utah Territorial Supreme Court in 1884.[75] He presided over that court during the most intense period of the polygamy raids, earning him a reputation as a stern but essentially fair-minded judge, in contrast to earlier anti-Mormon crusaders on the territorial bench.[76] Upon Utah's admission to the Union in 1896, he was chosen chief justice of the new state supreme court, serving until 1899 when he entered private practice in Salt Lake City.[77] Given his reputation as a widely respected hero of the federal government's legal victories over the Church, the choice of Zane gave a certain gravitas to Smurthwaite and Musser's suit.

Joseph F. Smith was represented by Franklin S. Richards. The son of apostle Franklin D. Richards, Richards had planned on a medical career. That changed after a conversation with Brigham Young in which the aging president urged him to study law instead. Young said, "[T]he time will come when the Latter-day Saints will need lawyers of their own to defend them in the Courts and strive with fearless inspiration to maintain their constitutional rights."[78] Richards abandoned medicine and, after a course of self-directed study, was admitted to the Utah bar in 1874. The timing of his entry into the legal profession couldn't have been better for a young Latter-day Saint attorney. He became the Church's general counsel in 1880, just as the hard fought legal battles over the polygamy raids were beginning. He argued the Church's position before the territorial courts, as well as handled its numerous appeals before the United States Supreme Court.[79] In addition, he worked with George Q. Cannon and others as an emissary for Church leaders with legal and political leaders in the East. By 1905, he was an experienced attorney in the prime of his career with decades of experience defending the interests of his church in court.

---

75. See Goodwin, *History of the Bench and Bar of Utah*, 221.

76. See Thomas G. Alexander, "Charles S. Zane: Apostle of a New Era," *Utah Historical Quarterly* 34, no. 3 (Fall 1966): 290–314..

77. Goodwin, *History of the Bench and Bar of Utah*, 221.

78. Quoted in Ken Driggs, "'Lawyers of Their Own to Defend Them': The Legal Career of Franklin Snyder Richards," *Journal of Mormon History* 21, no. 2 (October 1, 1995): 88.

79. See Driggs, "'Lawyers of Their Own to Defend Them'"; Goodwin, *History of the Bench and Bar of Utah*, 189. In cases before the US Supreme Court, the Church generally retained a prominent member of the Supreme Court bar to argue the case with Richards.

Richard struck a confident air with reporters when the suit was filed. "I feel assured in saying the whole matter will come to nil," he said. "I do not wish my words to be taken as casting any reflection upon such an able practitioner as Judge Zane, but nevertheless, I cannot see any other result." He went on to say, "I had a long talk with President Smith last night, but this matter was not touched upon. As you know, I represent the Mormon church in all legal matters, and for that reason these papers have been turned over to me." Finally, as a good advocate, he ended by trying to change the public framing of the case away from grasping hierarchs speculating with the money of widows and orphans. He said: "The tithings are purely voluntary; they are not forced. They are never diverted from church work. Just so long as the tithings are properly used for the furthering of church and religious ends steps to prevent their voluntary contribution are absurd. The Mormon church has nothing to fear."[80] Despite the lawyer's confident public face, Joseph F. Smith was concerned. Richards later wrote, "President Smith was considerably disturbed in his mind about the suit and offered to employ additional counsel." Richards, however, insisted that "we were entirely able to win the case ourselves."[81]

The Legal Arguments

The surviving case file contains no briefing by the parties, and one must therefore reconstruct the legal theories in the lawsuit from pleadings and newspaper reports of oral arguments. Zane's initial theory seems to have been that the Church was a legal entity of which Joseph F. Smith was the trustee.[82] As members of the corporation, Smurthwaite and Musser were entitled to demand an accounting and obtain an injunction against the wayward custodian of the Church's funds. The idea seems to have been that, as a matter of law, the Church was an inherently religious entity, and it would be *ultra vires*—beyond the corporation's legal powers—for it to use funds for any commercial activities. In this he would seem to have been on good legal ground, given the 1897 Utah law limiting religious corporations to activities set out in their articles of incorporation.

80. "Suit to Compel an Accounting of Tithing Cause of Great Interest; Judge Richards Talks of the Case," *Salt Lake Telegram*, April 8, 1905, 1.

81. Franklin S. Richards, Memorandum, "Musser-Smurthwaite Suit against President Smith to Enjoin Him from Investing Church Funds in Secular Enterprises, 1905–1906," Church History Library.

82. See Complaint, Smurthwaite v. Church.

This view of the case is buttressed by the presence of Musser in the suit. Smurthwaite was the primary mover in suing the Church, and it is possible that Musser was added as a plaintiff to forestall the argument that because of his excommunication, Smurthwaite was no longer a member of the corporation and therefore lacked standing to sue.

Richards responded by filing a demurrer insisting that "the Church of Jesus Christ of Latter Day Saints [*sic*] is improperly made defendant . . . because the said Church is a voluntary religious association, and not a corporation or legal entity."[83] In this, Richards was correct. Thirteen years before, as territorial chief justice, Zane had presided over the proceedings in the territorial supreme court confirming that the Church's 1850 incorporation had been nullified by Congress. Perhaps because he and his clients were aware of the flurry of local incorporations by wards and stakes, Zane seems to have assumed that the Church had incorporated under Utah law subsequent to statehood. This was not the case. As a result of his error, Zane had to shift the ground of his legal theory. He could no longer rely directly on Church articles of incorporation and the Utah statute.

He filed an amended complaint which dropped the allegation that the Church had been incorporated under Utah law and added the rest of the First Presidency and the presiding bishop as additional defendants.[84] His new theory of the case relied on an ordinary trust argument. At common law, a trust is created when a settlor confers property on a trustee with the expressed intention that the property be used for the benefit of some specifically identifiable beneficiary. Zane seems to have reasoned that tithe payers were settlors who conveyed property to church officials as trustees on behalf of church members. Trustees owe strict fiduciary duties to beneficiaries, who have standing to sue trustees if they fail to use the property as intended by the settlors. However, the trust is a very flexible device. Its

83. Demurrer, Smurthwaite v. Church. A demurrer is a motion in which a defendant, rather than contesting the factual accuracy of the complaint's assertions as would be done in an answer, claims that even if all of the factual claims in the complaint are correct, the plaintiff is still not entitled to a remedy. Richards's motion was open to the objection that it wasn't truly a demurrer because he denied that the Church was incorporated under Utah law, as was asserted in the complaint. This could be characterized as a factual question calling for a trial and thus outside the scope of a demurrer. However, Zane chose not to contest this point, in all likelihood because he realized that it was pointless to do so because Richards was correct.

84. Amended Complaint, Smurthwaite v. Church.

primary purpose is to advance the intentions of the settlor, which must be determined by the court to know the scope of the beneficiaries' rights. This meant that Smurthwaite and Musser had to provide evidence as to the intention of the specific settlors/tithe payers under whose trust they were suing.

In his demurrer to Zane's amended complaint, Richards demanded that the identity and intentions of these tithe payers be set out with specificity.[85] In support of his argument, he seems to have cited two cases to the court.[86] The first was *Pulpress v. African Methodist Episcopal Church*,[87] a case decided by the Pennsylvania Supreme Court in 1864. It grew out of a dispute over a bequest to the AME churches around Pittsburgh. The plaintiffs argued that the trustees in the case, the pastor and trustees of the largest AME church in the city, were using the bequested property entirely for the benefit of the large urban church rather than to help the outlying rural congregations. The original bequest, however, had simply stated that the property was for the use of "the African Methodist Church." Accordingly, the court ruled that the exercise of discretion by church leaders could not be attacked because there was no more specific deed limiting their discretion. The attractions of the case to Richards were obvious. It suggested that so long as property was used for the church, its use could not be attacked without a more specific deed. He also cited *Penfield v. Skinner*, a Vermont case involving a trust created for the education of poor boys in the ministry.[88] The court found that so long as the property was not diverted to another use, the particular way in which it was spent in support of such poor boys couldn't be attacked wihtout a specific deed.

Smurthwaite's case was heard before Judge Charles W. Morse. Morse was born in Cambridge, Illinois.[89] His family moved to Kansas when he

85. Demurrer to Amended Complaint, Smurthwaite v. Church.

86. In many ways the nineteenth century was a golden age of church litigation, as numerous denominations and congregations divided over not only theology, but also the politics of slavery and emancipation in the run up to the Civil War and during its aftermath. See Kellen Funk, "Church Corporations and the Conflict of Laws in Antebellum America," *Journal of Law and Religion* 32, no. 2 (2017): 263–84. This is the body of case law from which Richards drew his arguments. Interestingly, Richards never seems to have raised the rule against perpetuities in objection to Zane's trust theory. See discussion supra note 26.

87. Pulpress v. African Methodist Episcopal Church, 48 Pa. 208 (1864).

88. Penfield v. Skinner, 11 Vt. 296 (1839).

89. "Annual Meeting Issue," *Utah Bar Bulletin*, 1938, 6.

was a teenager, and it was there that he studied law and was admitted to the bar in 1880.[90] Although he was moderately successful in local politics in Kansas, in 1888 he "yielded to the call of the further West." Once in Utah, he was active in Republican politics but arrived in the territory too late to be caught up in the bonanza of legal business created by the federal crusade against polygamy. Religiously he was described as a "spiritually minded man," and he served as the president of the board of trustees of the First Methodist Episcopal Church in Salt Lake City, a post that may have given him some practical insight into the issues involved in the case. In 1905 he had been on the bench for four years, and he would serve for another eleven years before retiring into private practice.[91]

Judge Morse accepted Richards's theory of the case. In a six-page written opinion, he sided with Smith on Richards's demurrer, writing:

> It is well settled by an almost unbroken line of decisions that the civil courts will take jurisdiction of suits to prevent the misappropriation of church funds or property, or of any attempted application of the same, not warranted by the terms upon which the fund was created or the property acquired, or of the rules and regulation of the society. But before the courts will interfere to exercise a visitorial control over the management, disposal or investment of such property or funds, it must clearly appear from the averments of the bill, that the acts complained of are unwarranted or unauthorized, and that the trust repose in those to whom the management and control of such property of fund has been committed, is being or is about to be violated.[92]

He cited both *Pulpress v. African Methodist Episcopal Church* and *Penfield v. Skinner*. He pointed out that none of the pleadings or arguments in the case suggested that the Church's investments were illegal, "nor was it contended that any of the trust property was being . . . appropriated by the defendants."[93] However, in ruling for Richards and the Church, Morse had not disposed of the case. Zane was free to amend his complaint once again and allege new facts that could give rise to a valid cause of action. This is exactly what he did on December 16, 1905.[94]

The court's ruling left Zane in a difficult position. His trust theory required that there be some specific evidence of the settlors' intentions being violated by Joseph F. Smith as trustee-in-trust. In his opinion, Morse

90. "Annual Meeting Issue," 6; Goodwin, *History of the Bench and Bar of Utah*, 178.
91. "Annual Meeting Issue," 6.
92. Decision upon Demurrer to Complaint, Smurthwaite v. Church.
93. Decision upon Demurrer to Complaint, Smurthwaite v. Church.
94. See Second Amended Complaint, Smurthwaite v. Church.

stated that one could look to the articles of incorporation or other controlling ecclesiastical documents for evidence of such an intent.[95] However, as Zane acknowledged in his second amended complaint: "[T]he Church of Jesus Christ of Latter Day Saints [*sic*] is a voluntary religious association and has no constitution or by laws and has no articles of association; nor has said Church adopted any rule or rules, regulation or regulations designating the purpose or purposes to which the Church fund in the hands of the said trustee-in-trust may or can be devoted."[96]

Accordingly, Zane adopted two new theories of the case. The first was that donations to religious associations could not be used "otherwise than for Church purposes." There was a default rule that governed when a settlor was silent as to his or her intentions, Zane argued. This rule required the court to divine between "Church purposes" and merely "secular purposes," ruling that the latter violated the fiduciary duties of the trustee. Unfortunately for his case, Zane couldn't seem to point to any legal authority in support of this argument. His second theory was more ambitious. He argued that "it is a violation of public policy for said church or its trustee to engage in various kinds of secular business by the use of Church funds and is therefore unlawful."[97] The advantage of this argument is that it did not require Zane to provide evidence of tithe payers' intentions. Rather, he was claiming that even if tithe payers intended to allow the Church to invest in secular businesses, it was unlawful for the Church to do so. Again, the disadvantage of this argument was that he couldn't point to any legal authority directly stating that Utah had such a public policy.

Richards filed another demurrer, and an oral argument on the second amended complaint was heard in July 1906.[98] Richards's response was straightforward. He denied that any default rule or public policy of the kind Zane contended for existed. He pointed out that churches frequently engaged in secular business. Richards told the court:

> While churches did not engage extensively in such business . . . the Methodist Church was in the book business and other business and there was no law against it. Counsel might say it is very bad taste, but I don't know how far I would take issue with him in engaging in certain kinds of business; but we are not here to discuss this question. It is a question of law. It cannot engage in

95. See Decision upon Demurrer to Complaint, Smurthwaite v. Church.

96. Second Amended Complaint, Smurthwaite v. Church.

97. Second Amended Complaint, Smurthwaite v. Church.

98. See Demurrer to Second Amended Complaint, Smurthwaite v. Church; "Joseph F. Smith and the Tithes," *Salt Lake Tribune*, July 7, 1906.

> business that would be subversive of good government or public morals, but it is lawful to engage in legitimate business and it is not against public policy.[99]

Richards's example of the Methodists was well chosen. In the mid-nineteenth century, the combined Methodist Book Concern was the largest commercial publisher in the world.[100] Furthermore, it had been the object of a bitter dispute when Methodism split apart over the issue of slavery in the years before the Civil War.[101] All of this was likely familiar to Judge Morse, a devout Methodist. Richards ended with a sly parting shot against Zane. Almost twenty years before, as territorial chief justice, Zane had decided the two cases involving the disincorporation of the Church under the Edmunds-Tucker Act.[102] In that litigation, George Romney and other members of the Church sought to intervene in the litigation to assert their rights as beneficiaries of any property held in trust for the Church. Their application was denied because, in the words of Richards, the court held that "the contributions having been made to the church that the individual members had no further interest in them."[103] In other words, Zane had ruled that the tithes were gifts rather than the corpus of a trust created by tithe payers as trust settlors. Thus, Richards had the fun of citing judge Zane as negative precedent against lawyer Zane.

In his argument, Richards conceded that tithing funds had to be used for church purposes. He disputed that this was confined to the maintenance of religious buildings, payment of Church officers, and support for the poor, the purposes that Zane was willing to acknowledge as legitimate. Zane insisted, however, that "all legal principles are a definition."[104] It wasn't sufficient for Richards to assert that investments were for Church purposes. The defendants must either point to articles of incorporation or the like explicitly allowing investments in secular businesses, Zane argued, or else the court ought to use a definition of "Church purposes" that excluded business activities. He then went on to argue that regardless of any idiosyncratic definition that might be offered as to "Church purposes,"

99. "Joseph F. Smith and the Tithes."

100. See Gordon, "The First Disestablishment," 364.

101. Gordon, 361–63.

102. See United States v. Church of Jesus Christ of Latter-day Saints, 5 Utah 361 (1887); United States v. Late Corporation of the Church of Jesus Christ of Latter-day Saints, 8 Utah 310 (1892).

103. "Joseph F. Smith and the Tithes."

104. "Joseph F. Smith and the Tithes."

the public policy of Utah prohibited churches from carrying on business practices.

In support of the existence of such a public policy, Zane pointed to two sources in Utah law. The first was the state constitution, which stated, "no corporation shall engage in any business other than that expressly authorized in its charter, or articles of incorporation."[105] The second was the state corporation code, which provided for the incorporation of religious corporations but limited them to the activities specified in their corporate charters.[106] The statutory sections, however, did not explicitly limit the ability of religious corporations to be involved in profit-making enterprises. Rather, he pointed to section 346 of the code, which stated merely that "corporations not for pecuniary profit shall have power . . . to receive and hold such property. . . as may be necessary to carry on or promote the objects of the corporation, society, or association."[107] Zane sought to bolster his argument by retreating into aphorism, insisting that "law is the perfection of human reason" and that it would not be reasonable to allow unincorporated religious societies to engage in commerce while forbidding such commerce to incorporated societies.[108] He ended with a parade of horribles that would result from the position argued for by Richards:

> It would be a beautiful sight to behold the Presbyterian church, and the Mormon church, and the Catholic church, and the Methodist church engage in a scramble of trickery of business as it is carried on too often. It necessarily follows if this church has the right to do it then every other church has, and I say there is no church that I know in the United States that engages in all kinds of business, and no corporation does so. . . . I confess that the idea of this church engaging in all kinds of business is an alarming one. I know that in the middle ages, and comparatively modern times in Europe, the church

105. Utah Const. art. XII, § 10 (1896); "Joseph F. Smith and the Tithes."

106. Rev. Stat. Utah. §§ 342–44 (1897); "Joseph F. Smith and the Tithes."

107. Rev. Stat. Utah § 346 (1897); "Joseph F. Smith and the Tithes."

108. "Joseph F. Smith and the Tithes." The aphorism that "law is the perfection of human reason" is often ascribed to the seventeenth-century English jurist Edward Coke, although I have been unable to locate any place where Coke actually says this. It is likely a distillation—or a corruption—of his famous claim in the *Prohibitions Del La Roy*, Coke Rep. 63, 65 (K.B. 1607), that law cases are "decided not by natural reason but by the artificiall reason and judgment of Law. . . . And that the Law was the Golden metwand and measure to try the Causes of the Subjects." Regardless, Zane's reliance on the well-worn aphorism signaled both his legal erudition and his inability to find any more helpful precedent for his client. This would not have gone unnoticed by Judge Morse.

> undertook to do almost everything and it resulted in cutting off a great many heads, and breaking up of a great many people on wheels and so on, but the churches of this country are limited to the purpose of their organization.[109]

In short, the position of the Church was un-American and dangerous to civil liberty.

Judge Morse was never given a chance to rule on the second amended complaint. Before he could issue a decision, Zane filed a motion asking to withdraw the suit on the grounds that his clients were no longer willing to post the appeal bond necessary to continue the litigation.[110] It is also possible that Zane withdrew the second amended complaint because he persuaded his clients that they were unlikely to prevail. A dismissal of the case prior to the court's decision would be without prejudice, meaning it could be filed again. Indeed, after Morse granted Zane's motion to withdraw the case, Smurthwaite told the press that he and Musser contemplated refiling in federal court.[111] (Nothing seems to have come of this idea.) At the end of the day, Zane's second amended complaint contained no new factual allegations, and Morse's decision on the earlier amended complaint suggested that Zane was unlikely to persuade the court. Withdrawal of the case avoided handing the Church a clear victory and left open the implicit threat of future litigation.

Aftermath

When *Smurthwaite v. Smith* was dismissed in 1906, Franklin S. Richards had been thinking deeply about the legal status of the Church for more than a quarter century. When the suit was filed, most Church property was held by ward or stake corporations. Originally, these corporations were governed by cumbersome articles of incorporation and bylaws. This structure created a variety of risks. First, relatively complex corporate formalities had to be maintained or the wards and stakes risked losing their corporate charters. Second, the acquisition and transfer of property required that the complicated internal governance procedures of the corporations be followed exactly or risk invalidity. Third, upon the death or release of ward or stake officers serving as corporate trustees, relatively strict legal formalities had to be observed to replace them. Finally,

109. "Joseph F. Smith and the Tithes."

110. Smurthwaite v. Church.

111. "Investing Tithing Funds of Saints," *Salt Lake Tribune*, November 23, 1906, 12.

because the corporations were self-governing entities, there was a risk that the Church hierarchy could lose control over Church property if enough local congregants wished to go their own way. All of these factors likely contributed to John Taylor's hesitance to form such corporations in the early 1880s; and his insistence that the governing board of trustees be as large as possible under the then-existing Utah territorial law likely reflected concern about concentrating power over Church property in the hands of local leaders.

By 1901, Richards had found a solution to these problems. Borrowing the strategy adopted by the Catholic hierarchy in the United States, he proposed that stake and ward corporations be reorganized as corporations sole.[112] The corporation sole would consist of a single person, either the stake president or the bishop. Furthermore, the identity of this person would be defined in terms of their ecclesiastical status. In other words, a bishop who was released or had died would automatically cease to be the occupant of the corporation, which would continue to exist until his successor was chosen by the Church hierarchy. This eliminated the risk of title to Church property passing by operation of law to the heirs of Church leaders and the risk of rogue leaders taking control of Church assets. Richards later wrote:

> It occurred to me that this system was admirably adapted to our condition, and after giving the matter careful consideration, I suggested it . . . to the First Presidency. After much deliberation they decided to adopt this plan, which involved the necessity of getting the legislatures of states where our wards and stakes were located to enact laws providing for the creation of corporations sole to hold title to church property. We finally succeeded, after much effort and persuasion in getting laws passed in Idaho, Utah, Nevada, Arizona, and Wyoming providing for corporations sole.[113]

In 1901 Rulon S. Wells, a member of the First Council of the Seventy then serving in the Utah House of Representatives, introduced a bill pro-

---

112. See Dignan, *A History of the Legal Incorporation of Catholic Church Property*, 215–16; F. W. Maitland, "Corporation Sole," *Law Quarterly Review* 16, no. 4 (1900): 335–54; M. W. S., "The Corporation Sole," *Michigan Law Review* 26, no. 5 (1928): 545–51.

113. Franklin S. Richards, "Corporations and Land Titles," Memorandum to the Presiding Bishop and the First Presidency, November 2, 1931, typescript, Church History Library.

viding for the creation of corporations sole, which passed unanimously.[114] It is clear that this statute was originally intended only for the use of wards and stakes. Thus, while only an "arch-bishop, bishop, overseer, presiding elder, rabbi or clergyman"[115] could formally be a member of the corporation, the corporation could not dispose of property without "the consent of the majority of the members of the church or religious society present at a meeting duly called for that purpose."[116] Such a procedure would clearly be too cumbersome for use by the president of the Church.

However, Richards's thinking on this topic was continuing to develop. In 1903, almost certainly at the discreet request of the Church, the Utah legislature replaced the 1901 statute with a new law governing corporations sole.[117] By this point, Richards was clearly thinking of providing a corporate existence above the stake and ward level. The religious officials allowed to incorporate as a corporation sole now included "bishop, president, trustee-in-trust, and president of stake." The inclusion of the term "trustee in trust" is particularly telling, because this term was a neologism coined in Nauvoo for the president of the Church. However, it is also clear that the Church hierarchy had not yet decided to avail itself of incorporation. The evidence for this can be seen in the statute. Incorporating the trustee-in-trust as a corporation sole would eliminate the possibility of a

---

114. See "Church and Charitable Incorporations," in *Laws of the State of Utah* (1901) (Salt Lake City: Deseret News, 1901), 78–79; see also Andrew Jenson, "Wells, Rulon Seymour," in *Latter-Day Saint Biographical Encyclopedia* (Salt Lake City: Andrew Jenson History Co., 1901).

115. "Church and Charitable Incorporations," 78, § 2.

116. "Church and Charitable Incorporations," 78, § 4.

117. See "Incorporation of Churches and Religious Societies," in *Laws of the State of Utah* (1903) (Provo: Skelton Publishing, 1903), 62–63. While Richards did not explicitly claim authorship of the 1903 law, he did claim authorship of the 1901 law. See Richards, "Corporations and Land Titles." There is very good reason to suppose that the 1903 law was authored and introduced in the state legislature at his request. The law was introduced by William Newjent Williams, an English convert to the Church who was married to Clarissa W. Smith, daughter of apostle and counselor to Brigham Young, George A. Smith. Williams served as a missionary in Australia, and he was a high priest at the time he introduced the law. Clarissa was the treasurer of the church-wide Relief Society organization. In short, he was precisely the kind of loyal and well-connected Latter-day Saint that the Church would have used to get the law introduced. It was passed unanimously by the legislature. See Utah Senate Journal, 1903; *Biographical Record of Salt Lake City and Vicinity* (Chicago: National Historical Record Co., 1902), 279–81.

dispute between the Church and the heirs of a deceased president like the kind that had broken out upon the deaths of Joseph Smith and Brigham Young. Richards, however, inserted a provision in the law providing that in the case of "a trustee in trust . . . who at the time of his death . . . was holding the title to trust property for the use or benefit of any church . . . and not incorporated as a corporation sole . . . the title to any and all such property . . . shall not revert to the donor, nor vest in the heirs of such deceased person, but shall . . . vest in the person appointed to fill such vacancy."[118] In other words, the statute solved this problem without requiring the hierarchy to decide on whether to incorporate. Likewise, the 1901 provision requiring a vote by church members prior to the conveyancing of Church property was eliminated from the 1903 version of the law. Thus, when *Smurthwaite v. Smith* was being fought, an alternative legal identity for the president of the Church had been created but not yet assumed.

Richards did not explicitly reference the *Smurthwaite* case in his accounts of the legal structure of the Church.[119] However, the case illustrates the problems created when the top hierarchy of the Church was left without any formal legal existence. Joseph F. Smith was styled as a trustee-in-trust, but in *Smurthwaite* Richards clearly wanted to resist the idea that the president of the Church was a trustee in the ordinary common-law sense. He could not be a trustee on behalf of the Church as a legal beneficiary because the Church did not exist as a legal entity. At the same time, to say that he held Church property as a trustee for every church member exposed him to enormous potential liability and created an opportunity for ecclesiastical disputes by disgruntled members to spill over into the courts. As it had developed in the nineteenth century, however, the traditional assumptions of corporate law that applied to churches were essentially hostile to the hierarchical priesthood structure of Latter-day Saint ecclesiology. In particular, the emphasis on congregational structure worked awkwardly for denominational rather than congregational buildings such as temples or mission homes. Likewise, the law's emphasis on lay control created a system in which ecclesiastical disputes could be refought in the courts, as happened repeatedly in other denominations during the

118. "Incorporation of Churches and Religious Societies," 63, § 9.

119. See Richards, "Corporations and Land Titles"; Franklin S. Richards, "Address Delivered by President Franklin S. Richards to the High Priests Quorum of the Ensign Stake, Sunday November 13, 1932," typescript, Church History Library.

nineteenth century.[120] The *Smurthwaite* case was an effort to apply this basic approach to the Church, and in winning the case, Richards provided the Church hierarchy with the time to develop an alternative.

Ten years after the *Smurthwaite* case, the solution that had been latent in Utah law since 1903 was adopted when the Corporation of the Presiding Bishop of the Church of Jesus Christ of Latter-day Saints was organized. Seven years later, in 1923, Richards created the Corporation of the President of the Church of Jesus Christ of Latter-day Saints, finally providing a formal legal structure for the Church completely independent of the personal identity of the hierarchy. For most of the twentieth century, this dual structure of corporations sole provided the legal framework for the Church. In 2019, after more than a century, the Corporation of the President was merged into the Corporation of the Presiding Bishop, which was renamed The Church of Jesus Christ of Latter-day Saints. Thus, for the first time since 1862, there was an operating legal entity bearing that name. However, The Church of Jesus Christ of Latter-day Saints as a legal matter remained a corporation sole, meaning that in 2019 it had but a single member—Russell M. Nelson—who became the incumbent of the corporation sole after the merger of the earlier entities. This odd structure is a legacy of Mormonism's effort to find a legal structure less infected with Protestant ecclesiology than that which was on offer in the legal world when it was born. It may also be, in part, a legacy of the long-forgotten dispute over salt between Charles Smurthwaite and Joseph F. Smith.

120. See Gordon, "The First Disestablishment"; Funk, "Church Corporations and the Conflict of Laws in Antebellum America."

CHAPTER 7

Time, Eternity, and Real Estate: Mormon Law in Secular Court and the Opacity of Religion

I. Introduction

Modern lawyers are prone to see law as a monopoly of the secular state. Historically, this assumption is questionable at best, and if we accept Lon Fuller's capacious definition of law as "the enterprise of subjecting human conduct to the governance of rules,"[1] the world is filled with non-state legal systems. Some of the most important examples of such alternative legal systems are religious communities that promulgate rules governing the lives of believers.[2] One common area where religious authorities legislate is in the field of marriage and family.[3] How secular legal regimes relate to such religious bodies of law is one of the persistent questions for jurisprudence in a pluralistic society.

In the United States, no religious group's sacred marriage rules have had a more fraught relationship with the secular legal system than the Latter-day Saints. This can be seen most clearly in the federal government's grueling legal crusade to suppress Mormon polygamy in the closing decades of the nineteenth century. However, Mormon polygamy was but one part of a complex set of theological ideas and religious practices that defined Latter-day Saint marriages in the nineteenth century. Marriage it-

---

1. Lon L. Fuller, *The Morality of Law*, revised edition (New Haven: Yale University Press, 1969), 106.

2. The most obvious examples are Judaism and Islam, both of which place a heavy spiritual emphasis on the explication of religious law and fidelity to it. See generally Chaim Saiman, *Halakhah: The Rabbinic Idea of Law* (Princeton: Princeton University Press, 2018) (discussing the religious significance of Jewish law); Noel J. Coulson, *A History of Islamic Law* (Edinburgh: Edinburgh University Press, 1964) (providing a history of Islamic law).

3. See generally Perry Dane, "The Intersecting Worlds of Religious and Secular Marriage," in *Law and Religion: Current Legal Issues* 2001, vol. 4 (Oxford: Oxford University Press, 2001), 287–407 (discussing the legal intersection between secular and religious conceptions of marriage).

self was integrated into a sprawling religious worldview that linked certain ritual acts—sealings—to salvation and one's status in the afterlife. The result was a marriage system that purported to bridge mortality and eternity and where every marriage ritual was performed with at least one eye—and often two—on life after death. In 1902, the Utah Supreme Court was forced to grapple with the legal significance of these rituals in *Hilton v. Roylance*,[4] a case that purported to apply Mormon marriage rules while fundamentally misunderstanding them.

Hilton v. Roylance is worthy of study for two reasons.[5] First, there is the inherent interest of the case's colorful story. In the simplest terms, the case involved the legal consequences of a deathbed union between a dying young woman and a diffident older man that was aimed at securing the young woman's place in the soon-to-be-confronted afterlife. When she unexpectedly recovered, legal chaos resulted. Before the case had run its course, it spawned litigation that grabbed headlines for a decade, generated a politically motivated sex-crime prosecution, and involved a cast of characters that included the first president of the University of Utah, the highest echelons of The Church of Jesus Christ of Latter-day Saints, the shrewd mother of eleven children, and a private investigator working for a consortium of anti-Mormon Protestants. Ultimately, the courts would consider the legal significance of a college professor's sexual powers and embark on a clumsy effort to provide an authoritative interpretation of some of the most esoteric aspects of Mormon theology. In 1968 the whole affair was turned into a musical farce that ran on Broadway for five performances, drawing withering critical scorn from the *New York Times*. In short, it's a good story.

Second, the case illustrates the difficulty created by the mutual incomprehension of secular and religious legal systems. Initially, the Latter-day Saints sought to opt out of a system of secular marriage law that they saw as, at best, irrelevant and, at worst, hostile to their religious marriage system. Unsurprisingly, the secular law could not be escaped in the end.

---

4. 25 Utah 129 (1902).

5. Hilton v. Roylance has appeared previously in legal scholarship, but there is no scholarly treatment of the background of the case. See, e.g., Goran Lind, *Common Law Marriage: A Legal Institution for Cohabitation* (New York: Oxford University Press, 2008), 479 (discussing Hilton v. Roylance); C. Z. Lincoln, *The Civil Law and the Church*, ATLA Monograph Preservation Program (Nashville: Abingdon Press, 1916), 412 (same as previous); "Recent Important Decisions," *Michigan Law Review* 1, no. 5 (1903): 414 (same as previous).

For its part, the Utah Supreme Court proved unable to accurately grasp Latter-day Saint practices because it approached those practices using a simplified set of ideas based on its own jurisprudential and religious assumptions. The result is a cautionary tale about the opacity of religious communities to legal authorities and the inevitable distortions that the law's simplified view of social reality risks, particularly in the case of believers already suspicious of the secular state.

This chapter proceeds as follows: part II provides an overview of the legal and religious context of the case. Part III recounts the events that led to *Hilton v. Roylance*. Part IV examines the litigation and its aftermath. Part V reflects on some of the broader questions that the case raises, and part VI concludes.

II. The Law and Religion of Marriage in Early Utah

In July 1847, an advanced party of Mormon pioneers arrived in the valley of the Great Salt Lake. Refugees from the United States, they were fleeing chronic conflict with their neighbors and more than a decade of intermittent violence in Ohio, Missouri, and Illinois. At the time of their arrival, what would become Utah was formally part of Mexico, but in less than a year, the Treaty of Guadalupe-Hidalgo ended the Mexican-American War and transferred the territory to the victorious United States.[6] Despite the legal change in sovereignty, however, de facto power lay with a Mormon-created polity called the State of Deseret.[7] In 1850, Congress organized Deseret into the Territory of Utah.[8] While Utah rapidly built up a population equaling or surpassing that of other western territories that were admitted to the Union as states, the Latter-day Saints would languish under a territorial government for two generations until Utah was granted statehood in 1896.

The Latter-day Saint practice of plural marriage accounted for the long period of political subordination. Polygamy had haunted the radical

---

6. See generally Treaty of Peace, Friendship, Limits and Settlement, February 2, 1848, 9 Stat. 922.

7. See Eugene E. Campbell, "Governmental Beginnings," in *Utah's History*, ed. Richard D. Poll et al. (Provo: Brigham Young University Press, 1978), 153–74 (recounting the earliest government structures in Utah).

8. See generally Utah Territory Organic Act, Sept. 9, 1850, 9 Stat. 453 (establishing a territorial government in Utah).

fringes of Protestantism for centuries.[9] Most spectacularly, the apocalyptic Anabaptist theocracy of Munster, which was bloodily suppressed by the armies of the Catholic Church in 1535, practiced polygamy in imitation of the biblical patriarchs.[10] While forever tainted by its association with Anabaptism, Protestant thinkers as diverse as Martin Luther and John Milton were willing to affirm that, in light of the precedent of biblical polygamy, plural marriage could be licit for Christians.[11] Throughout the eighteenth and nineteenth centuries, religious radicals of various stripes experimented in theory and in practice with alternative forms of marriage. Beginning in the early 1840s, Mormonism's founding prophet, Joseph Smith, introduced the practice of polygamy among a tight group of close associates.[12] This was accompanied by increasingly elaborate religious teachings on marriage. In his theology, couples who were ritually "sealed" in mortality were promised that their marriage would persist after death into the eternities, with salvation and blessings in the hereafter.[13]

After the murder of Smith in 1844 and their arrival in the Great Basin, the Latter-day Saints created a legal regime in Territorial Utah to accommodate their marriage practices. The territorial legislature very pointedly

---

9. See John Cairncross, *After Polygamy Was Made a Sin: The Social History of Christian Polygamy* (London: Rooutledge & Kegan Paul, 1974), 1–54 (recounting arguments around polygamy in the Radical Reformation).

10. For a comparison of Anabaptism with early Mormonism, including a discussion of plural marriage, see D. Michael Quinn, "Socio-Religious Radicalism of the Mormon Church: A Parallel to the Anabaptists," in *New Views of Mormon History: A Collection of Essays in Honor of Leonard J. Arrington*, ed. Davis Bitton and Maureen Ursenbach Beecher (Salt Lake City: University of Utah Press, 1987).

11. See generally John Alfred Faulkner, "Luther and the Bigamous Marriage of Philip of Hesse," *The American Journal of Theology* 17, no. 2 (1913): 206–31; John S. Tanner, "Milton and the Early Mormon Defense of Polygamy," *Milton Quarterly* 21, no. 2 (1987): 41–46.

12. See Linda King Newell and Valeen Tippetts Avery, *Mormon Enigma: Emma Hale Smith*, 2nd ed. (Urbana: University of Illinois Press, 1994), 98 (recounting Joseph Smith's introduction of plural marriage).

13. See Jonathan A. Stapley, *The Power of Godliness: Mormon Liturgy and Cosmology* (New York: Oxford University Press, 2018), 34–56 (recounting Joseph Smith's sealing theology and its relationship to eternal marriage and polygamy); Rex Eugene Cooper, *Promises Made to the Fathers: Mormon Covenant Organization* (Salt Lake City: University of Utah Press, 1990), 100–131 (same as previous).

refused to pass any statute governing marriage.[14] Utah legislation was literally silent on the question of how one became married until 1888, more than forty years after the first arrival of the Latter-day Saints. In 1887, Congress passed the Edmund-Tucker Act, the final round in an increasingly harsh series of laws aimed at the suppression of Mormon polygamy that began with the 1862 Morrill Anti-bigamy Act.[15] As part of the Edmunds-Tucker Act, Congress instructed the Utah Territorial legislature to pass a marriage statute, which it did the following year, adopting a law largely indistinguishable from that of other jurisdictions.[16] Prior to 1888, however, marriage in Mormon country was legally informal and seems to have been governed by the common-law principle of *per verba de presenti*, under which the law recognized any present intention to marry as forming a presumptively valid union.[17] In practice this meant that the law largely deferred to religious authorities on questions of marriage formation.

Perhaps surprisingly, given their emphasis on the idea of eternal marriage, nineteenth-century Latter-day Saints had a liberal attitude toward divorce. Polygamy produced many unhappy unions, and Brigham Young, who succeeded Joseph Smith as prophet and president of the Church, believed that it was better for unhappy couples to separate. It was par-

14. The Latter-day Saints, however, did pass a territorial law granting a charter of incorporation to their church that specified that marriages solemnized by the Church's authority could not be legally questioned. This provision was repealed by Congress in 1862, and the entire charter was revoked by Congress in 1887. See Nathan B. Oman, "'Established Agreeable to the Laws of Our Country': Mormonism, Church Corporations, and the Long Legacy of America's First Disestablishment," *Journal of Law and Religion* 36, no. 2 (2021): 219–21 (discussing the territorial incorporation of The Church of Jesus Christ of Latter-day Saints).

15. See Edmunds-Tucker Act, ch. 397, 24 Stat. 635 (1887).

16. See Edmunds-Tucker Act (1887) §§ 4, 9; An Act Regulating Marriage (March 8, 1888), in Laws of Utah 88 (1888).

17. See Kathryn Daynes, *More Wives than One: Transformation of the Mormon Marriage System, 1840–1910* (Urbana: University of Illinois Press, 2001), 55–66 (discussing marriage law and practice in nineteenth-century Utah); Lisa Madsen Pearson and Carol Cornwall Madsen, "Innovation and Accommodation: The Legal Status of Women in Territorial Utah, 1850–1896," in *Women In Utah History*, ed. Patricia Lyn Scott, Linda Thatcher, and Susan Allred Whetstone (Denver: University Press of Colorado, 2005), 36–81 (same as previous); Lyman D. Platt, "The History of Marriage in Utah, 1847–1905," *Genealogical Journal* 12, no. 1 (Spring 1983): 28–41 (same as previous).

ticularly easy for plural wives to obtain a divorce.[18] (Husbands of polygamous wives had a much more difficult time obtaining a separation; Young tended to assume that men seeking divorce from plural wives were immorally abandoning vulnerable women.) These attitudes crystalized in an unusually liberal territorial divorce statute that all but dispensed with the idea of fault.[19] Easy divorce under territorial law, however, understates the extent to which legal informality governed dissolution of marriage in nineteenth-century Utah. Many couples never used even the simple territorial legal procedures. Rather they obtained a "church divorce," which consisted of a petition to Church leaders to dissolve the marriage. If granted, the divorce would be memorialized as a contract of separation signed by both spouses before witnesses.[20] Such divorces were presumed to be valid, freeing couples to remarry.

The Latter-day Saint preference for "church divorces" had a number of sources. First, there was a general suspicion of secular law, which was seen as expensive, divisive, and dominated by a class of grasping, dishonest lawyers.[21] Hence, their ecclesiastical court system provided Latter-day Saints with a forum for the resolution of all civil disputes, including such matters as alimony and child support.[22] Second, after 1862, polygamous marriages in Utah were illegal under the Morrill Act.[23] Understandably, couples in polygamous unions were not eager to take their disputes to

---

18. See Daynes, *More Wives than One* (discussing divorce among nineteenth-century Latter-day Saints); Eugene E. Campbell and Bruce A. Campbell, "Divorce among Mormon Polygamists: Extent and Explanations," *Utah Historical Quarterly* 46 (Winter 1978): 4–23 (same as previous).

19. See An Act in Relation to Bills of Divorce (1852), in Acts, Resolutions, and Memorials Passed by the First Annual and Special Sessions of the Legislative Assembly of the Territory of Utah 82 (1852). See generally Richard I. Aaron, "Mormon Divorce and the Statutes of 1852: Questions for Divorce in the 1980's," *Journal of Contemporary Law* 8 (1982): 5–46 (discussing Utah's nineteenth-century divorce statute).

20. See Daynes, *More Wives than One*, 152–53 (discussing divorce procedures).

21. See Nathan B. Oman, "Preaching to the Court House and Judging in the Temple," *Brigham Young University Law Review* 2009, no. 1 (2009): 194–208 (discussing Latter-day Saint attitudes toward the legal profession in early Utah).

22. See Edwin Brown Firmage and Richard Collin Mangrum, *Zion in the Courts: A Legal History of the Church of Jesus Christ of Latter-Day Saints*, 1830–1900 (Urbana: University of Illinois Press, 1988), 322–36 (discussing divorce cases in Church courts).

23. See Morrill Anti-Bigamy Act, June 24, 1862, 12 Stat. 501.

secular fora that would create records which could potentially be used in a criminal prosecution. Finally, Mormon theology placed enormous importance on ecclesiastical authority over marriage, a system of belief in which secular law was largely an afterthought.

Lutheran and Protestant traditions had rejected the earlier Catholic idea that marriage was a sacrament.[24] Protestants thus reconceptualized marriage as an essentially civic and secular status rather than a mystical union blessed by the priesthood of the church. In many Protestant lands, authority over marriage moved entirely into the secular courts. Even under the Reformed tradition, which proved influential in America, churches were seen as having an important role in solemnizing marriage, and as a matter of theology, ultimate control of marriage remained with secular authorities.[25] Mormonism decisively rejected the Protestant theology of marriage.[26] While Latter-day Saints did not adopt Catholic sacramentalism, they denied that the state retained final authority over marriage.

Within Latter-day Saint theology, Smith and his successors had been given the sealing power Jesus conferred on his apostles in the New Testament with the promise that what they bound on earth would be bound in heaven and what they loosed on earth would be loosed in heaven.[27] They exercised this power through "sealing" rituals that were believed to be valid in the eternities. The most common kind of ritual sealings were weddings "for time and eternity," which were deemed to create marriages that would persist both in life and after death.[28] However, there were other kinds of sealings. Adoptive sealings created eternal connections between parents and children.[29] A sealing "for time only" created a marriage valid

24. See John Witte, *From Sacrament to Contract: Marriage, Religion, and Law in the Western Tradition*, 2nd ed. (Louisville: Westminster John Knox Press, 2012), 113–58 (discussing Lutheran theologies of marriage).

25. See Witte, 159–216 (discussing Calvinist theologies of marriage).

26. See Terryl L. Givens, *Feeding the Flock: The Foundations of Mormon Thought: Church and Praxis* (New York: Oxford University Press, 2017), 45–71 (summarizing Latter-day Saint sacramental theology).

27. See Matthew 16:19. "And I will give unto thee the keys of the kingdom of heaven: and whatsoever thou shalt bind on earth shall be bound in heaven: and whatsoever thou shalt loose on earth shall be loosed in heaven."

28. See generally Kathleen Flake, "The Development of Early Latter-Day Saint Marriage Rites, 1831–53," *Journal of Mormon History* 41, no. 1 (2015): 77–102 (summarzing the early development of Latter-day Saint marriage liturgy).

29. See Stapley, *The Power of Godliness*, 39.

in mortality but not in eternity.[30] Likewise, a sealing could be "for eternity only," meaning that a couple were not married in mortality—indeed they might be married to other people—but would be united in the hereafter.[31] The eternal significance of these sealings was sometimes explained in terms of the continuation of happy family relationships in the eternities, but nineteenth-century sealing theology was only partially centered on the idea of eternal families. Sealings were a mechanism by which people became connected in ritual kinship networks infused with divine power.[32] To be left outside of such a kinship network in the hereafter was to risk one's eternal salvation.[33]

The practical and theological complexity of nineteenth-century Mormon sealings is best illustrated by Brigham Young's sprawling marital arrangements. Young was America's most famous polygamist, and during his life he was sealed to fifty-five women.[34] Of these fifty-five women, sixteen had children with Young, and an additional seven lived in Young's household. The remaining women had a variety of relationships to Young. Eliza R. Snow, a leading Latter-day Saint intellectual and poet, was sealed to Brigham Young "for time" but had previously been sealed in eternity to Joseph Smith.[35] At times she lived independently of Young, and they don't seem to have had conjugal relations. Some women were sealed to Young for eternity but remained married to other men in mortality.[36] Other

---

30. See Laurel Thatcher Ulrich, *A House Full of Females: Plural Marriage and Women's Rights in Early Mormonism*, 1835–1870 (New York: Knopf, 2017), 132 (recounting Eliza R. Snow's sealing to Joseph Smith for eternity and to Brigham Young for time).

31. See Stapley, *The Power of Godliness*, 42 (recounting such a ritual).

32. See Stapley, 40–42.

33. See Stapley, 41–42 (discussing the law of adoption). See also Samuel M. Brown, "Early Mormon Adoption Theology and the Mechanics of Salvation," *Journal of Mormon History* 37, no. 3 (2011): 3–52 (discussing early Latter-day Saint sealing theologies); Jonathan A. Stapley, "Adoptive Sealing Ritual in Mormonism," *Journal of Mormon History* 37, no. 3 (2011): 53–117 (same as previous); Gordon Irving, "The Law of Adoption: One Phase of the Development of the Mormon Concept of Salvation, 1830–1900," *Brigham Young University Studies* 14, no. 3 (1974): 291–314 (same as previous).

34. See Jeffery Ogden Johnson, "Determining and Defining 'Wife': The Brigham Young Households," *Dialogue: A Journal of Mormon Thought* 20, no. 3 (1987): 57–70.

35. See Ulrich, *A House Full of Females*, 132.

36. See Johnson, "Determining and Defining 'Wife,'" 63–64.

women—including several who were quite old and one woman who was on her death bed—were sealed to Young for time and eternity, but never had an earthly, marital relationship with him, although he did provide financial support to some of them.[37] In addition to the fifty-five women to whom Young was sealed in his lifetime, numerous adult men were sealed to Young as "adopted" sons, meaning that they were part of Young's divine kinship network in the eternities and had an ill-defined, semi-ecclesiastical relationship with Young in mortality.[38] Married couples were also sealed to Young in adoptive rituals—although some of these husbands were themselves polygamists and not all of their wives were parties to adoptive sealings—which ceased between 1846 and Young's death in 1877. Finally, Latter-day Saints believed that living proxies could perform sealing rituals on behalf of those who were dead. Accordingly, after his death, numerous women—living and dead—were sealed to Young for eternity, as were large numbers of men—also living and dead—who were adopted into Young's eternal kin network. Young's situation was an extreme case, but it illustrates the complex and diverse way in which "sealings" could operate.

Latter-day Saint sealing practices began to simplify after 1890. In that year, Church President Wilford Woodruff issued the so-called Manifesto, publicly disavowing the practice of polygamy after three decades of increasingly intense legal pressure. Even so, some Mormon leaders continued to perform clandestine plural marriages until 1904, when top members of the Church's hierarchy were excommunicated over the practice and the Church began to aggressively discipline its members for polygamy. Less dramatically, in 1894 Woodruff repudiated the so-called law of adoption, insisting that thenceforth sealings should mirror mortal family relationships.[39] As a result, Mormonism's sealing theology in the twentieth century abandoned its earlier concern with eternal dynastic connections. Rather, it simplified to focus on the idea of continuing mortal families in the eternities. As a result, sealing practices largely—but not entirely—came to focus on marriages for time and eternity, and the earlier variety of sealings fell into desuetude.

After 1888, the legal formality around marriage increased precipitously in Mormon country. Utah was admitted to the Union in 1896.

---

37. See Johnson, 58–62.

38. See John G. Turner, *Brigham Young, Pioneer Prophet* (Cambridge: Belknap Press of Harvard University Press, 2012), 58–59 (discussing Brigham Young's practice of the law of adoption).

39. See Cooper, *Promises Made to the Fathers*, 198–99 (discussing the end of the law of adoption).

Although now free of direct Congressional supervision, Utahns evidenced no interest in returning to the informality of their pre-1888 law of marriage. The shift to legal formality was completed in 1899 when the Utah Supreme Court decided the case of *Norton v. Tufts*.[40] The case involved a convoluted series of marriages and real estate transactions that resulted in a lawsuit between a mortgage holder and two women, both of whom claimed to be the non-polygamous widows of the original mortgager.[41] Eleanor and Elbridge Tufts were married in 1869, but the marriage failed. A short time later the couple obtained a "church divorce."[42] Thereafter Elbridge married, was widowed, was married again to one Jennie Tufts, and was granted a mortgage to George Norton in some real estate acquired after the "church divorce."[43] For her part, Eleanor married John Wickel shortly after her "church divorce." Elbridge died in 1896, and Norton sought to foreclose the mortgage on the real estate in the possession of Jennie, Elbridge's third wife. Eleanor sued, arguing that despite the "church divorce" twenty-five years earlier, and no less than three subsequent marriages between the two of them, she was Elbridge's legal widow.[44] As such, she claimed dower rights in the real estate.[45] The case made its way to the Utah Supreme Court, which considered a number of legal arguments, including the claim that Eleanor could not assert dower rights because her twenty-five-year marriage to John, and the child they had together, proved that she was an adulteress.[46] Ultimately, the court held that the only way a couple in Utah could legally dissolve their marriage was by complying with the Utah divorce statute. Accordingly, "church divorces" were declared ineffective, and all of the marriages purportedly dissolved by such divorces remained valid.[47] The case was widely reported

40. 19 Utah 470 (1899).

41. 19 Utah at 472.

42. 19 Utah at 473.

43. 19 Utah at 474.

44. See 19 Utah at 474–75.

45. Dower rights refer to "[a]t common law, the right of a wife, upon her husband's death, to a life estate in one theory of the land that he owned in fee. With few exceptions, the wife could not be deprived of dower by any transfer made by her husband during his life time." Bryan A. Garner and Henry Campbell Black, eds., *Black's Law Dictionary*, 7th ed. (St. Paul: West Group, 1999), 507.

46. See 19 Utah at 475.

47. See 19 Utah at 477.

in Utah and came to the attention of a woman living in Salt Lake City named Annie Hilton.

III. The Love Story of Annie and John

Annie Hilton had been born as Annie Flora Armitage in Notting Hill, outside of London, in 1853.[48] In 1866, she joined The Church of Jesus Christ of Latter-day Saints, and six years later she chose to "gather to Zion" by emigrating to Utah.[49] She traveled with a large group of other Latter-day Saint immigrants aboard a ship called the *Minnesota*. Among the group was an American Latter-day Saint named John Park, twenty years Armitage's senior.[50]

Park was born in Ohio in 1833.[51] In 1857, he graduated from New York University with a medical degree.[52] He practiced medicine for a short time but soon gave it up and moved to Iowa to find work as a teacher.[53] It was here, according to family lore, that Park first became interested in Mormonism.[54] Eventually he traveled west to seek his fortunes in the gold fields outside of Denver.[55] When that project failed, he made his way to Utah, where he began teaching school and was baptized into The Church of Jesus Christ of Latter-day Saints in 1862.[56] The young educator came to the attention of Brigham Young and other Church leaders, and he was appointed president of the nascent University of Deseret, which would eventually because the University of Utah.[57] In 1871, the Church sent Park as a "missionary" to "visit the principal schools and colleges in the United States" before proceeding to "Germany and Switzerland . . . [to]

48. See Annie Flora Armitage, Details(visited January 4, 2022).

49. See Annie Flora, Ordinances, Details, FamilySearch.

50. See "How Dr. Park Wooed Miss Annie Armitage," *Salt Lake Herald-Republican*, October 12, 1900. See also British Mission Emigration Register 238, available online at https://saintsbysea.lib.byu.edu/mii/passenger/1923 (accessed January 5, 2022).

51. John Clifton Moffitt, *John Rocky Park in Utah's Frontier Culture* (n.p.: n.p., 1947), 6.

52. Moffitt, 7.

53. Moffitt, 7.

54. Ralph V. Chamberlin, *Memories of John Rockey Park* (Salt Lake City: University of Utah Alumni Association, 1949), 142.

55. Moffitt, *John Rocky Park in Utah's Frontier Culture*, 8.

56. Moffitt, 8–9.

57. Moffitt, 17.

visit all the best educational institutions in those countries."[58] He was returning from this fact-finding mission aboard the *Minnesota* when he first met Annie. Park and the 19-year-old Armitage struck up a friendship.[59] After the ship docked in New York City, John showed Annie the city before they parted and she proceeded by rail to Utah.[60]

As was often the case with young Latter-day Saint immigrants without families, upon her arrival in Salt Lake City, Annie was taken in by a local Mormon household, in this case by Emeline Free Young, one of the plural wives of Brigham Young.[61] While both Annie and John were devout Latter-day Saints in the early 1870s, they were ambivalent about polygamy.[62] In the much-married Mormon community of Utah, he was notable for being a bachelor at age 40, and while they were in New York City, John seems to have advised Annie against entering plural marriage.[63] If Annie felt conflicted about polygamy, the same thing could not be said of Emeline Free Young. Her family were early converts to Mormonism, and she was one of the first women to enter polygamy, marrying Brigham Young in Nauvoo, Illinois, in 1846 before the Mormon exodus to Utah.[64] Nor was she alone among her family in embracing polygamy. That same year, her sister Louisa married John D. Lee as a plural wife, and after divorcing him she was polygamously married a second time to Daniel H. Wells, Brigham Young's counselor in the governing First Presidency of the Church.[65] Wells was also married to another Free sister, Hannah, who had

58. "For Europe," *Salt Lake Herald-Republican*, September 26, 1871; See "Local and Other Matters," *Deseret Evening News*, November 13, 1872 (noting Park's return to Salt Lake City).

59. See "How Dr. Park Wooed Miss Annie Armitage."

60. See "How Dr. Park Wooed Miss Annie Armitage."

61. See "How Dr. Park Wooed Miss Annie Armitage." See also Emeline Free, Ordinances, FamilySearch (noting Emeline's marriage to Brigham Young).

62. See "Mrs. Hilton Testifies," *Salt Lake Tribune*, May 17, 1901 ("Dr. Park, she said, warned her about conditions in Utah and spoke of polygamy being practiced here. She told him she did not believe in polygamy, and he hold her he was very glad that she did not").

63. See Jeffery Ogden Johnson, "On the Edge: Mormonism's Single Men," *Dialogue: A Journal of Mormon Thought* 16, no. 3 (1983): 51–52 (discussing Park's status as a well-known bachelor); "Dr. Park Will Case Now On," *Deseret Evening News*, May 16, 1901 ("[H]e told me about polygamy and that I ought not to be in haste to get married").

64. See Emeline Free, Ordinances, FamilySearch.

65. Louisa Free, Ordinances, FamilySearch.

previously been polygamously married to a man that she later divorced.[66] Another sister, Sarah, was the polygamous wife of the son of Heber C. Kimball, one of Brigham Young's other counselors.[67] Finally, the Free sisters' father, Absalom, eventually followed the example of his daughters, contracting polygamous marriages in the 1850s and 1860s.[68]

Thus in 1872 Annie found herself living in the home of a member of Mormonism's ecclesiastical elite, a family that was deeply enmeshed in plural marriage and fiercely committed to the Church's sealing theology. At some point after Annie came to live with Emeline Free Young, John returned to Salt Lake City. A short time later, Annie became violently ill.[69] At times the sickness rendered her unconscious, and the household became convinced that she would die.[70] At this point Emeline began urging Annie to be sealed to "some good man" before she died.[71] "It would be better for her" in the hereafter, Emeline urged, if the ritual were performed.[72] Annie agreed and indicated that she wished to be sealed to John Park.[73] The diffident John was approached, and although initially uncomfortable lest he be seen as "taking advantage" of the young woman, he reluctantly agreed.[74] On December 5, 1872, Daniel H. Wells, Emeline's brother-in-law and Brigham Young's counselor, performed the sealing.[75]

It is difficult to determine the precise intentions of the parties. It is possible that some kind of romance developed between Park and Armitage during the journey from Europe to America, and that, as Annie told a

---

66. Hannah Corilla Free, Ordinances, FamilySearch.

67. Sarah Elvira Free, Ordinances, FamilySearch.

68. Absalom Pennington Free, Sr., Ordinances, FamilySearch.

69. See "How Dr. Park Wooed Miss Annie Armitage."

70. Transcript of Testimony, Mrs. Hannah C. Wells in Hilton v. Roylance, Case Files #3528 & #3601, Utah State Archives (hereafter Hilton v. Roylance Case File). The case file does not contain a complete record. Most notably, the transcripts of trial testimony have not survived. Wells's statement only exists in the record because a special deposition was taken in her case. Because of her advanced age, it was feared that she would die before trial. Thus, for testimony in the trial court we are dependent on newspaper reports.

71. See Hilton v. Roylance, 25 Utah 129, 134 (1902) (quoting testimony at trial).

72. "Dr. Park Will Case Now On."

73. See Transcript of Testimony, Mrs. Hannah C. Wells in Hilton v. Roylance Case File.

74. See "Park Will Case Begun," *Salt Lake Tribune*, May 6, 1901.

75. See "Park Will Case Begun."

newspaper nearly three decades later, John pursued her.[76] There are reasons to doubt, however, that the December 1872 sealing was understood by the parties as the deathbed union of two lovers. The moving force seems to have been Emeline Free Young, and both Annie and John were reluctant. When Annie recovered from her illness, witnesses later reported that John seemed annoyed.[77] The couple never lived together, Annie continued to use her maiden name, and there is nothing to suggest that the marriage was consummated.[78] Indeed, in subsequent litigation, attorneys asserted that John was "physically incapacitated from marriage,"[79] and Annie testified that at the time this fact was explained to her by Emeline and her sister Hannah.[80] It is difficult to know exactly to what this referred. The most likely meaning is that John was sexually impotent, but it is also possible that John was a closeted homosexual, although there is no explicit evidence that this was the case.[81] Whatever the situation, John seems to have had a habit of forming "romantic" attachments to women in situations where there was no risk of the relationship maturing into marriage and sexual activity. In addition to his deathbed sealing to Annie, according to family lore, John was "engaged" to a woman in the "Eastern States" who refused to marry him unless he abandoned Mormonism, which he refused to do. In another case he "formed an attachment" shortly after his arrival in Utah with a young woman who refused to marry because she

76. "How Dr. Park Wooed Miss Annie Armitage."

77. See "Park Was Annoyed," *Salt Lake Tribune*, January 5, 1901.

78. The one exception is when the couple later obtained a "church divorce" and Annie signed the separation agreement as "Anne Park." Hilton v. Roylance 25 Utah 129, 135 (1902) (reproducing the separation agreement).

79. "Park Will Case Begun."

80. "Mrs. Hilton Testifies," *Salt Lake Tribune*, May 17, 1901, at 5 ("Mrs. Hilton said Dr. Park told her there was an obstacle in the way to their living together. He did not state what the obstacle was but said that it was of such a nature that he could not explain it to a young girl. She afterward learned from Mrs. Young and Mrs. Wells that it was a physical disability under which the doctor labored").

81. While persistent same-sex relationships did exist among nineteenth-century Latter-day Saints, albeit without explicitly being labeled as homosexual unions, Park never seems to have been part of such a couple. See Johnson, "On the Edge," 51–52 (discussing Park's status as a life-long bachelor in nineteenth-century Utah); see generally D. Michael Quinn, *Same-Sex Dynamics among Nineteenth-Century Americans: A Mormon Example* (Urbana: University of Illinois Press, 1996) (discussing homosexuality among nineteenth-century Latter-day Saints).

had to care for an aged father.[82] The oblique later testimony about John's sexuality was not mere prurience. Impotence was a long-standing legal impediment to marriage, and John's sexual condition went to the question of the couple's state of mind under the principle of *per verba de presenti*. The most likely explanation for the sealing is that, similar to a deathbed rite such as extreme unction, it was seen as a ritual aimed primarily at securing Annie's position after death.

Whether this meant that the sealing was a marriage "for eternity only," rather than "for time and eternity" is another question. Either sort of union would have served the parties' theological purposes equally well, and given that everyone—including Annie—assumed that she was shortly going to die, it is possible that the parties simply didn't consider the question. Whether or not Park and Armitage would be married "for time" during the brief period between the ceremony and Annie's death would have been a question of little, if any, practical significance. Nevertheless, it was later reported that on the day of the sealing John recorded in his diary that he "notified [Daniel H. Wells] that I did not wish to marry her [i.e. Annie Armitage] but only to be sealed for eternity."[83] It is, however, now impossible to verify if this is true or if it was a later invention.[84] Finally, it is possible that John wished to be sealed only "for eternity," but that Daniel H. Wells performed the ceremony "for time and eternity." Later witnesses testified that Wells seemed annoyed with John's conduct in the affair.[85] It is possible that Wells saw John's behavior as evidencing a half-hearted or disrespectful attitude toward the sealing ritual. Alternatively, he may have seen John as making a distasteful effort to obtain the eternal blessings of the sealing without accepting the mortal responsibilities of matrimony.

---

82. See Chamberlin, *Memories of John Rockey Park*, 14 (discussing Park's romantic attachments in Iowa); R. S. Gifford, *History of William Charles Smith, Jr. and Clara Sloan Smith and Family* (n.p.: Stevenson's Genealogy Center, 1994), 163–64 (recounting the story of Park's romantic attachment to Elizabeth Wadley Smith when he was first a school teacher in Utah). Interestingly, given the legal controversy surrounding John's sealing to Annie and its alleged post-mortal implications, Park was posthumously sealed to Elizabeth Wadley Smith in 1917. Gifford, 164.

83. Quoted in Moffitt, *John Rocky Park in Utah's Frontier Culture*, 96.

84. The diary entry was quoted in a book published in 1947, seventy-five years after the event and after the precise nature of the sealing had become a cause to celebrate. The original diary, however, does not seem to have survived. See Moffitt, 95–96.

85. See Transcript of Testimony, Mrs. Hannah C. Wells in Hilton v. Roylance Case File.

Annie recovered from her illness. For a time, John continued to visit the convalescing young woman regularly, but the two had little in common and the visits soon ceased. For her part, Annie found that her sealing to John was a social embarrassment. She was teased about the matter by other young people, and the sealing may have scared off potential suitors.[86] In March 1873, at Annie's request, John obtained a "church divorce."[87] Again, the precise significance of this act is uncertain. It is possible that the two understood themselves as married "for time and eternity" and that the "church divorce" would dissolve their marriage. The "church divorce" in their case, however, was not accompanied by any proceeding before a Church court to establish John's alimony obligations, something that was quite common in such cases.[88] Although there was some inconsistency in practice, Church leaders were generally hostile toward men who left economically vulnerable wives in divorce.[89] In the case of Annie and John's sealing, however, Annie was never economically dependent on John, and Church leaders may have seen the "church divorce" in this case as an annulment. The other possibility is that while the sealing was "for eternity only," the "church divorce" was necessary to dissolve the sealing and thus render Annie eligible in the Mormon marriage market. While Annie would have been free to marry "for time" without dissolving a sealing "for eternity only" to John, she may have needed to get the sealing cancelled to be sealed to a husband "for time and eternity." The most likely explanation is that neither Annie nor John had a fine-grained theological understanding of their "church divorce." It was enough that the sealing created social awkwardness, and the "church divorce" eliminated that awkwardness.

After March 1873, John and Annie do not seem to have had any interaction. In 1875, Annie was sealed "for time and eternity" to another English convert to Mormonism, William Hilton.[90] William became a policeman in Salt Lake City, and eventually the couple had twelve children.[91] As the federal government's legal crusade against Mormon polygamy reached white-hot intensity in the 1880s, the couple seems to have

86. See "How Dr. Park Wooed Miss Annie Armitage."

87. See "Park Will Case Begun" (reproducing the divorce certificate).

88. See Firmage and Mangrum, *Zion in the Courts*, 325–29 (discussing divorce proceedings in church courts).

89. See Firmage and Mangrum, 326–27 (recounting the case of a husband required to provide support to his adulterous ex-wife because of her vulnerability).

90. Annie Flora Armitage, Ordinances, FamilySearch.

91. See Annie Flora Armitage, Details, FamilySearch.

become disenchanted with Mormonism over plural marriage.[92] In 1887, as Congress was passing the Edmunds-Tucker Act, they ceased baptizing their new children, indicating their status us lapsed Latter-day Saints.[93] For his part, John Park never married but pursued a successful career as an educator and investor. At the time of his death in September 1900, he was not only the former president of the University of Utah but also the state superintendent of education.[94] He acquired a substantial fortune in real estate and other investments in Utah and Idaho.[95] He remained a Later-day Saint throughout his life, but he had an ambivalent relationship with his church. He reportedly clashed with Brigham Young over the dangers of a secular education for young Latter-day Saints, although in the end he persuaded the aging patriarch that such education was not only necessary but spiritually valuable.[96] Later in life he told his non-Mormon relatives that he avoided Latter-day Saint meetings because he was often called on to deliver impromptu sermons.[97] He defended his religion mainly in terms of its social and moral utility rather than a burning conviction of the truth of its theology. As one of his nieces later wrote, "Uncle Rockey [i.e. John Park] said that for him Mormonism was a very satisfactory, practical, and livable religion; but he could understand the feelings of those who did not

---

92. According to family lore, "Annie and William came to Utah from England as converts to the Mormon Church because of some instances concerning polygamy they become distant." Beth Blake Parrish, "Annie Armitage and William Hilton," FamilySearch, accessed January 15, 2022, https://www.familysearch.org/tree/person/memories/K27T-ZW8.

93. According to Mormon practice, children of Latter-day Saint families are supposed to baptized sometime shortly after their eighth birthday. Church records show that the Hiltons stopped baptizing their children in 1886 or 1887. Compare Rosa Ellen Hilton, Ordinances, FamilySearch (a daughter born to Annie and William in 1876, who according to Mormon practice should have been baptized around 1884, and was baptized in 1884) with Alice Minne Hilton, Ordinances, FamilySearch (a daughter born to Annie and William in 1878, who according to Mormon and previous Hilton family practice should have been baptized around 1886 or 1887 but was not).

94. See Darrell S. Willey, "Utah's Frontier Architect of Social Destiny: John R. Park," *Peabody Journal of Education* 38, no. 2 (1960): 100–106.

95. See Moffitt, *John Rocky Park in Utah's Frontier Culture*, 91–93 (discussing Park's business activities).

96. See Chamberlin, *Memories of John Rockey Park*, 155–56.

97. See Chamberlin, 142.

like it . . ."[98] When he died the public schools throughout the state were closed in mourning.[99]

Two months later, on December 5, 1900, Annie Armitage Hilton filed suit in Utah District Court in Salt Lake County, claiming to be the legal widow of John R. Park.[100]

IV. *Hilton v. Roylance*

A. Litigation in District Court

Shortly before his death, John Park executed a will leaving his property to the University of Utah.[101] While he never married, he did raise three foster children, who were disappointed to discover that they would inherit nothing under the will.[102] However, Park had sought to provide for his foster daughter, Rosa Roylance, by transferring real property to her before his death.[103] Annie sued Roylance. She argued that because she was John's wife, he could not transfer real property free of her dower rights without her consent.[104] Because Annie never extinguished her dower rights, she was entitled to one third of the property conveyed to Roylance. In addition, the Park estate sued Annie to quiet title in a case that was tried with Annie's suit against Roylance, and in her counterclaim Annie demanded a one-third interest as her dower rights in the real property of the estate, as well as a living allowance out of the estate until it was wound down.[105]

Annie's primary motive in prosecuting the suit seems to have been economic. She took umbrage in the press at the suggestion that there was any "jobbery" in her suit.[106] She only wished to vindicate her rights, she insisted. However, given the assiduousness with which she pursued Park's

---

98. Chamberlin, 145.

99. See "Schools Close Tomorrow," *Ogden Daily Standard*, October 2, 1900.

100. See "To Break the Will," *Salt Lake Herald-Republican*, December 6, 1900. See also Plaintiff's Amended Complaint, in Hilton v. Roylance Case File.

101. See "Another Cloud Arises," *Salt Lake Herald-Republican*, October 17, 1900.

102. See "Another Cloud Arises."

103. See Plaintiff's Amended Complaint, in Hilton v. Roylance Case File.

104. See Plaintiff's Amended Complaint.

105. See Stewart v. Hilton, Complaint, in Hilton v. Roylance Case File; Stewart v. Hilton, Amended Answer, in Hilton v. Roylance Case File.

106. See "'Sealing' is Legal Marriage, Says the Supreme Court," *Salt Lake Herald-Republican*, July 22, 1902, at 1 ("There have been intimations of jobbery in this matter, but I was only after my rights, and, thanks to my attorneys, I got them").

assets, it is implausible to suppose that she was vindicating any abstract conception of rights. Within the Hilton family, the case seems to have been seen in economic terms. When the Utah Supreme Court sided with Annie, William Hilton, an anti-polygamist who had just been adjudged to have spent nearly three decades in an adulterous and bigamous relationship, cheered, and the Hilton children shouted, "Now we shall have a new house!"[107] However, Annie's motives were not entirely mercenary. At trial she testified that she felt wronged by John in the divorce.[108] This sense of wrong presumably didn't flow from the effort to dissolve the union, which was made at her instigation. More likely she was mortified to discover in 1899, when *Norton v. Tufts* was decided, that she had been living in a legally illicit relationship for decades, and she blamed John's legal incompetence for creating the mess.[109] She may have seen obtaining John's property as a way of posthumously vindicating the wrong that she had suffered at his hands.

In light of the Utah Supreme Court's recent decision in *Norton v. Tufts*, the defendants made no effort to argue that Annie's suit was barred by her "church divorce" from John in 1873. Rather, they argued:

> John R. Park and the said plaintiff were "sealed," that is, they thereby went through a sealing ceremony whereby they agreed to be husband and wife after death and not before . . . [they] were then, members of what is known as the "Mormon" Church and it is a tenet of said church that a man and a woman may be sealed so that they will be husband and wife after death, that is, in eternity.[110]

Under the principle of *per verba de presenti* governing the legal validity of marriages in Utah prior to 1888, the legally important fact was whether in the sealing ceremony Annie and John manifested agreement to a *present* intent to marry. Annie claimed that this was the parties' intent in 1872.

---

107. "'Sealing' Is Legal Marriage, Says the Supreme Court."

108. See "Mrs. Hilton Testifies," *Salt Lake Tribune*, May 17, 1901, at 5 ("Q: You yourself were the one to resurrect this story about your relation to Dr. Park? A. No sir; the story was repeated in my presence, which humilated me thereby. I felt that I had beenwronged—wronged by Dr. Park in giving me a bogus diorce, and if I had any rights, I wanted to know it").

109. Even in 1873, John could have obtained a legally valid divorce by complying with the Utah territorial divorce statute rather than obtaining a church divorce.

110. See Hilton v. Roylance, Amended Answer, in Hilton v. Roylance Case File.

The defendants denied that any such intention existed because the marriage was to take effect in the *future* after both parties were dead.[111]

As with the allegation in *Norton v. Tufts* that remarriage constituted adultery, there were immediately accusations that Annie's union with William Hilton constituted legal adultery.[112] In the legal hothouse of late nineteenth- and early twentieth-century Utah, this was not simply an accusation of private immorality. Rather, during the anti-polygamy crusades of the 1870s and 1880s, adultery was a crime that was often used to prosecute polygamists, particularly plural wives.[113] In the case of women, these indictments had a particular sting, as adultery was also the crime for which prostitutes were routinely prosecuted. The effort to brand Mormon wives as whores was not accidental.[114] With the 1890 Manifesto and President Cleveland's blanket pardon for pre-Manifesto polygamy issued in 1891, it was hoped that the specter of legal battles over plural marriage had been put to rest.[115] This, however, was not the case for two reasons. First, there was disagreement over what "abandoning" polygamy meant. Some anti-polygamists believed that husbands and plural wives must separate or face continued prosecution for unlawful cohabitation. Other anti-polygamists, however, were content to let plural marriage die out gradually, so long as no new polygamous marriages were formed. For their part, most polygamist husbands refused to sever ties to their wives and those who did so were widely regarded by Church leaders and other Latter-day Saints as abandoning their families. The result was a situation where continued criminal prosecution hovered as an ever-present threat. The second problem was that,

---

111. The alternative principle of *per futuro subsequente copula*, adopted by the common law in some states, held that a marriage could be formed when an agreement to marry in the future, such as a formal engagement, was followed by sexual intercourse. However, no Utah case adopted this principle. Furthermore, while a sealing for eternity might conceivably constitute such a future agreement, there was never any suggestion that Annie and John consummated their union.

112. See "To Accuse Mrs. Hilton," *Salt Lake Tribune*, December 7, 1900; "Mrs. Hilton's Case," *Salt Lake Herald-Republican*, December 8, 1900; "Sequel to Dower Interest Case," *Deseret Evening News*, December 7, 1900.

113. See Sarah Barringer Gordon, *The Mormon Question: Polygamy and Constitutional Conflict in Nineteenth-Century America* (Chapel Hill: University of North Carolina Press, 2002), 164–66 (discussing the dynamics around prosecuting plural wives for adultery).

114. See Gordon, 166.

115. See "Polygamy," in *Public Papers of President Grover Cleveland*, 263–264 (Sept. 25, 1894) (pardoning Mormon polygamists).

notwithstanding the Manifesto, some Latter-day Saint leaders continued to perform plural marriages, either in jurisdictions—Canada, Mexico, and the high seas—deemed not to be covered by the Manifesto or else secretly within the United States.[116] The Church did not begin to move decisively to end all new plural marriages until 1904, when it began excommunicating those who advocated, performed, or entered into such marriages.

Post-Manifesto polygamy was thus very much a live issue in Mormon country in the 1890s and 1900s. In 1898, Brigham Roberts, a polygamist Church leader, was elected to Congress, which voted in 1899 to deny him his seat.[117] In 1903, Utah chose Reed Smoot, a monogamist Mormon apostle, to fill one of its Senate seats.[118] The choice proved explosive. The Senate launched a massive investigation of Mormon affairs in Utah that lasted from 1904 to 1907, and Smoot retained his seat only after President Theodore Roosevelt intervened with fellow Republicans to defend Smoot after the investigating committee recommended that he be expelled from the Senate.[119] One of the moving forces behind these controversies was a Utah resident named Charles Mostyn Owen.[120] Trained as a civil engineer, Owen was a professional anti-polygamy activist during the late 1890s and early 1900s.[121] In 1899 the *New York Journal* hired him as an investigator in its effort to exclude Roberts from Congress, and later that year he also swore out a criminal complaint against Roberts.[122] Thereafter, he worked as a private investigator

116. See B. Carmon Hardy, *Solemn Covenant: The Mormon Polygamous Passage* (Urbana and Chicago: University of Illinois Press, 1992), 206–43.

117. See generally R. Davis Bitton, "The B. H. Roberts Case of 1898–1900," *Utah Historical Quarterly* 25, no. 1 (1957): 27–46 (recounting B. H. Roberts's political career and the aftermath of his election to the US House of Representatives).

118. See generally Kathleen Flake, *The Politics of American Religious Identity: The Seating of Senator Reed Smoot, Mormon Apostle* (Chapel Hill: University of North Carolina Press, 2004); Harvard S. Heath, "The Reed Smoot Hearings: A Quest for Legitimacy," *Journal of Mormon History* 33, no. 2 (2007): 1–80.

119. Flake, *The Politics of American Religious Identity*, 143–45.

120. Flake described him as "the protestants' investigator and Utah's resident rumormonger." Flake, 143–45.

121. See Brian Q. Cannon, "Shaping BYU: The Presidential Administration and Legacy of Benjamin Cluff Jr.," *Brigham Young University Studies* 48, no. 2 (2009): 26 (referring to Owen as "an investigator hired by Protestant opponents of Smoot and the Mormons").

122. See "Charge Against Roberts," *The Gilspin Observer*, October 19, 1899. See also Proceedings Before the Committee on Privileges and Elections of the United States Senate in the Matter of the Protests Against the Right of Hon.

for various anti-Mormon Protestants who hired him to ferret out information on post-Manifesto polygamy, and he filed dozens of affidavits in Utah, Idaho, and Wyoming in an effort to see Mormon polygamists prosecuted on various grounds.[123] As part of his efforts to demonize Latter-day Saints during the Smoot Hearings, Owen also posed in Mormon temple robes for national reporters in mockery of Latter-day Saint rituals.[124] At the time of Annie's suit, he was working for the Womans' Interdenominational Council of New York as an anti-Mormon investigator.[125]

In December 1900, Annie's lawsuit caught Owen's attention. Despite the fact that the Hiltons were no longer observant Latter-day Saints and seemed to have left the Church over polygamy, Owen swore out a criminal complaint against Annie for adultery with the Salt Lake County Attorney on December 7, 1900, two days after Annie filed suit.[126] The county attorney took up the case, a warrant for her arrest was issued, and she was criminally indicted.[127] Her attorney claimed that Owen was motivated "by a spirit of revenge or an effort to intimidate her into abandoning her claims."[128] This is unlikely. There is no evidence to suggest any connection between Owen, Roylance, or the Park estate.[129] Rather, Annie was caught

---

Reed Smoot, a Senator from the State of Utah, to Hold is Seat, 59th Cong. 2:396 (1906) (testimony of Charles Mostyn Owen).

123. See Cannon, "Shaping BYU," 26 (referring to Owen as a professional anti-polygamy investigator). See generally Charles Mostyn Owen Collection, Church History Library, The Church of Jesus Christ of Latter-day Saints, Salt Lake City, Utah (containing copies of correspondence, court documents, and surveillance notes from Owen's extensive polygamy-hunting activities); see Charles Mostyn Owen Collection, Folder 20, Church History Library, Church of Jesus Christ of Latter-day Saints, Salt Lake City, Utah (containing copies of numerous affidavits filed by Owen)

124. See Flake, *The Politics of American Religious Identity*, 82 (recounting the story).

125. See Proceedings Before the Committee on Privileges and Elections of the United States Senate in the Matter of the Protests Against the Right of Hon. Reed Smoot, a Senator from the State of Utah, to Hold is Seat, 59th Cong. 2:396 (1906) (testimony of Charles Mostyn Owen).

126. See "Sequel to Dower Interest Case."

127. See "Sequel to Dower Interest Case"; "Marriage Relations Not Disturbed by Decision," *Salt Lake Herald-Republican*, July 23, 1902.

128. "Sequel to Dower Interest Case."

129. However, the ultimate party in interest in the litigation against the estate was the University of Utah, the beneficiary under Park's will, and thus the state government that indicted Annie.

up in the logic of Owen's anti-polygamy crusade. It was enough that her situation resulted from Latter-day Saint sealing and divorce practices. Upon reading of Annie's suit, Owen reportedly said, "If it be true that this woman was the wife of Dr. Park when he died, she has committed adultery and ought to be prosecuted for it."[130]

Annie and her husband, however, had anticipated such action. In late October 1900, they traveled to Wayne County in the remote desert reaches of central Utah and obtained a marriage license under which they secretly married before a justice of the peace in Salt Lake City five days later.[131] According to the Hiltons, the time-consuming procedure of obtaining the marriage license hundreds of miles from their home was to keep the second marriage secret from their children.[132] They may also have worried that a readily available public record of their second marriage might have prejudiced Annie's suit in some way.[133] The careful planning, however, paid off. Armed with the marriage license, Annie was able to persuade the government to drop the criminal case after an election replaced the previous county attorney.[134]

At trial, the basic problem was to establish the intention of the parties to the December 1872 sealing. Daniel H. Wells had produced a certificate for the couple, but in a move almost calculated to generate legal ambi-

---

130. "Sequel to Dower Interest Case."

131. See Marriage License issued to William Hilton and Annie Armitage, October 29, 1900, County Book A, Page 56, Wayne County, Utah, copy in Family History Library, The Church of Jesus Christ of Latter-day Saints, Salt Lake City, Utah (showing that a marriage license was issued in Wayne County for a marriage performed by a Justice of the Peace seven days later and several hundred miles north, in Salt Lake City). See also "Will Not Wed Again," *Salt Lake Tribune*, July 23, 1902.

132. See "Will Not Wed Again" ("I am perfectly willing that it should come out although even our own children were in ignorance of it").

133. It is striking that no word of the Hiltons' second marriage appears in the press until the day after the Utah Supreme Court handed Annie victory in her suit. She won her case on July 22, 1902, and news of her second marriage appeared in the press the following day. See "Will Not Wed Again." Compare Hilton v. Roylance, 25 Utah 660 (1902) (issued July 22, 1902). Her attorney pointedly did not disclose the fact of the second marriage when Annie was first indicted, but her civil lawsuit was still before the courts. See "Sequel to Dower Interest Case" (quoting Annie's attorney, who makes no mention of the October 1900 marriage).

134. See "Marriage Relations Not Disturbed by Decision."

guity, it stated merely that he had performed a "sealing."[135] It made no mention of marriage and did not specify if the sealing was "for time and eternity," "for time only," or "for eternity only." Of the five witnesses of the ceremony—Annie Armitage, John Park, Emeline Free Young, Hannah Free Wells, and Daniel H. Wells—three of them (Park, Young, and Wells) were dead. That left only Annie and an aged Hannah Wells available to testify. To further complicate matters, the so-called dead man's statute precluded testimony of Park's intentions in the case against his estate.[136] In 1900, Hannah Wells was seventy-one years old, but she was sufficiently frail that the attorneys in the case moved rapidly to depose her and preserve her testimony, most likely for fear that she might die before a full trial was possible.[137] (She lived until 1913.)[138] Other witnesses testified to events surrounding the sealing. Unfortunately, the trial transcripts did not survive, and newspapers provide only a partial record of the proceedings. Hannah proved a hostile witness. Her son stated in a letter to Annie's attorney that he saw her suit as "blackmail," and Hannah agreed to testify only after being threatened with a subpoena and a contempt order.[139] She testified to the sealing but resisted efforts by Annie's lawyers to characterize it as a marriage "for time and eternity."[140] For her part, Annie testified that while she was sick at the time, she regarded the sealing as a valid marriage.[141] When pressed, however, she admitted that her death was widely

135. See Hilton v. Roylance, 25 Utah at 134 (reproducing the sealing certificate).

136. See 188 Utah Comp. Laws § 3877 (Utah's Dead Man's Statute in force at the time of Hilton v. Roylance). See "Dr. Park Will Case Now On," *Deseret Evening News*, May 16, 1901, at 1 ("An objection was promptly raised [to Annie's testimony] by the counsel of the respondents in the will contest, on the grounds that the question was contrary to the rules of evidence, which prevent any person from testifying to a matter within the equal knowledge of a deceased person").

137. See Order in the Matter of the Application of Annie F. A. Hilton to Perpetuate the Testimony of Hannah Wells, Hilton v. Roylance Case File; "Testimony for Mrs. Hilton," *Salt Lake Tribune*, December 15, 1900.

138. Hannah Corilla Free, Details, FamilySearch.

139. See Copy of Letter to Hannah Wells from N. V. Jones, October 16, 1900, in Hilton v. Roylance Case File.

140. See, e.g., Transcript of Testimony, Mrs. Hannah C. Wells in Hilton v. Roylance Case File; "Dr. Park's Wedding," *Salt Lake Tribune*, January 4, 1901.

141. "Dr. Park Will Case Now On"; see "Mrs. Hilton Testifies."

expected at the time.[142] She also admitted to being informed of John's mysterious sexual disability and his reluctance to enter into the union.[143]

The judge treated the existence of the marriage as a question of fact that hinged on the intention of the parties. He concluded:

> That at the time of the alleged marriage the plaintiff and John R. Park were single; that they were friends of some years standing, but the friendship had not ripened into or been impressed by a courtship, a declaration of love and reciprocity. At the time, the woman was in extremis, thought by those present and by herself to be in a state of immediate physical dissolution. The only thought of them all seemed to be the spiritual or future welfare of the one passing from this into the next would.[144]

The ceremony, he concluded, was "a religious function—a sealing having relation to things spiritual and not temporal."[145] Accordingly, he held that Annie and John had never been married, and he dismissed both lawsuits.

Annie and her attorneys appealed to the Utah Supreme Court.

B. Litigation in the Utah Supreme Court

The Utah Supreme Court began its opinion by rehearsing the basic facts of the case without discussing the complex history of marriage law in Utah. The court asserted that while marriage could be differentiated from normal contracts by the state's special interest in the status, it was nevertheless created by the agreement of the parties:

> [C]onsent, which, as we have seen, constitutes the contract to marry, may be given in writing or verbally, or may be inferred from the acts of the parties and the ceremony performed.[146]

The court went on to endorse an objective theory of consent. "[N]o secret reservation of one of the parties, entertained at the ceremony, unknown to the other party, can serve the party entertaining it to avoid the marriage."[147] To this point, the analysis largely tracks the approach taken by the district court. Marriage is formed by the mutual consent of the parties applying

142. "Dr. Park Will Case Now On"; see "Mrs. Hilton Testifies."

143. "Mrs. Hilton Testifies."

144. In the Third Judicial District Court (Division No. 1), State of Utah, County of Salt Lake, Hilton v. Roylance, Opinion of Judge Hall, July 11, 1901, in Hilton v. Roylance Case File.

145. See Opinion of Judge Hall.

146. Hilton v. Roylance, 25 Utah 129, 138 (1902).

147. Hilton v. Roylance, 25 Utah 129, 140 (1902).

an analysis analogous to that of contract cases. In the district court, this meant determining what the parties individually intended by focusing on the fragmentary evidence from the 1872 ceremony. Indeed, at trial some effort was made to introduce into evidence statements from Church leaders and Mormon scripture as to the meaning of "sealing," and the court refused to admit the evidence.[148] In addition, the trial court issued a subpoena to Charles Penrose, the editor of the Church-owned *Deseret Evening News* and a frequent participant in the highest councils of the Church.[149] (He would be called as an apostle, a member of the Church's second highest governing council, in 1904.)[150] He was presumably being called to explain the content of Mormon theology. However, the court seems to have refused to allow him to testify.[151]

In contrast, the Utah Supreme Court chose to dive into the substantive content of Mormon theology without any expert guidance. "The parties," the court wrote, ". . . must be held to have consented to and intended whatever their language and acts indicate."[152] The court went on to insist, "The most important subject of interest in this case, therefore, is what was meant by the term sealed or 'sealing ceremony.'"[153] However, for the court the important question was not the meaning subjectively assigned to these terms by the parties. Rather, it was the meaning assigned to these terms by The Church of Jesus Christ of Latter-day Saints.

> The church, as an organized ecclesiastical body, had the right to declare and adapt tenets rules, and ordinances, not inconsistent with or repugnant to the laws of the land, for its own governance and guidance and conduct of its members; and the same are binding upon the members, and will be respected by the courts in passing upon questions relating to ecclesiastical affairs.[154]

---

148. Hilton v. Roylance, 25 Utah 129, 143–144 (1902).

149. See Subpoena Issued to Charles W. Penrose, May 20, 1901, in Hilton v. Roylance Case File. The return indicates that the subpoena was served on Penrose by the deputy sheriff.

150. See "Charles W. Penrose," Church Historian's Press, accessed January 6, 2022, https://www.churchhistorianspress.org/the-first-fifty-years-of-relief-society/people/charles-william-penrose.

151. None of the newspaper reports on the first trial in Hilton v. Roylance mention Charles Penrose as a witness, although the trial was big news at the time and the newspapers produced lengthy accounts of the testimony. See, e.g., "Dr. Park Will Case Now On"; "Mrs. Hilton Testifies."

152. Hilton v. Roylance, 25 Utah at 142.

153. Hilton v. Roylance, 25 Utah at 142.

154. Hilton v. Roylance, 25 Utah at 142–143.

The Utah Supreme Court thus focused its attention on the institutional rather than the subjective meaning of sealings. Indeed, such institutional meaning controlled over the subjective intention of the parties.

There are a number of reasons why the Utah Supreme Court's approach to the question diverged from that taken by the district court. First, Annie's case was a suit in equity. The dower rights that she was asserting were formally a common-law property interest that had traditionally been enforced using the common-law writ of right.[155] However, the remedy that Annie sought in the lower court was a partition of the real estate, an equitable remedy.[156] Furthermore, the case turned on the underlying validity of her purported marriage to John. Although, in the absence of a marriage statute in Utah before 1888, Annie and John were governed by "common law marriage," the idea of common-law marriage was, ironically enough, first articulated by Chancellor James Kent before the New York Court of Chancery and was thus an equitable doctrine.[157] The distinction between law and equity was important because it defined the scope of the Utah Supreme Court's jurisdiction on appeal. As the Utah law in force at the time put it, "In equity cases the appeal may be on questions of both law and fact, [but] in cases of law the appeal shall be on questions of law alone."[158] Thus, the Supreme Court felt free to ignore the district court's factual findings as to the intentions of the parties in the 1872 sealing.

Contemporary American courts are disallowed from inquiring into matters of theology.[159] Such inquiries now violate the religion clauses of the First Amendment to the US Constitution.[160] However, in the nineteenth century this was not the case. The courts were frequently called on to adjudicate cases involving religious doctrines. This happened most

155. See Maybury v. Brien, 40 U.S. 21 (1841) ("Dower is a legal right, and whether it be claimed by suit at law or in equity the principle is the same").

156. See Hilton v. Roylance, Amended Complaint, in Hilton v. Roylance Case File.

157. See Fenton v. Reed, 4 Johns 52 (1809) (recognizing the validity of "common law" marriages). See generally Ariela R. Dubler, "Governing Through Contract: Common Law Marriage in the Nineteenth Century," *Yale Law Journal* 107, no. 6 (1998): 1885–1920 (discussing "common law marriage" in the nineteenth century).

158. Utah Rev. Stat § 3300 (1898).

159. See Serbian Eastern Orthodox Dioceses for the U.S. of America and Canada v. Milivojevich, 426 U.S. 696, 708–709 (1976) (stating that the courts cannot make theological inquiries).

160. See United States v. Ballard, 322 U.S. 78, 87 (1944) (holding that theological inquiries by secular courts violate the First Amendment).

frequently in disputes over church property.[161] This issue became particularly important as congregations, and in some cases whole denominations, split apart over slavery and the Civil War.[162] In 1871, the US Supreme Court decided in *Watson v. Jones*[163] that where ecclesiastical authorities had adjudicated a question, secular courts should defer to their decisions. The court stated:

> It cannot be supposed that judges of the civil courts can be as competent in the ecclesiastical law and religious faith of all these bodies as the ablest men in each are in reference to their own. It would therefore be an appeal from the more learned tribunal in the law which should decide the case, to one which is less so.[164]

Watson v. Jones, however, was not decided on constitutional grounds. The deferential approach of the US Supreme Court in *Watson* coexisted with cases where courts were much more confident in their ability to decide matters of religious doctrine and practice.

For much of the nineteenth century, American courts treated religious rules and doctrines in much the same manner as the law of a foreign jurisdiction, to be applied using ideas taken from conflict of law analysis.[165] An early and influential example of such analysis can be found in *Gable v. Miller*.[166] The case involved a dispute over control of the German Reformed Church in New York City. The court decided that the outcome turned on which of the two disputing factions remained true to the original theological vision of those who had set up the congregation. Accordingly, the trial and appellate courts in the case generated a massive

---

161. See generally Victor Manuel Muñiz-Fraticelli, "Neutral Principles and Legal Pluralism," in *Democracy, Religion, and Commerce: Private Markets and the Public Regulation of Religion*, ed. Nathan B. Oman and Kathleen Flake (New York: Routledge, 2023) (discussing the judicial resolution of church property cases).

162. See generally Mark A. Noll, *The Civil War as a Theological Crisis* (Chapel Hill: The University of North Carolina Press, 1900) (discussing the theological conflicts of the Civil War era); see Mark DeWolfe Howe, *The Garden and the Wilderness: Religion and Government in American Constitutional History* (Chicago: University of Chicago Press, 1965), 75 (discussing nineteenth-century legal disputes over church property).

163. 80 U.S. 679 (1871).

164. 80 U.S. 729 (1871).

165. See generally Kellen Funk, "Church Corporations and the Conflict of Laws in Antebellum America," *Journal of Law and Religion* 32, no. 2 (2017): 263–84.

166. 2 Denio 493 (N.Y. 1845).

record of expert testimony from ministers and produced hundreds of pages of dense theological analysis of the nuances of Calvinist and Lutheran soteriology.[167] *Gable v. Miller* was not an outlier. "From 1830 until the Civil War, nearly every divisive point of Protestant theology . . . came into court . . . including sabbatarianism, trinitiarianism, the inheritability of sin, and real presence of Christ in the Euchrist—and those are just the cases from New York."[168] Judicial enthusiasm for theological interpretation, in turn, flowed from a particular vision of religious freedom. As Kellen Funk has observed:

> [B]egin with the notion that at bottom religious freedom assumes that there can exist an alternative legal order to the legal order of one or another American state. Such reasoning seems to accord with the understanding of this earlier era and what is remarkable about these cases is that state judges respected these alternative legal systems enough to actually enforce their rules in American courts. . . . In this sense religious freedom was a corporate freedom the right of an aggregate to see its institutional rules and actions validated in the state courts.[169]

The Utah Supreme Court in *Hilton v. Roylance* took this more aggressive approach. First the court agreed to consider documentary evidence refused below. Its analysis focused on three kinds of sources. First, it looked to the Doctrine and Covenants, a canonized book of Latter-day Saint scripture containing written revelations recorded by Church founder Joseph Smith.[170] Second, it perused written reports of sermons delivered by Church leaders.[171] Finally, the court consulted books published by Latter-day Saint authors with varying levels of theological authority.[172] The court treated section 132 of the Doctrine and Covenants as the controlling Mormon authority on the meaning of sealings. "We have not been referred to nor have our researches disclosed any other law or regulation of the Mormon Church for the solemnization of marriages of its members," the court wrote. "It must therefore be regarded as the

167. See Funk, "Church Corporations and the Conflict of Laws," 274–78 (recounting the litigation).

168. Funk, 279–289 (collecting citations).

169. Funk, 278.

170. See Hilton, 25 Utah at 148–49.

171. See Hilton, 25 Utah at 150–54.

172. See Hilton, 25 Utah at 154–55.

ecclesiastical law for contracting and solemnizing all marriages which are celebrated through the instrumentality of that church."[173]

The revelation relied on by the court was recorded by Joseph Smith in 1843 as part of his effort to implement polygamy among the Latter-day Saints. The text declares

> All covenants contracts, bonds, obligations, oaths vows, performances connections, associations or expectations, that are not made, and connections, associations, or expectations, that are not made, and entered into, and sealed by the Holy Spirit of promise of him who is anointed, both as well for time and for eternity . . . are of no efficacy virtue, or force, in and after the resurrection from the dead; for all contracts that are not made unto this end have an end when men are dead.[174]

The revelation goes on to discuss this power to "seal . . . by the Holy Spirit of Promise" in terms of marriage for time and eternity.[175] Based on the fact that only such marriages were discussed in the revelation, the court went on to confidently conclude that "neither a sealing nor marriage for time whereby the parties are to become husband and wife for this world only, nor a sealing or marriage for eternity, whereby the parties are not to become husband and wife until after death (that is in the next would) was authorized by this revealed law."[176] Accordingly, Annie and John could not have intended to have been sealed merely for eternity, as, according to the court, no such sealings existed among the Latter-day Saints.[177] The court thus concluded that Annie and John had been legally married by Daniel H. Wells in 1872, and in light of the invalidity of their 1873 "church divorce" they remained married at the time of Park's death.[178]

C. The Aftermath of Hilton v. Roylance

The Utah Supreme Court's decision in July 1902 was not the end of the legal controversy over the sealing of Annie and John. It was not even the end of the beginning. Litigation would continue until 1910 and would eventually spill across the border into the neighboring state of Idaho. Furthermore, The Church of Jesus Christ of Latter-day Saints

---

173. Hilton, 25 Utah at 148–49.
174. Hilton, 25 Utah at 148–47.
175. Hilton, 25 Utah at 147.
176. Hilton, 25 Utah at 149.
177. Hilton, 25 Utah at 156.
178. See Hilton, 25 Utah at 159.

did not fail to notice the Utah Supreme Court's effort to authoritatively interpret Mormon scripture and practice.

The day after the decision came down, Charles Penrose, editor of the Church's *Deseret Evening News*, blasted the court's foray into Latter-day Saint theology. "We do not know whether the hot weather has an effect upon courts as well as upon some individuals," he wrote, "but the decision just handed down from the Supreme Court of the State in the Hilton case appeared to the average mind like an emanation from heated brains." The editorial went on to affirm that the Church did indeed perform sealings for eternity only, going on to say, "To the Mormon mind the decision will appear utterly absurd, and we believe the general public will not have a very different opinion."[179] Privately, however, high Church leaders were not entirely comfortable with Penrose's decision to come out swinging against the court. Anthon Lund, then a counselor in the First Presidency, the Church's highest governing council, confided to his diary that while he agreed with Penrose that in the past, sealings for eternity only had been performed, the Church had abandoned the practice and it would have been better to remain silent.[180] He was worried that Penrose's article might lead to a general attack on the legal validity of Latter-day Saint sealing rituals as legal marriages. "I think it is bad to spring this question to the world. It may give rise to the query: 'Can you provide that this sealing was for time otherwise you claim that it is not a marriage!'"[181]

The public hostility of the Church's newspaper did not go unnoticed, and the Park estate petitioned the Utah Supreme Court to rehear the case. The court denied the petition in September, leading to another editorial attack from Penrose.[182] Penrose reaffirmed the declaration in his earlier editorial that the court had erred in holding that sealings for eternity only were not practiced within the Church. He went on to write:

> 'We speak that which we do know and testify of that which we have seen,' and we say that, however right the court may have been to determine that a legal marriage was contracted between Dr. Park and Miss Armitage, the court was wrong in its attempt to declare, judicially, the doctrine and prac-

179. "Who Would Have Thought It," *Deseret Evening News*, July 22, 1902.

180. See Anthon H. Lund, *Danish Apostle: The Diaries of Anthon H. Lund, 1890–1921*, ed. John P. Hatch (Salt Lake City: Signature Books, 2006), 197–98 (discussing the case and Penrose's editorial).

181. Lund, 198.

182. See "The Mrs. Hilton-Dr. Park Case," *Deseret Evening News*, September 2, 1902; "Law and Gospel," *Deseret Evening News*, September 9, 1902.

> tices of the Church of Jesus Christ of Latter-day Saints in reference to the sealing ordinances. Judicial opinions on strictly legal propositions, when uttered by a court of last resort, stand as law. But disquisitions from the bench on purely religious and doctrinal questions are not final, neither are they reliable or bind in in law or in the Gospel.[183]

Despite Annie's victory before the Utah Supreme Court, the Park estate continued to drag its feet, and not simply by petitioning the court for a rehearing. It wasn't until nearly a year after the court issued its decision that the lower court issued a report on how to partition the Park estate.[184] Frustrated by the delay, Annie expanded her litigation strategy by suing additional transferees of real property, bringing suit against George Thatcher and William McCormick in December 1902 for a dower interest in property that they acquired from John.[185] In the McCormick case, the defendant—who had not been a party to the original litigation—again argued that the 1872 sealing was intended for eternity only. Charles Penrose was again called to testify, but this time the lower court allowed him to take the stand. The day before Penrose testified, Lund confided in his diary, "I hope that he [Charles Penrose] does not defend his statement that there are sealings for eternity and not for time."[186] Lund was to be disappointed. Penrose was unequivocal, testifying, "There may be a marriage without a sealing, there may be a sealing for time alone, there be a sealing for time and eternity, there may be a sealing which relates to eternity and not to time. I will add that then in 1872 such ordinances might be performed."[187] Penrose testified that he personally had witnessed

---

183. "Law and Gospel."

184. See "Park-Hilton Case Up," *Salt Lake Tribune*, June 6, 1903.

185. "Mrs. Hilton Sues for Dower Right," *Salt Lake Tribune*, December 14, 1902.

186. Lund, *Danish Apostle*, 253.

187. Transcript on Appeal 112, in Case File Hilton v. Stewart, Idaho Supreme Court, 1908, Idaho State Archives. Trial transcripts do not survive in the Utah State Archives for district courts in this period. However, attorneys for the Park estate in an Idaho case tried to introduce portions of the trial transcripts from Hilton v. Roylance and Hilton v. McCormick into evidence. This evidence was excluded, and the estate appealed to the Idaho Supreme Court, where the Transcript on Appeal contains testimony from the two Utah cases. See Transcript on Appeal 92-233 in Case File Hilton v. Stewart, Idaho Supreme Court, 1908, Idaho State Archives. See also "Time or Eternity?" *Salt Lake Tribune*, November 20, 1903 (recounting Penrose's testimony).

several sealings for eternity only.[188] The district court sided with the defendant. In an opinion that made no mention of the Utah Supreme Court's decision in *Hilton v. Roylance*, the lower court concluded that "the sealing was for eternity and the divorce dissolved that relation. The subject being wholly spiritual, and having nothing whatever to do with things temporal, the parties could assume to dissolve the relation between themselves at pleasure."[189] The court went on to hold "both as a matter of law and of fact"[190] that "by the doctrines and usages of the 'Mormon' church a sealing for eternity only is not a marriage. That John R. Park was never married to the plaintiff."[191]

Annie's attorneys chose not to appeal the McCormick decision, likely to avoid presenting the Utah Supreme Court with an opportunity to reconsider its conclusions about sealings for eternity in light of what seemed to be clear and at least quasi-authoritative statements from the Church. The Park estate, however, took notice of the case and tried to introduce Penrose's testimony in the McCormick case in the litigation with Annie. In addition, as part of the ongoing Smoot Hearings in Washington, DC, Church president Joseph F. Smith had also testified before the US Senate's Committee on Privileges and Elections about the existence of sealings for eternity only, although he stated that for "twenty years or more" the practice had "fallen into disuse . . . [although] I do not know that it could be said to have fallen absolutely into disuse."[192] The Park estate also tried to introduce these statements. The Utah Supreme Court, however, rejected

188. See Transcript on Appeal, in Case File Hilton v. Stewart, Idaho Supreme Court, 1908, Idaho State Archives.

189. "Hall Against Supreme Court," *Salt Lake Herald-Republican*, April 14, 1904 (reprinting the text of the trial court's opinion).

190. "Hall Against Supreme Court."

191. "Hall Against Supreme Court." In the case against George Thatcher, the defendant argued that Annie's dower rights failed to survive the acts of the Utah legislature abolishing dower rights, then reinstating them at Congressional behest, and finally codifying them. The case eventually made its way to the Utah Supreme Court, which rejected the defendant's arguments. See Hilton v. Thatcher, 31 Utah 360 (1907) (upholding the continuing vitality of Hilton's dower rights).

192. See Proceedings Before the Committee on Privileges and Elections of the United States Senate in the Matter of the Protests Against the Right of Hon. Reed Smoot, a Senator from the State of Utah, to Hold is Seat, 59th Cong. 1:185 (1906) (testimony of Joseph F. Smith).

these efforts, holding that for the estate the matter was *res judicata*.[193] However, the court also doubled down on its position, stating somewhat oddly that because Joseph F. Smith, president of the Church, testified in the Smoot Hearings "I heard of . . . one or two instances of that kind [i.e. sealings for eternity only]" that its earlier decision had been correct.[194] Annie also sued the Park estate in Idaho, where Park had owned land, claiming she was entitled to one half of the value of the property. Again, the estate's lawyers tried to introduce evidence from the McCormick case, but the Idaho courts held that they had to accept the conclusion of the Utah Supreme Court regarding the validity of the 1872 marriage as *res judicata*.[195] For their part, no doubt rattled by the victory of the defendant in the McCormick case, Annie's lawyers abandoned their earlier strategy of going after Park's transferees, who were not bound by the conclusions in *Hilton v. Roylance* because they had not been a party to the earlier lawsuit.[196] Rather, they argued that Annie was entitled to one third of the value of all real property transferred by Park during their marriage out of the estate. This argument was also rejected by the Utah Supreme Court, which insisted that dower rights were in rem and had to be pursued against transferees who now owned the land in question.[197]

This forced Annie's lawyers to return to the strategy of suing John's transferees. They did so, instituting eight separate lawsuits in March 1907.[198] However, this strategy ultimately proved unsuccessful. Upon appeal, the Utah Supreme Court held that the transferees were not bound by its holding in *Hilton v. Roylance* under the doctrine of *res judicata*.[199] Rather than revisiting its interpretation of Mormon theology, however, the Utah Supreme Court chose to dispose of the case in a decidedly

---

193. See In re Park Estate, 29 Utah 257 (1907) (rejecting the estate's effort to relitigate the question of sealings for eternity).

194. See In re Park Estate, 29 Utah at 263.

195. See Hilton v. Stewart, 15 Idaho 150 (1908) (holding that the Idaho courts would not question the validity of a marriage judged to be valid by the Utah courts and denying the estate's efforts to introduce evidence from the McCormick case).

196. They were, of course, bound by *Hilton v. Roylance* as legal precedent, but the case was not *res judicata* (binding) as to its specific factual holding regarding Annie's and John's intentions with regard to the 1872 sealing.

197. See In re Park Estate, 31 Utah 255 (1906).

198. See "Mrs. Hilton Sues for Park Estate," *Salt Lake Tribune*, June 25, 1908.

199. See Hilton v. Snyder, 37 Utah 384 (1910) (holding that third parties to the suit in Hilton v. Roylance were not bound by its factual conclusions).

lawyerly fashion. Instead of admitting its error or doubling down on its clearly threadbare interpretation of Latter-day Saint practice, the court held that Annie was estopped from pursuing claims against third parties because from 1873 on, she had held herself out as not being married to John, and John's transferees were entitled to rely on her representations.[200] Thus, at the conclusion of a decade of litigation, Annie was able to recover one-third of the value of the property of the estate in Utah as dower rights and one-half of the value of the parcel of land held by John in Idaho at the time of his death. However, with the exception of her successful suit against Roylance, she was unable to recover against any of the other property that John had owned during their "marriage."

V. Law and the Opacity of Religion

Law has a tendency to simplify and flatten social reality. The late Justice Antonin Scalia once remarked, "The main business of a lawyer is to take the romance, the mystery, the irony, the ambiguity out of everything he touches."[201] There are good reasons for this. Judges and lawyers are not historians or social scientists. They are certainly not prophets or theologians. They are practical men and women who, at their best, are making a good faith effort to decide cases according to pre-existing rules, a process that requires only that they be able to discern legally relevant facts. Nobody is paying a lawyer get at a full understanding of social reality. Holmes famously described the project in these terms:

> The process is one . . . eliminating . . . all the dramatic elements with which his client's story has clothed it, and retaining only the facts of legal import, up to the final analyses and abstract universals of theoretic jurisprudence. The reason why a lawyer does not mention that his client wore a white hat when he made a contract, while Mrs. Quickly would be sure to dwell upon it along with the parcel gilt goblet and the sea-coal fire, is that he forsees that the public force will act in the same way whatever his client had upon his head.[202]

This tendency toward simplification, however, is not merely a product of legal analysis. Rather, the flattening effect of modern law is but one

---

200. See Hilton v. Sloan, 37 Utah 359 (1910) (holding that Hilton's claims were estopped).

201. "Justice Antonin Scalia: In his own words," BBC, February 14, 2016, https://www.bbc.com/news/world-us-canada-35571825.

202. Oliver Wendell Holmes, Jr., "The Path of the Law," *Harvard Law Review* 10 (1897): 458.

aspect of the persistent demand of modern states for a simplified vision of social reality.

One of the hallmarks of modernity has been the growing social ambitions of the secular state. Modern governments want to adjust society in order to improve it. This requires that social reality be made legible to government actors. Society, however, is a bewilderingly complicated thing, and bureaucratic actors—including those bedecked out in judicial robes—have no hope of grasping it without simplifying stories. This process, which James Scott has called "seeing like a state," involves both a distorted view of social practices and an urge to remake those practices in a simpler, more legible form.[203] Sometimes this is beneficent process. To take a pedestrian example, the passage of Article 9 of the Uniform Commercial Code replaced a bewildering variety of financing devices that had grown organically out of commercial practice with a single, simplified law of secured transactions.[204] No one lamented the decline of pledges, chattel mortgages, and hypothecations because Article 9 not only rendered debt relations more legible to the state but also to commercial actors, who benefited from decreased information costs.

At times, however, communities resist the state's efforts at simplification both because they derive important value from their own internal complexities and because they can be particularly opaque to state actors. This is often the case with religion. Religious communities often make strong claims to ultimate authority, which attracts the suspicious attention of the state, creating feedback that has been aptly described by Jacob Levy:

> State overreach forces associations and groups into a defensive posture; they raise barriers to entry, become more opaque to outside monitoring, demand more conservative and loyal behavior from their members. Local elite power, the opaqueness of intermediate social groups, and the oppositional character of many group identities make it difficult for states to regulate intra-group life in any fine-grained way and motivate more aggressive state action. And so on.[205]

---

203. See generally James C. Scott, *Seeing like a State: How Certain Schemes to Improve the Human Condition Have Failed* (New Haven: Yale University Press, 1999).

204. See Grant Gilmore, *Security Interests in Personal Property* (Boston: Little Brown & Co., 1965), 1:5–287 (discussing the immensely complicated system of pre-Article 9 security devices).

205. Jacob T. Levy, *Rationalism, Pluralism, and Freedom* (Oxford: Oxford University Press, 2015), 61.

Religious practice is also opaque for less politically fraught reasons. A religious practice that is legible to the state in Scott's terms is one that is subject to simplifying assumptions about what religion is. In its crudest form, state actors will simply view all religious practices through their native religious assumptions. Witness the way in which American law persistently understands "religion" as a legal category through analogies to Protestant Christianity.[206] More subtly, religion becomes more legible when it is seen in terms of a simple set of coherent doctrines that are consistent over time and subscribed to in their entirety by a homogeneous group of religious believers. This is religion that courts can "look up" with the help of a competent librarian. The reality, however, is that the content of religious belief and the meaning of religious practices evolves over time, often in discontinuous ways, and believers almost always have an idiosyncratic, often ambivalent, and generally imperfectly thought-out relationship to their own religious tradition.

All of these factors were on display in *Hilton v. Roylance*. The court erred badly in its interpretation of Latter-day Saint theology and practice. The well-documented sealing practices of nineteenth-century Latter-day Saints show that sealings "for eternity only" were certainly possible. The court sought to validate its interpretation of the Doctrine and Covenants by pointing to sermons by Church leaders in which sealings were referred to as marriages for time and eternity.[207] No one, however, disputed that Latter-day Saints could be sealed for time and eternity. Just before the Utah Supreme Court handed down its decision, an editorial in the Church-controlled *Deseret Evening News* had defended the district court's decision from critical eastern newspapers by explaining that while ordinarily sealings were "for time and for all eternity," in some cases it was possible to have "simply a sealing for the next world, carrying with it 'no duty of marriage,' responsibility or contract for this world."[208]

The court erred about the content of Latter-day Saint theology for three reasons. First, it ignored the plain meaning of the text of Doctrine and Covenants 132, from which its opinion quoted. Second, it misunderstood the relationship between scripture and authoritative practice in the Latter-day Saint tradition. Finally, at the time that the court wrote,

---

206. See Nathan B. Oman, "How To Judge Sharia Contracts: A Guide to Islamic Marriage Agreements in American Courts," *Utah Law Review* 2011 (2011): 292–93 (discussing and documenting this tendency).

207. See Hilton, 25 Utah at 153.

208. "A Misapprehension," *Deseret Evening News*, July 29, 1901.

Latter-day Saint sealing practices were in flux. Hence, in part the court was anachronistically imposing the sealing practices and theology that was emerging in 1902 back on to the very different Mormonism of 1872.

The language initially quoted from Doctrine and Covenants 132 by the court speaks of the sealing power in extremely broad terms. Rather than confining the term to marriages of a single sort, it speaks of "all covenants, contracts, oaths, obligations, oaths, vows, performances connections associations or expectations" (D&C 132:7) It then goes on to discuss the specific case of marriage. The text, far from confining the term "sealing" to marriages for time and eternity, explicitly refers to sealings in terms of a broader understanding of what sorts of relationships could be subject to sealing. This textual structure makes sense within the historical context in which the revelation was originally given. While it was later canonized as authoritative for the Church as a whole, the revelation was originally directed at a single person: Joseph Smith's first wife, Emma Smith.[209] By 1842, Joseph had introduced a complex set of rituals that were often referred to as "sealings" or "anointings."[210] Emma had accepted the legitimacy of these rituals but remained violently opposed to the practice of polygamy.[211] Hence, rhetorically, the 1842 revelation was intentionally nesting the idea of marriage sealings within the context of a broader set of sealing rituals. This is why, contrary to the court's interpretation, the text of the revelation does not present the term "sealing" as applied solely to marriage ceremonies.

Its approach to Latter-day Saint theology reveals a deeper misunderstanding by the court about how religious authority works within the Latter-day Saint tradition. The court took an essentially Protestant ap-

---

209. See Newell and Avery, *Mormon Enigma*, 151–52.

210. These rituals became the basis for modern Latter-day Saint temple rituals. These were described thus in the Church's 2021 Handbook:

> The endowment is received in two parts. In the first part, a person receives a preliminary ordinance called the initiatory. The initiatory is also known as the washing and anointing (see Exodus 29:4–9). . . . In the second part of the endowment, the plan of salvation is taught, including the Creation, the Fall of Adam and Eve, the Atonement of Jesus Christ, the Apostasy, and the Restoration. Members also receive instruction on how to return to the Lord's presence.

General Handbook: Serving in the Church of Jesus Christ of Latter-day Saints, 27.2 (2022), available at https://www.churchofjesuschrist.org/study/manual/general-handbook (accessed January 6, 2022).

211. See Newell and Avery, *Mormon Enigma*, 140–43.

proach, assuming that Latter-day Saint beliefs and practices were deduced from scripture. In the case of the Doctrine and Covenants, the book of Mormon scripture on which the court relied, this assumption gets the relationship backwards. Mormonism began in the late 1820s when a young Joseph Smith announced that he had been receiving visions and revelations.[212] In 1830, Smith and his followers formally organized as a church.[213] Central to their theological identity was the conviction that continuing revelation meant that the scriptural canon was open. Until his murder in 1844, Smith continually refashioned Mormon theology and practice, issuing a flood of written revelations and oral teachings to his followers.[214] In 1835, the Church sought to codify its theology and practice by publishing a curated collection of Smith's revelations as the Doctrine and Covenants.[215] This book was formally accepted as scripture by the Church, but it was an ex post effort to organize practices and teachings rather than a set of textual first principles from which those practices and theologies were derived.[216] Final authority remained with Smith and his successors as "prophets, seers, and revelators" for the Church rather than with a corpus of scriptural texts. Indeed, by 1844, the 1835 Doctrine and Covenants was already out of date, missing materials on the key innovations Smith had made in the intervening decade.[217]

The revelation on marriage discussed by the court is a key example of this process. The text of the revelation discusses both the theology of sealing and of plural marriage, but it was not used to introduce either idea. Rather, Smith introduced the former idea in public sermons and the

---

212. See generally Richard Lyman Bushman, *Joseph Smith and the Beginnings of Mormonism* (Urbana: University of Illinois Press, 1984).

213. See Oman, "'Established Agreeable to the Laws of Our Country,'" 210.

214. See Thomas G. Alexander, "The Reconstruction of Mormon Doctrine: From Joseph Smith to Progressive Theology," *Sunstone* 5, no. 4 (August 1980): 24–33 (discussing the iterated and at times discontinuous nature of the theology of Joseph Smith and his successors).

215. See Richard E. Turley Jr. and William W. Slaughter, *How We Got the Doctrine and Covenants* (Salt Lake City: Deseret Book, 2015), 101–15.

216. See Nathan B. Oman, "'I Will Give Unto You My Law': Section 42 as a Legal Text and the Paradoxes of Divine Law," in *Embracing the Law: Reading Doctrine and Covenants 42*, ed. Jeremiah John and Joseph M. Spencer, 2017, 4–6 (discussing how the 1835 Doctrine and Covenants was compiled in an attempt to codify then-current Church doctrines and practices).

217. See Turley and Slaughter, *How We Got the Doctrine and Covenants*, 4–15.

latter idea through private conversations.[218] In both cases, it was Smith's personal authority as prophet rather than an appeal to the Doctrine and Covenants that underwrote the practice. In Smith's lifetime and for years after his death, the text of the revelation that would become Doctrine and Covenants 132 was not widely known among Latter-day Saints. Rather, their understanding of sealing practice came through public teachings and private instructions from Church leaders. Indeed, when Annie and John were sealed by Daniel H. Wells in 1872, Joseph Smith's 1842 revelation was not formally part of Mormon scripture. Rather, their version of the Doctrine and Covenants would have been based on the 1835 edition, which contains no material on sealing. Section 132 was only added to the Mormon canon in 1880, when the Church formally adopted a new edition of the Doctrine and Covenants.[219] The addition of the 1842 revelation to the 1880 Doctrine and Covenants, in turn, was not a matter of announcing any new doctrines or revelations. The new edition of the Doctrine and Covenants was an effort to bring Mormon scripture more into line with then-current Latter-day Saint theology and practice.[220] However, the updating was only partial, in part because for important Latter-day Saint doctrines and practices there simply weren't any revelatory texts to include and in part because a comprehensive scriptural codification was neither necessary nor desired. Ultimate theological authority remained with the Church's prophetic hierarchy, not its prophetic texts.

Finally, Latter-day Saint theology was going through a quiet, and sometimes not-so-quiet, revolution as the court was deciding *Hilton v. Roylance*. The case came in the midst of the Church's painful transition from polygamy to monogamy. This transition required a revolution in not only the Church's marriage practices but also in the sealing theology that underlay those practices. Nineteenth-century Latter-day Saints saw the purpose of sealing ordinances partially in terms of maintaining family relationships in the eternities and partially in terms of creating sav-

---

218. See Richard Lyman Bushman, *Joseph Smith: Rough Stone Rolling* (New York: Alfred A. Knopf, 2005), 48–49. See also Gary James Bergera, "The Earliest Eternal Sealings for Civilly Married Couples Living and Dead," *Dialogue: A Journal of Mormon Thought* 35, no. 3 (Fall 2002): 41–66.

219. See Turley and Slaughter, *How We Got the Doctrine and Covenants*, 4–15.

220. See generally Brian C. Passantino, "Orson Pratt and the Expansion of the Doctrine and Covenants" (master's thesis, Logan, Utah, Utah State University, 2020) (discussing the historical background to the expansion of the Doctrine and Covenants in the 1870s).

ing ritual connections to webs of priesthood power. When Emeline Free Young urged the dying Annie Armitage to be sealed to someone before it was too late, she likely had this latter purpose in mind. She was not trying to ensure that the then non-existent Park-Armitage marriage would persist in the eternities. Beginning in the 1890s, however, the idea of eternal families came to completely eclipse the idea of sealing into saving priesthood networks. This shift took two forms. The first of these began in 1877 when Latter-day Saints dedicated their first temple in Utah. Thereafter, except in exceptional circumstances, sealing rituals were to be confined to these sacred building from which all but faithful Latter-day Saints were excluded. Temple rituals, in turn, were esoteric rites covered by oaths of secrecy and extremely strong norms of confidentiality. This shift emerged as an issue in Annie's lawsuit. Latter-day Saint witnesses resolutely refused to testify about the wording of sealing rituals, even though such wording would have been highly relevant for determining Annie and John's intentions in December 1872.[221] This is because while Annie and John were sealed in Emeline Free Young's home, by 1901 such sealing ordinances were confined to temples and, according to the witnesses, were covered by secrecy oaths. Heightened norms of reticence around temple rituals made it more difficult to perpetuate older ideas because discussing them publicly became increasingly taboo.

The second shift was desuetude. Latter-day Saint sealing practices simplified after the 1890s, and the earlier ritual complexity was gradually forgotten. This process was facilitated by a strategic use of Protestant ideas about scripture. While insisting that the canon of scripture was open and that the president of the Church had the right to authoritative revelations, in practice Latter-day Saints increasingly emphasized the authority of their own scriptures as the twentieth century progressed.[222] This made it easy to allow older sealing practices that were not in the Doctrine and Covenants

221. See "Temple Against Court," *Salt Lake Tribune*, May 21, 1901.

222. In the mid-twentieth century, some Latter-day Saint leaders and theologians developed a view of scripture similar to that of propounded by Protestant fundamentalists. Hence, Bruce R. McConkie wrote in a widely used theological reference:

> The four volumes of scripture are the standards, and the measuring rods, the gauges by which all things are judged. Since they are the will, mind, word, and voice of the Lord, they are true; consequently, all doctrine, all philosophy, all history, and all matters whatever nature with which they deal are truly and accurately presented.

to fall into disuse. The Church also produced a number of theological syntheses that, while lacking prophetic authority, came to define Latter-day Saint beliefs through sheer ease of reference and the fact that they were published with the imprimatur of the Church.[223] These works maintained a discrete silence about the complexity of nineteenth-century sealing practices, presenting sealing entirely in terms of eternal families.[224] The Utah Supreme Court's opinion relied heavily on James E. Talmage's *The Articles of Faith*, an early and hugely influential example of such a work. In some ways the Utah Supreme Court modelled its approach to Latter-day Saint theology on Talmage's 1899 work, an approach that diverged from the Mormonism of the 1870s when Annie and John were sealed. The court was thus guilty of reading Mormonism's emerging twentieth-century theology of sealing back into the nineteenth century. In fairness to the court, it was a move that Latter-day Saint leaders and writers were beginning to make and would make repeatedly over the following decades.

VI. Conclusion

In September 1968, a new musical, "Woman is My Idea" opened on Broadway. The vanity project of a wealthy Latter-day Saint named Don C. Liljenquist, the play retold the story of *Hilton v. Roylance* with music and song.[225] It was Liljenquist's first production on Broadway because, as

---

Bruce R. McConkie, *Mormon Doctrine*, 2nd ed. (Salt Lake City: Bookcraft, 1966), 764–65. Even at the time, however, McConkie's theology did not command universal assent among members or high Church leaders. See Gregory A. Prince and William Robert Wright, *David O. McKay and the Rise of Modern Mormonism* (Salt Lake City: University of Utah Press, 2005), 49–53 (discussing Church President David O. McKay's reservations about McConkie's Mormon doctrine). It does, however, reflect an extreme manifestation of an intellectual trajectory that was already underway when the Utah Supreme Court handed down Hilton v. Roylance.

223. See Thomas G. Alexander, *Mormonism in Transition: A History of the Latter-Day Saints, 1890–1930* (Urbana: University of Illinois Press, 1996), 289–321 (discussing Latter-day Saints' theological retrenchment at the opening of the twentieth century).

224. See James E. Talmage, *The Articles of Faith* (The Church of Jesus Christ of Latter-day Saints, 1963), 444–46 (discussing "celestial marriage" in terms of "a solemn agreement which is to extend beyond the grave").

225. See "Out of the Shadows: Lara Parker," Collinsport Historical Society, accessed January 14, 2022, http://www.collinsporthistoricalsociety.com/2013/06/

the playbill pompously explained, he hadn't wished to come to New York "until he could write and direct both comedy and tragedy."[226] Annie was changed to Emily and she became an orphan rather than an immigrant.[227] However, John R. Park remained, and the basic story of the deathbed sealing and unexpected recovery was transformed into a domestic comedy of a charmingly sly ingenue pursuing a reluctant bachelor. Brigham Young made a cameo appearance, usurping Daniel H. Wells's historical role. There was also a singing, polygamous lawyer and a crusading federal judge.[228] By all accounts it was a wretched musical. *The New York Times* described it as "one of those unsurprising plays only a mother could love. The author's mother at that."[229] The reviewer went on to write, "Mr. Lilienquist himself directed, and it would be unfair to place the blame on him as director for the sluggish pace he so clearly perpetrated as the author."[230] Even *Dialogue*, a leading Latter-day Saint journal, panned the production.[231] It had five performances before closing. The female lead reported, "I was relieved I didn't have to go back to the play and perform it again."[232] *Hilton v. Roylance*, it would seem, was not the stuff of which great musical theater is made.

It does, however, work well as a colorful legal story and as a case study of the opacity of religion to the law. A full recounting of the story in

---

out-of-shadows-lara-parker.html ("It was actually written, bankrolled and directed by a man who was a Mormon who felt he'd written this wonderful play. It cost a fortune, and you can imagine how critics feel about vanity productions"). Lara Parker played the role of Emily (Annie) in the play. It was not her only brush with a Latter-day Saint playwright. Later in her career, she had a role in Galactica: 1980, a follow on to Latter-day Saint Glen Larson's Battlestar Galactica, a science fiction story that included a number of Mormon tropes and Easter eggs.

226. "Woman is My Idea," Playbill, accessed January 14, 2022, https://www.playbill.com/productions/woman-is-my-ideabroadway-belasco-theatre-1968.

227. See Clive Barnes, "The Theater: Mormons," *The New York Times*, September 28, 1968 (summarizing the plot); Mark Woodworth, "Broadway Runs Comedy on U's First President," *Daily Utah Chronicle*, October 3, 1968 (same as previous).

228. The music, alas, does not survive, but I like to believe that the two of them performed a rousing male duet about the Morrill Anti-Bigamy Act.

229. Barnes, "The Theater: Mormons."

230. Barnes "The Theater: Mormons."

231. See C. Lowell Lees, "A Mormon Play on Broadway," *Dialogue: A Journal of Mormon Thought* 4, no. 1 (1969): 110 ("The crux of the failure was the plot of the play and its writing").

232. "Out of the Shadows," Collinsport Historical Society.

Hilton v. Roylance reveals a religious story punctuated by ambivalent and complex responses to a shifting religious tradition. Both Annie and John were hustled into the deathbed sealing in part by their own sense of religious devotion but just as much by the forceful if well-meaning cajoling of Emmeline Free Young and her sister Hannah. These two women seem to have been the only actors in the drama with a clear and unambiguous theological agenda. Yet even as they deftly maneuvered Annie and John within their theological and ritual world, that world was rapidly evolving and would be largely transformed three decades later when Annie's suit forced the courts to grapple with the legal significance of the sealing. Using the tools of a historian, it's possible to capture some of the complexity of the events.

However, such nuance proved beyond the capacity of the Utah Supreme Court. Determining title to real estate required that it impose a set of simple meanings on the confused religious ritual of thirty years previous. The intent of the parties had to be discerned and that intent had to be boiled down to a simple binary of present consent to be married, yes or no. Likewise, the "objective" meaning of the sealing ordinance had to be simplified into terms that the court could understand and use. It thus rendered Latter-day Saint practices in its own image, working from Protestant assumptions about religious texts to recast Mormon scripture into a code that could be legally parsed by the court. Given its refusal—or inability—to obtain expert, insider guidance on the religious questions, the court's failure of understanding was unsurprising. Courts must inevitably simplify social reality to make it legible to the law. In this, religious practices are no different than any other complex social arrangement that must pass through the epistemic meat grinder of the state. There are problems that arise when courts treat religion as a black box that is utterly beyond their ken. Such "modesty" by the courts presents its own risk of misunderstanding.[233] At times, courts will need to rush in where angels tread and seek to understand the meaning of religious acts on their own terms. When they do so, however, they should proceed cautiously, and ideally obtain help from some expert guides rather than presume to interpret religious texts and practices unaided.

---

233. See Oman, "How To Judge Sharia Contracts" (discussing how American courts have failed to understand the meaning of Islamic marriage contracts because the courts have failed to understand the relationship between those contracts and Islamic law).

CHAPTER 8

"The Blessing That's Anticipated Here Will Be Realized in the Next Life": The Development of Modern Latter-day Saint Marital Sealing Rules

Sealing rules, which govern wedding rituals in Latter-day Saint temples, constitute a hitherto unstudied religious law of marriage that has continued to evolve from the first introduction of sealing rituals in the 1840s to the present.[1] This chapter provides an account of the development of contemporary sealing rules. That story begins in 1888. In that year Utah passed its first marriage statute, making marriage law in Mormon country essentially indistinguishable from the rest of the United States for the first time.[2] Prior to 1888, for practical purposes, sealings simply were legal marriages, although after 1862 plural sealings violated the Morrill Anti-Bigamy Act. During the territorial period, couples could dissolve their marriages by obtaining a "church divorce" in which the president of the Church granted a divorce petition that was then memorialized using a preprinted contract of separation.[3] Between 1888 and 1899, when the

---

1. "Sealings" refer to Latter-day Saint religious rituals in which a Mormon priesthood holder with special authority creates a bond between two or more people that will persist in the eternities. While other kinds of sealings have been performed at various times, most sealings are either marriage sealings that marry a couple for "time and eternity" or sealings of parents to children that vouchsafe intergenerational family connections in the eternities.

2. Prior to 1888, territorial Utah had no marriage statute. As a legal matter, the territory used the informal rule of "common law marriage" as its sole law of marriage. In 1887, as part of the anti-polygamy Edmunds-Tucker Act, Congress required Utah to pass a marriage statute, which it did in 1888, adopting a law that was indistinguishable from those passed in other American jurisdictions. See Edmunds-Tucker Act (1887) §§ 4, 9, 24 Stat. 635 (1887) (criminalizing consanguineous marriages within the fourth degree and marriages not registered in a local court); An Act Regulating Marriage (March 8, 1888), in Laws of Utah 88 (1888).

3. After 1852, there was a parallel procedure in nineteenth-century Utah under which couples could also obtain a divorce from the secular probate courts. See An Act in Relation to Bills of Divorce (1852) § 2, in *Acts, Resolutions, and Memorials Passed by the First Annual and Special Sessions of the Legislative Assembly*

Utah Supreme Court declared that church divorces lacked any legal efficacy, the Latter-day Saints had to begin clearly differentiating the religious rules governing sealings from the secular legal rules governing marriage.[4] This process had two parts. First, the Church had to adapt its marriage practices to a new secular regime that, after 1890, it no longer sought to challenge. Second, it had to determine how its sealing practices would function in a world where sealings were no longer necessarily synonymous with legal marriages. This process was complicated by the practice of proxy sealings for deceased ancestors, which meant rules had to be promulgated for both the living and the dead. In addition, the abandonment of polygamy, which began in 1890, influenced sealing rules. In 1904, the Church began moving decisively to impose monogamy as an internal ecclesiastical standard on Latter-day Saints, although it would take decades to expel internal dissidents who continued to practice polygamy. Despite these efforts, however, new sealing rules based on allegiance to plural marriage would be promulgated in the 1920s and 1930s. These rules were not a continuation of nineteenth-century practice. Rather, they were an invention of the first part of the twentieth century. Later, those rules came under pressure from shifts in both theology and practice as Mormonism moved further and further away from nineteenth-century polygamy.

It would be a mistake to imagine that sealing rules represent a simple working out of the implications of Mormon theology. First, Latter-day Saint theology has evolved over time, and often the rules reflect theological ambivalence rather than a single, well-worked-out theological position. Second, the rules have been shaped by legal and institutional pressures. As is often the case in legal systems, Latter-day Saint sealing practices represent a layering of rules promulgated at different times in response to different concerns. Each new layer supplements and modifies the previous layer without repealing it. The result is a corpus juris that tries to respond to practical demands but is filled with tensions and inconsistencies.

There are basically three strata of sealing rules that have survived into the present. The first layer was promulgated as part of the Church's abandonment of plural marriage. These rules emphasize the centralization of sealing authority in the face of polygamist diehards, a desire to

---

of the Territory of Utah 82 (1852). See generally Richard I. Aaron, "Mormon Divorce and the Statutes of 1852: Questions for Divorce in the 1980's," *Journal of Contemporary Law* 8 (1982): 5–46.

4. See Norton v. Tufts, 19 Utah 470 (1899) (holding that "church divorces" had no effect on the legal validity of marriages).

avoid conflict with secular marriage law, and a continuing commitment to polygamy in the hereafter. They were largely put in place by the 1930s. The second stratum was promulgated in the second half of the twentieth century. These rules focus on posthumous sealings and were vital in facilitating temple worship as a regular and lifelong part of Latter-day Saint practice, something that began in earnest with the Church's first international temples in the 1950s. These rules represent a liberalization of posthumous sealing practices and, at least for deceased persons, abandon the earlier rules' implied commitment to polygamy in the eternities. The ironic result of this new layer of rules is that while modern sealing rules for living persons seem to have a strong implicit assumption of polygamy after death, sealing rules for dead people do not. This shift reflects the needs of mass temple worship and a waning theological commitment to plural marriage. Finally, there is a third stratum laid down at the end of the twentieth century and beginning of the twenty-first century that responds to the sexual revolution by accommodating the rise of no-fault divorce and making efforts at the margins to mitigate the gender inegalitarianism of earlier rules without fundamentally rewriting them. The result is a system of sealing rules that maintains continuity while adapting to meet practical demands, but which cannot be mapped onto a single, consistent theological vision.

Law and Early Twentieth Century Sealing Rules

The story of modern sealing rules begins with the demise of the legal regime governing marriage that the Latter-day Saints created in territorial Utah. Under American law, marriage is generally a matter of state or territorial law and is governed by a local marriage statute. However, American jurisdictions have blessed less formal unions. In the 1809 case of *Fenton v. Reed*, the New York Supreme Court declared that "proof of an actual marriage was not necessary" and that "no formal solemnization of marriage was necessary."[5] Rather, despite the clear language of the New York marriage statute, Chancellor James Kent held that "[a] marriage may be proved . . . from cohabitation, reputation, acknowledgment of the parties, reception in the family, and other circumstances from which marriage may

5. Fenton v. Reed, 4 Johns 52 (N.Y. Sup. Ct. 1809) (per curiam). Scholars have identified James Kent as the author of the opinion. See Ariela R. Dubler, "Governing Through Contract: Common Law Marriage in the Nineteenth Century," *Yale Law Journal* 107, no. 6 (1998): 1885n5.

be inferred." While such "common law marriages" remained controversial throughout the nineteenth century, a majority of American jurisdictions came to recognize marriage *per verbe de presenti*—simply meaning a stated present agreement to be married—as valid.[6]

In territorial Utah, the Latter-day Saints chose not to adopt a marriage statute of any kind.[7] Rather, a provision in the charter of incorporation granted to the Church by the first territorial legislature simply stated that the Church had the authority to "solemnize marriage compatible with the revelations of Jesus," which acts "may not legally be questioned."[8] In part, early Utah legislation may have been motivated by a desire to eliminate public records of polygamous unions that might lead to criminal prosecution, although section 4 of the Church's charter required each Latter-day Saint congregation to keep "a registry of marriages, births, and death."[9] However, criminal prosecutions were a remote risk in the early

---

6. See Dubler, 1886. There were also states in which a promise to marry in the future coupled with subsequent sexual intercourse constituted marriage. This was the so-called marriage *per verba de future cum copula*. See Dubler, 1889n18. "Common law marriage" required courts to engage in interpretive gymnastics to avoid the language of state marriage statutes that seemed to clearly require formalities. The US Supreme Court summarized these moves in the 1877 case of *Meister v. Moore*, which construed an 1838 Michigan statute:

> Such formal provisions may be construed as merely directory, instead of being treated as destructive of a common law right to form the marriage relation by words of present assent. And such, we think, has been the rule generally adopted in construing statutes regulating marriage.

Meister v. Moore, 96 U.S. 76, 79 (1877). American courts also misread the English common law, which did not in fact provide a general recognition of informal relationships as marriages in ways suggested by the US Supreme Court and other American tribunals. See generally Peter Lucas, "Common Law Marriage," *The Cambridge Law Journal* 49, no. 1 (1990): 117–34.

7. See generally Lyman D. Platt, "The History of Marriage in Utah, 1847–1905," *Genealogical Journal* 12, no. 1 (Spring 1983): 28–41.

8. See Nathan B. Oman, "'Established Agreeable to the Laws of Our Country': Mormonism, Church Corporations, and the Long Legacy of America's First Disestablishment," *Journal of Law and Religion* 36, no. 2 (2021): 219–21 (discussing the Church's territorial corporate charter).

9. This argument is made by Lisa Madsen Pearson and Carol Cornwall Madsen, "Innovation and Accommodation: The Legal Status of Women in Territorial Utah, 1850–1896," in *Women In Utah History*, ed. Patricia Lyn Scott, Linda Thatcher, and Susan Allred Whetstone (University Press of Colorado, 2005), 44.

1850s. American authorities were too distant to exercise direct control over the Saints, all law enforcement was firmly in Mormon hands, and bigamy would not be made a crime in the territories until 1862, at which time Congress revoked the marriage provisions in the Church's charter. More likely, Utah law simply represented an extreme manifestation of the trend toward informality around marriage that had long been present in American law more generally.[10] Thus in territorial Utah, there wasn't any distinction between a sealing and a legal marriage. For legal purposes, sealings simply were marriages. There were no additional legal formalities, such as obtaining a marriage license, that were required.

In 1887, in the final round of its anti-polygamy legislation, Congress enacted the Edmunds-Tucker Act. The law levied criminal punishments against anyone performing a marriage that was not recorded with the local court.[11] In response, the Utah territorial legislature finally enacted a marriage statute in 1888.[12] The law abandoned the principle of marriage *verba de presenti*, invalidating marriages "when not solemnized by an authorized person,"[13] which was restricted to "ministers of the gospel . . . in regular communion with any religious society" or judges.[14] Marriages could only be performed after first obtaining a marriage license from the local probate court, and those performing the marriage had to provide a certificate to the court at the conclusion of the ceremony. Criminal punishments were levied against those who performed marriages without a license or in violation of the act.[15] Absent compliance with new legal formalities, sealings were no longer legal marriages.

When the Latter-day Saints arrived in the Great Basin, they were far less reticent in legislating on divorce than they were in legislating on marriage. In 1852, the Utah territorial legislature adopted a law modeled

---

10. It is striking that a catalogue of the territorial library published in 1852 lists numerous legal treatises including such standard works as Kent's *Commentaries* and Blackstone's *Commentaries*. See *Catalogue of the Utah Territorial Library, October 1852* (Great Salt Lake City: Brigham H. Young, Printer, 1852). Notably absent is Tapping Reeve's *The Law of Baron and Femme*, the standard American treatise on marriage law in the first half of the nineteenth century. Indeed, the catalogue does not list any legal titles related to marriage.

11. See Edmunds-Tucker Act (1887) §§ 4, 9, 24 Stat. 635 (1887).

12. See An Act Regulating Marriage (March 8, 1888), in Laws of Utah 88 (1888).

13. An Act Regulating Marriage (March 8, 1888) § 2(3), in Laws of Utah 88 (1888).

14. See An Act Regulating Marriage (March 8, 1888) § 7, in Laws of Utah 88 (1888).

15. See An Act Regulating Marriage (March 8, 1888) §§ 12–14, in Laws of Utah 88 (1888).

on Iowa's liberal divorce statute. In practice, however, Utah divorce was often even less formal than this statute suggested. The 1852 law granted jurisdiction over divorce to the locally staffed probate courts.[16] But married couples often petitioned the Church president for divorce rather than going to court.[17] While Brigham Young preached against divorce, he was quite lenient in granting separation to couples, particularly when plural wives sought divorce. He was considerably less sympathetic to polygamous husbands who wished to leave their wives. In all cases, Young required that those wishing to divorce pay a fee to the Church, apparently to discourage frivolous petitions.[18] Latter-day Saints assumed that a church divorce had all of the legal consequences of a divorce and cast the final separation not as an ecclesiastical decree but as a formal contract. The language of such contracts was standardized and eventually, the Church produced preprinted forms.[19]

This Latter-day Saint divorce regime was challenged in the courts, creating legal uncertainty into the early twentieth century. In 1892, a pension commissioner in the Department of the Interior denied benefits to the widow of a Mormon battalion pensioner on the grounds that the "Mormon divorce" from his first wife was invalid, and therefore the two had never been married. On appeal, the administrator took it as established that the "Mormon divorce" was invalid but reasoned that after the first wife died a common-law marriage came into existence between the

---

16. See An Act in Relation to Bills of Divorce (1852) § 1, in *Acts, Resolutions, and Memorials Passed by the First Annual and Special Sessions of the Legislative Assembly of the Territory of Utah* 82 (1852).

17. See generally Eugene E. Campbell and Bruce A. Campbell, "Divorce among Mormon Polygamists: Extent and Explanations," *Utah Historical Quarterly* 46 (Winter 1978): 4–23. See also Kathryn Daynes, *More Wives than One: Transformation of the Mormon Marriage System, 1840–1910* (Urbana: University of Illinois Press, 2001), 141–59.

18. Brigham Young said, "I tell a man he has to give me ten dollars if he wants a divorce. For what? My services? No, for his foolishness." JD 17:119.

19. They were signed before witnesses, generally clerks in the Church headquarters offices, and read:

> Know all persons by these presents that we, the undersigned . . . do hereby mutually covenant, promise, and agree to dissolve all the relations which have hitherto existed between us as husband and wife, and to keep ourselves separate and apart from each other, from this time forth.

Quoted in Hilton v. Roylance, 25 Utah 129, 135 (1902).

veteran and his second wife, even though their original marriage had been bigamous and therefore invalid.[20] The issue soon arose in litigation over dower rights, where wives who had obtained church divorces against their husbands subsequently asserted legal rights as lawful widows.[21] The Utah Supreme Court ruled in 1899 that such divorces were invalid, which had the effect of divesting subsequent wives who believed that they had been their husband's "legal wife" of dower rights.

Thus, after 1888, it became necessary to clearly separate sealing rules from secular law. The shape of Mormonism's post-polygamous future was the central issue in the initial development of these rules. With the 1904 Second Manifesto, the First Presidency set itself against efforts to continue performing polygamous marriages in secret.[22] The centralizing of sealing authority in the hands of the First Presidency and its agents was emphasized, a move that coincided with an increasing emphasis on new claims to be able to dissolve sealings. At the same time, the Church began creating clear rules for priesthood leaders performing legal marriages that were not sealings. In 1901, Mormon elders "working in the Court House" were appointed to marry people outside the temple as "the Presidency thought it would be better to have the people married by some of our own Elders."[23] In 1908, in response to legislation in Idaho, the First Presidency declared that only bishops and stake presidents could perform legal marriages outside of temples.[24] In 1913, bishops and stake presidents were provided with a liturgy to be used in such ceremonies. At the time, the First Presidency was struggling to suppress the activities of polygamist diehards, including former apostle Mathias Cowley and bishops and stake

---

20. "Former Utah Marriages," *Salt Lake Herald-Republican*, December 28, 1892 (reprinting the final appellate decision from the Department of the Interior). Compare Fenton v. Reed, 4 Johns 52 (N.Y. Ch. 1809) (Kent, Ch.) (a leading "common law marriage" case holding that a marriage that was bigamous at the time of the wedding was subsequently validated after the death of the first spouse).

21. "Dower" refers to the common law right of a widow to claim one-third of her husband's real property upon his death, regardless of wills or unconsented to inter vivos transfers.

22. See James R. Clark, ed., *Messages of the First Presidency* (Salt Lake City: Bookcraft, Inc., 1965), 4:84 (hereinafter MFP) (the so-called Second Manifesto).

23. See Anthon Lund Diary, Church History Library, Salt Lake City, Utah, (typescript copy in the author's possession) March 28, 1901 (hereinafter Lund Diary).

24. See MFP 4:176–77. See also Revised Codes of Idaho § 2622 (John F. MacLane, comp. 1908).

patriarchs who were purporting to perform polygamous sealings.[25] The 1913 liturgy makes clear that the marriages performed by bishops and stake presidents were not sealings.[26]

In 1913, the Church also provided instructions to local leaders on temple sealings for the first time.[27] The primary concern was that no living sealing should purport to marry people in a situation where a marriage would be invalid or illegal. The Church declared that "it must be understood that the marriage ceremony [in the temple] will not be performed unless the contracting parties have complied with the law in securing a proper license from the county clerk within the state where the Temple is located."[28] Indeed, until well into the twentieth century, Church leaders were so anxious that a temple sealing for a living couple not be performed in cases of a colorable conflict with secular laws that sealing rules became more restrictive than the secular law itself. Hence, a temple sealing could not be performed for a couple unless it conformed with the law of marriage in the jurisdiction where the temple was located, even in the case of couples already married in another jurisdiction whose marriage would be recognized as legally valid in the jurisdiction where the temple was located.[29] For example, if State A, where a temple was located, required that a person wait a year after obtaining a divorce before re-marrying but State B allowed divorced persons to remarry immediately, then a couple married in State B six months after a divorce would have to wait a year before being sealed in the temple, even though under well-established legal rules

25. Cowley resigned from the Quorum of the Twelve in 1905 at the request of Church President Joseph F. Smith because of his unwillingness to abandon the practice of polygamy and the threat that the public disclosure of his activities presented to the Church in light of the Reed Smoot hearings. He continued to advocate plural marriage, and in 1911 the Church suspended the use of his priesthood. He continued to meet with proto-Mormon fundamentalists until the mid-1920s, when he broke ties with them. His priesthood was restored in 1936.

26. The Church of Jesus Christ of Latter-day Saints, *Circular of Instructions* (Salt Lake City: The Church of Jesus Christ of Latter-day Saints, 1913), 47.

27. For background on the development of Church handbooks, see Michael Harold Paulos, "'Does Not Purport to Comprehend All Matters of Church Government': The LDS 'General Handbook of Instructions,' 1899–2006," *Journal of Mormon History* 38, no. 4 (2012): 200–225.

28. The Church of Jesus Christ of Latter-day Saints, *1913 Handbook*, 22.

29. See The Church of Jesus Christ of Latter-day Saints, *General Handbook of Instructions* (Salt Lake City: The Church of Jesus Christ of Latter-day Saints, 1960), 70.

State A would recognize as valid the marriage performed in State B.[30] The rule was later simplified to require that couples simply be legally married before being sealed if they were not going to be married in the temple.[31]

Complications also arose in situations where the existence of a civil marriage was doubtful. An early example of this problem arose in New Zealand.[32] Beginning in the 1880s, missionaries succeeded in baptizing a large number of Maori converts. The legal informality around Maori marriage customs made it difficult for American missionaries to decide who was married in the eyes of the Church.[33] In 1897, President Wilford Woodruff instructed, "Where couples living together as man and wife have observed the requirement of their people, tribe or nation, their union should be respected by our brethren."[34] Woodruff's letter was soon for-

---

30. See, e.g., Bogen v. Bogen, 261 N.W.2d 606 (Minn. 1977) (validating a Nebraska marriage under Minnesota law, even though the Nebraska union would have been invalid in Minnesota because it was entered into too soon after a divorce ending a previous marriage); Garrett v. Chapman, 449 P.2d 856 (Or. 1969) (same as previous). See Russell J. Weintraub, *Commentary on the Conflict of Laws*, 5th ed., University Textbook Series (New York: Foundation Press Thomson/West, 2006), 307–10 (discussing the basic rules regarding state recognition of marriages performed in other states).

31. See The Church of Jesus Christ of Latter-day Saints, *General Handbook of Instructions* (Salt Lake City: The Church of Jesus Christ of Latter-day Saints, 1963), 79–80 (simplifying the earlier rule to require only that those being married in the temple have a valid marriage license, and dropping special legal requirements for sealings related to previously performed marriages).

32. See generally Marjorie Newton, "From Tolerance to 'House Cleanin': LDS Leadership Response to Maori Marriage Customs, 1890–1990," *Journal of Mormon History* 22, no. 2 (1996): 72–91.

33. Maori tribal rules governing marriage and divorce were informal by western standards. Marriages were generally contracted by a simple agreement, and divorce by mutual agreement was also allowed, although it was often expected that some payment would accompany the end of a union. Unsurprisingly, Maoris generally did not avail themselves of the family law promulgated by New Zealand's European settlers. This was combined with relatively lax attitudes toward premarital sex and the acceptance of polygamous unions. See Newton, 72–75.

34. Newton, 78–79. This respectful attitude toward Maori custom did not persist. When couples informally dissolved their union by agreement, American elders often treated subsequent unions as illicit. In addition, Wilford Woodruff's 1897 decision seems to have been forgotten. Accordingly, the Church in New Zealand went through periods of acceptance of Maori marriage rules—such as the presidency of future apostle Matthew Cowley in the 1940s—and periods of

gotten, however, and controversy continued. It was only after the New Zealand government moved aggressively to bring Maori families under its law by forcing them to legally formalize their unions that the issue faded within the Church. Similar problems arose in other jurisdictions. The Church adopted a rule of recognizing informal marriages only if local law did so, with the result that comparable Latter-day Saint unions in different legal jurisdictions would be treated differently. In a 1935 letter to the European Mission, the First Presidency wrote:

> In a country in which common law marriage is recognized as legal, and the children resulting from such marriages are recorded as legitimate offspring, the Church will recognize such marriage under the conditions attaching in recognition by the law of the land. . . . [In countries without such legal rules] a couple so living are [*sic*] certainly not living in honorable wedlock, and therefore cannot be recognized by the Church as married people.[35]

This rule was extended to non-European countries as well, notably in 1942 to Brazil, setting a precedent for other Latin American countries where informal marriage without legal recognition is common due to the difficulty of obtaining legal divorces.[36]

Changing Theologies and the First Modern Sealing Rules

In addition to adaptations to new legal environments and changing Latter-day Saint attitudes toward marriage law, the birth of modern sealing rules at the end of the nineteenth century came in a period of theological flux. During the nineteenth century, what can be called kingdom theology dominated sealing practices.[37] Kingdom theology can be seen most clearly in the law of adoption, where sealings between non-biologically related adults were designed to bind individuals in eternal, dynastic struc-

---

"house cleaning" when American mission presidents required that couples either formalize their unions under New Zealand law or face Church discipline. See Newton, 84–87.

35. Quoted in response accompanying Letter of David. A Smith, President of the Canadian Mission, to the First Presidency, Feb. 28, 1941, Church History Library, Salt Lake City, Utah.

36. Letter of the First Presidency to William W. Seegmiller, President of the Brazil Mission, July 31, 1942, Church History Library, Salt Lake City, Utah.

37. To be clear, nineteenth-century Latter-day Saints did not use the term "kingdom theology," which is adopted here for ease of reference.

tures with patriarchal heads.[38] This idea also motivated marital sealings.[39] Where modern Latter-day Saints think of such sealings in terms of "eternal families" using ideas of companionate marriage and nuclear families, their nineteenth-century forebearers thought in terms of kingdoms and sacral networks. This explains, for example, the bewildering variety of Brigham Young's plural marriages.[40] Fifty-five women were sealed to Young. Only sixteen of these women bore Young children. Twenty-three of the women belonged to Young's households, although some of these wives likely did not have a sexual relationship with Young. The other women were sealed into Young's eternal kingdom without becoming part of his earthly family. Some of these women were much older when they were sealed to Young, including one woman sealed on her deathbed. Some of them held themselves out as "wife of President Young" without being part of his household. Some of the women were sealed to Young while continuing to be married to other men, presumably to be included in Young's post-mortal dynasty.

This theology of sealings was further complicated by the possibility of posthumous sealings by proxy.[41] These posthumous marriage sealings could follow mortal marriages but need not do so. There was initially great concern about the mortal worthiness of those for whom posthumous sealings were to be performed. Should a woman be sealed to a man who was known to be an adulterer, abuser, or apostate? In such cases women

38. See Rex Eugene Cooper, *Promises Made to the Fathers: Mormon Covenant Organization* (Salt Lake City: University of Utah Press, 1990), 198–99; Jonathan A. Stapley, "Adoptive Sealing Ritual in Mormonism," *Journal of Mormon History* 37, no. 3 (2011): 53–117; Samuel M. Brown, "Early Mormon Adoption Theology and the Mechanics of Salvation," *Journal of Mormon History* 37, no. 3 (2011): 3–52; Gordon Irving, "The Law of Adoption: One Phase of the Development of the Mormon Concept of Salvation, 1830–1900," *Brigham Young University Studies* 14, no. 3 (1974): 291–314.

39. See generally J. Spencer Fluhman, "'A Subject That Can Bear Investigation': Anguish, Faith, and Joseph Smith's Youngest Plural Wife," in *No Weapon Shall Prosper: New Light on Sensitive Issues*, ed. Robert L. Millet (Provo: Religious Studies Center, Brigham Young University, 2011), 105–19.

40. See generally Jeffery Ogden Johnson, "Determining and Defining 'Wife': The Brigham Young Households," *Dialogue: A Journal of Mormon Thought* 20, no. 3 (1987): 57–70.

41. Prior to 1877, proxy marriage sealings were performed in the Endowment House in Salt Lake City, but between the abandonment of the Nauvoo Temple in 1846 and the dedication of the St. George Temple in 1877, no "law of adoption" sealings were performed for either the living or the dead.

were often posthumously sealed to a righteous descendent or prominent Church leader.[42] Such sealings were less a matter of creating eternal families that mirrored mortal families than of using marriage sealings along with adoptive sealings to knit together post-mortal kingdoms. Thus, for most of the nineteenth century, proxy temple sealings bore only the most limited relationship to earthly families. Latter-day Saints who were unable to be sealed to spouses and children while alive could be sealed by proxy after death. However, ancestors beyond the last generation before the Mormon baptism of a descendant were not sealed along family lines. Rather, they were "adopted" into a priesthood line by being sealed directly to a Latter-day Saint descendant or to a high Church leader.[43]

Kingdom theology went into decline after 1894 when Wilford Woodruff rejected the law of adoption, announcing, "We want the Latter-day Saints from this time to trace their genealogies as far as they can, and to be sealed to their fathers and mothers. Have children sealed to their parents and run this chain through as far as you can get it."[44] Lorenzo Snow, president of the newly dedicated Salt Lake Temple, issued a set of rules implementing the new sealing regime.[45] At the heart of these rules was the idea of "heirship." Snow's rules declared "in performance of work for the dead the right of heirship (blood relationship) shall be sacredly

---

42. For example, in response to one inquiry, Wilford Woodruff wrote in 1889:

> If your sister, while alive, did not feel that she wished to be sealed to her living husband for eternity, and if she did not express any preference on that matter other than the ones you mentioned, you should then make a choice in her behalf, and have sealed to some faithful man in the Church, either living or dead, and have her children adopted into his family.

Quoted in Devery S. Anderson, ed., *The Development of LDS Temple Worship, 1846–2000: A Documentary History* (Salt Lake City: Signature Books, 2011), 81.

43. See Jonathan A. Stapley, *The Power of Godliness: Mormon Liturgy and Cosmology* (New York: Oxford University Press, 2018), 41–42.

44. Brian H. Stuy, ed., *Collected Discourses Delivered by President Wilford Woodruff, His Two Counselors, the Twelve Apostles, and Others* (Woodland Hills: B. H. S. Publishing, 1987), 4:73.

45. The Salt Lake Temple was dedicated in 1893 after forty years of construction. Until 1938, the president of the Salt Lake Temple was always either an apostle or a member of the First Presidency. During this period, the president of the Salt Lake Temple acted as a kind of de facto director of Church-wide temple work under the direction of the First Presidency.

regarded."[46] As Joseph F. Smith, who succeeded Snow as president of the Salt Lake Temple, explained in his amendments to Snow's guidelines, "As a rule, the eldest MALE representative of the family who is a member of the church is the recognized heir."[47] Later, women were allowed to become heirs for family lines that failed to terminate in a male Latter-day Saint descendant.[48] As it developed, these heirs had the right and obligation to perform or authorize the sealing of all ancestors in the four patrilineal lines emanating from their four grandparents.[49] An heir, however, was not to perform sealings along collateral lines.[50] The goal of the rule was to avoid duplicative proxy ordinances and perhaps initially to retain some continuity with the older, more patriarchal model of kingdom theology sealings by according a special status to living family patriarchs.[51]

---

46. These instructions were given to Church members in the preface to blank genealogical record books prepared by the Church and published by Deseret Book. Members were expected to record proxy temple work performed for deceased ancestors in these books. See, e.g., Bollinger family temple ordinance book, Church History Library, Salt Lake City, Utah; Temple Record Book, MS 22011, Church History Library, Salt Lake City, Utah; Alice Hatch Keeler, Family and temple record book, Church History Library, Salt Lake City, Utah. Copies of the family record books published prior to 1894 do not contain instructions relating to the idea of "heirship." See George Halliday family record and autobiography, 1884, BYU Special Collections, Provo, Utah.

47. Joseph F. Smith, Instructions Concerning Temple Ordinance Work, Church History Library, Salt Lake City, Utah.

48. See *Lessons in Genealogy* (Salt Lake City: Genealogical Society of Utah, 1915), 30 (discussing female heirship).

49. See Duncan M. McAllister, "Heirship in Temple Work," *Utah Genealogical and Historical Magazine*, April 1912; "The Heir and Relationship," *Utah Genealogical and Historical Magazine*, July 1918. This seems to have been the rule for female heirs as well, meaning that such heirs were supposed to perform proxy ordinances along patrilineal lines.

50. Heirs were authorized to perform proxy ordinances for deceased persons in the immediate families of those in their direct patrilineal lines, e.g., paternal great-great-aunts.

51. According to a much later source, the idea of heirship was originally adopted in the St. George Temple as a way of simplifying indexing by allowing all ordinances to be indexed under the name of a single heir rather than producing "an index book almost as large as the original record." "Heirship and Relationship to Temple Work," *Utah Genealogical and Historical Magazine*, July 1933, 124. This suggests that the idea of heirship may have predated Wilford Woodruff's 1894 revelation ending the law of adoption. The idea, however, does not show

The system of heirship had the consequence of ensuring that men and women married to multiple persons during their lifetimes would be sealed posthumously to all of their spouses, provided that the unions resulted in a patrilineal line of descendants. Imagine that Mary Able married John Baker and had a son, Robert Baker. The male descendants of Robert Baker would result in Heir #1, who would then perform proxy sealings for his Baker ancestors, including a posthumous sealing between Mary and John. Now suppose that Mary either divorced John or was widowed. She subsequently married a second time to Paul Carpenter and had a second son, Joseph Carpenter. Joseph Carpenter's descendants would eventually end in Heir #2, who would then perform proxy sealings for all of his Carpenter ancestors, including a posthumous sealing between Mary and Paul. Given the difficulty of retrieving temple records, Heir #1 and Heir #2 might be unaware of one another's work. However, if the system functioned as envisioned, Mary Able would be sealed to both John Baker and Paul Carpenter. The rules would operate the same way for men married to multiple women while alive. Thus, at the beginning of the twentieth century, posthumous sealing rules at least implicitly contemplated multiple proxy sealings for both men and women.

The precise theological significance of these multiple sealings was never fully specified, particularly because if the system of heirship functioned as envisioned, a single descendant might never confront the complex reality of multiple ancestor marriages because the heir was only supposed to concern himself with the sealing of ancestors from whom he was directly descended. In practice, of course, things were often messier, with Latter-day Saints performing proxy sealings for collateral ancestors from whom they were not directly descended. When forced to confront the reality of both polygynous and polyandrous proxy sealings, early twentieth-century Latter-day Saints tended to assume that the polygynous sealings could be easily assimilated into a regime of postmortal patriarchal polygamy, while the polyandrous sealings were conceptualized as offering women a choice as to which of her mortal husbands she would have in the eternities.[52]

---

up in the printed temple instructions prepared for temple patrons in the 1880s. See George Halliday family record and autobiography, 1884, BYU Special Collections, Provo, Utah. By the early 1930s, heirship was presented as a mere bookkeeping convention devoid of theological significance.

52. This same approach was applied to multiple sealings by living women. See, e.g., Lund Diary, Oct. 23, 1902 (after approving a second sealing for a woman

At the opening of the twentieth century, sealing rules for living couples mirrored those for proxy sealings. This was not an innovation, but rather a continuation of nineteenth-century practice. This can be seen in the approach taken to second sealings after a first marriage ended in divorce. During the nineteenth century, there was no single understanding about the relationship between a church divorce and sealing ordinances. While the belief in polygamy presented no theological challenge to a living man being sealed to multiple women for eternity, during her life a woman could also be sealed to multiple men without any formal Church action to dissolve the earlier sealings. Rather, divorce rendered a woman eligible for a second sealing. In 1874, Brigham Young explicitly denied that the church divorces he granted dissolved marriage sealings, saying, "It takes a higher power than a bill of divorce [in a church divorce] to take a woman from a man who is a good man and honors his Priesthood."[53] Thus, until the end of the nineteenth century, a church divorce was a matter of ending an earthly union and managing such practical matters as alimony, child custody, and child support. It left sealings unchanged, resulting in numerous living women being sealed to two or more men. Therefore, for example, in an 1869 sermon, Young opined that the final status of a woman sealed to multiple men in mortality would be sorted out by God in the eternities based on the righteousness of her various husbands.[54]

The same dynamic can be seen in the interaction of sealing rules with secular divorce proceedings. Throughout the territorial period, couples could obtain a divorce from secular authorities by filing a petition in a local probate court.[55] While probate judges were occasionally also Church leaders, parties to probate court cases understood themselves as taking part

---

whose first husband had died, Lund recorded, "The President said these things must be guarded but he considered a woman should have her choice").

53. Richard S. Van Wagoner, ed., *The Complete Discourses of Brigham Young*, 5 vols consecutively paginated (Salt Lake City: The Smith-Pettit Foundation, 2009), 3043 (hereinafter *CDBY*). In this sermon, Young goes on to quote verbatim from the preprinted church divorce certificates issued by the Church, making clear that the bill of divorce to which he refers is a church divorce, not a secular divorce. Compare Hilton v. Roylance, 25 Utah 129, 135 (1902) (transcribing the language used on the "bill of divorce" issued as part of a church divorce).

54. *CDBY*, 2692.

55. See Pearson and Madsen, "Innovation and Accommodation"; Aaron, "Mormon Divorce and the Statutes of 1852"; Campbell and Campbell, "Divorce Among Mormon Polygamists."

in a secular rather than an ecclesiastical proceeding.[56] These probate court divorces frequently dissolved marriages formed by a sealing ordinance. Probate court and genealogical records reveal a number of women who were sealed, divorced in a secular proceeding, and then sealed a second time.[57] A review of Brigham Young's records show that none of the women

---

56. See James B. Allen, "The Unusual Jurisdiction of County Probate Courts in the Territory of Utah," *Utah Historical Quarterly* 36 (1968): 132–42; Elizabeth D. Gee, "Justice for All or for the 'Elect'? The Utah County Probate Court, 1855–72," *Utah Historical Quarterly* 48, no. 2 (1980): 129–47; Jay Emerson Powell, "An Analysis of the Nature of the Salt Lake County Probate Court's Role in Aggravating Anti-Mormon Sentiment, 1852–1855" (honors thesis, Department of History, University of Utah, 1968), on file with Howard W. Hunter Law Library, Brigham Young University; Jeffery Ogden Johnson, "Was Being a Probate Judge in Pioneer Utah a Church Calling" (Mormon History Association Annual Meeting, Casper, Wyoming, 2006).

57. Probate courts were organized on the county level in Territorial Utah. Prior to 1874, they had expansive jurisdiction, hearing a variety of cases. The judges and clerks often lacked legal training. This has resulted in often jumbled, disorganized, and incomplete records. Nevertheless, digital copies of these records are available through Ancestry.com. The author's research assistant, Katy Naef, a William & Mary law student and professional genealogist, combed these records for divorce cases. She then checked the names of women that she discovered against records available through FamilySearch to identify women whose probate court divorces ended sealed marriages and who were then subsequently sealed a second time to a new husband. Naef discovered the following women who met this profile: Isabel Wilkins McCleve (sealed to Daniel Richmond Mott 1870.01.24; divorced (Sevier County) Daniel Mott 1874.05.09; sealed to Jabez Erastus Durfree, 1880.06.24); Mary Thorp (sealed to Joseph Morris date unknown; divorced (Sanpete County), 1854.04.06; sealed to Henry Beal 1857.02.14); Eliza Pennington (sealed to William Coombs date unknown; divorced (Sanpete County) 1867; sealed to Nephi Robertson 1869.03.22); Joanna McKenna (sealed to Seth Childs date unknown; divorced (Sanpete County) 1868.02.10; sealed to Lars Christian Madsen 1870.04.06); Mariah Davidson (sealed (perhaps) to M. D. Hambleton; divorced (Sanpete County) 1852.09.13; sealed to Seth George Dodge 1853.04.28); and, Mary Ogden (sealed to Oscar Swanigan 1872.02.26; divorced Francis Perkins (Sevier County) 1872.06.15; sealed to Jens Larsen Brown 1875.06.02). In the case of Mary Ogden, the person to whom she was sealed has a different name than the person from whom she divorced. The sealing information on FamilySearch may be erroneous. Another possibility is that Francis Perkins was a husband from whom she separated without a secular divorce, she was sealed to Oscar Swanigan, and then she filed the divorce action against Perkins to "clean up" her legal affairs shortly after her second marriage. There is no evidence in the

in a sample of such cases sought a church divorce in addition to her secular divorce.[58] Rather, the secular divorce rendered the woman eligible for a second sealing without an intervening action by the president of the Church to "cancel" the previous sealing. For example, Isabel McCleve was born in Ireland in 1843. She joined the Church in the British Isles and "gathered to Zion" in 1856. She was part of one of the successful handcart companies that completed their journey ahead of the ill-fated Martin and Wiley companies that summer. Among the rescuers sent out to relieve those parties was Daniel Richmond Mott, whom Isabel married in 1860 as a plural wife. In 1870, Isabel and Daniel were sealed in the Endowment House in Salt Lake City. In 1874, Isabel successfully sued for divorce from Daniel in the Sevier County probate court. Six years later she was sealed a second time as the plural wife of Jabez Erastus Durfree, a man eleven years her junior who had been married to Daniel Mott's niece.[59] There is no record of Isabel seeking a church divorce, despite being sealed to both Daniel and Jabez.

Toward the end of the century, a new understanding emerged. In contrast to Brigham Young's approach, a belief developed that the sealing power included the authority to cancel sealings. As marriage law in Utah

---

Brigham Young papers, however, of a church divorce from Swanigan dissolving Ogden's second marriage. Naef's review of the probate court records was not comprehensive. There were likely additional women whose first (sealed) marriages ended in a secular divorce before the probate courts who were subsequently sealed to a second spouse. Our goal was to find a manageable sample to check against the closed Brigham Young divorce records held in the Church History Library of The Church of Jesus Christ of Latter-day Saints in Salt Lake City, Utah.

58. Brigham Young's correspondence relating to church divorces, held by the Church History Library of the Church of Jesus Christ of Latter-day Saints in Salt Lake City, Utah, is currently closed to researchers. Each church divorce resulted in a triplicate set of preprinted divorce certificates, one of which was retained for the records of the Church. The correspondence and these certificates were systematically arranged by husband's name. Email of Library Consultant & Certified Archivist, Church History Library, to the author, February 22, 2022 (copy in the author's possession). At the author's request, employees of the Church History Library searched the correspondence and certificates for the names of the women and their husbands in supra note 57. No record of a church divorce appears in these cases. Email of Library Consultant & Certified Archivist, Church History Library, to the author, July 26, 2022 (copy in the author's possession).

59. This biography is reconstructed from information available on FamilySearch as well as the Sevier County Probate Court records, which are available through Ancestry.com.

formalized in the late 1880s, people began questioning the legal validity of church divorces.[60] Even after 1890, however, the First Presidency continued to deal with legacy plural marriages. These couples could not avail themselves of secular fora to resolve the concrete disputes over property and child custody that separation provoked. Hence, even after church divorces were understood to be legally invalid, they likely continued to be used to resolve precisely the questions involved in secular legal proceedings, rather than the status of a previous marriage sealing. The shift in the treatment of church divorces for monogamous couples, who could avail themselves of the secular legal system, raised new questions. If church divorces lacked legal effect in these cases, what was their purpose? In 1895, Joseph F. Smith, then a counselor in the First Presidency, suggested to an associate "that where the President gives a divorce it disunites the couple for time and eternity, for the same power which unites them together dissolves the bond."[61] After *Norton v. Tufts* declared that church divorces lacked any legal efficacy, the First Presidency continued to grant church divorces, which came to be understood as dissolving temple sealings. In addition, after Wilford Woodruff announced the revelation ending the law of adoption in 1894, he received numerous questions from people who had been sealed to high Church leaders under the previous regime and now wished to be sealed to family members. Woodruff generally responded by allowing the family sealings and instructing temple presidents to note the cancellation of the previous sealings.[62]

---

60. For example, the plaintiff in *Norton v. Tufts* was informed in 1891 that her church divorce was invalid, although the Utah Supreme Court did not pass on the issue until 1899. See Norton v. Tufts, 19 Utah 470, 474 (1899).

61. Abraham H. Cannon, *Candid Insights of a Mormon Apostle: The Diaries of Abraham H. Cannon 1889–1895*, ed. Edward Leo Lyman (Salt Lake City: Signature Books, 2010), 744.

62. For example, immediately after the announcement ending the law of adoption, the daughter of a deceased woman who had been sealed to Orson Pratt rather than her husband sought permission to seal her mother to her father. Woodruff wrote to Lorenzo Snow, president of the Salt Lake Temple, instructing him to allow the woman to perform the temple ordinances for her parents. "Please cancel the sealing, which was done November of last year, so that Sister Sampson may be free to do the necessary work for her parents. Also please cancel the adoptions in this case." Letter of Wilford Woodruff to Lorenzo Snow, April 24, 1894, Leonard Arrington Papers, Utah State University Special Collections, Logan, Utah. See also Wilford Woodruff to M. W. Merrill, president of the Logan Temple, May 1, 1894, Leonard Arrington Papers, Utah State University

New Rules in a New Century

These shifts cemented the idea that the president of the Church could cancel previously performed sealings. Gradually, the nomenclature changed. "Church divorce" became "temple divorce,"[63] and by the opening decades of the twentieth century, the First Presidency was frequently considering requests to "cancel" sealings.[64] Initially the cancellation of a previous sealing was not necessary to render someone—male or female—eligible for a second sealing after death or divorce ended a first marriage.[65] Rather, cancellation of sealing was an extraordinary action reserved for cases of abuse or apostasy. In internal deliberations, the First Presidency expressed unease with sealings for widows whose first husbands died in full

---

Special Collections, Logan, Utah (cancelling the sealing of Mary Proctor Harker to apostle Angus M. Cannon so she could be sealed to her husband). Generally, Woodruff seems to have instructed temple presidents to leave adoptive sealings unchanged unless a request was made by family members to change the sealings. See Letter of Wilford Woodruff to J. D. T. McAllister, president of the Manti Temple, April 26, 1894, Leonard Arrington Papers, Utah State University Special Collections, Logan, Utah; Letter of Wilford Woodruff to David H. Cannon, president of the St. George Temple, May 4, 1894, Leonard Arrington Papers, Utah State University Special Collections, Logan, Utah. See also Anderson, *The Development of LDS Temple Worship*, 98 (reproducing correspondence between John Nicholson and Wilford Woodruff dated June 14, 1894, on this question).

63. See The Church of Jesus Christ of Latter-day Saints, *Handbook of Instructions for Stake Presidencies, Bishops and Counselors, Stake and Ward Clerks and Other Church Officers* (Salt Lake City: The Church of Jesus Christ of Latter-day Saints, 1944), 82.

64. See, e.g., Lund Diaries, Oct. 23, 1901; Lund Diaries, May 23, 1912; Lund Diaries, July 28, 1919.

65. For example, in one case the First Presidency counseled that a woman wait before being sealed a second time:

> A sister applied to have her marriage with her dead husband canceled. It was concluded not to cancel, but to allow her sealing to the husband she has now. I suggested that she wait a year longer and that she may better know her own feelings. This the brethren thought wise. The President said these things must be guarded but he considered a woman should have her choice.

Lund Diary, Oct. 23, 1902. Compare *CDBY*, 2692 (an 1869 sermon in which Brigham Young discusses women who have been sealed to multiple men).

fellowship with the Church but generally allowed the second sealing.[66] As the century progressed, however, cancellation of sealings was formalized in a way that ironically emphasized the continuing theological vitality of plural marriage at precisely the moment when, in practical terms, the Church was moving decisively to stamp out polygamist diehards in its own ranks.

Beginning in 1913, Church handbooks began containing instructions for bishops and stake presidents on sealing practices that became increasingly elaborate over time. In the 1920s, George F. Richards, an apostle and the president of the Salt Lake Temple, was tasked with bringing greater consistency to temple practices.[67] He authored rule books that governed all temples, beginning in 1923 with a compilation from available records of how previous cases had been treated.[68] During this period, a new rule seems to have developed under which a woman could be sealed to only one man. This rule appeared in the handbook for the first time in 1944 but seems to have been in place at least a decade earlier.[69] By 1933, apostle

66. For example, the First Presidency wrote to one woman:

> If you desire in your heart to be sealed to the young man referred to in yours of the 20th inst., we know of no reason why this may not be done, provided you have no children by your first husband (a widower) of whom you were sealed. Under the circumstances, and in the even of this being done, the record of your sealing to your first husband need not be disturbed.

Transcript First Presidency Letterpress Book, May 25, 1912, Scott Kenney Papers, University of Utah Special Collections, Salt Lake City, Utah.

67. See Thomas G. Alexander, *Mormonism in Transition: A History of the Latter-Day Saints, 1890–1930* (Urbana: University of Illinois Press, 1996), 315–18 (discussing George F. Richards's work in reforming temple procedures).

68. See Dale C. Mouritsen, "A Symbol of New Directions: George Franklin Richards and the Mormon Church, 1861–1950" (Ph.D. dissertation, Provo, Utah, Brigham Young University, 1982), 202–3 (discussing Richards's systemization of temple practices). See also Minerva Richards Tate Robinson, Sarah Richards Cannon, and Mamie Richards Silver, *Life of George F. Richards* (Provo: J. Grant Stevenson, 1965), 84 (noting that Richards "correlated decisions and rulings from a number of letters, papers, manuscripts and books and indexed them so that they could be more readily found when needed").

69. The first appearance of the rule stated:

> Bishops should make sure that in case of a divorced person being recommended for temple marriage, a final divorce decree has been secured; and if the individual was married in the temple previously that a temple divorce was granted in the case of a woman. However, a man married in the temple

Melvin J. Ballard explained in a letter that when a woman who was previously sealed remarries, the second marriage could be for time only.[70] This marked a shift to a rule under which a woman could be sealed to only one man. In 1934, the Church announced a new rule applying the same approach to proxy sealings. "In sealing the dead," it read, "a woman is to be sealed to her first husband."[71] Under the new rule, however, it was still possible for a man, living or dead, to be sealed to multiple women.[72]

Thus, the formal sealing rules apparently adopted in the early 1930s allowed living men to be sealed to two or more women so long as such sealings did not involve bigamy or efforts to form polygamous households. This occurred when a man was sealed to a second wife after his first marriage was ended by divorce or death. These rules have remained unchanged since the early twentieth century. The result is that many living Latter-day Saint males are "married in eternity" to two or more living women, even though any effort to practice polygamy while alive would result in automatic excommunication from the Church. The connection between modern sealing rules and nineteenth-century polygamy is emphasized by the gender asymmetry of the rules. In contrast to men, by the 1930s women were not ordinarily allowed to be sealed to a second spouse without first obtaining a cancellation of the previous sealing from the president of the Church. The result is that under the rules that have been in place since the 1930s, a living woman ordinarily cannot be sealed to two or more men. Thus, just at the moment when the Church was making its final push to systematically excommunicate all post-Manifesto

---

> who has had a civil but not a temple divorce may be recommended for temple marriage without first having the previous sealing annulled.

The Church of Jesus Christ of Latter-day Saints, *1944 Handbook*, 82. The handbook contained no guidance on the treatment of widows who had been sealed to their dead husbands and wished to be sealed a second time after remarrying.

70. Quoted in Anderson, *The Development of LDS Temple Worship*, 233.

71. George F. Richards, Joseph Fielding Smith, and Joseph Christenson, "Preparation of Temple Sheets," *Deseret News*, January 20, 1934, sec. Church Department. The rule was published as part of instructions printed in the *Deseret News* and promulgated under the names of the Salt Lake Temple presidency. George F. Richards was still president of the Salt Lake Temple at the time.

72. See The Church of Jesus Christ of Latter-day Saints, *1944 Handbook*, 82.

polygamists, its sealing rules were arguably becoming more explicit in their commitment to post-mortal polygamy.[73]

Despite a general policy requiring women to obtain a cancellation of a previous sealing before remarrying in the temple, the First Presidency retained its prerogative to make exceptions, and throughout the twentieth century it allowed living women in exceptional circumstances to be sealed to multiple men without first cancelling the previous sealing. This seems to have happened most commonly in the case of widows. For example, in 1959 Church President David O. McKay considered the case of a widow who had been sealed to her first husband but not her second husband. Citing a precedent by former Church President Joseph F. Smith, he allowed the second sealing.[74] After World War II, the First Presidency faced numerous cases involving young widows whose first husbands, to whom they had been sealed, were killed in the war and who now desired to be sealed to a second husband. In such cases, the second sealing was allowed without cancelling the first sealing.[75] As late as 1968, the First Presidency was still dealing with such cases from World War II.[76]

---

73. Interestingly, in contrast to the elaborate rules on multiple sealings, the Church in the modern era has never sought to articulate internal rules on other issues of marital capacity for living sealings. Hence, there are no sealing rules on questions such as age, parental consent, consanguinity, or affinity. All such questions have been outsourced to secular legal regimes through the requirement that sealings between living persons may only be performed either when a civil marriage has already occurred or where the sealing ceremony itself will constitute a valid civil marriage. For proxy sealings there are unpublished rules on consanguinity and affinity. These rules cannot be accessed directly. Rather, they are encoded into the software that Church members use to submit names of ancestors for approval to perform proxy temple ordinances. Thus, the contemporary Church of Jesus Christ of Latter-day Saints is perhaps unique in having what amounts to a body of religious law governing marriage that exists entirely as computer code. Compare Lawrence Lessig, *Code: And Other Laws of Cyberspace, Version 2.0*, 2nd ed. (New York: Basic Books, 2006).

74. David O. McKay Diary, May 8, 1959, Special Collections, University of Utah, Salt Lake City, Utah.

75. See Edwin B. Firmage, *An Abundant Life: The Memoirs of Hugh B. Brown*, 2nd edition (Salt Lake City: Signature Books, 2018), 117–20.

76. For example, David O. McKay approved the sealing of Catherine Cutler Poulter and William Ivins Poulter. The coupled had been married but not sealed in 1946. At the time Catherine was a young widow. Her first husband, Samuel Ship Musser, was killed in Yemen in 1944. They had been sealed in the Salt

In addition to promulgating rules for living sealings, the practice of proxy temple ordinances meant that the Church also had to deal with rules for posthumous sealings. The availability of such sealings was an important way in which Mormonism managed its transition to monogamy. While the First Presidency was consistently hostile to living polygamous sealings after 1904, it had a more permissive attitude toward posthumous polygamous sealings. In the decades after the Manifesto, some couples who desired to be married polygamously would make promises to be posthumously sealed as soon as one of them died.[77] In 1909, apostle George F. Richards was encouraging his fellow monogamist apostles to have some "good dead woman sealed to them while they are here and can look after their own interests."[78] As late as 1950, apostle Joseph Fielding Smith sealed apostle Ezra Taft Benson to Benson's deceased cousin, with Benson's then-living wife acting, at her request, as proxy.[79] The persistence of polygynous sealings for men under the rules created in the first half of the twentieth century is unsurprising. Both Joseph F. Smith and Heber J. Grant, the successive Church presidents between 1901 and 1945, suffered on the polygamist Underground during the Raid of the 1880s and remained theologically committed to polygamy until their deaths, despite waging an increasingly bitter struggle against its continued practice within the Church after 1904.[80] Formalizing sealing rules around the idea of eternal polygamy may have been a way of managing the dissonance they no doubt experienced as victims of anti-polygamy persecution in the 1880s,

---

Lake Temple exactly one day short of a year previously. In 1968, Catherine and William were allowed to be sealed without canceling Catherine's previous sealing to Samuel. See David O. McKay Diary, Oct. 21, 1968, David O. McKay Collection, Special Collections, University of Utah, Salt Lake City, Utah; Catherine McEwan Cutler, Timeline, FamilySearch.

77. See, e.g., Lund Diary, Oct. 13, 1915.

78. Quoted in Alexander, *Mormonism in Transition*, 315.

79. See Gary James Bergera, "'Weak-Kneed Republicans and Socialist Democrats': Ezra Taft Benson as U.S. Secretary of Agriculture, 1953–61, Part 2," *Dialogue: A Journal of Mormon Thought* 41, no. 4 (2008): 83n6. There were other cases as well. In addition to reporting a posthumous polygamous sealing between George F. Richards and the deceased daughter of an associate in 1907, Thomas Alexander notes, "The extent of the practice is not currently known, but some posthumous sealings to living authorities continued as late as April 1925." Alexander, *Mormonism in Transition*, 315.

80. See generally B. Carmon Hardy, *Solemn Covenant: The Mormon Polygamous Passage* (Urbana and Chicago: University of Illinois Press, 1992).

who in the twentieth century found themselves cooperating with law enforcement to prosecute polygamist diehards. It wasn't until 1945 that the Church would have its first monogamous president.

Twentieth-Century Shifts in Rules and Theology

The mid-twentieth century saw the second wave of innovations in sealing practices. Prior to David O. McKay's administration, temples were concentrated in areas of Latter-day Saint settlement, and while there was a focus on the importance of temple marriage, regular temple worship was not an important part of Latter-day Saint practice.[81] This changed with the expansion of temple building, particularly internationally with the dedications of the London, Swiss, and New Zealand temples.[82] Increasingly, Church members were counseled, where possible, to attend the temple regularly. This shift required a massive scaling up of the performance of posthumous sealings and other ordinances. Without such an increase in proxy sealings, there wouldn't be anything for patrons to do when they arrived at temples to worship because, despite the Church's emphasis on genealogy, only a minority of Latter-day Saints actively submit the names of ancestors for temple work. After 1934, in doing temple ordinances for a deceased woman who had been married multiple times during her lifetime, temple patrons were to seal her to her first husband only. Exceptions were possible if one could determine which of the husbands the wife would have chosen to be sealed to in life. Such intentions often proved impossible to discern in the case of deceased Latter-day Saints, and for non-Latter-day Saints the inquiry was wholly fictitious as such people could never have formed intentions regarding temple sealings in their lifetimes.

---

81. One dramatic example of this shift is that prior to David O. McKay's administration, temple worship was sufficiently uncommon among Latter-day Saints that it was standard practice to pay patrons to perform ordinances on behalf of deceased ancestors. See, e.g., George F. Richards, Joseph Fielding Smith, and Joseph Christenson, "Preparation of Temple Sheets," *Deseret News*, January 6, 1934, sec. Church Department ("When proxies have to be obtained to act in endowments for the dead, it is customary to pay 50 cents for a male name and 40 cents for a female name").

82. See Gregory A. Prince and William Robert Wright, *David O. McKay and the Rise of Modern Mormonism* (Salt Lake City: University of Utah Press, 2005), 261–64 (discussing the construction of temples in the United Kingdom, Switzerland, and New Zealand).

The logistics of mass temple work placed pressure on the 1934 rule. Members submitting the names of deceased ancestors were unable to provide enough proxy work to keep up with the increasing demand for temple worship. By 1959, temples were limiting worship sessions to conserve names, and by 1960 most temples only had a sufficient supply of names to operate for four to six weeks.[83] The Church responded in 1962 by beginning the mass extraction of names from genealogical records such as parish registers, matching names from several records together to form family groups, and sending those names directly to the temple.[84] This program ensured that temples would always have a supply of names for patrons who wished to perform ordinances. There was no way, however, of ensuring that women would be sealed to only their first husbands, and multiple sealings by deceased women were allowed.[85] In 1969, David O. McKay extended this rule more generally, deciding that the rule for living sealings for women—which by then allowed a woman to be sealed to only one man—were unworkable for proxy work.[86] Rather, deceased women

83. See James B. Allen, Jessie L. Embry, and Kahlile B. Mehr, *Hearts Turned to the Fathers: A History of the Genealogical Society of Utah, 1894–1994* (Provo: Brigham Young University Studies, 1995), loc 3473.

84. See Allen, Embry, and Mehr, loc. 3473.

85. Presumably the difficulty lay in the fact that when names were submitted to the temple there was no way of knowing whether any particular marriage was the woman's first marriage, given that there was no way of knowing whether all of the genealogical records in which marriages by the woman appeared had been indexed. Such a problem, of course, existed under the older system of individuals researching their own ancestors, but the name extraction program involved such a huge volume of names that this issue became acute. See David O. McKay, *Confidence amid Change: The Presidential Diaries of David O. McKay, 1951–1970*, ed. Harvard S. Heath (Salt Lake City: Signature Books, 2019), 789–91 (reproducing First Presidency minutes in which then-apostle Howard W. Hunter references the decision to allow multiple sealings for the names of women provided by the name extraction program).

86. The First Presidency was briefed on the issue by then-apostle and later president of the Church Howard W. Hunter, who noted that the rule of sealing a woman to her first husband was largely arbitrary and that using computers to extract names for proxy sealing ordinances resulted in multiple sealings of women to their various husbands and that this had previously been approved by the First Presidency. He argued, successfully, that this approach should be extended more generally. See McKay, 789–91 (reproducing the minutes of the First Presidency meeting where this action was taken).

were to be sealed by proxy to all of the men to whom they had been sealed while living.[87] Initially the rule did not apply to deceased Latter-day Saint women who had been sealed while alive, but eventually such women could also be sealed to multiple husbands after death.[88] Without acknowledging or perhaps realizing it, the Church thus returned to something like the position that had existed in the early twentieth century, albeit without the idea of heirship. The shift, by simplifying the process of deciding which ordinances to perform for deceased women, eased the name crunch at temples, facilitating regular temple attendance by Latter-day Saints. In short, when forced to choose between clearly insisting on post-mortal polygamy or some other precise model of family relationships for the hereafter and being able to perform mass temple work, President McKay chose mass temple work.

The result was a marriage regime that bifurcated the rules between the living and the dead. Rules for the living were based on a kind of vestigial pseudo-polygamy that allowed a man to be sealed to all of the women to whom he had been married, even after the marriages had ended in divorce, but a divorced woman could only be sealed a second time after successfully petitioning the First Presidency for a cancellation of the previous sealing. Such cancellations were routinely granted to women seeking a second sealing, but in the absence of such a petition by an ex-wife, it was difficult for a man to obtain the cancellation of a sealing after a divorce. For proxy sealings, however, the rules for men and women were symmetrical. Both men and women would be sealed to all of the spouses to whom they had been married while living, even though in theory those sealings could create a web of polygynous and polyandrous relationships in the eternities that didn't correspond to any configuration of earthly conjugal relationships.

While the basic structure for living sealings put in place under Heber J. Grant has remained stable to the present, there has been a waning of theological commitment to the idea of continuing eternal polygamy. As

87. See McKay, 791.

88. The new rule first appeared in the handbook in 1976. See The Church of Jesus Christ of Latter-day Saints, *General Handbook of Instructions* (Salt Lake City: The Church of Jesus Christ of Latter-day Saints, 1976), 62 (stating that a woman "not having been sealed to any of her husbands during her lifetime" may be sealed to all of her husbands after death). In 1989, the permissive rule was expanded to Latter-day Saint women who had been sealed to one husband while alive. See The Church of Jesus Christ of Latter-day Saints, *General Handbook of Instructions* (Salt Lake City: The Church of Jesus Christ of Latter-day Saints, 1989), 6–6.

sealing theology came to be articulated in the twentieth century, three conditions must be met in order for a marriage to be valid in the eternities. First, a sealing ordinance in mortality or posthumously by proxy must be performed by someone holding the sealing keys.[89] Second, the couple must accept the sealings in eternity.[90] During the twentieth century, Church leaders, largely in response to women and men dismayed by the continued vitality of sealings to ex-spouses from whom they were estranged, had insisted that in the eternities no one will be forced into a relationship with anyone.[91] Third, the sealing ordinance must be ratified by God through the "Holy Spirit of promise."[92] This understanding of the significance of sealings thus leaves open the question of any particular sealing's eternal validity. Theologically, the presence of multiple sealings need not imply any polygamous relationship in the eternities. In addition, as the direct memory of nineteenth-century polygamy and the fierce theological insistence of its apologists faded, many Latter-day Saints came to see plural marriage as a temporary expedient in God's plan. President David O. McKay said, "[H]aving more than one wife is not a principle

89. As explained in one widely cited reference:

> Those keys belong to the President of the Church—to the prophet, seer, and revelator. That sacred power is with the Church now. . . . There are relatively few men who hold this sealing power upon the earth at any given time—in each temple are brethren who have been given the sealing power. No one can get it except from the prophet, seer, and revelator and President of the Church of Jesus Christ of Latter-day Saints.

Boyd K. Packer, *The Holy Temple* (Salt Lake City: Deseret Book Company, 2019), 75.

90. Church leaders have also spoken of the contingency of a sealing's effect on parties' choices in terms of personal righteousness. See, e.g., Joseph Fielding Smith, *Doctrines of Salvation*, ed. Bruce R. McConkie (Salt Lake City: Bookcraft, 1974), 2:98 ("If one or both of these covenanting persons break that covenant by which they were sealed by the Holy Spirit of promise, then the Spirit withdraws the seal and the guilty party or parties stand as if there had been no sealing or promise given").

91. See The Church of Jesus Christ of Latter-day Saints, *General Handbook: Serving in The Church of Jesus Christ of Latter-Day Saints* (Salt Lake City: The Church of Jesus Christ of Latter-day Saints, 2021), 38.4 ("The sealing is not compulsory in the post-mortal life for either a man or a woman").

92. See Smith, *Doctrines of Salvation*, 2:98 ("When a man or woman, in all sincerity, enter into a covenant of marriage for time and eternity . . . the Holy Ghost—who is the Spirit of promise—bears record and ratifies that sealing. In other words, he seals the promises appertaining to the marriage covenant upon them").

but a practice. The principle of the eternity of the marriage covenant revealed to the Prophet [Joseph Smith] and all the blessings pertaining to that may be obtained by a man with one wife."[93] Eugene England, a prominent Latter-day Saint intellectual, no doubt spoke for many rank-and-file members when he insisted on monogamy as the eternal standard and polygamy as a temporary variation.[94] England wrote:

> It is possible and spiritually healing, I believe, to affirm our polygynous ancestors for their obedient sacrifices and courageous achievements, which made the foundation of the restored church secure—and yet to reject the expectation of future polygyny. For too many of us, that expectation undermines the foundations of our present identities as women and men and diverts us from the difficult struggle for complete fidelity to our marriages that the gospel standard of morality and the expectation of celestial marriage as the basis of godhood require.[95]

There are also theological problems with equating modern sealing practices with the surreptitious continuation of polygamy in the hereafter. Contemporary plural sealing practices within the Church do not comply with nineteenth century requirements for plural marriage. Most notably, Joseph Smith's canonized revelation on polygamy requires the consent of a first wife to a polygamous second marriage (see D&C 132:61), and while often ignored in practice, in theory this was the rule for polygamous sealings prior to 1890.[96] Throughout the post-Manifesto period, however, the

---

93. McKay, *Confidence amid Change*, 136 (reproducing minutes from a February 3, 1956, First Presidency meeting) (emphasis in original). A few weeks later, McKay carefully parsed Joseph Smith's canonized revelation on plural marriage (D&C 132) in a talk to the First Presidency. He argued that the "every blessing pertaining to the salvation and exaltation of man" in the revelation applied to "the eternity of the marriage covenants; it was not polygamy." Polygamy, according to McKay's reading of the text, was merely a temporarily authorized practice. See McKay, 138 (reproducing minutes of a February 29, 1956, First Presidency meeting).

94. See generally Eugene England, "On Fidelity, Polygamy, and Celestial Marriage," *Dialogue: A Journal of Mormon Thought* 35, no. 1 (2002): 43–61.

95. England, 61.

96. See Daynes, *More Wives than One*, 203 ("A first wife's permission was supposed to be sought before her husband married other wives, but she could veto additional marriages only if she had sound and valid reasons"). Between 1968 and 1976, however, there was a rule in place for men seeking sealing clearance after a first divorce. Their petition to the First Presidency had to attach a written statement from their former spouses that would "state whether or not the divorced wife has any objections to the sealing of the applicant to another

Church has not required that a divorced wife who remains sealed to her ex-husband give her consent to a second sealing.[97]

There were further theological complexities in the understanding of temple sealings that contributed to a hesitancy to cancel sealings for divorced couples. Latter-day Saints generally speak of temple sealings as synonymous with the idea of marriages and will often speak of "temple weddings." However, liturgically two things happen in a temple sealing. First, husband and wife are declared to be married to one another for eternity. Second, the participants are blessed individually with "immortality and eternal lives" and "kingdoms, thrones, principalities, powers dominions, and exaltations."[98] The cancellation of a sealing dissolves both the eternal marriage and revokes the individual blessings. Presidents of the Church have been hesitant to cancel sealings and revoke those blessings. Thus, cancellation of sealings has not been issued as a matter of course in cases of divorce, and presidents of the Church have been loath to cancel temple blessings of deceased persons absent special circumstances. Rather than relying on the idea of eternal polygamy, in official sources Church leaders have explained the reluctance to cancel temple sealings in terms of preserving individual blessings rather than conjugal unions in the eternities. In 2021, the Church's general handbook declared:

> Members who are divorced but still sealed to the former spouse are often troubled by the thought of the sealing. The sealing is not compulsory in the post-mortal life for either a man or a woman. However, those who keep their covenants will retain the individual blessings provided by the sealing. This is the case even if the spouse has broken covenants or withdrawn from the marriage. Once a cancellation of sealings has been approved by the First Presidency, individual blessings pertaining to the sealing are no longer in force.[99]

---

person and the reasons if there are objections." The Church of Jesus Christ of Latter-day Saints, *General Handbook of Instructions* (Salt Lake City: The Church of Jesus Christ of Latter-day Saints, 1968), 94.

97. See The Church of Jesus Christ of Latter-day Saints, *1976 Handbook*, 58–59 ("It is not necessary to cancel the sealing or receive permission of the former wife if living to permit the sealing of the subsequent wife provided the divorce is final"). Note that this language dispensed with the short-lived rule promulgated in 1968 in which an ex-wife could voice her objections to a husband's second sealing. However, even under that rule an ex-wife's permission was not necessary for a man to be sealed a second time after divorce.

98. Quoted in Anderson, *The Development of LDS Temple Worship*, 102.

99. The Church of Jesus Christ of Latter-day Saints, *2021 Handbook*, 38.4.

Nevertheless, from the 1930s onward the Church has retained the rule allowing multiple sealings for living men but not for living women.

The creation of parallel but different sealing rules for men and women depending on whether they are living or dead creates complications when a couple straddles the grave, with one spouse living and another spouse deceased. For example, may a living man who has already been sealed once be sealed to a deceased wife who has been sealed to another man?[100] The rules in these cases suggest an effort to maintain the distinction between the living and posthumous sealing regimes. Thus, a deceased woman may not be sealed to multiple husbands until all of the men to whom she was married while alive are dead.[101] A man—like a woman—may choose to be sealed to a spouse who remains sealed to a previous spouse. However, a man—unlike a woman—must wait until he dies and have someone else perform the sealing on his behalf.

It is not clear how stable the dual track sealing rules for living and deceased women will be in the future. Pastorally it creates a problem because theological appeals to polygamy exacerbate rather than dissipate the anxieties of those caught up in the rules.[102] Contemporary Church leaders have said very little in response to such anxieties and do not purport to explain the precise meaning of multiple sealings. Hence, for example, then-apostle Dallin H. Oaks, who was sealed to a second wife in 2000 after being widowed, in answer to the question of the eternal status of his multiple sealings, said:

> [F]or people who live in the belief, as I do, that marriage relations can be for eternity, then you must say, "What will life *be* in the next life, when your married to more than one wife for eternity?" I have to say I don't know.

---

100. For example, suppose that Jack and Jill are married and sealed in the temple. Jack dies, and Jill remarries John, but they are not sealed because she does not wish to cancel her sealing to Jack. Jill then dies, and John remarries Joan, to whom he is sealed. May John be sealed by proxy to Jill now that she is dead? If not, may he be sealed to her posthumously once he also dies?

101. The Church of Jesus Christ of Latter-day Saints, *Church Handbook of Instructions: Book 1, Stake Presidencies and Bishoprics* (Salt Lake City: The Church of Jesus Christ of Latter-day Saints, 1998), 73; The Church of Jesus Christ of Latter-day Saints, *General Handbook: Serving in The Church of Jesus Christ of Latter-Day Saints* (Salt Lake City: The Church of Jesus Christ of Latter-day Saints, 2021), 38.4.1.7.

102. See generally Carol Lynn Pearson, *The Ghost of Eternal Polygamy: Haunting the Hearts and Heaven of Mormon Women and Men* (n.p.: Pivot Point Books, 2016).

> But I know that I've made those covenants, and I believe if I am true to the covenants that the blessing that's anticipated here will be realized in the next life. How? Why, I don't know.[103]

Recent Developments and Future Prospects

The Church has also tried to mitigate some of the gender asymmetry created by the rules. The trend since the 1970s has been toward a simplification of Church procedures around temple marriage. However, sealing rules continue to require that divorced women petition the First Presidency for a cancellation of sealing before being sealed to a new husband. In 1998, the Church promulgated a rule that required divorced men to petition the First Presidency as well before being sealed a second time, although a cancellation of the previous sealing is still not required.[104] The current sealing rules thus create a regime of procedural equality between men and women while maintaining the earlier rules of substantive inequality when it comes to second sealings.

Further changes could come in two ways. First, the First Presidency could relax its current stance toward cancelling sealings after divorce. Such cancellations could be granted as a matter of course when sought by either

103. "Elder Oaks Interview Transcript from PBS Documentary," Newsroom, The Church of Jesus Christ of Latter-day Saints, July 20, 2007, http://newsroom.churchofjesuschrist.org/article/elder-oaks-interview-transcript-from-pbs-documentary.

104. See The Church of Jesus Christ of Latter-day Saints, *1998 Handbook*, 73. There are complications here. Until 1983, any member who went through a divorce had to obtain a "divorce clearance" from the First Presidency before obtaining a temple recommend for any purpose. The Church of Jesus Christ of Latter-day Saints, *1976 Handbook*, 57–58. Thus, before a man could be sealed a second time, he would have to make a petition to the First Presidency—although this petition might have happened well before the second sealing, when he simply applied for an ordinary temple recommend after his divorce. This process of "divorce clearance" was dropped in 1983. See The Church of Jesus Christ of Latter-day Saints, *General Handbook of Instructions* (Salt Lake City: The Church of Jesus Christ of Latter-day Saints, 1983), 34–35, 40–41. Prior to 1983, there was greater procedural symmetry between men and women seeking a second sealing after a divorce. Both men and women would have to seek permission from the First Presidency, although a woman would have to petition the First Presidency twice, once for a "divorce clearance" and again for a "cancellation of sealing," while a man would only have to petition the First Presidency once for a "divorce clearance."

men or women, regardless of whether there is the immediate prospect of remarriage in the temple for a woman. One consequence of the current rules is that it is easier for a woman to obtain a cancellation of her sealing to an ex-husband than it is for a man, for whom it is all but impossible to obtain a cancellation unless his ex-wife wishes to be sealed to a second husband. However, because sealings involve both personal blessings and marriage for eternity, it seems unlikely that the First Presidency would adopt such a course. Furthermore, even if a cancellation of sealing was granted as a matter of course in cases of divorce, inequality would remain between widows and widowers, with the latter being able to be sealed to a second spouse but the former not.

The second option would be to extend the current regime of posthumous sealings to living women, returning to the nineteenth and early-twentieth century's more permissive stance toward multiple sealings for living women. If the Church took this approach, then both men and women could be sealed to multiple people while living, provided such sealings did not involve efforts to practice polygamy. This rule would also be an extension of the procedural regime of gender equality to substantive rules. Such a change, however, would have its own complications. First, it would deepen the theological ambiguity around the status of post-mortal relationships. This ambiguity already exists under current posthumous sealing practices. Given the vagaries of human relationships and family structures, such ambiguity is ineradicable. However, it is likely that such a move would further emphasize the way in which sealing practices and theology not only converge with and support the ideal of companionate marriage, but also diverge from and undermine that ideal. Second, a permissive rule toward multiple living sealings by living women could exacerbate concerns about eternal connections with estranged ex-spouses. Currently this concern is most acute for men, who have the greatest difficulty in obtaining a cancellation of sealing, although it is shared by divorced women. A shift to a permissive sealing rule for women would place women in an analogous position. Indeed, a permissive rule would make it even less likely that a cancellation of sealing could be obtained because such cancellations would no longer be readily obtainable—as they are now—in the case of a divorced woman who wishes to remarry in the temple.

Secular law has also impacted Latter-day Saint sealing practices in the late twentieth century. This can be seen in the reaction of sealing rules to the revolution in American divorce law. Nineteenth-century Latter-day Saints had a relatively easy-going legal attitude toward divorce, something that was carried forward into early twentieth century temple practices, which did not create special rules for divorced persons until 1944.[105] However, as the century progressed this attitude shifted as legal rules were simplified and divorce became more common. In 1960, the Church adopted a rule that Church members who divorced were ineligible to enter the temple without first obtaining clearance from the First Presidency.[106] Given that prior to the 1970s, divorce required a showing of fault such as adultery or cruelty, the rule may have been motivated by an assumption that most divorces involved serious moral lapses by a least one of the spouses.[107] However, the rule almost immediately came under pressure. First, the Latter-day Saint population was growing rapidly, and the rule no doubt placed substantial administrative burdens on the First Presidency. Second, with the passage of no-fault divorce statutes beginning in the 1970s, the frequency of divorce increased, and it no longer created a strong presumption of adultery or other serious moral lapses. Accordingly, First Presidency approval of temple recommends for divorced members was first confined only to those members who had been sealed in the temple, then only to divorces involving adultery or abuse, and finally in 1983 the question was left entirely to local leaders.[108]

Another place where the influence of secular laws can be seen is in the rules governing temple sealings after a marriage ceremony outside of the temple. Throughout the twentieth century, Church leaders had a strong preference that members be married in the temple. Accordingly, it was not possible to obtain a civil marriage outside of the temple and then immediately be sealed. Rather, Church rules imposed a one-year waiting period on couples between a non-temple marriage and their eligibility to be sealed in

105. See The Church of Jesus Christ of Latter-day Saints, *1944 Handbook*, 82.

106. See The Church of Jesus Christ of Latter-day Saints, *1960 Handbook*, 67–68.

107. See Howard A. Krom, "California's Divorce Law Reform: An Historical Analysis Family Law Act of 1969," *Pacific Law Journal* 1, no. 1 (1970): 156–81 (recounting the passage of the first no-fault divorce statute in the United States).

108. See The Church of Jesus Christ of Latter-day Saints, *1963 Handbook*, 79 (confining divorce clearance procedures to members who had previously been sealed in the temple); The Church of Jesus Christ of Latter-day Saints, *1968 Handbook*; The Church of Jesus Christ of Latter-day Saints, *1976 Handbook*, 58 (stating that divorce clearance is not required where the divorce was caused by a moral transgression of one of the parties and the non-transgressing party is seeking a temple recommend); The Church of Jesus Christ of Latter-day Saints, *1983 Handbook*, 34–35, 40–41 (dropping rules for divorce clearance for issuing temple recommends).

the temple.[109] However, legal complications soon appeared. This happened first in Mexico. Mexican Latter-day Saints traveling to be married in temples in the United States found that the process of proving the validity of their foreign marriage in Mexico was expensive and complex. Accordingly, the Church relaxed its rules to allow Mexican Latter-day Saints to be sealed in the temple immediately after being married in Mexico.[110] Following Lutheran and anti-clerical strands in the civil law tradition, many European countries require that all marriages be performed in public before a secular official. Numerous countries throughout the world that have adopted the civil law have similar rules. As the Church expanded internationally after World War II, and especially after the dedication of the Swiss Temple in 1955, it became clear that temple rules based on the American legal assumptions that one could easily perform a legally valid marriage within the temple would not work internationally. Accordingly, waiting periods for temple sealings were dropped in these countries.[111] In 2019, the same rule was adopted for the United States, bringing marriage and sealing norms among American Latter-day Saints into conformity with long-standing Latter-day Saint practice in civil law jurisdictions.[112]

Conclusion

During the nineteenth century, there was no sharp distinction between Utah marriage law and Latter-day Saint sealing practices. Theologically, Latter-day Saints believed that sealings had eternal consequences that merely civil marriages did not have, and civil marriages without sealings were possible. However, under Utah law, sealings simply were marriages, and until the end of the century it was assumed that a church divorce was a legal act that dissolved a legal marriage. After 1888 this changed as marriage law formalized and sealing rules came uncoupled from secular

109. See The Church of Jesus Christ of Latter-day Saints, *1968 Handbook*, 100.

110. See The Church of Jesus Christ of Latter-day Saints, *1976 Handbook*, 55–54.

111. See The Church of Jesus Christ of Latter-day Saints, *1976 Handbook*, 55 (stating the rule requiring a one-year wait between civil marriages outside the temple and a sealing does not apply "[w]here civil law requires that marriages be performed outside the temple, provided the couple goes to the temple for their sealing within such reasonable time after their civil marriage as travel permits. This includes civil marriages in Japan and the temple districts of London, Switzerland, and New Zealand temples").

112. See The Church of Jesus Christ of Latter-day Saints, *2021 Handbook*, 27.3, 38.3.

marriage. At the same time, Latter-day Saint sealing theology underwent a revolutionary change in 1894 when Wilford Woodruff announced the end of the law of adoption, which marked the abandonment of nineteenth-century kingdom theology. This is the setting from which the modern rules governing marriage sealings in The Church of Jesus Christ of Latter-day Saints emerged. These rules constitute a de facto ecclesiastical law of marriage for Latter-day Saints both living and dead. Over the course of the twentieth century, those rules have evolved in the face of shifts in theological understanding and the practical requirements of modern Mormonism. The result is a set of bifurcated rules in which the living and the dead are subject to substantially different regimes, neither of which rest on a fully articulated theological foundation. Rather, the rules grew organically over time, with each set of changes retaining continuity with the past while introducing innovations that sometimes repudiated the theological assumptions behind earlier rules that were retained. This process has allowed the Church to adapt to changing patterns of worship, but the resulting system is not without problems, and it is by no means clear that it will remain stable in the future.

CHAPTER 9

International Legal Experience and the Mormon Theology of the State, 1945–2012

I. Introduction

By spring 1945, the Third Reich had reached its Gotterdammerung. The previous summer, Allied Armies under Dwight D. Eisenhower landed in Normandy and began driving toward the Fatherland. The Red Army had been pushing west toward Berlin since its victory over the final German offensive at the Battle of Kursk in August 1943. On April 30, Hitler committed suicide in his bunker, and Germany surrendered seven days later. War continued on the other side of the globe. The American strategy of island hopping had culminated in the 1944 recapture of the Philippines and the final destruction of the Imperial Japanese Navy at the Battle of Leyte Gulf. On April 1, 1945, American forces landed on Okinawa, a Japanese island 340 miles south of the home archipelago. After eighty-two days and over 142,000 deaths, the Americans declared victory. Six weeks later, the United States dropped atomic bombs on Hiroshima and Nagasaki. On September 2, 1945, the Japanese formally surrendered on the deck of an American battleship in Tokyo Bay. The war was over.

That same month, the First Presidency of The Church of Jesus Christ of Latter-day Saints began discreetly calling men to serve as mission presidents. Beginning in 1939, the Church shut down its overseas missions and recalled American Mormons serving as missionaries back to the United States. As war spread across the globe, the American government exercised extensive control over the US economy, imposing rationing and labor controls. Not surprisingly, religious proselytizing was far down on the wartime government's list of priorities, and the Church ceased virtually all formal missionary work. The mission presidents sent forth by the First Presidency in September 1945 would help to create a very different kind of Mormonism than that which had existed before World War II. In 1945, there were roughly 980,000 Mormons, living mainly in the Intermountain West. Taking advantage of the *Pax Americana* wrought by the United States' victory and the tense stability of the Cold War, the Church would seek to establish itself as a global institution. By 2013, the Church would claim more than fifteen million baptized members, with the majority living outside of the United States.

While little remembered today, President George Albert Smith pointed toward the Church's postwar emphasis on international growth in December 1947. In a front-page *Church News* editorial, he stated:

> I assure every man and woman of the Church that you have a great obligation to spread the word of the Lord abroad and to carry the truth to every land and clime so that the power of the Priesthood will be made manifest among our Father's children in many places where it has never yet even been heard of.[1]

In the succeeding decades, Mormons would carry out this injunction by expanding the scope of missionary work, establishing the Church in dozens of countries where it had never previously functioned. This expansion, however, transformed the Church both institutionally and ideologically. Twenty years after Smith's 1947 editorial, Elder Franklin D. Richards remarked, "We are now 20 years into this new era of growth and development, and growth and development mean change. We must not resist change, as we believe that God 'will yet reveal many great and important things pertaining to the Kingdom of God.'"[2]

In discussing the interaction between law and religion, scholars and others often speak as if religion is a given, a phenomenon exogenous to law. We then ask how the law reacts to religion, either regulating it, accommodating it, or perhaps being controlled by it. Implicit in this view is the sense that law is the agent reacting to religion. The Mormon experience, however, provides an example of what this approach misses. The law not only reacts to religion but also shapes it. Religious traditions are not static. They evolve and reinterpret themselves over time in reaction to the world in which religious believers find themselves. Law is one of the factors that can force religious change. The Church's abandonment of polygamy in the face of legal pressure from the United States' government is a dramatic example of this kind of change. Less understood is the way that law has driven shifts in Mormon theological discourse in the twentieth century. Thus, beyond any particular interest it may offer, the story of law and the international expansion of Mormonism since 1945 provides an example of the more general phenomenon of how law precipitates religious change.

This chapter has three goals. The first is to provide a basic narrative of postwar Mormon expansion, identifying the basic periods and major developments. The second is to summarize the main legal issues provoked

---

1. George Albert Smith, "Looking Ahead: Into a New Century of Growth and Development," *The Church News*, December 20, 1947.

2. Franklin D. Richards, "Looking Ahead," *Conference Report*, October 1967, 146.

by this expansion. The scholarship on Mormon legal history has overwhelmingly focused on the nineteenth-century experience of the Latter-day Saints, resulting in general agreement about the basic structure of the narrative: We can divide the period between the lifetime of Joseph Smith, and the subsequent legal experience of the Church in Utah. During Smith's lifetime, his personal difficulties dominate the story, particularly in the high-stakes legal maneuvering in Nauvoo that ultimately led to his murder;[3] but once in Utah, the legal story focuses on the efforts of the Mormons to create an independent commonwealth and the struggle with the federal government over polygamy. There is no similar narrative for Mormon legal experience in the twentieth century. This chapter fills this gap by providing an overview of the legal issues involved in the postwar international expansion of the Church. The third goal is to advance an argument about the relationship between this legal experience and the development of Mormon discourse in the last half of the twentieth century.

As the Church expanded into new regions of the globe, it confronted non-American legal systems. Some of these new legal environments were quite similar to the United States, while others were very different. All of them placed pressure on the Church and affected the development of Mormon discourse in the last half of the twentieth century. In particular, international legal challenges created incentives that tended to moderate Mormon theologies of the state. By the turn of the twenty-first century, the dominant theology of the state in Mormon discourse was quietist and non-confrontational, a marked contrast from the theodemocratic ambitions of the nineteenth century or the Cold War apocalypticism popular among many Mormons in the middle of the twentieth century. Just as law proved decisive in the development of Mormon belief and practice in the nineteenth century—particularly Mormon doctrines surrounding plural

3. See generally Gordon A. Madsen and John W. Welch, eds., *Sustaining the Law: Joseph Smith's Legal Encounters* (Provo: BYU Studies, 2014); Edwin Brown Firmage and Richard Collin Mangrum, *Zion in the Courts: A Legal History of the Church of Jesus Christ of Latter-Day Saints, 1830–1900* (Urbana: University of Illinois Press, 1988); Dallin H. Oaks and Marvin S. Hill, *Carthage Conspiracy: The Trial of the Accused Assassins of Joseph Smith* (Urbana: University of Illinois Press, 1975); John S. Dinger, "Joseph Smith and the Development of Habeas Corpus in Nauvoo, 1841–44," *Journal of Mormon History* 36, no. 3 (July 1, 2010): 135–71; Marvin S. Hill, "Carthage Conspiracy Reconsidered: A Second Look at the Murder of Joseph and Hyrum Smith," *Journal of the Illinois State Historical Society* 97, no. 2 (July 1, 2004): 107–34.

marriage—in the twentieth century, law had again exerted its influence on Mormon teachings.

II. The International Expansion of Mormonism Since 1945

A. Pre-1945 Mormon Expansion

In 1945, despite over a century of international missionary work and well-established Mormon branches in a few European cities, the Church remained an overwhelmingly American institution. The first international Mormon missionaries were Joseph Smith Sr. and Don Carlos Smith—Joseph Smith's father and brother—who traveled across the international border from New York to Canada to preach the Restoration in September 1830.[4] A more ambitious effort came in 1837 with the first Mormon proselytizing mission to England. This was followed by an even more concerted effort by the Mormon apostles in 1839–1841.[5] From England, Mormon missionary work expanded to continental Europe, where it enjoyed particular success in Scandinavia.[6] The result was a wave of conversions and emigration to Mormon settlements in America, as European Saints[7] followed the counsel of successive Mormon prophets to "gather to Zion." During the nineteenth century, missionaries from England and the United States also sought to spread Mormonism beyond Europe and North America. Their efforts were mainly confined to outposts of the British Empire, such as the British West Indies, South Africa, India, Australia, and New Zealand. There were also sporadic efforts at missionary work in Latin America, and there was also a more sustained effort in Hawaii and other Pacific Islands.[8]

---

4. Richard Lyman Bushman, *Joseph Smith: Rough Stone Rolling* (New York: Alfred A. Knopf, 2005), 114.

5. See generally James B Allen, Ronald K. Esplin, and David J. Whittaker, *Men with a Mission, 1837–1841: The Quorum of the Twelve Apostles in the British Isles* (Salt Lake City: Deseret Book Co., 1992).

6. See generally William Mulder, *Homeward to Zion: The Mormon Migration from Scandinavia* (Minneapolis: University of Minnesota Press, 2000).

7. Mormon terminology follows the New Testament in which "Saint," rather than denoting a person of special spiritual merit, refers to any member of the Church.

8. See generally R. Lanier Britsch, *Nothing More Heroic: The Compelling Story of the First Latter-Day Saint Missionaries in India* (Salt Lake City: Deseret Book Co., 1999); R. Lanier Britsch, *From the East: The History of the Latter-Day Saints in Asia* (Salt Lake City: Deseret Book Co., 1998).

With the passing of the nineteenth century, the Mormon doctrine of a literal gathering to the Zion of the Intermountain West went into decline. This decline came gradually and without any clear theological rationale or justification. In its 1907 Christmas Letter to the Dutch Saints, for example, the First Presidency stated that "the policy of the Church is not to entice or encourage people to leave their native lands; but to remain faithful and true in their allegiance to their governments and to be good citizens."[9] In 1921, the First Presidency renewed its counsel, this time to the English Mission, stating their objections in economic terms.

> We are constrained to call your attention to the state of unemployment prevailing in America generally, and especially as it affects the western States, including Utah. This state of things is hard enough on our people here that are out of work, living in rented houses, but is particularly hard on our European immigrants who have come here during the last two or three months without sufficient means of support . . .[10]

Even so, Church growth beyond the borders of nineteenth-century Mormon settlements in Utah and surrounding states remained anemic. In 1945, the prototypical Mormon congregation outside of the United States would most likely have been a small branch located in Western Europe or among Western European communities in other countries, like the whites of South Africa or the German communities of southern Brazil, Paraguay, and Argentina. The one large-scale exception to the racially white complexion of international Mormonism was the long-time presence of the Church in Polynesia, which dated back to nineteenth-century missionary successes in the Sandwich Islands (Hawaii) and New Zealand.[11] In the years after 1945, this all began to change.

B. The Postwar Period

The postwar expansion of the Church can be usefully divided into three periods. The first period extended from 1945 until the succession of Spencer W. Kimball to the Church presidency in 1973. The dominant

9. James R. Clark, ed., *The Messages of the First Presidency of the Church of Jesus Christ of Latter-Day Saints*, vol. 4 (Salt Lake City: Bookcraft, Inc., 1970), 165.

10. James R. Clark, ed., *Messages of the First Presidency of the Church of Jesus Christ of Latter-Day Saints*, vol. 5 (Salt Lake City: Bookcraft, Inc., 1976), 199–200.

11. See R. Lanier Britsch, *Moramona: The Mormons in Hawaii* (Laie: Institute for Polynesian Studies, 1989); R. Lanier Britsch, *Unto the Islands of the Sea: A History of the Latter-Day Saints in the Pacific* (Salt Lake City: Deseret Book Co., 1986).

leader in this period was President David O. McKay. Before World War II, the Church beyond the United States operated very differently than the Church within the United States. With the exception of the Mormon colonies in Canada and Mexico, there were no non-American stakes of the Church. (A stake is a collection of congregations similar to a Catholic Diocese that is administered by local priesthood leaders rather missionaries sent by Church headquarters.) Mormons met in small branches, often presided over by American missionaries, and local ecclesiastical authority almost always resided with an American-born mission president.[12] Furthermore the number of missionaries was relatively small compared to the postwar years.[13] The Church's physical footprint was similarly subdued. Church units met in rented spaces or in small buildings built by local members without any support from Church headquarters.[14]

This changed in the postwar years. The Church expanded its missionary program, doubling the number of prewar missionaries by 1946 and steadily increasing its proselytizing force thereafter. The growth in missionaries reflected more than a growth in church population. Rather, missionary service became a more common and salient feature of Mormon life.[15] The Church matched the increased missionary force with an expanded building program.[16] For the first time, non-American Latter-day Saints began to meet in chapels owned and built by the Church. More strikingly, the Church began building temples overseas, beginning in Switzerland, London, and New Zealand. When these buildings were constructed, there was not a single international Mormon stake outside of the Canadian and Mexican colonies. Thus, the early international temples were self-

---

12. See, e.g., Ross Geddes, "Before Stakehood: The Mission Years in Brisbane, Australia," *Journal of Mormon History* 22, no. 2 (October 1, 1996): 92–119; Kahlile Mehr, "Enduring Believers: Czechoslovakia and the LDS Church, 1884–1990," *Journal of Mormon History* 18, no. 2 (October 1, 1992): 111–54.

13. *Church Almanac 2013* (Deseret Book, 2012), 210.

14. See Gregory A. Prince and Wm. Robert Wright, *David O. McKay and the Rise of Modern Mormonism* (Salt Lake City: University of Utah Press, 2005), 199–200.

15. For example, in 1939 there was roughly one missionary for every two wards or branches in the Church. In the postwar period that number shifted to something more like 1.25 missionaries per ward or branch. This figure is calculated using numbers in *Church Almanac 2013*.

16. Prince and Wright, *David O. McKay and the Rise of Modern Mormonism*, 199–226.

consciously conceptualized as anchors for future growth.[17] Finally, and perhaps most importantly, the decision was made to establish the full program of the Church beyond the borders of the United States. Non-American Mormons would no longer inhabit an ecclesiastically liminal "mission field." Instead, beginning in 1958 with Auckland, New Zealand, the Church began organizing stakes beyond the United States with the same kind of autonomous local leadership seen in the Mormon heartland of the Intermountain West.[18]

The second period began with Spencer W. Kimball's succession to the presidency of the Church in 1973. David O. McKay and many of his associates in the leadership of the Church came from long-time Utah families and had long careers as prewar general authorities. Kimball, in contrast, came from the borderlands of the Mormon corridor in Thatcher, Arizona, where he'd spent much of his life in a more culturally diverse milieu of non-Mormon Anglos, Hispanics, and Native Americans. Called as an apostle in 1943, he spent his entire career as a general authority in the internationally expansive postwar Church. Strikingly, both of his counselors were born outside of the United States, albeit in the Mormon colonies.[19] This period was marked by a number of developments. By far the most important was the 1978 revelation abandoning Mormonism's ban on ordaining Black men to its lay priesthood. This facilitated international growth in two ways.[20] First, it made possible the staffing of the Church with local leaders in areas with large Black populations. Second, it allowed the Church to distance itself from past racism, making itself more appealing to converts, especially in Africa and Latin America where Church growth

---

17. The Church had constructed one temple beyond the borders of the United States prior to World War II: the Cardston, Alberta, temple, which served the Canadian colonies.

18. James B Allen and Glen M. Leonard, *The Story of the Latter-Day Saints* (Salt Lake City: Deseret Book Co., 1992), 606–9.

19. Marion G. Romney was born in the Mexico in the Mormon colonies at Colonia Juarez. N. Eldon Tanner was a Canadian who had served in the Alberta provincial government before being called as a general authority.

20. Edward L Kimball, *Lengthen Your Stride: The Presidency of Spencer W. Kimball* (Salt Lake City: Deseret Book Co., 2005), 236–45; compare Prince and Wright, *David O. McKay and the Rise of Modern Mormonism*, 75–94 (discussing the administrative and proselyting difficulties created by the ban during David O. McKay's administration).

expanded in this era.[21] Kimball also moved far more aggressively than his predecessors to gain access to countries previously closed to Mormonism, tapping former US Treasury Secretary David Kennedy, a Latter-day Saint, as his personal diplomatic envoy.[22] For example, during this period the Church gained formal recognition in communist Poland and was allowed to build its only temple behind the Iron Curtain in Freiberg, Germany.[23]

The third period of postwar expansion began with the fall of the Berlin Wall in 1989. Unquestionably, the dominant figure in this period was President Gordon B. Hinckley.[24] Hinckley became an apostle in 1961, a period corresponding with the organization of the first international stakes. He was called as a counselor to the ailing Kimball in 1981 and continued to serve in the first presidencies of the aged and largely inactive Ezra Taft Benson and Howard W. Hunter, before becoming president of the Church in 1995. Hence, from the early 1980s on, the day-to-day operations of the Church were largely in the hands of Hinckley. This period saw three main developments. The first was the expansion of missionary efforts in new countries, especially those in the former Soviet bloc. The second was an expansion in the number of temples around the world. Particularly after 1997, the Church built small buildings to put temple worship within relatively easy distance of the majority of Latter-day

---

21. Strikingly, it was in the decade immediately after the 1978 revelation that sociologist Rodney Stark claimed Mormonism represented a "new world religion." Rodney Stark, "The Rise of a New World Faith," *Review of Religious Research* 26, no. 1 (September 1, 1984): 18–27; compare Rodney Stark, "So Far, So Good: A Brief Assessment of Mormon Membership Projections," *Review of Religious Research* 38, no. 2 (December 1, 1996): 175–78. See also sources cited infra at note 26.

22. Kimball, *Lengthen Your Stride*, 130–33; Martin B. Hickman, *David Matthew Kennedy: Banker, Statesman, Churchman* (Salt Lake City: Deseret Book Co., in cooperation with the David M. Kennedy Center for International Studies, 1987); Kahlile Mehr, "An LDS International Trio, 1974–97," *Journal of Mormon History* 25, no. 2 (October 1, 1999): 102–6.

23. Kimball, *Lengthen Your Stride*, 138 (discussing Church recognition in Poland); Raymond M. Kuehne, "The Freiberg Temple: An Unexpected Legacy of a Communist State and a Faithful People," *Dialogue: A Journal of Mormon Thought* 37, no. 2 (Summer 2004): 95–131.

24. See generally Sheri L Dew, *Go Forward with Faith: The Biography of Gordon B. Hinckley* (Salt Lake City: Deseret Book Co., 1996).

Saints.[25] Finally, this era saw the sharp exponential growth in Church membership taper off. The Church continued to grow but at a more modest rate. Much of the statistical growth in previous years was revealed to be hollow, with very high attrition rates among converts.[26] The Church responded in various ways. Two apostles—Dallin H. Oaks and Jeffery R. Holland—were dispatched to live in the Philippines and Chile, respectively, to supervise massive retrenchment and reorganization.[27] Recently, the Church has subtly redesigned its missionary program. It has jettisoned pre-scripted missionary "discussions" in favor of a more flexible approach to teaching.[28] There has also been a shift away from baptismal statistics as a metric of success to an emphasis on "real growth" of the Church.[29] Finally, in 2012, Hinckley's successor, President Thomas S. Monson, lowered the minimum age for missionaries. This led to an increase in the number of missionaries generally and female missionaries in particular.[30]

III. Legal Challenges and International Expansion

As the Church has expanded beyond the United States, it has faced many legal challenges. Providing a concise summary of these challenges is difficult for a number of reasons. First, there is a great deal of ambiguity

---

25. For an account of the introduction of these small temples, see Virginia Hatch Romney, *The Colonia Juárez Temple: A Prophet's Inspiration* (Provo: Religious Studies Center, Brigham Young University, 2009).

26. Rick Phillips, "Rethinking the International Expansion of Mormonism," *Nova Religio: The Journal of Alternative and Emergent Religions* 10, no. 1 (August 1, 2006): 52–68; David Clark Knowlton, "How Many Members Are There Really? Two Censuses and the Meaning of LDS Membership in Chile and Mexico," *Dialogue: A Journal of Mormon Thought* 38, no. 2 (Summer 2005): 53–78.

27. Carrie A. Moore, "2 Apostles Assigned to Live Outside U.S.," *Deseret News*, April 10, 2002, http://www.deseretnews.com/article/906937/2-apostles-assigned-to-live-outside-US.html.

28. See generally The Church of Jesus Christ of Latter-day Saints, *Preach My Gospel: A Guide to Missionary Service*, 2004 edition (Salt Lake City: Intellectual Reserve, 2004).

29. Heather Whittle Church Wrigley, "Worldwide Leadership Training Highlights Path to Real Growth," *Ensign*, March 2012, http://www.lds.org/ensign/2012/03/worldwide-leadership-training-highlights-path-to-real-growth; Richard C. Edgley, "The Rescue for Real Growth," *Ensign*, May 2012, http://www.lds.org/general-conference/2012/04/the-rescue-for-real-growth.

30. Laurie Goodstein, "Young Mormon Women Jump at the Chance to Become Missionaries at 19," *The New York Times*, November 2, 2012, sec. U.S.

about what counts as "legal," especially outside the advanced democracies of the developed world. Most people think of "law" in Weberian terms as the subjugation of the state's monopoly on the legitimate use of force to a system of formal rules enforced by specialized, rule-following bureaucracies.[31] On this view, state and private action are sharply differentiated, as are law and politics. To be sure, the distinction between law and politics has been strenuously questioned even in mature legal systems like in the United States. In countries where states and the rule of law are weak, however, insisting on a sharp distinction between law and politics makes little sense. Often, law has little meaning beyond the discretion of local political elites. The problem of defining the boundaries of law points toward the other difficulty: the many different contexts in which the Church has operated during the postwar period. The differences of institutions, legal cultures, and political pressures faced by the Church in different countries make generalizations difficult. Nevertheless, the Church did face a series of broadly similar legal challenges as it expanded internationally. First, it faced restrictions on missionaries' and general authorities' ability to enter countries, most commonly in the form of visa restrictions. Second, it faced laws limiting missionaries' ability to proselytize. Third, it faced laws restricting Church members from meeting and worshiping together. Finally, it faced challenges in acquiring and owning property for Church buildings.

A. Legal Challenges Faced by the Church

Among the first steps in establishing the Church in a new country has been for missionaries and Church leaders to enter the country. This has often been preceded by the baptism of a national abroad who then assists the Church's initial access to a country or by Latter-day Saint expatriates who introduce Mormonism to the country.[32] Governments, however, often restricted access to foreign missionaries. For example, in 1963 the Church sought to establish a mission in Nigeria to serve self-proclaimed Mormon congregations that had formed after reading materials about the

---

31. Max Weber, *Max Weber on Law in Economy and Society*, ed. Max Rheinstein, trans. Edward Albert Shils (New York: Touchstone Book, 1954).

32. For example, the first missionaries to enter Slovenia, which declared independence from Yugoslavia in 1991, were aided by Albin Lotric, a Slovenian national who had joined the Church in Norway. Jeffery G. Moore, Oral History Interview, interview by Jeff Anderson, transcript, November 22, 1991, Church History Library.

Church and its doctrines.[33] The effort was blocked when the Nigerian government refused to issue visas to the assigned mission president.[34] During most of the Cold War, the Church was unable to send missionaries to most of the nations behind the Iron Curtain, although there were notable exceptions—Poland and the German Democratic Republic—as well as sporadic visits by Church authorities.[35] Some governments only allow missionaries to visit on short-term tourist visas or require local citizens to formally invite missionaries into the country. In the 1990s, for example, Russian converts frequently spent hours waiting in long lines to fill out the paperwork necessary to formally invite foreign missionaries into the country.[36]

In some instances, governments have expelled missionaries after previously allowing them. In 1946, the Church sent missionaries into Czechoslovakia to re-establish missionary work in that country.[37] After a communist coup in 1948, however, the secret police began monitoring missionaries, and in 1950 two missionaries were arrested and imprisoned for a month on suspicion of espionage. The government passed a law banning non-Czech pastors and all American missionaries were withdrawn after the release of the two imprisoned elders.[38] Similarly, Mormon missionaries were expelled from Ghana by the government in 1989, although foreign LDS missionaries were allowed back into the country a year later.[39] In other cases,

33. Prince and Wright, *David O. McKay and the Rise of Modern Mormonism*, 81–94; James B. Allen, "Would-Be Saints: West Africa Before the 1978 Priesthood Revelation," *Journal of Mormon History* 17 (January 1, 1991): 207–47.

34. Allen, "Would-Be Saints," 228–30.

35. Raymond M. Kuehne, *Mormons as Citizens of a Communist State: A Documentary History of the Church of Jesus Christ of Latter-Day Saints in East Germany, 1945–1990* (Salt Lake City: University of Utah Press, 2010), 331–34; Mehr, "An LDS International Trio, 1974–97," 107. In 1978, the Church also sent missionaries into Yugoslavia. They arrived on student visas and could answer questions but could not openly proselytize. They wore ordinary clothes and grew their hair to their shoulders to avoid drawing undue attention. Mehr, 112.

36. Gary Browning, "Out of Obscurity: The Emergence of The Church of Jesus Christ of Latter-Day Saints in 'That Vast Empire' of Russia," *Brigham Young University Studies* 33, no. 4 (1993): 678.

37. Mehr, "Enduring Believers," 140.

38. Mehr, 141.

39. Emmanuel A. Kissi, *Walking in the Sand: A History of the Church of Jesus Christ of Latter-Day Saints in Ghana*, ed. Matthew K Heiss (Provo: Brigham Young University Press, 2004), xxvii–xxviii.

visas have been so difficult to obtain that the Church has simply withdrawn non-native missionaries. This happened in 2005, for example, when the Church withdrew over two hundred missionaries from Venezuela as a result of actions committed by the government of Hugo Chavez.[40]

Second, the Church has faced restrictions on missionaries' ability to openly proselytize. For example, the Church obtained permission to send missionaries to Poland and Yugoslavia in the 1970s, but the government would not allow them to proselytize.[41] More recently, the Church called missionaries to work among members in Israel, many of whom are Eastern European guest workers and European and North American expatriates, but the Church does not allow them to proselytize.[42] The situation in Israel illustrates the complex relationship between legal and other pressures on the Church. The Israeli Supreme Court has recognized a basic right to religious conversion, and religious proselytizing is legal under Israeli law, subject to various restrictions.[43] Beginning in 1979, however, Brigham Young University, a Church-sponsored school, sought to build a study abroad center in Jerusalem. The building became hugely controversial in Israel, with conservative groups opposing it and claiming it was part of a broader effort to evangelize Jews to Mormonism. The Knesset Interior Committee took up the issue and demanded a pledge from the Church not to proselytize as a condition for being allowed to build the center. The Mormons agreed, and in 1985 Jeffery R. Holland, then the president of Brigham Young University, promised on behalf of the Church

---

40. United States Commission on International Religious Freedom, "Annual Report 2009" (Washington, DC: US Department of State, 2009), 216.

41. Kimball, *Lengthen Your Stride*, 138; Mehr, "An LDS International Trio, 1974–97," 112.

42. Joseph Bentley, Conversation with Elder Joseph Bentley, Jerusalem Branch, interview by Nathan B. Oman, June 2011. At the time of this conversation, Elder Bentley and his wife were serving as missionaries in Israel.

43. See HCJ 1031/93 Passaro (Goldstein) v. Minister of the Interior [1995] IsrSC 49(4) 661 (Isr.). For an English language summary of the case, see Rahel Rimon, "Non-Orthodox Conversions in Israel," *Justice: The International Association of Jewish Lawyers and Jurists* 1 (December 1997): 43–48. A 1977 law prohibits inducing religious conversation by offering something of value. See Penal Law Amendment (Enticement to Change Religion), 5738-1977; Peter G. Danchin, "Of Prophets and Proselytes: Freedom of Religion and the Conflict of Rights in International Law," *Havard International Law Journal* 49, no. Summer, 2008 (Summer 2008): 279n114.

that Mormons in Israel would refrain from proselytizing, regardless of Israeli law.[44]

Third, the Church has faced restrictions on the ability of Latter-day Saints to meet and worship together. In some cases, restrictions on proselytizing have included restrictions on public meetings.[45] In other cases, Church members were allowed to meet but were subject to varying levels of harassment. During its history, for example, the German Democratic Republic generally allowed Latter-day Saints to meet for worship services, only occasionally prohibiting services. However, the police frequently monitored services, which scared away some members. In other cases, the police required onerous and detailed reports from Church leaders on each meeting.[46] In 1989 the government in Ghana issued decrees prohibiting all church meetings, rescinding the decrees in 1990.[47] In Nicaragua, hostility toward the Church spiked in the 1980s in response to the Reagan administration's support for the right-wing Contra rebels that were battling the socialist Sandinista government. Anti-American hostility by local Sandinista leaders was directed against Nicaraguan Mormons, who lost control of their own meetinghouses. Thereafter, according to one Latter-day Saint, "We met in secret in the homes of some members. . . . We always met in the house of members. . . . We didn't meet very often."[48]

Finally, the Church has faced restrictions on its ability to own and use property. As the Church has expanded beyond the United States, it has had to fragment its legal personality in order to own property. Mexico,

---

44. The details are recounted in Matthew L. Sandgren, "Extending Religious Freedoms Abroad: Difficulties Experienced by Minority Religions," *Tulsa Journal of Comparative and International Law* 8 (2001): 268–72.

45. See, e.g., Mehr, "Enduring Believers," 134.

46. Kuehne, *Mormons as Citizens of a Communist State*, 69–70.

47. Kissi, *Walking in the Sand*, 181, 239.

48. Quoted in Henri Gooren, "Latter-Day Saints under Siege: The Unique Experience of Nicaraguan Mormons," *Dialogue: A Journal of Mormon Thought* 40, no. 3 (Fall 2007): 145. According to Gooren:

> Between 1982 and 1990, most members were afraid to tell co-workers or relatives that they were Mormons. Mormons in Nicaragua were effectively under siege from their own government. In the process, only the most committed core members remained. All the other members, active and inactive, put their LDS identity on hold or took on membership in another church.

Gooren, 147.

for example, has legal restrictions on foreigners' ability to own land.[49] Furthermore, successive waves of Mexican reform in the nineteenth and early twentieth centuries directed at the land holdings of the Catholic Church resulted in mortmain provisions complicating the ecclesiastical ownership of land.[50] Other jurisdictions often have legal prerequisites for church ownership of property. Accordingly, one of the first legal tasks for the Church, upon entering a new country, was to incorporate or otherwise gain the ability to own land.[51] This has often required a native member or a group of members to be the formal titleholders for Church property. Furthermore, the process of registration has often been chaotic, with early missionaries and Church leaders not fully understanding the legal status that they obtained.[52]

In many countries, especially in Europe, there is a hierarchy of possible legal statuses that a church can have. At the bottom are simple non-profit corporations that allow a religious organization to own property and carry out basic collective actions. At the top are well-established churches that may receive financial support from the government or can enter into formal

---

49. See Mexican Const. art. 27(I) ("[F]oreigners may not acquire direct ownership of lands and water within a boundary of one hundred kilometers along the border and fifty along the beach. . . .").

50. William D. Signet, "Grading a Revolution: 100 Years of Mexican Land Reform," *Law & Business Review of the Americas* 16 (2010): 487–93.

51. For example, in Albania the Church created an entity called The Liahona Foundation of The Church of Jesus Christ of Latter-day Saints, which gives the Church a legal personality under Albanian law. David and Joan Haymond, Oral History with David and Joan Haymond, interview by Matthew K. Heiss, transcript, March 12, 1996, 14–15, Church History Library.

52. As one long-time leader of the Church in Belgium has noted:

> Indeed the understanding behind "recognition" can be bizarre. In Belgium an American mission president confirmed in a letter that the Church was officially recognized as a Church (copy in my possession). He based his claim on the fact that the Church had registered as a non-profit organization (something anyone can do) and the statutes had appeared in the State Paper. In the Netherlands I was shown the "official document recognition": a perfunctory form-letter from the Dutch Ministry acknowledging receipt of the Church's request for recognition, sent shortly after the request has been submitted.

Wilfried Decoo, "Issues in Writing European History and in Building the Church in Europe," *Journal of Mormon History* 23, no. 1 (April 1, 1997): 165n20.

concordats with the state.[53] In addition to these concrete legal benefits, the higher levels of official recognition confer a certain social legitimacy on a religion, something that can be of particular importance in Europe, where an active anti-cult movement targets the Church from time to time.[54] For most of its history in Europe, the Church was content with its legal status as long as it could own property and carry out basic church functions. In the final decades of the twentieth century, however, this approach shifted. In 1979, for example, the Catholic Church reached a concordat on education with the post-Franco government in Spain. In 1992, the Spanish government entered into similar agreements with the largest Jewish, Muslim, and Evangelical Christian groups in the country. In the wake of the 1992 agreements, the Church sought unsuccessfully to gain the same status.[55]

In owning property, the Church has faced legal challenges ranging from the regulatory issues it might face in the United States to the confiscation of Church property by revolutionary militias. One of the first major legal problems related to land ownership that the Church faced in the postwar period involved the tax status of the London Temple, which was litigated to the House of Lords in *Church of Jesus Christ of Latter-day Saints v. Henning*.[56] If *Henning* is close to the kind of legal issues faced by the Church in the United States, then the experience of the Church in Nicaragua in the 1980s represents the opposite end of the spectrum. Responding to widespread allegations that the Church was associated with the CIA, which was supporting the Contra insurgency against the Sandinista regime in the country, local Sandinista party bosses occupied

---

53. See Cole Durham, "Legal Status of Religious Organizations: A Comparative Overview," *The Review of Faith & International Affairs*, Summer 2010, 3–14.

54. See Massimo Introvigne, "Blacklisting or Greenlisting? A European Perspective on the New Cult Wars," *Nova Religio: The Journal of Alternative and Emergent Religions* 2, no. 1 (October 1, 1998): 16–23.

55. See Javier Martínez-Torrón, "School and Religion in Spain," *Journal of Church and State* 47, no. 1 (2005): 138n11.

56. [1964] AC 420. In 2008, the Church re-litigated the issue to the House of Lords for the Preston Temple in order to set up an appeal to the European Court of Human Rights. See Gallagher v. Church of Jesus Christ of Latter-day Saints, [2008] UKHL 56. See also Justin Gau and Ruth Arlow, "Gallagher v. Church of Jesus Christ of Latter-Day Saints," *Ecclesiastical Law Journal* 9, no. 2 (2007): 241–42. The appeal to Strasbourg proved unsuccessful. See Church of Jesus Christ of Latter-day Saints v. United Kingdom, Application No. 7552/09 (April 6, 2014) (European Court of Human Rights).

LDS meetinghouses without formal legal support but with the connivance of government officials.[57]

Individual Latter-day Saints have also faced legal problems not directly related to the institutional Church but flowing out of their Mormon faith. For example, in 2008, the Court of Appeals (Civil Division) of the United Kingdom heard an appeal by a Muslim convert to Mormonism from Afghanistan who sought asylum in Britain, arguing that he would face religious persecution if forced to return to his homeland.[58] There are similar cases in other countries.[59] In Belgium, Mormons employed by Catholic schools lost their jobs because of their religion. In these cases, the members found other employment rather than pursuing legal claims under Belgian law. Belgian Latter-day Saints have also found their religion used against them in divorce proceedings, where courts have awarded custody of children to non-Mormon parents to avoid religious indoctrination or have placed restrictions on religious activities during child visits.[60] In these cases, Latter-day Saints receive no formal assistance from the Church.[61] Church attorneys represent the Church as an institution, and Church handbooks discourage local priesthood leaders from becoming involved in members' legal proceedings.[62] Furthermore, in some contexts—

57. Gooren, "Latter-Day Saints under Siege: The Unique Experience of Nicaraguan Mormons," 142–45.

58. See MT (Afghanistan) v. The Secretary of State for the Home Department, [2008] EWCA Civ 65. The convert in this case was successful in obtaining a rehearing before an immigration judge after his first, unsuccessful bid for asylum.

59. In New Zealand, a Russian convert sought asylum on the grounds that he would face persecution if returned to his home country. The New Zealand court found that while Mormons were subject to discrimination in Russia, this harassment did not rise to the level of persecution. See IF, Refugee Appeal No. 70097/96, Refugee Status Appeals Authority, New Zealand, 26 March 1997.

60. Wilfried Decoo to Nathan B. Oman, "Legal Problems of Non-American Mormons," October 15, 2013.

61. The Church does provide welfare assistance to members that are struggling economically, including cash assistance in some cases. The Church does not permit welfare funds to be spent on attorneys. However, the fungibility of money means that Church assistance for food, shelter, and the like may in some cases indirectly help to defray legal expenses.

62. "To avoid implicating the Church in legal matters to which it is not a party, leaders should avoid testifying in civil or criminal cases reviewing the conduct of members over whom they preside." The Church of Jesus Christ of Latter-day Saints, *Church Handbook of Instructions: Book 1, Stake Presidencies and Bishoprics*

such as discrimination by religious employers—the Church's institutional interests are not necessarily aligned with the interest of members. So, for example, in *Obst v. Germany*, the Church successfully defended its right to dismiss an employee for failing to comply with Church standards before the European Court of Human Rights, arguing that religious discrimination was necessary to maintain its institutional integrity.[63]

B. Causes of the Church's Legal Challenges

Given the unique political and legal cultures of the various jurisdictions in which the Church has operated in the postwar era, it is difficult to generalize about the causes of the legal difficulties that Mormonism has faced. There have been, however, at least three recurring themes. The first is the difficulty of fitting the programs of the Church into legal systems that have specific assumptions about how religions operate, which are at odds with Latter-day Saint practice. This results in attempts to shove the square peg of Mormonism into the round hole of a foreign legal system. The second source of legal friction has been the Church's status as an American institution. Despite its efforts to internationalize, Mormonism is generally regarded as an American church. Accordingly, it has often proved a lightning rod for international resentments against American government policies and American cultural influence. Finally, the Church has found itself caught up in political and legal disputes internal to the societies where it has sought to expand. In many cases all three factors are present, reinforcing one another.

The difficulty of fitting Latter-day Saint practices into legal systems with differing assumptions about how religions should behave has been a recurring theme in Mormon legal history. For example, it took the Church nearly a century to find an adequate way of owning property in

---

(Salt Lake City: The Church of Jesus Christ of Latter-day Saints, 2006), 66. This policy, however, does not always preclude members and Church leaders from providing assistance in legal proceedings. For example, in the New Zealand case discussed in supra note 71, the Latter-day Saint asylum seeker was supported by testimony from a local Mormon.

63. See Obst v. Germany, Application No. 425/03 (Dec. 23, 2010) (European Court of Human Rights). For an account of the historical and theological importance of institutional autonomy for the Church, see Cole Durham and Nathan B. Oman, "A Century of Mormon Theory and Practice in Church-State Relations: Constancy Amidst Change" (November 7, 2006), http://papers.ssrn.com/sol3/papers.cfm?abstract_id=942567.

the United States. During the nineteenth century, American law had a strong Protestant and congregational bias and sharply limited the ability of churches to own property. The assumption was that a church corporation would exist for a single congregation that might own a glebe or other income-producing asset to pay a single pastor. The law assumed that all churches were decentralized like the Congregationalists or the Baptists. The Mormon church operated as a single, integrated community in which resources could be centralized under the control of general authorities.[64] During the lifetime of Joseph Smith, this proved impossible. In Utah, the Mormons abandoned the American congregational model in favor of a corporate charter that gave the Church unlimited power to hold property.[65] Congress, however, nullified this statute in 1862, and Church property was thereafter held in a complex network of local corporations or priesthood leaders acting as trustees for the Church.[66] It was only in the early twentieth century that the Church assumed its modern form as a corporation sole.

---

64. The Mormon settlement of Nauvoo provides an example of this problem. Joseph Smith, on the credit of the Church, borrowed money to purchase land for the city in Illinois. The hope was that this loan could then be repaid from the revenues of the Church, which consisted of tithing and receipts from the retail sale of lots in Nauvoo. Glen M. Leonard, *Nauvoo: Place of Peace, People of Promise* (Salt Lake City: Deseret Book Co., 2002), 54–61. Under Illinois law at the time, however, it was impossible for a church corporation to own such extensive assets. Jesse St. Cyr, "A Brief Corporate History of The Church of Jesus Christ of Latter-Day Saints, 1829–1901" (Paper, Mormon History Association, Sacramento, California, May 24, 2008), 25–27. The result was a hopeless entanglement of Church and personal assets in Joseph Smith's estate upon his death. Dallin H. Oaks and Joseph I. Bentley, "Joseph Smith and Legal Process: In the Wake of the Steamboat Nauvoo," *Brigham Young University Studies* 19, no. 2 (1979): 1–33.

65. The charter is reproduced in Dale L. Morgan, *The State of Deseret* (Logan: Utah State University Press with the Utah State Historical Society, 1987), 185.

66. Paul G. Kauper and Stephen C. Ellis, "Religious Corporations and the Law," *Michigan Law Review* 71, no. 8 (August 1, 1973): 1516–20; St. Cyr, "A Brief Corporate History of The Church of Jesus Christ of Latter-Day Saints, 1829–1901," 29. According to Kauper and Ellis:

> The early corporate history of the Mormon Church is a prime example of governmental regulation with a vengeance. The federal government effectively stripped the Mormon Church of the use of the corporate privilege primarily because of the Church's advocacy of polygamy, a form of marriage considered by many non-Mormons to be immoral.

Kauper and Ellis, "Religious Corporations and the Law," 1516.

The 1964 decision of the House of Lords in *Church of Jesus of Christ of Latter-day Saints v. Henning* illustrates a similar dynamic. Beginning in the seventeenth century, the English government began assessing local property taxes to finance poor relief. Property belonging to the Church of England was exempt from this tax, but properties belonging to dissenting sects were assessed for the tax. In 1833, parliament eliminated the special treatment for the Church of England by exempting all "public places of worship" from assessment, and the exemption was codified in subsequent English revenue law. After the London Temple was dedicated in 1958, the local English taxing authority took the position that the temple did not qualify as a "public place of worship" because it was closed to everyone except members in good standing. The House of Lords rejected the Church's argument that public worship meant corporate as opposed to private, household worship and accepted the local taxing authority's interpretation of the law. As the Church's barrister pointed out, this placed the London Temple in the odd position of being the only house of worship in the United Kingdom subject to taxation.

In some instances, friction was exacerbated by a lack of legal sophistication on the part of the Church. For example, the Church had been organized as a *Verein*, a kind of non-profit corporation, under prewar German law.[67] After the war, the Church reorganized itself in the Federal Republic of Germany by obtaining a corporation under the laws of one of the West German Lander. Under West Germany's federal constitution, this corporation could act for the Church throughout the Federal Republic. The Church then dissolved its *Verein*. The law of the German Democratic Republic, however, continued to recognize prewar *Verein* in at least some situations. Thus, as a result of what Church leaders thought of as a minor bit of bureaucratic tidying up in West Germany, the Church lost its legal existence in East Germany.[68] Thereafter, local leaders in East Germany repeatedly petitioned communist authorities for recognition, and Church

67. Kuehne, *Mormons as Citizens of a Communist State*, 59. The organization had taken place in 1938 and resulted in a legal entity called Vereign Der Deutschen Mission der Kirche Jesu Christi Der Heiligen der Letzten Tage.

68. Spencer W. Kimball recorded in his diary on August 25, 1955:

> When we incorporated in West Germany we had to relinquish our association status and did not realize what that would do to our status in East Germany, but it seems to have had the effect of disenfranchising us there and losing for us our recognition. . . . Cannot buy buildings. Difficulty getting land.

Quoted in Kuehne, 60.

property was either held by individuals in trust for the Church or by legal entities that lacked general recognition in the GDR. The Church dissolved its *Verein* in 1952 and did not gain general recognition again in the GDR until 1985.[69] Over the course of the postwar period, however, the Church gradually professionalized its international legal operations. In the late 1970s, it began opening area offices in cities such as Frankfurt or Hong Kong and developed a cadre of internal attorneys to handle Church affairs and develop long-term relationships with competent local law firms.[70]

As an American denomination, the Church has often served as a target of convenience for those hostile to American policies and cultural influence. Initially, the Church enjoyed much of the international goodwill directed toward the United States in the immediate postwar years. But as the Cold War continued, confrontation with the Soviets and other communist movements pushed the United States to take actions that ultimately dissipated much of this goodwill, particularly in the Third World countries where the Church was expanding most rapidly. In 1953 the CIA, in cooperation with Britain's MI-6, toppled the elected government in Iran after it sought closer ties with the Soviet Union. Thereafter, the CIA supported a coup in Guatemala (1954) and worked covertly to overthrow Fidel Castro's regime, culminating in the disastrous Bay of Pigs invasion of 1961. The CIA also made covert interventions in Iraq (1960–1963), the Dominican Republic (1961), and South Vietnam (1963). In addition, the United States backed often-brutal anti-communist strongmen, most notably in South Korea and Chile, where the Nixon administration tacitly sup-

69. Kuehne, 60–61.

70. Perry H. Cunningham, "Area, Area Presidency," in *Encyclopedia of Mormonism* (New York: Macmillian Co., 1992); Mehr, "An LDS International Trio, 1974–97," 119. The year-end summaries prepared by Randy Ayers, a Church lawyer who worked first in Frankfurt and later in Chile, provide a rare document giving a flavor for the kinds of tasks Church attorneys in area offices have performed. Ayers recounts traveling throughout Russia and Ukraine to acquire property on behalf of the Church and to negotiate with local government officials over the construction of LDS buildings. His recounting of his Chilean experience provides less detail, but it also focuses mainly on issues related to the purchase of land and the construction of buildings. See Randy Ayre, "1993 in Review" (Manuscript, Salt Lake City, Utah, n.d.), Church History Library; Randy Ayre, "1994 in Review" (Manuscript, Salt Lake City, Utah, n.d.), Church History Library; Randy Ayre, "2001 Year in Review" (Manuscript, Salt Lake City, Utah, n.d.), Church History Library; Randy Ayre, "2005 Year in Review" (Manuscript, Salt Lake City, Utah, n.d.), Church History Library.

ported Agusto Pinochet's violent coup against Salvador Allende's elected government. Eventually, American involvement went beyond the covert machinations of the CIA. Across the Third World, the United States faced off against the Soviet Union in a series of bloody proxy wars in southern Asia, Africa, and Central America. The United States also fought a full-fledged war in Vietnam from 1964 to 1973.[71] Deeply unpopular both at home and abroad, Vietnam generated hostility and suspicion toward the United States across the world more than any other single event.

Anti-American sentiment directed against the Church has sometimes been violent. In 1977, there was an unsuccessful attempt to assassinate Church President Spencer W. Kimball with a bomb during a visit to Santiago, Chile. Chilean officials foiled the plot, killing three of the plotters. In all likelihood, the plotters were seeking to embarrass the Pinochet government by killing a prominent American leader.[72] More tragically, in the 1980s and early 1990s, leftist guerilla groups murdered both American and Latin American missionaries in Peru and Bolivia.[73] In addition, dozens of Church buildings in Bolivia, Peru, Chile, and Colombia were bombed in the 1980s.[74] Although all of these groups had complex local ideologies, they were also driven by hostility toward American policies in Latin America and historical resentment against the *gringos* and *yanquis*.[75] Elsewhere, it was quite common for Mormon missionaries to be identified in the media or political debate as CIA agents.[76] At times, this diffuse association be-

---

71. Dating the beginning of the Vietnam War is tricky. American military personnel were involved in Indochinese conflicts as early as 1955, and there was a substantial military presence beginning in 1961–1962. 1964, however, was the year in which the Gulf of Tonkin incident prompted Congressional authorization for military operations in Southeast Asia. American troops were withdrawn in 1973, again as a result of Congressional action, and Saigon fell in 1975, marking the final victory for North Vietnam.

72. The assassination attempt and its connection with Pinochet's government is discussed in Kimball, *Lengthen Your Stride*, 16–17.

73. David Clark Knowlton, "Missionaries and Terror: The Assassination of Two Elders in Bolivia," *Sunstone*, August 1989.

74. David Clark Knowlton, "Mormonism in Latin America: Toward the Twenty-First Century," *Dialogue: A Journal of Mormon Thought* 29 (Spring 1992): 169; David Clark Knowlton, "Mormonism and Guerrillas in Bolivia," *Journal of Mormon History* 32, no. 3 (October 1, 2006): 180–208.

75. Knowlton, "Mormonism and Guerrillas in Bolivia."

76. For example, on rumors surrounding Mormon missionaries and the CIA in India, see Britsch, *From the East*, 542–43. For a detailed analysis of the politics

tween espionage and Mormonism led to concrete action, as when Mormon missionaries were arrested as spies by the Czechoslovakian government in 1950.[77] It has also led to overt symbolic actions against the Church by politicians eager to exploit popular resentment against the United States. For example, in the early 1980s, leftist MPs made Mormonism the topic of questions in the Finnish parliament, and in 1970 when a *coup d'etat* brought the populist general Juan Jose Torres to power in Bolivia, he threatened to ban Mormonism in the country, insisting that it was an agent for American imperialism. (A right-wing military putsch deposed Torres in 1971 before he could act on these threats.)[78]

Finally, the Church has been subject to legal pressure because of internal political or social dynamics in the countries where it has sought to expand. Two examples illustrate this dynamic. On December 8, 1989, the Church sent the first full-time missionaries from Finland into the Soviet Union. The Mormons were not the only group moving into the rapidly crumbling Soviet bloc in this era. Mikhail Gorbechev's policy of *glasnost,* which eased restrictions on religion, and the subsequent dissolution of the Soviet Union, led to a religious land rush in Central and Eastern Europe.[79] American churches were particularly aggressive in proselytizing the former communist world, with Baptists, Seventh Day Adventists, and Jehovah's Witnesses all sending missionaries into the former Soviet bloc.

This led to a backlash as the Russian Orthodox Church recovered from Soviet era repression and the public odium of forced cooperation with the communist state.[80] In the 1990s, the Russian economy went into free fall and a mafia-infested economic oligarchy emerged, souring the

---

of Mormonism and espionage in Finland, see Kim B. Östman, "The Mormon Espionage Scare and Its Coverage in Finland, 1982–84," *Journal of Mormon History* 34, no. 1 (January 1, 2008): 82–117. For a general discussion of the relationship between religion and espionage, see Nikolas K. Gvosdev, "Espionage and the Ecclesia," *Journal of Church and State* 42 (2000): 803–23.

77. See Mehr, "Enduring Believers," 142.

78. Knowlton, "Mormonism and Guerrillas in Bolivia," 187.

79. Emily B. Baran, "Negotiating the Limits of Religious Pluralism in Post-Soviet Russia: The Anticult Movement in the Russian Orthodox Church, 1990–2004," *Russian Review* 65, no. 4 (October 1, 2006): 639–40.

80. See Baran, "Negotiating the Limits of Religious Pluralism in Post-Soviet Russia"; W. Cole Durham, Natalie J. Petersen, and Elizabeth A. Sewell, "Introduction: A Comparative Analysis of Religious Association Laws in Post-Communist Europe," in *Laws on Religion and the State in Post-Communist Europe*, by W. Cole Durham and Silvio Ferrari, Law and Religion Studies 2 (Leuven: Peeters, 2004), xi.

optimism about Western-inspired reforms. The sense of social and cultural dissolution was exacerbated by Russia's two bloody wars (1994–1996 and 1999–2000) against the breakaway province of Chechnya and the resulting terrorist attacks in Moscow and elsewhere. This hostility often focused on western churches, including the Mormon Church.[81] In 1996, Alexander Lebed, a former general, ran in the presidential elections on a nationalist and authoritarian platform.[82] After finishing third, he was

81. Metropolitan Kirill of Smolensk and Kaliningrad stated the Russian Orthodox Church's reaction to religious proselytizing before the World Conference of Churches Conference on World Mission and Evangelism in November 1996:

> As soon as freedom of missionary work was allowed, a crusade began against the Russian church, even as it began recovering from a prolonged disease, standing on its feet with weakened muscles. Hordes of missionaries dashed in, believing the former Soviet Union to be a vast missionary territory. They behaved as though no local churches existed, no Gospel was being proclaimed. They began preaching without even making an effort to familiarize themselves with the Russian cultural heritage or to learn the Russian language. In most cases the intention was not to preach Christ and the Gospel, but to tear our faithful away from their traditional churches and recruit them into their own communities. Perhaps these missionaries sincerely believed that they were dealing with non-Christian or atheistic communist people, no suspecting that our culture was formed by Christianity and that our Christianity survived through the blood of martyrs and confessors, through the courage of bishops, theologians, and laypeople asserting their faith.
>
> Missionaries from abroad came with dollars, buying people with so-called humanitarian aid and promises to send them abroad for study or rest. We expected our fellow Christians would support and help us in our own missionary service. In reality, however, they have started fighting with our church, like boxers in a ring with their pumped-up muscles, deliver blows. The annual budget of some of the invading missionary organizations amounts to dozens of millions of dollars. They have bought time on radio and television and have used their financial resources to the utmost in order to buy people.

Metropolitan Kirill, "Gospel and Culture," in *Proselytism and Orthodoxy in Russia: The New War for Souls*, ed. John Witte, Jr. and Michael Bourdeaux (Maryknoll: Obis Books, 1999), 73. For a summary of the attitudes of cultural hostility toward Mormon missionaries, see Decoo, "Issues in Writing European History and in Building the Church in Europe," 154–57.

82. Lebed famously claimed that Russia could benefit from a military dictatorship modeled on that of Augusto Pinochet.

installed by his rival, President Boris Yeltsin, as security chief. In a widely reported speech before a nationalist rally, he said:

> We have established traditional religions—Russian Orthodox, Islam, Buddhism. As to all these Mormons, Aum Supreme Truth, all this is mold and scum that is artificially brought into our country with the purpose of perverting, corrupting and breaking up our state.[83]

Lebed's linking of Mormons with Aum Supreme Truth, a Japanese group associated with fatal gas attacks in a Tokyo subway, was telling. Beginning in the 1990s, Russian activists—many of them associated with the Russian Orthodox Church—began forming ties with American and Western European anti-cult activists. In the 1990s and 2000s, these ties generated a political movement within Russia directed against so-called "totalitarian cults" that allegedly corrupted the morals of their victims through brainwashing, thus undermining Russian society.[84]

In 1997, the Russian Duma passed a new law governing religious associations.[85] It threatened to revoke the status of all religious groups that could not demonstrate a presence within the country for fifteen years, limiting their ability to hold property or publish their views. The law provoked widespread concern in the United States. Senator Gordon Smith, a Mormon representing Oregon, introduced a law that would make US foreign aid contingent on a finding that "the Russian Federation has enacted no statute or promulgated no executive order that would discriminate . . . against religious minorities . . . in violation of accepted international agreements on human rights and religious freedoms."[86] Acting indepen-

---

83. Richard Boudreaux, "Yeltsin Aide Denounces Foreigners, Urges Curbs," *Los Angeles Times*, June 28, 1996.

84. See Baran, "Negotiating the Limits of Religious Pluralism in Post-Soviet Russia," 638.

85. An unofficial English translation of the law has been published in W. Cole Durham and Silvio Ferrari, eds., *Laws on Religion and the State in Post-Communist Europe*, Law and Religion Studies 2 (Leuven: Peeters, 2004), 279–300; For background on the law, see generally T. Jeremy Gunn, "Caesar's Sword: The 1997 Law of the Russian Federation on the Freedom of Conscience and Religious Associations," *Emory International Law Review* 12 (1998): 43. For an early but comprehensive analysis of the law's provisions, see W. Cole Durham and Lauren B. Homer, "Russia's 1997 Law on Freedom of Conscience and Religious Associations: An Analytical Appraisal," *Emory International Law Review* 12 (1998): 101–246.

86. See Congressional Record S7518 (July 16, 1997). For a discussion of the Smith Amendment, see Durham and Homer, "Russia's 1997 Law on Freedom of

dently of the Church, another Mormon Senator, Utah's Robert F. Bennett, traveled to Russia on behalf of the US State Department, where he met with the chairman of the Duma committee on religious affairs, President Yeltsin's chief of staff, and lawyers from the Russian Ministry of Justice. These officials assured him that—despite its language—the law would not be applied to Mormons and other new religions.[87] In addition, officials from the Church's Area Office in Frankfurt flew to Moscow to lobby members of the Duma.[88] Shortly after the law was passed, the Church was recognized under an exemption in the law for "centralized religious organizations," a provision originally designed to exempt the Russian Orthodox Church from the law's restrictions on other religious groups.[89] Notwithstanding official recognition, however, the US State Department reported that after the passage of the 1997 law, the Church routinely faced difficulties with officials in proselytizing and obtaining property.[90]

Conscience and Religious Associations: An Analytical Appraisal," 237–40.

87. Robert F. Bennett, Conversation with Former Senator Robert F. Bennett, interview by Nathan B. Oman, November 15, 2013. Bennett also met with an official he described as "the secretary of state for the Russian Orthodox Church," who claimed that the law would exclude new religious groups but only for fifteen years, enough time to give the Russian Orthodox Church "breathing space."

88. Bennett.

89. Mark Elliott and Sharyl Corrado, "The 1997 Russian Law on Religion: The Impact on Protestants," *Religion, State & Society* 27, no. 1 (1999): 111–12. Indeed, Elliott and Carrado concluded in 1999 that "Mormons actually appear for the moment to be enjoying something of a privileged status, despite the minimal responses of the Russian people to their missionaries." Elliott and Corrado, 111. For a summary of the treatment of religious minorities under the law during its first ten years, see Wallace L. Daniel and Christopher Marsh, "Russia's 1997 Law on Freedom of Conscience in Context and Retrospect," *Journal of Church and State* 49, no. 1 (2007): 5–18.

90. Government officials obstruct efforts to rent or build property; see United States Commission on International Religious Freedom, "Annual Report 2013" (Washington, DC: US Department of State, 2013), 256–57; renting and building places of worship is difficult, United States Commission on International Religious Freedom, "Annual Report 2012" (Washington, DC: US Department of State, 2012), 318; government officials take an inordinate interest in fire and other safety regulations to assess fines and shut down services, United States Commission on International Religious Freedom, "Annual Report 2011" (Washington, DC: US Department of State, 2011), 293; difficulty in obtaining places of worship, restrictions on visas for missionaries, vandalism of a Church building, and perception that law enforcement will not protect Church

The experience of the Church in West Africa provides another example of legal difficulties flowing out of unique local political concerns. As early as the 1950s, people in Nigeria and other West African countries found materials about the Church and began converting to "Mormonism" without baptism or any interaction with missionaries.[91] Within the religious economy of sub-Saharan Africa, such religious entrepreneurialism based on new religious texts and revelations is fairly common, and reflects widespread syncretism and "Africanization" of foreign religious traditions.[92] When Church leaders in Salt Lake City became aware of these African Mormons, they had to decide how to respond given the Church's policy at the time of denying the priesthood to Blacks.[93] After nearly a decade of internal debate, President David O. McKay decided to open missionary work in Nigeria.[94] At this point, however, the Church faced legal difficulties in the country. Nigerian students studying abroad had learned about

---

services or property, United States Commission on International Religious Freedom, "Annual Report 2010" (Washington, DC: US Department of State, 2010), 279–81; difficulty obtaining worship space, United States Commission on International Religious Freedom, "Annual Report 2009," 183; pro-Kremlin demonstrations outside Mormon building in Saratov, United States Commission on International Religious Freedom, "Annual Report 2008" (Washington, DC: US Department of State, 2008), 254; chronic problems obtaining legal recognition United States Commission on International Religious Freedom, "Annual Report 2007" (Washington, DC: US Department of State, 2007), 50; government officials warn that Mormons are a threat to "spiritual security," United States Commission on International Religious Freedom, "Annual Report 2006" (Washington, DC: US Department of State, 2006), 155; Mormons and other minority religions must secure permission of local Russian Orthodox leaders before being allowed by the government to obtain places of worship, United States Commission on International Religious Freedom, "Annual Report 2005" (Washington, DC: US Department of State, 2005), 91.

91. Kissi, *Walking in the Sand*, 3–4; See Prince and Wright, *David O. McKay and the Rise of Modern Mormonism*, 81–82; Allen, "Would-Be Saints," 211–12.

92. See Philip Jenkins, "Letting Go: Understanding Mormon Growth in Africa," *Journal of Mormon History* 35, no. 2 (April 1, 2009): 1–25; Rosalind I. J. Hackett, "Prophets, 'False Prophets,' and the African State: Emergent Issues of Religious Freedom and Conflict," *Nova Religio: The Journal of Alternative and Emergent Religions* 4, no. 2 (April 1, 2001): 187–212.

93. Prince and Wright, *David O. McKay and the Rise of Modern Mormonism*, 81–83; Allen, "Would-Be Saints," 213–16.

94. Prince and Wright, *David O. McKay and the Rise of Modern Mormonism*, 82–88; Allen, "Would-Be Saints," 227.

the Church and denounced attempts to formally introduce Mormonism into Nigeria. A local newspaper, *The Nigerian Outlook*, published an editorial entitled "Evil Saints." It read:

> [Mormons] believe as a cardinal [tenet] of their faith that the Negro race is not equal to any other race in the eyes of God. . . . Our correspondent has gone into great pains to expose this organization because he fears it may come to Nigeria thoroughly disguised. . . . These so-called Latter Day Saints must be recognized for what they are—godless Herrenvolkism—and must not be allowed into the country.[95]

The government responded by restricting visas for potential missionaries, and the Church eventually abandoned the proposed Nigerian mission.[96] The West African Mormons had to wait until November 1978 for baptism.[97]

Given the Church's priesthood ban and the racist theology that was commonly used to defend it in the postwar years, the Nigerian government's negative reaction to Mormon proselytizing is understandable.[98] *The Nigerian Outlook*, however, framed the issue in uniquely African terms. Africans, especially in the immediate post-colonial period, were sensitive to how European churches had generated racial hierarchies, the so-called veranda missionaries.[99] More telling was the association of Mormonism with "Herrenvolkism." Herrenvolk means "master race," and in the African context it was associated with Apartheid in South Africa, especial-

95. Quoted in Allen, "Would-Be Saints," 230.

96. The Nigerian government's action in restricting visas was not the only reason for abandoning the proposed Nigerian mission. There was also disagreement in high Church councils about the wisdom of organizing Mormon congregations where there could be no local leadership. Finally, the proposed African mission came at a time when rumors were circulating in the American media that the Church was about to abandon its racial restrictions on the priesthood. Some in the Quorum of the Twelve were eager to quell these rumors and thought opening a mission in West Africa would lend them credence. Prince and Wright, *David O. McKay and the Rise of Modern Mormonism*, 92–94.

97. Allen, "Would-Be Saints," 246.

98. For an example of the kind of racial theologizing common within Mormonism at the time, see John Lewis Lund, *The Church and the Negro* (Salt Lake City: Paramount Publishers, 1967); For a discussion that places Mormon racial teachings in a historical and social perspective, see Armand L. Mauss, *All Abraham's Children: Changing Mormon Conceptions of Race and Lineage* (Urbana: University of Illinois Press, 2003).

99. Jenkins, "Letting Go," 19.

ly with its most strident proponents among the Afrikaner population.[100] The editor of *The Nigerian Outlook* was thus viewing Mormonism's racial theologizing through a peculiarly uniquely West African lens—one that saw itself fighting for a new post-colonial space between the tradition of European imperialism to the north and Apartheid to the south.

In the decade after the 1978 revelation on the priesthood, Mormon missionaries were particularly successful in Ghana, a former British colony west of Nigeria.[101] As is often the case throughout sub-Saharan Africa, politics in Ghana can become infused with religious content.[102] The country's first post-independence leader created a quasi-religious cult of personality. A pro-government newspaper, for example, insisted that "the whole phenomenon of Nkrumah's emergence is second to none in the history of world messiahs from Buddha and Mohammed to Christ."[103] Thereafter, different regimes took different positions vis-à-vis Ghana's religious culture, sometimes favoring mainline religious establishments and sometimes cultivating indigenous African religions or syncretic local forms of Christianity. In 1981, J. J. Rawlins led a successful military coup. He actively sought to legitimate his regime religiously, calling the coup a "Holy War" and garnering the popular nickname of "Junior Jesus."[104] His regime soon found itself in conflict with mainline Christian churches, and in 1989 the government promulgated a law requiring that all churches register with a Religious Affairs Committee, which was given discretion to recognize the churches or not. Unrecognized churches were forbidden from operating.[105]

As soon as the government announced the new law, it banned all actions of the Church in Ghana and expelled its foreign missionaries.[106]

---

100. The term was also used by the Nazis to designate the Aryan master race. In Nigeria, however, the reference was likely South African rather than German.

101. Kissi, *Walking in the Sand*, 51.

102. See Abamfo Ofori Atiemo, *Religion and the Inculturation of Human Rights in Ghana* (New York: Bloomsbury Academic, 2013), 85–111; Hackett, "Prophets, 'False Prophets,' and the African State."

103. Quoted in Atiemo, *Religion and the Inculturation of Human Rights in Ghana*, 87–88.

104. Atiemo, 92.

105. Atiemo, 93; E. K. Quashigah, "Legislating Religious Liberty: The Ghanaian Experience," *Brigham Young University Law Review* 2001 (2001): 589–607; Elom Dovlo, "Religion and the Public Sphere: Challenges and Opportunities in Ghanaian Lawmaking, 1989–2004," *Brigham Young University Law Review* 2005 (2005): 629–58.

106. Kissi, *Walking in the Sand*, 51.

The government also outlawed three other religious groups: the Jehovah's Witnesses and two indigenous religious movements, the Nyamae Sompa Church of Ekwam-krom and the Jesus Christ Church of Dzorwulu.[107] The reasons for banning the Church are unclear. The pro-government press attacked the Church as racist, accused the missionaries of being CIA agents, and suggested that the Church was buying converts with "posh cars" and lavish buildings.[108] The 1989 law, however, seems to have been primarily directed against mainline Christian denominations.[109] It proved unenforceable against these groups, and was ultimately invalidated by the country's 1992 constitution.[110] It seems likely that the government chose to make an example of four relatively weak religious organizations—two foreign and two indigenous—to intimidate the larger mainline denominations.[111] The so-called "freeze" of the Church in Ghana lasted eighteen months. The Church lost many members, and its property was vandalized. Local leaders, however, maintained basic Church organization and, assisted by representatives from Church headquarters, negotiated an end to the "freeze" and the return of missionaries in 1990.[112]

---

107. Atiemo, *Religion and the Inculturation of Human Rights in Ghana*, 94.

108. Kissi, *Walking in the Sand*, 199. Abamfo Ofori Atiemo, the head of the religious studies department at the University of Ghana, Legon, wrote:

> The LDS suffered apparently on the basis of suspicion and alleged misdeeds in countries where they had been before coming to Ghana. It is clear also that public sentiments against these bodies played an important role in influencing the decision of the government. One of the official reasons given for the promulgation of the law was to protect the public from 'too many bogus churches' and to control corruption.

Atiemo, *Religion and the Inculturation of Human Rights in Ghana*, 94. Kissi, the local leader of the Church during the "freeze" who subsequently became a general authority of the Church, speculates that the government's action may have been instigated by local ministers and anti-Mormon propaganda from America. Ed Decker, a prominent anti-Mormon activist, has confirmed that his organization was active in Ghana at the time. Kissi, *Walking in the Sand*, 187.

109. Dovlo, "Religion and the Public Sphere: Challenges and Opportunities in Ghanaian Lawmaking, 1989–2004," 643–44.

110. Dovlo, 645–46.

111. In the absence of more direct sources on the government's motivations, however, this conclusion is necessarily speculative.

112. Kissi, *Walking in the Sand*, 263.

IV. Law and the Mormon Theology of the State

It is impossible to recount the development of Mormon theology in the nineteenth century without acknowledging the profound influence of the law on Latter-day Saint teachings. Most dramatically, the concerted effort of the federal government to suppress polygamy from 1862 to 1890 forced the Church to abandon the practice of plural marriage and ultimately its teaching of it as well. The power of the law, however, was also deployed against other aspects of the nineteenth-century Mormon commonwealth. Forced to abandon theocratic ambitions, the Church reinterpreted Zion in less literal terms and postponed its utopian hopes to an ever-receding millennium. For the Latter-day Saints, the American ideal of a religiously neutral law and an autonomous religious sphere free of government coercion proved illusory. Law was a causal force in the development of Mormon practices and teachings.[113]

Law was also a powerful influence on Mormon teachings in the latter half of the twentieth century. As Mormonism achieved a grudging cultural acceptance in the United States after 1904, it could avail itself of the freedom of religion, speech, and association protected by the First Amendment of the US constitution. At the same time, the Supreme Court steadily began expanding those freedoms. In 1938, the Court signaled the beginnings of its mid-century "rights revolution" with the famous footnote 4 of *United States v. Carolene Products*,[114] stating that the deferential attitude of the courts toward legislation entrenched by the constitutional settlement of the New Deal didn't extend to laws aimed at "discrete and insular minorities."[115] By the late 1960s and 1970s, this judicial attitude

---

113. See Elizabeth Harmer-Dionne, "Once a Peculiar People: Cognitive Dissonance and the Suppression of Mormon Polygamy As a Case Study Negating the Belief-Action Distinction," *Stanford Law Review* 50, no. 4 (April 1, 1998): 1295–1347.

114. 304 U.S. 144 (1938).

115. 304 U.S. 152–153n4. Footnote 4 is widely recognized as the most famous footnote in American law and has been the subject of massive scholarly literature. For a summary see Felix Gilam, "The Famous Footnote Four: A History of the Carolene Products Footnote," *South Texas Law Review* 46 (2004): 163–255. For historical treatments of the "rights revolution" in general in American constitutional law, see Gerald N Rosenberg, *The Hollow Hope: Can Courts Bring about Social Change?* (Chicago: University of Chicago Press, 2008); Charles R. Epp, *The Rights Revolution: Lawyers, Activists, and Supreme Courts in Comparative Perspective* (Chicago: University of Chicago Press, 1998).

had produced decisions such as *Sherbert v. Verner*,[116] *Wisconsin v. Yoder*,[117] and *National Labor Relations Board v. Catholic Bishop of Chicago*,[118] all of which took a deferential stance toward individual and institutional religious practice. Indeed, the Church was an important agent in creating the post-rights revolution religion clause jurisprudence, fighting the case of *Amos v. Presiding Bishop of the Church of Jesus Christ of Latter-day Saints*[119] to the Supreme Court, establishing the legitimacy of statutory exemptions designed to accommodate religious practice and protect the independence of religious institutions.[120]

It is one of the unappreciated ironies of Mormon history, however, that just at the moment when Mormonism had, after more than a century of struggle and accommodation, achieved maximum freedom and flexibility under American law, the Church was increasingly constrained and influenced by non-American legal systems. In navigating this bewildering new legal environment, the Church had to change. The changes, however, went beyond ecclesiastical structures or an increasingly professionalized apparatus of international lawyers. Interactions with non-American legal systems also had an influence on Mormon teachings. In particular, the necessity of accommodating Mormonism to a multiplicity of legal regimes required Church leaders to articulate a largely apolitical Mormon theology of the state, one that emphasized the role of Latter-day Saints as good citizens and sought to reassure skeptical government officials that the Church was uninterested in operating as an agent of radical political or social change. This apolitical theology of the state triumphed over the apocalyptic millennialism of the nineteenth-century Church.

116. 374 U.S. 398 (1963) (holding that laws burdening the free exercise of religion—in this case a law requiring a Seventh Day Adventist to work on the Adventist Sabbath—were subject to strict scrutiny).

117. 406 U.S. 205 (1972) (holding that Old Order Amish could be excused from compulsory education laws on the basis of freedom of religion).

118. 440 U.S. 490 (1979) (holding that religious institutions were constitutionally protected from invasive laws governing their administration).

119. 483 U.S. 327 (1987) (holding that the exemption of religious institutions from laws prohibiting discrimination on the basis of religion did not violate the Establishment Clause of the first amendment).

120. Compare Obst v. Germany, Application No. 425/03 (Dec. 23, 2010) (European Court of Human Rights).

A. Earlier Mormon Theologies of the State

During much of the nineteenth century, the dominant Mormon theology of the state was theodemocratic.[121] Originally articulated by Joseph Smith during the Nauvoo period, it envisioned the Mormon community as the Kingdom of God on Earth, a government-in-waiting ready to step into the breach when the imminent end times destroyed all secular competitors. A regime of theodemocracy would be put in place to build Zion in the last days and redeem all human communities that survived the coming deluge. With fierce literalism and commitment to Joseph's vision, Brigham Young sought to realize the Mormon Kingdom in the isolation of the Intermountain West.[122] Mormon theodemocracy, however, was already declining in the decades after the Civil War and ended in the first decade of the twentieth century during the Smoot Hearings.[123] In effect, President Joseph F. Smith committed the Church to behaving like an ordinary Protestant denomination. Theocratic ambitions were abandoned along with polygamy, the expansive jurisdiction of Church courts over civil disputes, and the cooperative economic institutions of Brigham Young's Deseret.[124]

In the immediate postwar period and for a decade or two thereafter, the main Mormon theology of the state could be called Cold War apocalypticism. The most articulate proponent of this view was Ezra Taft Benson,

---

121. See Patrick Q. Mason, "God and the People: Theodemocracy in Nineteenth-Century Mormonism," *Journal of Church and State* 55, no. 3 (Summer 2013): 349–75. For accounts of Mormon governments and political maneuvering in the nineteenth century, see Morgan, *The State of Deseret*; Edward Leo Lyman, *Political Deliverance: The Mormon Quest for Utah Statehood* (Urbana: University of Illinois Press, 1986).

122. See John G Turner, *Brigham Young, Pioneer Prophet* (Cambridge: Belknap Press of Harvard University Press, 2012); Leonard J. Arrington, Feramorz Y. Fox, and Dean L. May, *Building the City of God: Community and Cooperation Among the Mormons*, 2nd ed. (Urbana: University of Illinois Press, 1992); Leonard Arrington, *Great Basin Kingdom: An Economic History of the Latter-Day Saints, 1830–1900* (Cambridge: Harvard University Press, 1958).

123. Kathleen Flake, *The Politics of American Religious Identity: The Seating of Senator Reed Smoot, Mormon Apostle* (Chapel Hill: University of North Carolina Press, 2004).

124. On the rise and fall of civil disputes in Mormon courts, see Nathan B. Oman, "Preaching to the Court House and Judging in the Temple," *Brigham Young University Law Review* 2009, no. 1 (2009): 157–224.

who leavened his Mormonism with the paranoid anti-communism of the John Birch Society.[125] Benson's output on the subject of communism and America was prodigious, but he was far from the only Church leader who made anti-communism an important theme in his preaching.[126] The dominant Church figures in the immediate postwar period—J. Reuben Clark and David O. McKay—were both staunch anti-communists.[127] In 1959, for example, McKay, speaking in the Church's general conference, quoted from Salt Lake City's arch-anticommunist police chief W. Cleon Skousen's book *The Naked Communist*:

> The conflict between communism and freedom is the problem of our time. It overshadows all other problems. This conflict mirrors our age, its toils, its tensions, its troubles, and its tasks. On the outcome of this conflict depends the future of mankind.[128]

He also added, "I admonish everyone to read that excellent book of Chief Skousen's."[129] Other general authorities admonished against communists who sought to "overthrow the government and forfeit all safeguards,"[130]insisted that "the spirit of communism is unquestionably wholly foreign to the spirit of true Americanism"[131] and affirmed that "knowledge of the [communist] enemy teaches us wariness and caution."[132] The Manichean struggle between good and evil in the last days, which was a consistent theme of the early theodemocratic vision,

---

125. See D. Michael Quinn, "Ezra Taft Benson and Mormon Political Conflicts," *Dialogue: A Journal of Mormon Thought* 26, no. 2 (Summer 1993): 1–88.

126. Ezra Taft Benson, *The Red Carpet* (Salt Lake City: Bookcraft, 1962); Ezra Taft Benson, *An Enemy Hath Done This* (Salt Lake City: Parliament Publishers, 1969); Ezra Taft Benson, *The Constitution: A Heavenly Banner* (Salt Lake City: Deseret Book Co., 1986); Ezra Taft Benson, *This Nation Shall Endure* (Salt Lake City: Deseret Book Co., 1977); Ezra Taft Benson, *Stand Up for Freedom* (Belmont: American Opinion, 1966); Ezra Taft Benson, *God Family Country: Our Three Great Loyalties* (Salt Lake City: Deseret Book Co., 1974); Ezra Taft Benson, *A Plea for America* (Salt Lake City: Deseret Book Co., 1975).

127. Prince and Wright, *David O. McKay and the Rise of Modern Mormonism*; D. Michael Quinn, *Elder Statesman: A Biography of J. Reuben Clark* (Salt Lake City: Signature Books, 2002).

128. David O. McKay, "Preach the Word," *Conference Report*, October 1959.

129. McKay.

130. Stephen L. Richards, "The Wayward," *Conference Report*, April 1957.

131. Joseph F. Merrill, "The Gloomy Outlook and a Remedy," *Conference Report*, October 1946.

132. Ezra Taft Benson, "The Threat of Communism," *Conference Report*, April 1960.

was transposed to the mid-century struggle between the superpowers. In the nineteenth century, American democracy had been identified with the degenerate end-times regimes. In the vision of Cold War apocalypticism, however, America became the primary agent of God's work in history. To be sure, she was an uncertain agent, in constant danger of moral and political collapse from within. The Church and Mormonism were cast as agents of American righteousness in the global struggle against satanic communism. Even Mormon liberals, such as Hugh B. Brown of the First Presidency, who opposed Benson's politics, sounded anti-communist themes in their sermons.

There are three things worth noting about Cold War apocalypticism. First, it was intensely political. It provided a tightly intertwined set of theological and political narratives in which Mormonism spoke to pressing current concerns. Second, it was intensely American. Indeed, at times it seemed to tie the destiny of the Church to the destiny of the United States. Finally, and ironically, it was intensely local. Despite the international scope of the superpower struggle, Cold War apocalypticism ultimately spoke to American anxieties. In other words, it not only associated the Church closely with America, but it was also almost exclusively directed toward an American audience.

B. A Quietist Mormon Theology of the State

As the Church continued to expand, however, Cold War apocalypticism proved a theological luxury that Mormonism could not afford. Domestically, the fiery anti-communist rhetoric backfired. In July, 1965, for example, the NAACP adopted a resolution at its national conference that called on all Third World nations "to refuse to grant visas to missionaries and representatives of The Church of Jesus Christ of Latter-day Saints . . . until such time as the doctrine of non-white inferiority is changed and rescinded by that church and a positive policy of support for civil rights is taken."[133] Although the NAACP was critical of the Church's racial policies, the resolution itself was passed at the urging of the Utah chapter of the NAACP in response to Ezra Taft Benson accusing the civil rights movement of acting as a communist front.[134] As the Cold War eroded the immediate postwar goodwill toward the United States abroad, any close association of the Church with American policy became a liability. This

133. Quoted in Quinn, "Ezra Taft Benson and Mormon Political Conflicts," 35.
134. Quinn, 35.

was especially true as Mormonism moved into the Third World, a geopolitically liminal space between the superpowers. Mormon missionaries were seeking the same hearts and minds that American diplomats sought to win, but the Church found it best to decouple its efforts from US policy. This was especially true as it began to deal with governments that might or might not be friendly to the United States or, perhaps worse, governments that oscillated back and forth depending on the last coup or election. The Church's preferred strategy was to become as small a political and legal target as possible.

The Church sought to limit its exposure to legal and political hostility abroad by adopting an apolitical theology of the state. At its center was the Church's twelfth Article of Faith. In 1842, Joseph Smith concluded a letter to Joseph Wentworth, editor of *The Chicago Democrat*, with a list of Mormonism's basic beliefs, which became the Articles of Faith. The penultimate article declared, "We believe in being subject to kings, presidents, rulers, and magistrates, in obeying, honoring, and sustaining the law" (A of F 12). Written in Illinois amidst Smith's increasingly desperate legal maneuverings to avoid extradition to Missouri and the rising chorus of complaints about Mormon political machinations in the state, the statement made good political sense. Smith was pouring oil on troubled political waters. In the mid-twentieth century this text was repurposed to suit the rhetorical needs of the internationally expanding Church.

As early as 1950, Church leaders cited the twelfth Article of Faith in response to the expulsion of missionaries from Czechoslovakia.[135] In 1956, the First Presidency invoked the same text to negotiate legal requirements abroad. Stephen L. Richards, first counselor in the First Presidency, told a general conference audience that year:

> Within the past few weeks, in order to meet the requirements of a distant foreign country for the Church to hold property and otherwise carry forward its activities within that country, the First Presidency has caused to be prepared and submitted to the governing authority of the foreign country a statement of beliefs and objections of the Church.[136]

After repeating the twelfth Article of Faith, the statement affirmed that "the Church of Jesus Christ of Latter-day Saints builds and maintains churches, temples, educational institutions for all ages . . . It teaches loyalty to country

135. Joseph F. Merrill, "Repentance . . . or Slavery," *Conference Report*, April 1950.

136. Stephen L. Richards, "Our Message to the World," *Conference Report*, October 1956.

and fosters good citizenship in all communities where it is established."[137] Tellingly, the twelfth Article of Faith was invoked in a context where the Church was particularly vulnerable—the acquisition and use of real property. Hugh B. Brown, soon to be a counselor in the First Presidency, likewise told a general conference audience in the late 1950s that he had used the twelfth Article of Faith to answer questions about the Church's beliefs posed to him during the dedication of the London Temple.[138]

By the 1970s, this apolitical message was the dominant Mormon theology of the state. To be sure, there were still sermons and articles that drew on the images of Cold War apocalypticism,[139] but increasingly the message to both insiders and outsiders was that, above all, Mormons were law-abiding citizens uninterested in radical change.[140] The text of the twelfth Article of Faith is uniquely well suited for conveying this message for two reasons. First, the reference to "being subject to kings, presidents, rulers, and magistrates" is institutionally capacious. In contrast to philosophical liberalism, for example, it does not condition allegiance to the law on a particular institutional structure. If anything, the reference to "kings" and "rulers"—two models of authority that run counter to liberal ideas of legitimacy—suggest an almost unlimited allegiance to established authority.[141] Second, the emphasis on law as the primary mediator of

---

137. Richards.

138. Hugh B. Brown, "We Affirm Our Faith," *Conference Report*, October 1958.

139. It's worth noting that what I am calling Cold War apocalypticism went beyond Ezra Taft Benson's Mormonization of the paranoid visions of the John Birch Society. During the bicentennial celebrations of the United States in 1976, Spencer W. Kimball published a First Presidency message that was sharply critical of American materialism and castigated the United States and the Saints for being "a warlike people." See Spencer W. Kimball, "The False Gods We Worship," *Ensign*, June 1976.

140. This does not mean, of course, that this has always been an accurate description of the political beliefs of Latter-day Saints. Prior to the 1980s, for example, many Mormons in Nicaragua were supporters of the opposition Sandinistas, although many of these Latter-day Saints became disenchanted with the Sandinistas after they came to power and targeted the Church. See Gooren, "Latter-Day Saints under Siege: The Unique Experience of Nicaraguan Mormons."

141. Compare the twelfth Article of Faith, for example, with the Declaration of Independence. According to Jefferson's document:

> We hold these truths to be self-evident, that all men are created equal, that they are endowed by their Creator with certain unalienable Rights, that among these are Life, Liberty and the pursuit of Happiness.—That to se-

Latter-day Saint relationships to the state further suppresses any idea of political activism. Law has traditionally been presented as the antithesis of politics, a realm in which both obedience and authority are mediated through a system of impersonal principles that can be logically applied and obeyed without political judgment. To be sure, this ideal has always been something of an illusion, as critical theorists from Marx to realists of various stripes have been eager to point out. Still, as a rhetorical matter, invoking law as a central trope tends to emphasize the apolitical character of the Church.

Even at its most politically quietist, however, Mormon allegiance to established authority was not absolute. David Kennedy, who spent as much time thinking about these issues as any Latter-day Saint in the 1970s and 1980s, wrote:

> [S]o long as the government permits me to attend church, so long as it permits me to get on my knees in prayer, so long as it permits me to baptize for the remission of sins, so long as it permits me to partake of the sacrament of the Lord's Supper, and to obey the commandments of the Lord, so long as the government does not force me to commit crime, so long as I am not required to live separately from my wife and children, I can live as a Latter-day Saint within that political system.[142]

The Church has avoided states that cannot meet these minimal requirements, and thus has avoided direct conflict.[143] Still, Kennedy's formulation

---

> cure these rights, Governments are instituted among Men, deriving their just powers from the consent of the governed,—That whenever any Form of Government becomes destructive of these ends, it is the Right of the People to alter or to abolish it, and to institute new Government, laying its foundation on such principles and organizing its powers in such form, as to them shall seem most likely to effect their Safety and Happiness.

On this view the legitimacy of the government depends on both its procedural institutions—"deriving their just power from the consent of the governed"—and the substantive content of its acts—"secure these rights" and "effect their Safety and Happiness."

142. Quoted in Hickman, *David Matthew Kennedy*, 340–41.

143. For example, the Church's presence in the Islamic countries of the Middle East is muted, as is its presence in China. However, even in the Middle East there are Church units of expatriates and a smattering of local converts baptized abroad. In China, the population of native Latter-day Saints baptized abroad is sufficiently large enough that the Church has begun producing Chinese language materials giving them guidance on how to operate as Latter-day Saints within China. See "The Church of Jesus Christ of Latter-day Saints in China," The

provided a floor for the kinds of legal regimes within which the Church was willing to exist. Ideally, this near complete abandonment of a critical stance toward constituted authority reduced the probability of hostile action by the state directed against Latter-day Saints. Mormons, according to this apolitical theology, pose no threat to the powers that be, and those powers may safely ignore them.

As the legal experience of the Church in the last half of the twentieth century shows, however, its apolitical theology of the state has never been wholly successful. The Church has been unable to shed its widespread association with America in general and, to a lesser extent, with United States policy. In large part, this is an inevitable result of the Church's history and the geographic location of its administrative and demographic heartland. The American feel of the Church was further reinforced in the late 1960s and early 1970s by a comprehensive effort to simplify Church programs, known as correlation, which allowed the institution to focus its scarce resources but also homogenize Mormonism along lines that marked it as an American institution abroad.[144] In contrast to the international expansion of other denominations, Mormonism has made very few concessions to local culture in terms of worship or ecclesiastical structure. Given these factors, the rhetorical weight placed on an apolitical Mormon theology of the state has not surprisingly proven too great at times. With a few exceptions, it has protected Latter-day Saints from the kind violent persecution they suffered in the nineteenth century or that other religious groups have faced in the twentieth century. It has, however, not always shielded the Church from less dramatic forms of legal harassment.

Church of Jesus Christ of Latter-day Saints, accessed May 1, 2024, https://www.churchofjesuschrist.org/China. The website affirms:

> Over the years, the Church has built a strong relationship of trust with the People's Republic of China by always respecting the laws and traditions of that country. The Church teaches its members in each country to obey, honor, and sustain the law, to be good parents and exemplary citizens, and to make positive contributions to society.

It goes on to describe the restrictions under which native Chinese Latter-day Saints must function, including prohibitions on joint worship with expatriate Mormons in China, the distribution of Church literature, blogging or microblogging on religious subjects, and baptizing friends or family members in China.

144. For a discussion of the history of the correlation movement, see Allen and Leonard, *The Story of the Latter-Day Saints*, 593–624.

A 1994 general conference address by Russell M. Nelson of the Quorum of the Twelve Apostles nicely illustrates this problem. As early as the 1970s, before being called as an apostle, Nelson negotiated with governments in Eastern and Central Europe on behalf of the Church.[145] Nelson reported:

> While in Moscow in June 1991, in that spirit of preparation and with the sincere respect for leaders of other religious denominations, Elder Dallin H. Oaks and I had the privilege of meeting with the presiding official of the Russian Orthodox Church. We were accompanied by Elder Hans B. Ringger and the mission president, Gary L. Browning. Patriarch Aleksei was most gracious in sharing a memorable hour with us. We perceived the great difficulties endured for so many years by this kind man and his fellow believers. We thanked him for his perseverance and for his faith. Then we assured him of our good intensions and of the importance of the message that missionaries of The Church of Jesus Christ of Latter-day Saints would be teaching among his countrymen. We affirmed that ours is a global church and that we honor and obey the laws of each land in which we labor.[146]

This was essentially the same message that Hugh B. Brown had reported giving during the London Temple dedication over thirty years earlier. Yet as the political situation in Russia soured in the 1990s and the Russian Orthodox Church reasserted some influence over the law, Mormon protestations of apolitical law-abidingness proved insufficient to counter religious hostility. Indeed, despite the 1991 meeting with Oaks, Nelson, and Ringger and the assurances that they offered, Patriarch Aleksei was one of the most ardent supporters of the Duma's unsuccessful 1997 attempt to suppress new religions in Russia.[147]

V. Conclusion

After 1945, the Church went through some of the most dramatic changes in its history. Over the course of two generations, it transformed itself from a community concentrated overwhelmingly within the con-

---

145. See Mehr, "An LDS International Trio, 1974–97," 106; Browning, "Out of Obscurity: The Emergence of The Church of Jesus Christ of Latter-Day Saints in 'That Vast Empire' of Russia," 675–76; Kahlile Mehr, "Keeping Promises: The LDS Church Enters Bulgaria, 1990–1994," *Brigham Young University Studies* 36, no. 4 (1996): 71.

146. Russell M. Nelson, "Teach Us Tolerance and Love," *Ensign*, May 1994.

147. Daniel and Marsh, "Russia's 1997 Law on Freedom of Conscience in Context and Retrospect," 7.

fines of the Intermountain West into a global institution with ambitions to expand into every nation. This international expansion has created one of the unappreciated ironies of Mormon history. The postwar decades represent something of a high-water mark for the level of protection and autonomy enjoyed by the Church within the American legal system. Yet at precisely the moment when the Church successfully located itself within the legal culture of the United States, it found itself increasingly confronted by non-American legal systems. International expansion spawned a host of legal difficulties, and in trying to minimize itself as a target of potentially hostile governments, the Church crafted an apolitical theology of the state that has largely come to dominate internal and external Mormon discourse on the relationship between Latter-day Saints and legal authority. This late-twentieth century approach, however, has never entirely minimized the Church's exposure to legal hostility.

The Mormon experience illustrates the power of law in shaping religion. From 1862 until 1890, the federal government pursued a massive legal crusade against the Latter-day Saints in an effort to force the Church to abandon polygamy. These federal laws were ultimately successful, forcing a revolution in Mormon practice and theology. Since 1945 Mormon discourse has again responded to legal pressure, this time from a host of jurisdictions around the world. Both stories illustrate the complex interaction between law and religion. Religion is not a "given" to be punished, accommodated, or ignored by the state. Rather, religions are dynamic, constantly adapting and reinterpreting themselves in the face of these circumstances. This does not mean that the claims of religion are infinitely malleable. Even the Mormons, with their extremely deferential stance toward the law in the twentieth century, have been willing to articulate limits to the authority of the state. Nevertheless, their experience powerfully illustrates the role of law in shifting religious discourse over time.

Index

T

U

Also available from

GREG KOFFORD BOOKS

Joseph Smith's Polygamy, 3 Vols.

Brian Hales

Hardcover
Volume 1: History 978-1-58958-189-0
Volume 2: History 978-1-58958-548-5
Volume 3: Theology 978-1-58958-190-6

Perhaps the least understood part of Joseph Smith's life and teachings is his introduction of polygamy to the Saints in Nauvoo. Because of the persecution he knew it would bring, Joseph said little about it publicly and only taught it to his closest and most trusted friends and associates before his martyrdom.

In this three-volume work, Brian C. Hales provides the most comprehensive faithful examination of this much misunderstood period in LDS Church history. Drawing for the first time on every known account, Hales helps us understand the history and teachings surrounding this secretive practice and also addresses and corrects many of the numerous allegations and misrepresentations concerning it. Hales further discusses how polygamy was practiced during this time and why so many of the early Saints were willing to participate in it.

Joseph Smith's Polygamy is an essential resource in understanding this challenging and misunderstood practice of early Mormonism.

Praise for *Joseph Smith's Polygamy*:

"Brian Hales wants to face up to every question, every problem, every fear about plural marriage. His answers may not satisfy everyone, but he gives readers the relevant sources where answers, if they exist, are to be found. There has never been a more thorough examination of the polygamy idea." —Richard L. Bushman, author of *Joseph Smith: Rough Stone Rolling*

"Hales's massive and well documented three volume examination of the history and theology of Mormon plural marriage, as introduced and practiced during the life of Joseph Smith, will now be the standard against which all other treatments of this important subject will be measured." —Danel W. Bachman, author of "A Study of the Mormon Practice of Plural Marriage before the Death of Joseph Smith"

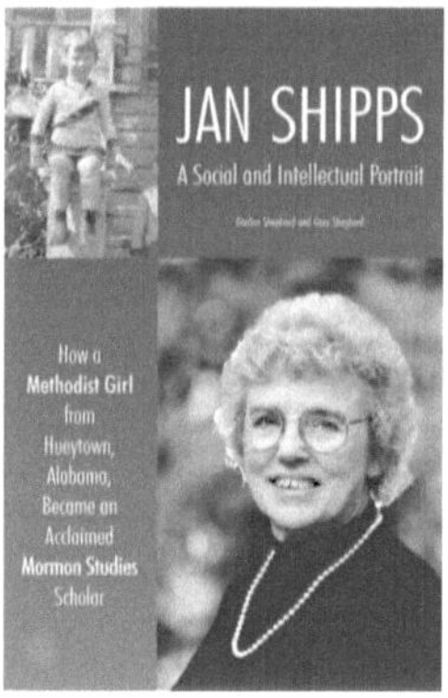

Jan Shipps: A Social and Intellectual Portrait: How a Methodist Girl from Hueytown, Alabama, Became an Acclaimed Mormon Studies Scholar

Gordon Shepherd and Gary Shepherd

Paperback, ISBN: 978-1-58958-767-0
Hardcover, ISBN: 978-1-58958-768-7

How did Jo Ann Barnett—a Methodist girl born and raised in Hueytown, Alabama, during the Great Depression and World War II—come to be Jan Shipps, a renowned non-Mormon historian and scholar of The Church of Jesus Christ of Latter-day Saints? In Jan Shipps: A Social and Intellectual Portrait, authors Gordon Shepherd and Gary Shepherd tell the story of how Shipps not only became an important and trusted authority in a field that was predominantly made up of Mormon men, but also the crucial role she played in legitimizing Mormon Studies as a credible academic field of study.

Praise for *Jan Shipps: A Social and Intellectual Portrait*:

"The person and work of Jan Shipps comprise one of the ten most important factors enabling Mormon Studies to eclipse its parochial past. Authors Gordon and Gary Shepherd have adroitly marshalled the tools of history and social science to lay bare how this unlikely event came to be. This is important reading for any who hope to understand Shipps or the emergence of the field in which she worked. Important also for any scholar feeling that the deck in a competitive academy is stacked against them." — Phil Barlow, Neal A. Maxwell Fellow at the Neal A. Maxwell Institute for Religious Scholarship at Brigham Young University.

"Jan Shipps deserves and the Shepherds are to be thanked for this celebration of her celebrated career. The authors rightly insist this is not a thorough treatment of Jan's life but rather an account of her role in the rise Mormon Studies in the late-twentieth century. It was a watershed time and Jan was a creator of and catalyst to much of the best scholarship which flowed from it. As such, there is much to learn here about Mormonism itself and those who studied it during this period." —Kathleen Flake, Richard Lyman Bushman Professor of Mormon Studies, University of Virginia

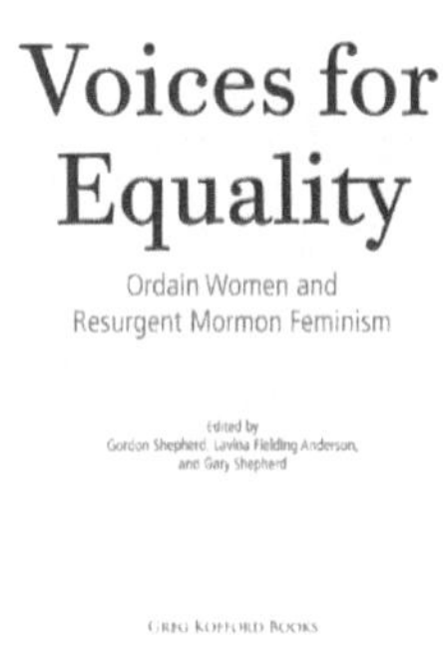

Voices for Equality: Ordain Women and Resurgent Mormon Feminism

Edited by Gordon Shepherd, Lavina Fielding Anderson, and Gary Shepherd

Paperback, ISBN: 978-1-58958-758-8

Praise for *Voices for Equality*:

"Timely, incisive, important—this book teaches us that our sometimes very personal struggles with gender and equality in Mormonism have profound and far-reaching significance. In these pages, some of Mormonism's finest researchers and thinkers bring a richness of historical and scholarly perspective and a powerful new survey of tens of thousands of Mormon people to bear on headline-making issues like women's ordination, sister missionaries, church discipline, the internet and faith, and change in the LDS church. They offer us a rare and precious opportunity to grasp the full significance of this moment. This book is a much needed mirror for our time."

— Joanna Brooks, co-editor of *Mormon Feminism: Essential Writings* and author of *The Book of Mormon Girl: A Memoir of an American Faith*

"*Voices for Equalty: Ordain Women and Resurgent Mormon Feminism* is a very important contribution to the discussion of Mormon feminism and the struggle for the ordination of women to the priesthood in the LDS Church. Anyone interested in this subject, any library concerned to be up-to-date on these issues, needs to have this book."

— Rosemary Radford Ruether, world-renowned feminist scholar and Catholic theologian, author of *Sexism and God-Talk: Toward a Feminist Theology and Women-Church: Theology* and *Practice of Feminist Liturgical Communities*

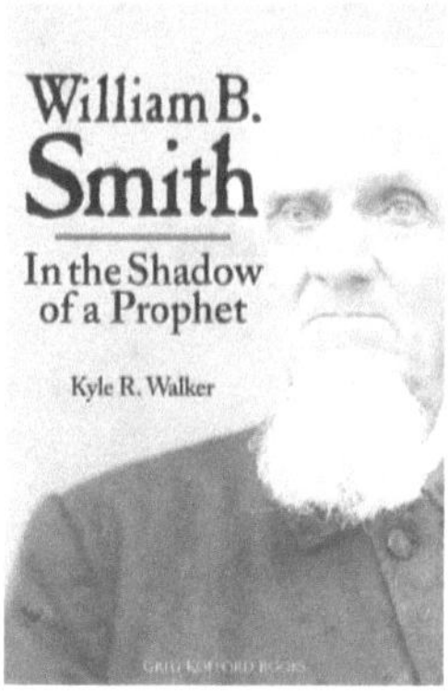

William B. Smith: In the Shadow of a Prophet

Kyle R. Walker

Paperback, ISBN: 978-1-58958-503-4

Younger brother of Joseph Smith, a member of the Quorum of the Twelve Apostles, and Church Patriarch for a time, William Smith had tumultuous yet devoted relationships with Joseph, his fellow members of the Twelve, and the LDS and RLDS (Community of Christ) churches. Walker's imposing biography examines not only William's complex life in detail, but also sheds additional light on the family dynamics of Joseph and Lucy Mack Smith, as well as the turbulent intersections between the LDS and RLDS churches. *William B. Smith: In the Shadow of a Prophet* is a vital contribution to Mormon history in both the LDS and RLDS traditions.

Praise for *William B. Smith*:

"Bullseye! Kyle Walker's biography of Joseph Smith Jr.'s lesser known younger brother William is right on target. It weaves a narrative that is searching, balanced, and comprehensive. Walker puts this former Mormon apostle solidly within a Smith family setting, and he hits the mark for anyone interested in Joseph Smith and his family. Walker's biography will become essential reading on leadership dynamics within Mormonism after Joseph Smith's death." — Mark Staker, author *Hearken, O Ye People: The Historical Setting of Joseph Smith's Ohio Revelations*

"This perceptive biography on William, the last remaining Smith brother, provides a thorough timeline of his life's journey and elucidates how his insatiable discontent eventually tempered the once irascible young man into a seasoned patriarch loved by those who knew him." — Erin B. Metcalfe, president (2014–15) John Whitmer Historical Association

"I suspect that this comprehensive treatment will serve as the definitive biography for years to come; it will certainly be difficult to improve upon." — Joe Steve Swick III, Association for Mormon Letters

www.ingramcontent.com/pod-product-compliance
Ingram Content Group UK Ltd.
Pitfield, Milton Keynes, MK11 3LW, UK
UKHW041854031026
15587UKWH00006B/1232/J

9 781589 588103